Community Interventions and AIDS

Community Interventions and AIDS

Edited by
Edison J. Trickett
Willo Pequegnat

UNIVERSITY PRESS

2005

OXFORD
UNIVERSITY PRESS

Oxford University Press, Inc., publishes works that further
Oxford University's objective of excellence
in research, scholarship, and education.

Oxford   New York
Auckland   Cape Town   Dar es Salaam   Hong Kong   Karachi
Kuala Lumpur   Madrid   Melbourne   Mexico City   Nairobi
New Delhi   Shanghai   Taipei   Toronto

With offices in
Argentina   Austria   Brazil   Chile   Czech Republic   France   Greece
Guatemala   Hungary   Italy   Japan   Poland   Portugal   Singapore
South Korea   Switzerland   Thailand   Turkey   Ukraine   Vietnam

Copyright © 2005 by Oxford University Press, Inc.

Published by Oxford University Press, Inc.
198 Madison Avenue, New York, New York 10016

www.oup.com

Oxford is a registered trademark of Oxford University Press

Library of Congress Cataloging-in-Publication Data
Community interventions and AIDS /
edited by Edison J. Trickett, Willo Pequegnat.
p. ; cm.
Includes bibliographical references and index.
ISBN 0-19-516023-1
ISBN-13 978-0-19-516023-9
1. AIDS (Disease)—Prevention.   2. Community health services.
I. Trickett, Edison J.   II. Pequegnat, Willo.
[DNLM: 1. Acquired Immunodeficiency Syndrome—prevention &
control.   2. HIV Infections—prevention & control.   3. Community
Health Services.   4. Consumer Participation.   5. Research
—methods.   6. Social Environment.   WC 503.7 C734 2005]
RA643.8.C65 2005
362.196'9792—dc22   2004019751

9 8 7 6 5 4 3 2 1

Printed in the United States of America
on acid-free paper

Foreword

In 1987, Randy Shilts published the widely acclaimed book *And the Band Played On*. In the prologue to the book, Shilts wrote the following:

> In those early years, the federal government viewed AIDS as a budget problem, local public health officials saw it as a political problem, gay leaders considered AIDS a public relations problem, and the news media regarded it as a homosexual problem that wouldn't interest anybody else. Consequently, few confronted AIDS for what it was, a profoundly threatening medical crisis. (p. xxiii)

At the time Shilts wrote this book, I was living in San Francisco and had occasion to see him speak several times about the contextual dimensions of the emerging epidemic. I also witnessed, first hand, the tragedy of HIV/AIDS in my community. Suffering and death, as well as inspiring stories of individual and collective action, confronted me daily. HIV/AIDS was front-and-center on the Bay Area stage. In the years that followed, my travels around the world made clear that HIV/AIDS was front-and-center on the stages of many countries.

The contextual dimensions of HIV/AIDS have increasingly appeared in public dialog about the disease. A Google Internet search of "AIDS and community context" and "community impact of AIDS," for example, generated over 1 million and 2 million "hits," respectively. Despite this public dialog, the contextual frame of the disease has not, until this book, been the focal point of a book for researchers and community service providers. As such, this book breaks new ground by bringing together research and practice, providing important texture and perspective to a pressing public health problem. In so doing, the editors and authors of this book have added immeasurably to our understanding of how individual disease is embedded in layers of context.

When HIV/AIDS first emerged, few could estimate the toll it would take on individuals, community ecologies, and the global community. Today, still, we do not know fully how future generations will be influenced by this epidemic and its aftermath. The effects of HIV/AIDS on the fabric of life are deep and expansive. However you define "community" and "community context," there is little question that HIV/AIDS cannot be understood by viewing it only from an individual level of analysis. Indeed, levers for effective intervention rest as much at the doorsteps of communities as in the labs of scientists. We learn much about the power of these levers in this book.

Today, over 500,000 Americans have died from AIDS and nearly 1 million have been diagnosed with AIDS. Worldwide, 40 million people are living with HIV/AIDS; 3 million die each year. These epidemiological data, though staggering, do not capture the full effect of HIV/AIDS. This disease is best understood and intervened upon via an ecological paradigm that considers multiple levels of analysis, dependence, and synergy. The editors and authors of this book have reminded us of this important fact and provided an illuminating, multidisciplinary, and coherent tour de force of the community context of HIV/AIDS.

David G. Altman

Preface

This book reflects an effort to articulate the intersection of two forces that, together, are shaping the social, political, and scientific landscape for the upcoming decades: the enormity of the ongoing AIDS crisis around the world and the emergence of participatory, community-based, and community focused behavioral and social science intervention as a response to that crisis. The AIDS pandemic shows little sign of abating, thus reinforcing the importance of addressing the complex issue of behavior change as a primary intervention and prevention strategy. The crisis has mobilized worldwide response on the part of governments and behavioral and social scientists.

Engagement with the populations, issues, and contexts affected by AIDS has pushed social and behavioral scientists to confront new challenges in multiple and varied cultures whose resources, traditions, and values have often diverged from those providing both the resources and the paradigmatic approaches toward intervention. It has made front-and-center the critical nature of developing an appreciation for the norms, structures, and traditions of the local context and the value of developing authentically collaborative working relationships with culturally and linguistically diverse people and places. Furthermore, this engagement has located social intervention squarely within a political context that has greatly affected what can be done and what is prohibited.

These activities, and the critical reflection that they have produced among AIDS interventionists, have called into question varied assumptions about how to conduct scientific inquiry and intervention. In so doing, a dialectic among differing perspectives on how to best attack the AIDS pandemic has arisen. It has arisen in terms of methods, levels of analysis of intervention, the kinds of relationships between outsiders and insiders involved in these community-based endeavors, and the very epistemology underlying what we consider as scientific knowledge. It has done so in the context of a broader set of challenges to positivism in the social and behavioral science literature over the past decades involving these same issues: the social construction of knowledge (Gergen, 1985), the research relationship as critical to the knowledge gained (Riger, 1992), and the role of context in defining the meaning of and options for behavior (Kingry-Westergaard & Kelly, 1990). Furthermore, it has coincided with movements in other fields toward a unified commitment to community-based participatory research and intervention (Minkler & Wallerstein, 2003). Thus, the fight to prevent AIDS has reflected both political and scientific agendas, each of which has challenged us to view and act on our world in different ways than we had before.

OVERVIEW OF CONTENTS

The purpose of this book is to reinforce and sharpen the political and scientific issues that are currently surrounding the AIDS pandemic and propose alternative models for future AIDS intervention. While the focus is on the behavioral and social science response, the political context in which it has occurred as both a provider of resources and constrainer of options is unmistakable. However, the primary focus is to provide a perspective for those behavioral and social scientists who have made a commitment to understanding and intervening in communities around the world. In addition, efforts are made throughout to implicate social policy in these endeavors; these efforts range from calls for specific kinds of programs such as needle exchange to the structure of external funding and its impact on how community intervention can be made to create local and enduring effects. The title of the book signals the belief that the community impact of intervention activity represents a primary goal of community-based AIDS interventions and a primary criterion by which such interventions should be judged.

The book begins with an overview of the "paradigm drift" (Beeker, Guenther-Grey, & Raj, 1998) toward a more community-oriented and empowerment-driven approach in AIDS intervention research. Chapter 1 sets the stage for the remainder of the book by elaborating on an ecological perspective from community psychology that highlights issues and themes articulated more fully in subsequent chapters. The next section of the book includes four chapters dealing with the related issues of community assessment and community impact. Chapter 2, by Hirokazu Yoshikawa, Patrick A. Wilson, John Peterson, and Marybeth Shinn, focuses on the multiple pathways that community-level interventions may lead to community-level impact. After highlighting the importance of defining the concept of "community," they outline six different potential intervention pathways that may lead to community-level impacts: 1) grassroots community mobilization; 2) the aggregation of subgroup-level change; 3) the aggregation of setting-level change; 4) organizational and institutional change; 5) change in public policy; and 6) the adoption and replication of interventions involving any of these pathways. In Chapter 3, Eric Stewart and Julian Rappaport focus on the contested nature by which varied AIDS narratives are constructed by differing groups. Drawing on Foucault's (1980) appreciation of the "insurrection of subjugated knowledges" (p. 81), they provide examples of how an exploration of community narratives can serve as a basis for the design of locally meaningful interventions that may have the same community-wide impact that early efforts in the San Francisco gay and lesbian community did in the mid 80s.

The following three chapters focus more directly on the relationship between community assessment and community intervention. Chapter 4, by Jeffrey Kelly, provides an overview of select community-level interventions

and a set of potential factors influencing their success. In Chapter 5, Carl
Latkin and Amy Knowlton direct attention to the social networks of individuals and AIDS interventions. Latkin and Knowlton's approach suggests that HIV/STI risk behaviors in communities are mediated by
microsocial influence processes that are amenable to intervention and that
potentially affect the diffusion of behavioral norms within a community.
Moreover, a network-oriented approach draws attention to the degree to
which community interventions are sufficiently socioculturally appropriate to be sustained over time. Examples of such interventions and implications for many more are offered. In Chapter 6, Robert Trotter and
Merrill Singer take a critical look at the emergence of rapid community assessment strategies in public health as a methodological response to developing relatively quick and accurate diagnoses of community problems
and designing locally supported intervention solutions. Here, emphasis
is on both the promise of this approach as well as its potential destruction
points as one approach to linking community assessment with community impact.

The next section of the book includes three chapters that draw attention
to differing perspectives and issues in community collaboration that have
implications for the community impact of interventions. In Chapter 7,
Merrill Singer and Margaret Weeks describe the critical role of long-term
institutional commitment in achieving community impact of interventions
through a description of a model developed by the Hispanic Health
Council and Institute for Community Research in Hartford, Connecticut,
over a 20-year period. The Hartford Model emphasizes community intervention based on long-term institutional commitment, community-based
partnerships and collaboration, a participatory action research approach,
and an interdisciplinary perspective. One means of assessing community
impact involves the degree to which interventions are sustained over time
after the initial program is ended. In Chapter 8, Jean Schensul focuses on
the complexities of the sustainability concept and links its feasibility to a
long-term, community-development perspective on community interventions. She suggests that the lack of emphasis on the question of sustainability inheres in the current culture of experimental science in which
communities are the sites, not objects, of intervention. She also asserts that
the model emphasizes internal validity, replication, and dissemination,
and that sustainability of effect and the development of infrastructure in
intervention sites are, at best, secondary concerns.

In the final chapter in this section, Chapter 9, Robin Miller and George
Greene look at the issues of community impact through the lens of those
responsible for operating community-based organizations. They suggest a
wide disconnect between current models of technology transfer of interventions to existing organizations and the important contextual contingencies in organizations that affect the relevance and adoption of externally
derived and validated interventions. They review literature suggesting that
lack of appreciation of the interests, ideologies, political constraints, and

resource limitations of community-based organizations severely limits the degree to which transported interventions are either relevant to or possible to incorporate into their ongoing functioning. They urge community interventionists to learn about the ongoing issues, histories, and hopes of such organizations as prelude to technology transfer.

The next two chapters in the book focus on methodological issues in community interventions designed to achieve community impact. Chapter 10, by Ralph DiClemente, Richard Crosby, and Gina Wingood, highlights some of the many theoretical and methodological challenges involved in designing and evaluating community-level change efforts. They discuss direct and indirect pathways through which community-level interventions may affect individual behavior and cite collaboration as a central component of the intervention process. In describing the many research challenges, they provide both a guide for future work and a set of issues that distinguish community-level from individual-level interventions. Next, in Chapter 11, Bruce Rapkin and Edison Trickett take a critical stance on the assumptions and implications for community impact of randomized clinical trials. They argue against the RCT being held up as a singular "gold standard," and clarify how methodological assumptions and implementation issues of the RCT are constrained when thinking of interventions involving community-level impact. They also provide design alternatives to further methodological efforts in this area.

Finally, in Chapter 12, Willo Pequegnat discusses future directions for community-based research deriving direction from the chapters themselves and her experience in the Office of AIDS Research on Mental Health at the National Institute of Mental Health. She provides an overview of concepts in need of further clarification in community-level interventions and outlines a series of research questions suggested by varied chapters in the book.

AUDIENCE

The book's manifest content makes it relevant for all who have a stake in AIDS research and community intervention: academic researchers/ interventionists concerned with being useful while contributing to scientific theory, community-based organizations facing decisions about how to allocate precious resources and what kinds of alliances to build with other agencies, graduate students intending to forge careers of commitment to alleviating the social devastation caused by AIDS, those responsible for graduate training, and funders who influence not only what kinds of community interventions are seen as potentially useful but also the nature of the relationships forged between externally funded interventionists and local community groups and organizations. To the degree that the emphasis on community impact encourages a rethinking of the basic perspectives underlying the science of community intervention, all these players have a critical stake in the dialectic such a change in perspective engenders. The chapters in the book provide a framework for such discussion.

Yet the book is also intended as a broader statement designed to stimulate discussion and debate about the nature of community research and intervention more broadly across such disciplines as public health, community health education, urban planning, psychology, sociology, anthropology, and philosophy of science. Taken as a piece, the book suggests an alternative perspective on how to gather valid knowledge, how to include community collaboration as part of the paradigm governing community intervention, and how and why to assess the multiple impacts of community interventions across levels of analysis in the community of concern. This perspective, burbling up relatively independently in varied discrete disciplines over decades, is currently taking shape as a potentially coherent set of assumptions that may serve to integrate varied disciplines concerned with understanding and affecting the community context in which we live our lives.

This book could not have been completed without the ongoing support of the Center for Mental Health Research on AIDS, National Institute of Mental Health and, more particularly, Dr. Ellen Stover, Director of that office. That office was responsible for developing and convening two meetings on the topic of the community impact of AIDS interventions in which the contours of the book were developed. In addition to those authors appearing in the book, the conferences included Drs. Thomas Coates, Linda Doll, Roberta Paikoff, Jeffrey Kelly, Bruce Rapkin, Dina Birman, Anthony D'Augelli, Richard Needle, Esther Sumartojo, Tony Whitehead, Elijah Anderson, Joseph Trimble, and Philippe Bourgois. We are indebted to them for their contribution to the overall set of ideas on which the book is based.

REFERENCES

Beeker, C., Guenther-Grey, C., & Raj, A. (1998). Community empowerment paradigm drift and the primary prevention of HIV/AIDS. *Social Science Medicine, 46*(7), 831–842.

Foucault, M. (1980). *Power/Knowledge: Selected interviews and other writings.* C. Gordon (Ed.). New York: Pantheon.

Gergen, K. (1985). The social constructionist movement in modern psychology. *American Psychologist, 40,* 266–275.

Kingry-Westergaard, C. & Kelly, J. G. (1990). A contextualist epistemology for ecological research. In P. Tolan, C. Keys, F. Chertok, & L. Jason (Eds.), *Researching community psychology* (pp. 23–32). Washington, DC: American Psychological Association.

Minkler, M. & Wallerstein, N. (Eds.) (2003). *Community-based participatory research for health.* San Francisco: Jossey-Bass.

Riger, S. (1992). Epistemological debates, feminist voices: Science, social values, and the study of women. *American Psychologist, 47*(6), 730–740.

Contents

Contributors

David G. Altman
  Center for Creative Leadership, Wake Forest University School of Medicine

Richard A. Crosby
  Emory Center for AIDS Research, Rollins School of Public Health

Ralph J. DiClemente
  Emory Center for AIDS Research, Emory University School of Medicine, Rollins School of Public Health

George J. Greene
  University of Illinois at Chicago

Jeffrey A. Kelly
  Center for AIDS Intervention Research (CAIR), Medical College of Wisconsin

Amy R. Knowlton
  Johns Hopkins School of Public Health

Carl A. Latkin
  Johns Hopkins School of Public Health

Robin Lin Miller
  University of Illinois at Chicago

Willo Pequegnat
  National Institute of Mental Health, USA

John L. Peterson
  Georgia State University

Bruce D. Rapkin
  Memorial Sloan-Kettering Cancer Center

Julian Rappaport
University of Illinois at Urbana-Champaign

Jean J. Schensul
Institute for Community Research

Marybeth Shinn
New York University

Merrill Singer
Hispanic Health Council

Eric Stewart
University of Georgia

Edison J. Trickett
University of Illinois at Chicago

Robert T. Trotter, II
Northern Arizona University

Margaret Weeks
Institute for Community Research

Patrick A. Wilson
New York University

Gina M. Wingood
Emory Center for AIDS Research, Rollins School of Public Health

Hirokazu Yoshikawa
New York University

Community Interventions and AIDS

1

Community Interventions and HIV/AIDS: Affecting the Community Context

Edison J. Trickett

When the AIDS epidemic first drew national attention in the United States, the dominant (though by no means exclusive) scientific response mirrored the "normal science" (Kuhn, 1970) paradigm of the time. Within psychology, the paradigm was reflected in what Sarason (1981) called the "acultural, asocial, and ahistorical" study of the individual. Epistemologically, it reflected the positivistic tradition characteristic of the history of psychology. This focus and epistemology has had its successes, and much is now known about how individually based interventions can be crafted to affect individual attitudes and self-reported sexual risk behaviors (Valdiserri, Ogden, & McCray, 2003; van Empelen, Kok, van Kesteren, van den Borne, Bos, & Schaalma, 2003).

However, over time, the substantive and epistemological limitations of this perspective as a basis for community intervention in HIV/AIDS have become more evident. This appreciation has fueled an exploration of alternative ways of approaching community intervention designed to affect the epidemic. Much of this impetus has been propelled by the phenomenon itself, the communities most affected by it, and its worldwide ramifications. HIV/AIDS community interventions have frequently involved poor, disenfranchised, stigmatized, and often, from the outside, "invisible" populations whose suspicion of outsider researchers is both deep and well-founded (Dunlop & Johnson, 1999; Sengupta et al., 2000). Engaging these communities in intervention efforts has necessitated a commitment on the part of interventionists to appreciate culture and confront race, class, and other palpable differences between interventionists and the communities in which they work. It has also forced interventionists to deal with the ramifications of the often-exploitive history of such communities with outsiders manifestly intending to help. Furthermore, it has required the development of relationships with community members both to learn about the community and to provide opportunities for the community to learn about the intervention team. It has encouraged the use of multiple methods to understand better the nature of the community context, to amplify the voices of those affected by the disease, and to provide process information about how the interventions were perceived and received. And it has provided a worldwide stage for the development of comparative knowledge about what worked, how, and for whom in countries with differing histories, resources, cultural traditions, and experiences with colonization and the colonizing effects of prior research conducted by outsiders (Cooke & Kothari, 2001).

This accumulated experience, propelled by the necessity of worldwide involvement in coping with the AIDS crisis, has resulted in a confrontation with the positivistic, individually focused intervention approach that has dominated behavioral science (Sarason, 1981). This confrontation has rippled through the paradigm of community-based research and intervention (Minkler & Wallerstein, 2003) and has provided the basis for alternative models. For example, the distanced and neutral stance of the researcher with respect to the people with whom he/she works is being replaced by the concept of collaboration between the researcher and the researched (Schensul, this volume; Singer & Weeks, this volume; Trickett & Espino, 2004). The emphasis on collaboration has, in turn, yielded an examination of how power is distributed and used in the community research and intervention process (Minkler & Wallerstein, 2003; Wallerstein, 1999). This confrontation with the power and possibilities of community collaboration has also surfaced the tension between traditional models of scientific objectivity and the value of local participation in defining both problems and solutions (Green & Mercer, 2001). The remainder of the book elaborates on many of these ripples.

The bottom line, however, is the emergence of cornerstones of a paradigm for community-based HIV/AIDS research and intervention that focuses on the integration of collaboration, culture, community, and context. This perspective was foreshadowed years ago by anthropologists and sociologists involved in the AIDS epidemic (Gagnon, 1989; Herdt, 1987; Herdt & Lindenbaum, 1992; Parker, 1987; Treichler, 1987), and much is owed to their commitment to understanding both the epidemic and response to it as a social and cultural as well as a biomedical issue (Treichler, 1992).

The current critique draws on the frameworks provided by this early literature. It is based partially on an unpacking of the often-implicit assumptions of individually based interventions. One assumption, for example, is the ability of individuals to transcend context (Rhodes, Stimson, & Quirk, 1996). Person-centered interventions leave untouched the ongoing noxious and multifaceted sets of environmental risk factors that contribute to both the incidence of risk behavior and "relapse" that occurs in individually based interventions over time (Altman, 1995b; Choi & Coates, 1994; Kegeles, Hays, & Coates, 1996; Latkin, 1998; Rhodes et al., 1996; Singer & Weeks, 1996; Tawil, Verster, & O'Reilly, 1995).

An additional focus of inquiry involves a rethinking of the goals of AIDS interventions in community settings to include community-level as well as individual-level changes in resources and capacity, and how the relationship between interventionists and community groups and organizations can affect those goals (Trickett & Espino, 2004). Individually based interventions have focused primarily on specific programs designed to change people, not on processes designed to change places. Thus, little attention has been paid conceptually or in program design to how to craft programs as enduring community resources (Trickett & Birman, 1989) and how to increase the capacity of local organizations to better fulfill their community missions with respect to AIDS/HIV (see Schensul, this volume). The individual-level perspective is further reflected in the decisions about what outcomes were of importance. Outcomes have been traditionally assessed through the individual behavior changes brought about by programs, not organizational or community level outcome measures. As a consequence, we know little, if anything, about the community impact brought about by the millions and millions of dollars directed toward person-based change in HIV/AIDS.

Another outgrowth of this individually based, positivistic perspective involves the increasing concern with such concepts as fidelity, transferability, sustainability, and community "buy-in." Fidelity has become central because of the assumption that interventions are theoretically supported by basic processes that have wide-niche breadth in terms of populations and contexts. Fidelity is thus defined by the processes operative in the technology of the intervention rather than in a more complex interaction of intervention technology, the social context within which it is implemented, and the implementation process itself (Kelly, et al., 2000). Whether or not fidelity is best conceptualized from this "within intervention" perspective is now being debated, and the multiple meanings of "evidence" around which fidelity is based discussed (Kellam & Langevin, 2003).

In like manner, transferability and sustainability have arisen as critical issues in no small measure because the research goals fostered by the individually based perspective have focused on demonstrating internal validity or "within intervention" technology under optimal conditions. The emerging emphasis of transportability and sustainability highlights the fact that neither were ever primary questions driving the development, implementation, and evaluation of interventions. The issue of transportability has sharpened an appreciation of the complexities of "what the intervention is" in community-based interventions. Such interventions include not only technology and manuals but also an infrastructure of professional expertise, inducements to participants, and a specific kind of synergistic relationship between interventionists and sites that also needs to be transported (Rotheram-Borus, Rebchook, Kelly, Adams, & Newmann, 2000).

A consideration of sustainability highlights the potential differences in the design and execution of interventions aimed at demonstrating change in an experimental context and interventions designed to become ongoing community resources. In addition, the sustainability issue has drawn attention to the unintended community ripples of interventions. Here, the ending of such projects, particularly when perceived as successful, has raised the issue of how to deal with community hopes and expectations for sustainability that might not be met. In addition, the short-term infusion of outside resources associated with community interventions often results in time-limited employment for local citizens that is withdrawn upon project completion. Together, these paradigm-related neglects of sustainability have contributed to the more fundamental disillusionment with researchers whose commitment to the locale ends with the successful completion of the project (Altman, 1995b).

The increasing emphasis on community "buy-in" stems from the dual concerns over community cooperation in researcher-defined projects and an appreciation of the potential role of citizens in implementing and adopting programs. The economic image suggested by "buy-in" is telling in that it suggests that the role of the researcher is to get the community to agree to buy something, a kind of product marketing of something presumably good for them. This stance, related to the push toward evidence-based practice, highlights the importance of understanding the contextual constraints over the nature and generalizability of evidence across time, culture, and context. Significantly, the concept of "researcher buy-in" to community needs and perspectives is not prominent in the published literature.

All these issues have become clear because of the commitment to responding to the magnitude of the epidemic within the acultural, ahistorical, and acontextual framework described by Sarason (1981). The wish to disseminate programs successfully tested in one location to other locations; the importance of sustaining useful programs after the cessation of external funding; and the frustration of seeing behavioral relapse over time around a life-threatening issue have all pushed the envelope in terms of seeking new alternative perspectives and methods to affect the course of the epidemic.

EPISTEMOLOGICAL AND CONCEPTUAL ALTERNATIVES

In response to the issues raised above, a new perspective is emerging. This perspective localizes interventions in specific sociocultural community contexts, focuses on how interventionists can collaborate with local citizens and organizations, and locates specific interventions in the context of a long-range strategy for community development. The overarching goal of this perspective is to participate in interventions that improve the resources of the community; that is, that create community-level impact.

Beeker, Guenther-Grey, and Raj (1998) reflect this movement in their essay "Community empowerment paradigm drift and the primary prevention of HIV/AIDS." They define this "paradigm drift" as follows: "A community empowerment intervention seeks to effect community-wide change in health-related behaviors by organizing communities to define their health problems, to identify the determinants of those problems, and to engage in effective individual and collective action to change those determinants. This definition is predicated on three assumptions: first, that health problems have multiple determinants, often including those that lie beyond individual volition and skill; second, that communities must participate in both the definition and solution of health problems; and third, that the success of an intervention depends on the capacity of the community to engage in effective action" (Beeker et al., 1998).

The remainder of this chapter outlines one general perspective reflecting this community empowerment paradigm drift and provides a general mind-set for the remainder of the book. The perspective rests on (a) a contextualist philosophy of science and (b) an ecological perspective on community intervention derived from community psychology. Together, they draw attention away from programs to places and focus on the issue of community impact of interventions.

ADOPTING A CONTEXTUALIST PHILOSOPHY OF SCIENCE

The contours of the contextualist philosophy of science are emerging more generally in the behavioral and social sciences (Gergen, 1985; Riger, 1992; Rosnow & Georgoudi, 1986; Kingry-Westergaard & Kelly, 1990) and are well summarized by Rosnow and Georgoudi (1986):

> The idea is that psychological knowledge is made concrete and is framed by relevant factors, relations, and conditions (the setting or context) within which, or among which, human acts unfold. Contextualism underscores the idea that human activity does not develop in a social vacuum, but rather it is rigorously situated within a sociohistorical and cultural context of meanings and relationships. Like a message that makes sense only in terms of the total context in which it occurs, human actions are embedded in a context of time, space, culture, and the local tacit rules of conduct . . . The idea of contextualism implies that to unlock the mysteries of what makes an event meaningful we must consider, via methodological and theoretical pluralism, the wider context that "allows" or "invites" the occurrence of that event and renders it socially intelligible. (pp. 4–5)

Shweder (1990) has put it more bluntly: "The ideas of a context-free environment, a meaning-free stimulus event, and a fixed meaning are probably best kept where they belong, along with placeless space, eventless time, and squared circles on that famous and fabulous list of impossible notions" (p. 8).

The research implications of this epistemology are outlined by McGuire (1983) in his contrast of contextualism with logical empiricism. McGuire offers the assumption that from a contextualist perspective, all hypotheses are true, even contradictory ones; the task is to uncover the range of contexts in which they hold. Some might be broadly true, some narrowly, but, quoting Blake's aphorism, he states, "Everything possible to be believed is an image of truth." This suggests that such issues as generalizability of intervention strategies and effects be approached less as an effort to discover acontextual basic processes and more as an attempt to discern the contexts across which relationships may be expected to generalize and those in which they may not.

Such a perspective redefines the goal of community research and intervention. Rather than viewing research as progressing in linear fashion toward truths generalizable across cultures, populations, contexts, and time, its primary purpose, even when testing theory-driven hypotheses, is to generate additional hypotheses about the contextual applicability and constraints of any specific piece of knowledge, or, in this instance, intervention. Thus, any empirical findings from a specific site or set of sites stimulate the question "Under what conditions would we expect current findings *not* to generalize?"

This larger epistemological framework situates many of the concerns evolving in the HIV/AIDS intervention literature within a broad philosophy of science perspective. It draws attention away from an exclusive or even primary "within paradigm" focus on internal validity of HIV/AIDS interventions. Instead, it concentrates on how the intervention meshes with the ongoing lives of those participating in it; what the relationship of the researchers to the population involves; how external resources that fund the intervention are themselves part of the context that may affect outcome; and how the broader local and indeed national culture within which the work is located insinuate their way into the intervention and its meaning to those involved. Each of these represents potential contextual constraints on the meaning, generalizability, and sustainability of interventions. In focusing on the intervention context, it also supports the potential value of an ecological perspective from which to approach community intervention aimed at community impact (Kingry-Westergaard & Kelly, 1990).

ADOPTING AN ECOLOGICAL PERSPECTIVE ON COMMUNITY INTERVENTION AND IMPACT

From a community psychology perspective, ecology directs attention to the community context and individual adaptation to that context. Its relevance to HIV/AIDS intervention is provided by Singer and Marxauch-Rodriquez (1996):

> The starting point for AIDS prevention is recognition that AIDS is only a cover term for a complex set of intertwined local epidemics that differentially impact diverse subgroups in varied local settings based on their sociopolitical location, social and sexual networks, specific configuration of risk behaviors (e.g., sexual practices and patterns), attitudes and beliefs, and prior health status (e.g., stressors, nutrition, exposure to other sexually transmitted diseases). (p. 141)

Aggleton (1993) adds: "HIV/AIDS health promotion is always context-bound, taking place within discrete communities and in specific settings. The impact of health promotion is always contingent, being mediated by social expectations, popular prejudices, and group norms" (p. 186). Both essays highlight the centrality of understanding local context as prelude to designing interventions that are responsive to the life demands and local culture of those for whom they are intended.

There is an increasing body of work in HIV/AIDS intervention consistent with the community impact goal, including multiple-component interventions with gay men (Kegeles et al., 1996) designed to orchestrate, integrate, and enhance local resources, and efforts to change social network and community norms around safe-sex behavior (Kelly et al., 1991; Kelly et al., 1992; Latkin, 1998; Latkin et al., 1995; Treadway & Yoakam, 1992). A review of this emerging literature is found throughout subsequent chapters in this book.

However, the general concern with community impact of interventions has been a central theme of community psychology over time (Kelly, 1970, 1971; Sarason, 1972). Much of this work has been guided by an ecological perspective and a contextualist philosophy of science (Rappaport, 1981, 1987; Trickett, 1996; Kingry-Westergaard & Kelly, 1990). Because the term ecology has multiple meanings within and across disciplines, it is useful to outline what is and is not meant by it in this chapter. Multiple ecological perspectives have been developed to describe the ecological context and its effects on individuals (Barker, 1968; Bronfenbrenner, 1979; Moos, 1974, 1979). The perspective underlying this chapter, however, flows from the ecological metaphor developed by Kelly (1968, 1970, 1971) and elaborated by colleagues (Trickett, 1996; Trickett & Birman, 1989; Trickett, Kelly, & Todd, 1972; Trickett, Kelly, & Vincent, 1985). In contrast to other perspectives, it was developed to link an appreciation of the community context with the designing of interventions intended to have community impact. The spirit of ecological inquiry (Trickett et al., 1985) was thus seen as combining the quest for knowledge with the spirit of using such knowledge in the service of community development.

Kelly's work draws on ecological processes developed in field biology, where the biological community, not the individual plant, is the level of analysis. The relevance of field biology as a source of analogy for human communities rests on two related building blocks: (a) the community as the level of analysis and (b) the role of the researcher as the "doting naturalist," attempting to understand how the community functions as a community. It is designed to serve as a guiding orientation for how to approach community intervention as an instance of community development. It is not intended to convey an inevitability that communities are as they are because of processes of natural selection that should be left uninterrupted as an expression of nature.

Within this perspective, the issue of community impact is highlighted by attention to three additive and complementary intervention-related activities: (1) environmental assessment of the community context and the ecology of individual lives in that context, (2) developing collaborative relationships between the interventionist and the setting or community where the intervention occurs, and (3) designing interventions whose goal is to create community resources (Trickett, 2002; Trickett & Birman, 1989; Trickett et al., 1985; Trickett & Schmid, 1993). Each of these interrelated and interactive activities commits the intervention team to crafting interventions responsive to and respectful of the local sociocultural context and its future. The spirit of these activities is commensurate with Altman's (1995a) description of the goals of a public-health perspective on community intervention: "(1) integrate interventions into a community infrastructure, (2) use comprehensive, multilevel intervention approaches, (3) facilitate community participation and promote community capacity-building, and (4) conduct thorough needs assessment/environmental reconnaissance in order to tailor interventions to the community context" (p. 229).

ENVIRONMENTAL ASSESSMENT: THE COMMUNITY CONTEXT AND THE ECOLOGY OF LIVES

Community Context

From an ecological perspective, the development of any community intervention begins with the question of what the community of concern is like. Regardless of whether the community is defined in terms of a single setting such as a school, a neighborhood, or a network of intravenous drug users, how it is structured, what norms govern behavior, what services are available, and how the community deals with marginalized groups within it becomes the knowledge on which interventions are designed, implemented, and evaluated. From this perspective, neither the most salient community issues in need of impact nor the possible strategies to achieve such impact can be discerned beforehand.

The importance of a fine-grained, differentiated appreciation of the community context is provided by Aggleton (1993). He reinforces the notion that communities are not homogeneous but rather "socially and culturally fragmented—by age, by class, by culture, and in some cases by gender . . . It is . . . absurd to talk about carrying out HIV/AIDS health promotion within the 'injecting drug using community', within the 'gay community', or even worse, within the 'heterosexual community'" (p. 195).

Kelly's ecological metaphor represents one effort to provide a roadmap for understanding the community in a differentiated manner. He focuses on four ecological processes: adaptation, cycling of resources, interdependence, and succession and their implications for understanding and intervention (Kelly, 1968; Trickett, 1996; Trickett & Birman, 1989; Trickett et al., 1972; Trickett et al., 1985). Together, they represent a framework for assessing community norms and structures, latent and manifest personal and social resources in the community, how differing aspects of the community fit together in reciprocal interaction, and the sociocultural history and future hopes of the community and its varying groups.

Each provides information relevant to the design and implementation of interventions. The adaptation principle, for example, directs attention to those aspects of the community that shape what is possible and permissible and what is not. The availability of certain behavior settings provides one such example of the opportunities and constraints facing individuals

in any particular community. For example, it might suggest the importance of looking for the venues where sexual encounters or risk behavior
is most likely to occur and assessing the norms governing sexual encounters in those venues.

In this regard, Matricka-Tyndale et al. (1997) discovered in Thailand
four contexts for the purchase of sexual services: brothels, festivals, sugar-
cane camps, and cattle markets. Latkin et al. (1994) identified five different
community settings, including residences and shooting galleries, that affected frequency of use and injection practices. Both studies link the design of interventions to identification of relevant social settings and the
social dynamics that characterize those settings (see also Latkin & Knowlton, this volume; Yoshikawa, Wilson, Peterson, & Shinn, this volume). Additionally, the attention paid to changing social and community norms
around safe-sex behavior (Kelly et al., 1991; Treadway & Yoakam, 1992)
rests on an appreciation of the critical role of local norms in promoting or
preventing risky behavior, as do efforts to alter norms in the social networks and support systems of at-risk individuals (Latkin, 1998; Latkin
et al., 1995; Power, Jones, Kearns, Ward, & Perera, 1995).

The second principle is the cycling of resources, drawing attention to
how resources in a community are defined, how they are managed, and
how they may be developed. Resources include people and community
settings that can contribute to local social problem solving (Trickett et al.,
1985). The focus on the resource value of individuals draws attention to
those who care about a particular community problem, have particular
skills or community savvy, and may serve as informal or formal community leaders around issues of concern. The connections among people and
their social networks represent a community-level resource because the
kinds of connections in a community shape the ways in which multiple resources may combine for community problem solving. One particular
resource embedded in community networks lies in what sociologists call
"weak ties" (Granovetter, 1983), those loose connections beyond one's cir-
cle of friends who link individuals to resources often outside the community; the "mole" downtown in the mayor's office, the funding source
outside the community, or the person whose sister in the suburbs is the
best lawyer in town for the issue of the moment.

In addition to people, social settings are also resources for information,
supportive social interactions, crisis resolution, and a sense of social integration. For example, Seibt et al. (1995) found a positive relationship between social attachment to the gay community and its institutions and
safe-sex behavior. They suggest the power of social integration into gay
culture as a protective factor and reinforce the importance of understanding the norms of that culture and how to foster their protective aspects.
Dowsett (1995) describes "community attachment strategies" to reach sexually active gay men "distanced or detached from the gay community"
(p. 247). Developed by gay organizations in Australia, this strategy used
community leaders, entertainers, and gay media to "link gay men to a safe

sex culture invoking the notion of a community acting to protect itself" (p. 247). As Dowsett describes it, "Safe sex culture cannot be reduced to sexual practice: it is context for practice and, as such, has been remarkably successful in sustaining a high degree of compliance for safe sex by most men with most partners most of the time in Australia" (p. 247).

The interdependence principle focuses on the interconnectedness of aspects of the community, of formal helping agencies and informal supportive networks of individuals at risk for HIV, of the cooperative or competitive connections among agencies that may influence how services are delivered, and of the compatibility of commitments of the intervention team and the expectations of community agencies. Attention to the ways in which varied aspects of the community are interdependent draws attention to the importance of anticipating and seeking out the inevitable unanticipated consequences of interventions. Understanding the potential for community ripple effects rests on an appreciation of how a particular intervention might impact the myriad forces, vested interests, and political agendas of agencies involved. From an ecological perspective, it is naïve to think that interventions affect only those directly involved as recipients or providers (Jewkes & Murcott, 1998). Thus, how different relevant facets of the community of interest fit together to form a coherent and ongoing context for individuals helps inform how to construct an integrative, community-level intervention strategy.

An example of how this might be accomplished at the agency level is provided by Singer and Weeks (this volume). Their description of the "Hartford Model" outlines the potential value of promoting and maintaining interdependencies among community agencies in the same locale. Here, the connections developed over time and across a variety of specific projects increase the ability to conduct multisetting community-wide interventions. Commitment to the community allows multiple projects to occur over time, with subsequent work building on prior efforts. Importantly, this longitudinal time commitment has provided an accumulated sense of trust among citizen groups, researchers, and agencies involved.

The importance of these long-term time perspectives on communities and intervention is highlighted by the final ecological principle, succession. Here emphasis is placed on both community history and hopes for the future, as interventions are crafted within the context of that history and with the hope that they will create a better future. The powerful role of culture and tradition frame the kinds of interventions that are acceptable and comprehensible from a community perspective. The potency of such forces is well articulated by several scholars (Freimuth et al., 2001; Sengupta et al., 2000; Stevenson & White, 1994) in their discussions of the historical antecedents of African-American suspicion of government-sponsored AIDS interventions fueled by the infamous Tuskegee experiment of years ago. Attention to this history provides a mind-set that can aid in developing interventions that are sufficiently congruent with community understandings and traditions to be seen as locally useful and worthy of preserving.

THE ECOLOGY OF LIVES: CONTEXTUAL AND CULTURAL INFLUENCES ON INDIVIDUAL EXPERIENCE

Community assessment is not only critical for identifying local norms, power structures, resources, and traditions but it also provides a context within which to appreciate the lived experience of those at risk for HIV/AIDS. From an ecology of lives perspective, the meaning of risk behavior cannot be separated from the sociocultural context in which it occurs. Further, that context is itself differentiated into varied life domains (Swindle & Moos, 1992), such that behavior in any one domain, such as sexual behavior, is understandable only in the context of other situations the individual must negotiate. As Kelly and Kalichman (1995) argue with respect to the interpersonal context of HIV risk behaviors, "research on situational antecedents of high-risk sex underscores the fact that sexual behavior does not occur in isolation from other events in people's lives, and that these other events can serve as important risk cofactors" (p. 911).

The ecology of lives as influencing sexual risk has received considerable attention in the AIDS literature across levels of analysis. Family ecology is discussed by Roth, Siegel, and Black (1994) in their essay on the particular concerns arising among children living in families with AIDS, and Rotheram-Borus and Fernandez (1995) view the distinctive developmental challenges faced by gay and lesbian youth as significant stressors that may lead to sexual risk behaviors (see also Doll & Beeker, 1996). Additional attention is brought to the adaptive demands of differing groups of individuals by Luna (1991) in describing the lives and associated survival demands of street youth in San Francisco and Rio de Janeiro, and Bletzer (1995) in his discussion of how ethnography informed interventions for Latino farm workers in Michigan.

A particularly nuanced portrayal of the link between context and risk behavior is provided by Campbell (2000) in her account of condom use among sex workers in South Africa. She focuses on factors that might influence a community-based peer education and condom distribution program. Her interviews with local sex workers draw attention to how the ongoing everyday organization of their "working and living conditions, as well as the strategies they use to construct positive social identities despite working in the most stigmatized of professions, serve to undermine their confidence in their ability to insist on condom use in sexual encounters with reluctant clients" (p. 479).

Much other work in this area focuses on the role of culture in defining the meaning of behavior, the role constraints associated with cultural identification, and the influence of cultural norms in the community on the expression of sexual risk behavior. For example, an ethnographic inquiry with Latinos (Carrier & Magana, 1991) combined field observations with interviews to map the kinds of behaviors in female prostitutes and male migrant laborers that were most likely associated with AIDS transmission. This inquiry found differences between Mexican-American and Anglo men in preferred sexual behaviors and in self-labeling as homosexual or bisexual, suggesting important differentiations in the subsequent intervention process. These same authors are among the few who comment on the implications of acculturation levels and styles for the development of sexual preferences. They suggest that greater social integration with Anglo Americans in adolescence would increase the likelihood of selecting them as later sexual partners, while greater Mexican-American adolescent social integration would tilt the scales toward later Mexican-American sexual involvement.

In addition, many other studies have documented the link between culture-linked norms and individual risk. Included here are issues such as familismo in Hispanic communities (Guyish & Sanstad, 1992) and the role of cultural norms and sex-role options for women, particularly around sexual decision making ('Amaro, 1995; Gupta & Weiss, 1993; Tawil et al., 1995). Economic influences on sexual behavior and risk are also prominent. For example, Weeks, Schensul, Williams, Singer, and Grier (1995) report that impoverished women of color accepted risky sexual behavior in order to maintain important economic as well as affectional ties with men (Weeks, Schensul, Williams, Singer, & Grier, 1995), while Carrier and Bolton (1991) and de Zalduondo (1991) discuss prostitution as an economic choice.

An extended example of the process of understanding the ecology of everyday lives is provided by Feldman, O'Hara, Baboo, Chitalu, and Lu (1997) in their development of a sociocultural model of behavior change relevant to the lives of adolescents from Zambia. These authors conducted extensive interviews with out-of-school and in-school male and female adolescents, including extensive inquiry into the social norms surrounding sex, the demands of their daily lives, and risk behaviors. They found links between socioeconomic and gender role-related factors. For example, many of the out-of-school girls spent time doing household chores at their parents' or relatives' homes without compensation, a situation that encouraged requesting cash or gifts for sexual favors from out-of-school boys. In addition, many were having sex with older men "who were asking for or performing a wider variety of sexual activities. We learned in a focus group discussion that it was not the money which necessarily drove the girls to these adult men, but rather it was increased (financial) security" (p. 462) they could provide in case of pregnancy and subsequent childbirth.

Additional research used local knowledge about culture-based values and preferences as a resource in the design of interventions. The rationale for such efforts is provided by Herdt and Boxer (1991): "Because national and local safe-sex campaigns are now reaching previously inaccessible communities, including hidden and marginal segments of our pluralistic society, the problem is to understand how these messages are perceived and received by different cultural communities" (p. 183). These same authors describe the crucial role of ethnographic knowledge as a basis for finding credible community sources to deliver interventions, locating them in familiar community institutions such as churches, and developing community outreach programs to reach populations not typically identified by service providers (see also Singer & Marxauch-Rodriquez, 1996).

From this same perspective, Airhihenbuwa, DiClemente, Wingood, and Lowe (1992) discuss the important role of ethnically based values of unity and cooperation and the significance of the extended family in African-American communities. They suggest that these resources can and should be incorporated into the design of interventions for African-American populations. They cite gender roles and the community mistrust of the White majority culture as important cultural influence on AIDS interventions that require additional attention.

Finally, in addition to a focus on context, culture, and settings, the ecology of lives also fosters insight into potential differences between the categories imposed by outside researchers and those individuals supposedly represented by those categories. For example, Singer and Weeks (1996) suggest that "lumping individuals of differing identities, cultures, and experiences into the same social category because they share a common potential route of infection and implementing uniform prevention programs targeted to these otherwise heterogeneous social groupings is not an effective way to make significant progress in halting the spread of AIDS" (p. 489). In addition, such externally imposed categories might lead "large numbers of individuals to be missed by prevention initiatives" (p. 489)

By drawing attention to the ways in which individuals adapt to and cope with their local contexts, the ecology of lives perspective embeds intervention activities within the constraints, meanings of high risk behaviors, and hopes of those for whom the interventions are intended. Applied to individual-level interventions, it increases the chances that the intervention will take hold and be viewed as showing commitment to understanding the community. The knowledge gained from approaching interventions in such a way, however, promotes an appreciation of community resources and community struggles. This knowledge, in turn, can provide a focus for community change efforts that simultaneously draw on community resources and settings while targeting extraindividual forces relevant to individual risk. Acquiring such knowledge requires the development of collaborative relationships between outside interventionists and community members and organizations. We now turn to the collaborative process.

BUILDING COLLABORATIVE RELATIONSHIPS AND EMPOWERING PROCESSES

Community assessment and attention to the ecology of lives represents only the first of the three fundamental tasks of an ecologically based approach to interventions striving for community impact. The second and third aspects of the ecological approach involve the development of collaborative relationships and the creation of empowering interventions. From an ecological perspective, the kind of relationship developed between the intervention team and the community is itself part of the intervention paradigm, as this relationship is a critical mediator of the intervention and its impact. In addition, the long-range goal of community impact suggests that while specific programs might indeed be developed and implemented, they are viewed not as ends in themselves but as opportunities to create additional community resources or capacity (Trickett & Birman, 1989; Trickett, 2002). Doing so draws attention to the ways in which local resources can be engaged in the intervention process and can, as a result, develop skills that can serve as a future community resource.

Collaboration as a Concept: Rationales, Aspirations, and Complexities

The collaboration concept has a long history in disciplines such as anthropology (Mead, 1969) and sociology (Whyte, 1964), and it has been central to community psychology since its inception. The intent has been to redefine the relationship between scholar and citizen from the image of "expert and client" to one of parties with differential expertise working together in a synergistic way to cope with community problems. The value of a collaborative stance rests on a variety of epistemological rationales and pragmatic aspirations consistent with the intervention goal of community impact.

With respect to epistemology, Argyris has long argued the case that the kind of relationship between researcher and subject affects the validity of knowledge gained. In his classic 1968 essay "Some unintended consequences of rigorous research," he likens the researcher-subject relationship found in controlled laboratory studies to one between workers and management in hierarchical organizations. Thus, the same kinds of unintended consequences found in laboratory research (Rosenthal, 1966), such as physical or psychological withdrawal from the research situation, and overt or covert hostility toward participation, are expected to occur in community research based on the same hierarchical and noncollaborative researcher-subject relationships.

Chavez, Duran, Baker, Avila, and Wallerstein (2003) discuss this epistemological issue more directly in their essay on the power dynamics of ethnicity, racism, and White privilege affecting the validity of information provided in community-based research. They distinguish among four different levels of community dialog (e.g., what researchers might hear) that reflect varying degrees of the authentic expression of beliefs and perspectives: public discourse, hidden transcripts (subordinates gathering outside the gaze of power and constructing a sharply critical and cultural discourse), coded defiance (veiled expression of hidden transcripts in public discourse), and open defiance. They further suggest that internalized oppression might lead community partners to say one thing (yes) and feel another (no).

The fundamental epistemological premise, however, is that unequal partnerships limit the range of valid information and thus may lead to the development of interventions based on invalid data. Collaboration is seen as a stance that can reduce researcher control over the research process and research participants and, as such, may provide a potential antidote to the creation of such interventions (see Booth & Booth, 1994; DiMatteo, Reiter, & Gambone, 1994, for empirical support). This epistemological perspective is reflected broadly in feminist theory (Harding, 1987; Riger, 1992), community psychology (Kingry-Westergaard & Kelly, 1990; Trickett, 1996), and social constructionist and contextualist philosophies of science (Jessor, Colby, & Shweder, 1996; Rosnow & Georguidi, 1986).

Collaboration is also seen within the HIV/AIDS literature as promoting locally useful as well as valid data. For example, Beeker, Guenther-Grey and Raj (1998) suggest that collaboration with communities results in a number of processes related to using knowledge generated through research. These include "greater buy-in from community leaders, better penetration of communities with more acceptable and culturally relevant messages, and greater sustainability of the intervention activities and efforts" (p. 834). Altman (1995b) provides additional rationales for collaboration as a means to generating useful knowledge, including the stimulating of research questions of importance to those living in the community and the information interventionists gather about the implementation of their interventions through close contact with community members involved in it. In addition, he suggests that it improves the chances for sustainability and, because of that, allows an assessment of long-term effects of the intervention over time.

Finally, through dialog between the "theory class" and citizens, collaboration can help reduce the disconnect between research and practice. Freudenberg et al. (1995), in their assessment of AIDS interventions in the United States, suggest a discrepancy between the scope and depth of published evaluations and community practice. Published evaluations were described as "too simplistic or superficial to make a significant impact on the continued transmission of infection or too unique to be valuable" (p. 300), while "the most creative, intensive, and innovative community-based interventions were rarely evaluated, leaving these programs to repeat the same mistakes, unable to share their successes or failures with others" (p. 300) (see Roussos & Fawcett, 2000, for a review of collaborative partnerships and community intervention).

While the collaboration concept involves a variety of approaches and definitions (Trickett & Espino, 2004), Israel, Schulz, Parker, and Becker (1998) suggest "each (approach) is explicitly committed to conducting research that will benefit the participants either through direct intervention or by using the results to inform action for change" (p. 175). Thus, "a fundamental characteristic of community-based research . . . is the emphasis on the participation and influence of nonacademic researchers in the process of creating knowledge" (p. 177).

The ecological perspective on collaboration is perhaps best captured by Singer (1993) in his description of participatory action research at the Hispanic Health Council in Hartford, Connecticut. In Singer's model, research

(1) is developed through a "perpetual discussion" between experienced re-searchers and experienced community health educators and activists, and con-sequently (2) tends to reflect issues, concerns or pressing problems as perceived by members of the community being researched, that (3) is carried out by a het-erogeneous research team; and (4) leads to recognition not only for the re-searchers but also for the community-based agency that sponsors it, as well as (5) a transfer of research skills to minority researchers, while (6) contributing to the intervention, public education, social development, advocacy and/or em-powerment goals of the sponsoring agency. (p. 19)

In touting the potential value of a collaborative stance, however, it is im-portant to clarify that in practice, it is a complex, context-bound phenome-non. For example, surveys of survey researchers (Weiss, 1977) suggest a common wisdom about the importance of hiring indigenous interviews. However, Huygens, Kajura, Seeley, and Barton (1996), in portraying the role of local interviewers in a series of HIV/AIDS related studies in Uganda, state that while "local interviewers played a crucial role in the translation of the questionnaire into Luganda and helped to a large ex-tent in understanding cultural meanings for the data collected . . . there is evidence to suggest that respondents were sometimes reluctant to talk to local interviewers about sensitive issues" (p. 225). At the same time, these authors also provide many examples of how anthropological un-derstanding can complement and enrich quantitative survey, such as clar-ifying that the term "abstinence" "was actually a concept that included various sexual practices (such as coitus interruptus and using a condom for over 20% of their sample)" (p. 228).

In addition, when it comes to collaboration as a concept, the devil is in the details. For example, collaboration can be constructed in such a way as to serve the will of the researcher rather than the needs and concerns of the community. Robertson and Minkler (1994) suggest that such is the case when community health interventions involve what they call "ma-nipulation and tokenistic forms of participation" (p. 305). Here, the agenda is defined and structured by researchers, who attempt to get com-munity members to "buy into" the externally defined agenda and aid in carrying it out "without the members of the community ever having de-cided whether these are the issues of interest to them" (p. 305) (see also Cooke & Kothari, 2001).

Finally, community collaboration can raise ethical issues not clearly covered by existing ethical codes based on the professional-client model. O'Neill (1989), for example, suggests that the redefinition of the role rela-tionship between professional and client as a collaborative one muddies to whom and for what the professional is accountable. Does the concept of human subjects protection invoke the same sets of accountability criteria when, as Margaret Mead (1969) pointed out, the relationship between interventionist and community member is more egalitarian and involves the sharing of power in decision making? What, for example, is the role of the researcher in HIV/AIDS work who, because of developing a close, collaborative relationship with someone who has disclosed that he is HIV positive, is in a situation observing that person about to engage in unprotected sex without telling the partner of his status (see Trickett, 2003 for additional emerging ethical issues related to collaborative inquiry)?

Collaboration, then, represents a critical component of community interventions designed for community impact for both epistemological and pragmatic reasons. However, it also represents a complex concept in need of extensive elaboration with respect to its varied meanings, its implications for the professional role of the interventionist (Krauss, Goldsamt, Bula, & Sember, 1997), and its role in creating sustainable community impact.

Creating Empowering Interventions

The third and final emphasis of an ecological perspective involves the development of interventions that create resources in the community. Such a definition includes both a sociopolitical appreciation of increased community clout to control local resources and such less overtly political outcomes as the development of new skills among members of key community organizations or the creation of new settings responsive to enduring community needs. To overly simplify, community assessment provides the content and community collaboration the process for the development of local skills, knowledge, and resources. This orchestrated integration makes a specific claim on collaboration to serve the goal of community development rather than as a means of getting a specific project done.

The goal of community empowerment is increasingly found in AIDS literature (Airhihenbuwa et al., 1992; Asthana & Oostvogels, 1996; Beeker et al., 1998; Freudenberg & Zimmerman, 1995), and a strong case has been made for the empowerment paradigm as a perspective that can affect community health and well-being more generally (Altman, 1995b; Rappaport, 1987). The general rationale for such a stance is provided by Hawe and colleagues (Hawe & Shiell, 2000; Hawe, Noort, King, & Jordens, 1997) in discussions of community health promotion. Their perspective on empowerment involves community capacity building, or the ability of the intervention to mobilize others in the community in an effort to "prolong and multiply health effects" (p. 29) of specific interventions.

Creating empowering interventions, then, involves creating programs and processes geared toward creating a change in community capacity. Change in community capacity, within an ecological perspective, rests on a knowledge of existing community structure and resources, ongoing collaborative relationships organized around the shared goal of community betterment, and the linking of interventions with community resources in a capacity-imparting manner. It requires a long-range time commitment (see Singer & Weeks, this volume) and a community-embedded vision for how specific intervention activities and programs can help define and promote subsequent local intervention agendas. It requires a "from the inside out" perspective on the tasks facing local community organizations who carry out such interventions (Miller & Greene, this volume). The ecological perspective of the current chapter represents one initial effort to provide a mindset and roadmap for approaching this task (Trickett & Birman, 1989).

However, as Beeker et al. (1998) point out, there are many fronts on which progress must be made if the goal of community interventions involves community impact. One such goal involves the conceptual articulation and subsequent assessment of such key concepts as community capacity and community empowerment in the community context. Recently, several efforts have been made to describe and operationalize such concepts. Laverack and Wallerstein (2001) outline a series of theoretical and practical questions guiding the intervention process from an empowerment perspective," including "who is the community in a program context?" and "how does the empowerment approach (to community development) influence stakeholder roles and responsibilities?" Goodman et al. (1998) provide a set of dimensions relevant to the community capacity construct, including the nature of citizen participation, the development of local skills, the ability to access and share resources, and the development of interorganizational networks. Additional essays focus on perception of individual, organizational, and community control (Israel, Checkoway, Shulz, & Zimmerman, 1994) and measuring the degree of community mobilization (Cheadle et al., 1998). Thus, the momentum described at the beginning of the chapter for alternative approaches to community intervention involving community impact in HIV/AIDS is complemented by work across varied areas of behavioral science.

CONCLUSION

From an ecological perspective, directing attention to the community impact of HIV/AIDS interventions represents first and foremost a paradigm-stretching or altering set of activities. It includes the development of conceptual frameworks for understanding the community context and the development of methods for doing so: It necessitates a multiple-method approach to understanding the ecology of the lives of those targeted for intervention, as well as those attempting to deliver them (see Miller & Greene, this volume); and it mandates the development of reciprocal, collaborative relationships in the design, conduct, and evaluation of interventions. In addition, it suggests that external agencies at the local, state, and national level who fund such work consider how to promote scientific accountability while remaining responsive to community-defined issues and influence over problem definition. One specific implication of this is adopting a time frame that supports local planning and the development of authentic and expedient collaborative relationships between interventionists and community groups and institutions.

The bottom line is that increasing community capacity, developing resources that can serve communities well over time, is not a 3- to 5-year project but an ongoing commitment. Sustainability of that commitment is a daunting yet critical task. The current chapter, and indeed the book, is intended as a stimulus for thought about how to embed current work on AIDS interventions within the critical task of community development. The intent and hope of the book is to provide ideas, examples, and issues that can further our understanding of and ability to appreciate the diversity and complexity of our communities while simultaneously contributing to our ability to become a resource to those living in them.

REFERENCES

Aggleton, P. (1993). Promoting whose health? Models of health promotion and education about HIV disease. *Advances in Medical Sociology, 3*, 185–200.

Airhihenbuwa, C., DiClemente, R., Wingood, G., & Lowe, A. (1992). HIV/AIDS education and prevention among African-Americans: A focus on culture. *AIDS Education and Prevention, 4*(3), 267–276.

Altman, D. (1995a). Strategies for community health intervention: Promises, paradoxes, pitfalls. *Psychosomatic Medicine, 57*, 226–233.

Altman, D. G. (1995b). Sustaining interventions in community systems: On the relationship between researchers and communities. *Health Psychology, 14*(6), 526–536.

Amaro, H. (1995). Love, Sex, and Power: Considering women's realities in HIV prevention. *American Psychologist, 50*(6), 437–447.

Argyris, C. (1968). Some unintended consequences of rigorous research. *Psychological Bulletin, 70*(3), 185–197.

Asthana, S. & Oostvogels, R. (1996). Community participation in HIV prevention: Problems and prospects for community-based strategies among female sex workers in Madras. *Social Science and Medicine, 43*(2), 133–148.

Barker, R. G. (1968). *Ecological psychology: Concepts and methods for studying the environment of human behavior.* Stanford, CA: Stanford University Press.

Beeker, C., Guenther-Grey, C., & Raj, A. (1998). Community empowerment paradigm drift and the primary prevention of HIV/AIDS. *Social Science Medicine, 46*(7), 831–842.

Bletzer, K. V. (1995). Use of ethnography in the evaluation and targeting of HIV/AIDS education among Latino farm workers. *AIDS Education and Prevention, 7*(2), 178–191.

Booth, T. & Booth, W. (1994). The use of depth interviewing with vulnerable subjects: Lessons from a research study of parents with learning difficulties. *Social Science Medicine, 39*(3), 415–424.

Bronfenbrenner, U. (1979). *The ecology of human development: Experiments by nature and design.* Cambridge: Harvard University Press.

Campbell, C. (2000). Selling sex in the time of AIDS: The psycho-social context of condom use by sex workers on a South African mine. *Social Science and Medicine, 50*, 479–494.

Carrier, J. & Bolton, R. (1991). Anthropological perspectives on sexuality and HIV prevention. *Annual Review of Sex Research, 2*, 49–75.

Carrier, J. M. & Magana, J. R. (1991). Use of ethnosexual data on men of Mexican origin for HIV/AIDS prevention programs. *Journal of Sex Research, 28*(2), 189–202.

Chavez, V., Duran, B., Baker, Q., Avila, M., & Wallerstein, N. (2003). The dance of race and privilege in community based participatory research. In M. Minkler & N. Wallerstein (Eds.) *Community-based participatory research for health* (pp. 81–97). San Francisco: Jossey-Bass.

Cheadle, A., Wagner, E., Anderman, C., Walls, M., McBride, C., Bell, M., et al. (1998). Measuring community mobilization in the Seattle minority youth health project. *Evaluation Review, 22*(6), 699–716.

Choi, K. H. & Coates, T. J. (1994). Prevention of HIV infection. *AIDS, 8*(10), 1371–1389.

Cooke, B. & Kothari, U. (Eds.). (2001). *Participation: The new tyranny*. London: Zed Books.

de Zalduondo, B. O. (1991). Prostitution viewed cross-culturally: Toward reconceptualizing sex work in AIDS intervention research. *Journal of Sex Research, 28*(2), 223–248.

DiMatteo, M. R., Reiter, R. C., & Gambone, J. C. (1994). Enhancing medication adherence through communication and informed collaborative choice. *Health Communication, 6*(4), 253–265.

Doll, L. S. & Beeker, C. (1996). Male bisexual behavior and HIV risk in the United States: Synthesis of research with implications for behavioral interventions. *AIDS Education and Prevention, 8*(3), 205–225.

Dowsett, G. (1995). Sexual contexts, HIV prevention and gay men. *Venereology, 8*(4), 243–250.

Dunlap, E. & Johnson, B. D. (1999). Gaining access to hidden populations: Strategies for gaining cooperation of drug sellers/dealers and their families in ethnographic research. *Drugs and Society, 14*(1-2), 127–149.

Feldman, D. A., O'Hara, P., Baboo, K. S., Chitalu, N. W., & Lu, Y. (1997). HIV prevention among Zambian adolescents: Developing a value utilization/norm change model. *Social Science and Medicine, 44*(4), 455–468.

Freimuth, V., Quinn, S. C., Thomas, S., Cole, G., Zook, E., & Duncan, T. (2001). African Americans' views on research and the Tuskegee Syphilis Study. *Social Science and Medicine, 52*, 797–808.

Freudenberg, N., Eng, E., Flay, B., Parcel, G., Rogers, T., & Wallerstein, N. (1995). Strengthening individual and community capacity to prevent disease and promote health: In search of relevant theories and principles. *Health Education Quarterly, 22*(3), 290–306.

Freudenberg, N. & Zimmerman, M. (1995). *AIDS prevention in the community: Lessons from the first decade*. Washington DC: American Public Health Association.

Gagnon, J. (1989). Disease and desire. *Daedelus, 118*, 44–77.

Gergen, K. (1985). The social constructionist movement in modern psychology. *American Psychologist, 40*, 266–275

Goodman, R. M., Speers, A. M., McLeroy, K., Fawcett, S., Kegler, M., Parker, E., et al. (1998). Identifying and defining the dimensions of community capacity to provide a basis for measurement. *Health Education and Behavior, 25*(3), 258–278.

Granovetter, M. (1983). The strength of weak ties: A network theory revisited. *Sociological Theory, 1*, 201–233.

Green, L. & Mercer, S. (2001). Can public health researchers and agencies reconcile the push from funding bodies and the pull from communities? *American Journal of Public Health, 91,* 1926–1929.

Gupta, G. R. & Weiss, E. (1993). Women's lives and sex: Implications for AIDS prevention. *Culture, Medicine, and Psychiatry, 17,* 399–412.

Guydish, J. & Sanstad, K. H. (1992). Behavior change among intravenous drug users: The role of community-based interventions. *Psychology of Addictive Behaviors, 6*(2), 91–99.

Harding, S. (1987). Introduction: Is there a feminist method? In S. Harding (Ed.), *Feminism and methodology* (pp. 1–14). Bloomington: Indiana University Press.

Hawe, P., Noort, M., King, L., & Jordens, C. (1997). Multiplying health gains: the critical role of capacity-building within health promotion programs. *Health Policy, 39,* 29–42.

Hawe, P. & Shiell, A. (2000). Social capital and health promotion: A review. *Social Science and Medicine, 51,* 871–885.

Herdt, G. (1987). AIDS and anthropology, *Anthropology Today, 3,* 1–3.

Herdt, G. & Boxer, A. M. (1991). Ethnographic issues in the study of AIDS. *Journal of Sex Research, 28*(2), 171–187.

Herdt, G. & Lindenbaum, S. (1992). *The time of AIDS: Social analysis, theory, and method.* Newbury Park, CA.: Sage.

Huygens, P., Kajura, E., Seeley, J., & Barton, T. (1996). Rethinking methods for the study of sexual behavior. *Social Science and Medicine, 42*(2), 221–231.

Israel, B, Checkoway, B., Shulz, A., & Zimmerman, M. (1994). Health education and community empowerment: Conceptualizing and measuring perceptions of individual, organizational, and community control. *Health Education Quarterly, 21*(2), 149–170.

Israel, B. A., Schulz, A. J., Parker, E. A., & Becker, A. B. (1998). Review of community-based research: Assessing partnership approaches to improve public health. *Annual Review of Public Health, 19,* 173–202.

Jessor, R., Colby, A., & Shweder, R. (Eds.) (1996). *Ethnography and Human Development.* Chicago: University of Chicago Press.

Jewkes, R. & Murcott, A. (1998). Community representatives: Representing the "Community"? *Social Science and Medicine, 46*(7), 843–858.

Kegeles, S. M., Hays, R. B., & Coates, T. J. (1996). The Mpowerment Project: A community-level HIV prevention intervention for young gay men. *American Journal of Public Health, 86*(8), 1129–1136.

Kellam, S. & Langevin, D. (2003). A framework for understanding "evidence" in prevention research and programs. *Prevention Science, 4*(3), 137–153.

Kelly, J., Heckman, T., Stevenson, L., Williams, P., Ertl, T., Hays, R., et al. (2000). Transfer of research-based HIV prevention interventions to community service providers: Fidelity and adaptation. *AIDS Education and Prevention, 12*(Suppl. A), 87–98.

Kelly, J. A. & Kalichman, S. C. (1995). Increased attention to human sexuality can improve HIV-AIDS prevention efforts: Key research issues and directions. *Journal of Consulting and Clinical Psychology, 63*(6), 907–918.

Kelly, J. A., St. Lawrence, J. S., Diaz, Y., Stevenson, L. Y, Hauth, A. C., Brasfield, T. L., et al. (1991). HIV risk behavior reduction following intervention with key option leaders of population: An experimental analysis. *American Journal of Public Health, 81*(2), 168–171.

Kelly, J. A., St. Lawrence, J. S., Stevenson, Y., Hauth, A. C., Kalichman, S. C., Diaz, Y. E., et al. (1992). Community AIDS/HIV risk reduction: The effects of endorsements by popular people in three cities. *American Journal of Public Health, 82*(11), 1483–1489.

Kelly, J. G. (1968). Toward an ecological conception of preventive interventions. In J. W. Carter, Jr. (Ed.). *Research contributions from psychology to community mental health.* New York, NY: Behavioral Publications.

Kelly, J. G. (1970). Toward an ecological conception of preventive interventions. In D. Adelson & B. Kalis (Eds.), *Community psychology and mental health* (pp. 126–145). Scranton, PA: Chandler.

Kelly, J. G. (1971). The quest for valid preventive interventions. In G. Rosenblum (Ed.), *Issues in community psychology and community mental health.* New York: Behavioral Publications.

Kingry-Westergaard, C. & Kelly, J. G. (1990). A contextualist epistemology for ecological research. In P. Tolan, C. Keys, F. Chertok, & L. Jason (Eds.), *Researching community psychology* (pp. 23–32). Washington, DC: American Psychological Association.

Krauss, B., Goldsamt, L., Bula, E., & Sember, R. (1997). The White researcher in the multicultural community: Lessons in HIV prevention education learned in the field. *Journal of Health Education, 28*(6), 567–571.

Kuhn, T. S. (1970). *The structure of scientific revolutions.* Chicago: University of Chicago Press.

Latkin, C. (1998). Outreach in natural settings: The use of peer leaders for HIV prevention among injecting drug users' networks. *Public Health Reports* (Suppl. 1), 151–159.

Latkin, C., Mandell, W., Oziemkowska, M., Celentano, D., Vlahov, D., Ensminger, M., et al. (1995). Using social network analysis to study patterns of drug use among urban drug users at high risk for HIV/AIDS. *Drug and Alcohol Dependence, 38,* 1–9.

Latkin, C., Mandell, W., Vlahov, D., Oziemkowska, M., Knowlton, A., & Celentano, D. (1994). My place, your place, or no place: Behavior settings as a risk factor for HIV-related injection practices of drug users in Baltimore, Maryland. *American Journal of Community Psychology, 22,* 415–430.

Laverack, G. & Wallerstein, N. (2001). Measuring community empowerment: A fresh look at organizational domains. *Health Promotion International, 16*(2), 179–185.

Luna, G. C. (1991). Street Youth: Adaptation and survival in the AIDS decade. *Journal of Adolescent Health, 12,* 511–514.

Maticka-Tyndale, E., Elkins, D., Haswell-Elkins, M., Ruikakoirn, D., Kuyyakanond, T., & Stam, K. (1997). Contexts and patterns of men's commercial sexual partnerships in Northeastern Thailand: Implications for AIDS prevention. *Social Science and Medicine, 44*(2), 199–213.

McGuire, W. J. (1983). A contextualist theory of knowledge: Its implications for innovation and reform in psychological research. In L. Berkowitz (Ed.), *Advances in Experimental Social Psychology* (Vol. 16, pp. 1–47). New York: Academic Press.

Mead, M. (1969). Research with human beings: A model derived from anthropological field practice. *Daedalus, 98*(2), 361–386.

Minkler, M. & Wallerstein, N. (Eds.) (2003). *Community-based participatory research for health.* San Francisco: Jossey-Bass.

Moos, R. H. (1974). *Evaluating treatment environments: A social ecological approach.* New York: Wiley.

Moos, R. H. (1979). *Evaluating educational environments.* San Francisco: Jossey-Bass.

O'Neill, P. (1989). Responsible to whom? Responsible for what? Some ethical issues in community intervention. *American Journal of Community Psychology, 17*(3), 323–341.

Parker, R. (1987). Acquired immunodeficiency syndrome in urban Brazil. *Medical Anthropology Quarterly, 1*, 155–175.

Power, R., Jones, S., Kearns, G., Ward., J., & Perera, J. (1995). Drug user networks, coping strategies, a HIV prevention in the community. *The Journal of Drug Issues, 25*(3), 565–581.

Rappaport, J. (1981). In praise of paradox: A social policy of empowerment over prevention. *American Journal of Community Psychology, 9*(1), 1–25.

Rappaport, J. (1987). Terms of empowerment/exemplars of prevention: Toward a theory for community psychology. *American Journal of Community Psychology, 15*(2), 121–148.

Rhodes, T., Stimson, G. V., & Quirk, A. (1996). Sex, drugs, intervention, and research: From the individual to the social. *Substance Use and Misuse, 31*(3), 375–407.

Riger, S. (1992). Epistemological debates, feminist voices: Science, social values, and the study of women. *American Psychologist, 47*(6), 730–740.

Robertson, A. & Minkler, M. (1994). New health promotion movement: A critical examination. *Health Education Quarterly, 21*(3), 295–312.

Rosenthal, R. (1966). *Experimenter Effects in Behavioral Research.* New York: Appleton-Century-Crofts.

Rosnow, R. & Georgoudi, M. (Eds.). (1986). *Contextualism and understanding in behavioral research.* NY: Praeger.

Roth, J., Siegel, R., & Black, S. (1994). Identifying the mental health needs of chil dren living in families with AIDS or HIV infection. *Community Mental Health Journal, 30*(6), 581–593.

Rotheram-Borus, M. J. & Fernandez, M. I. (1995). Sexual orientation and developmental challenges experienced by gay and lesbian youth. *Suicide and Life-Threatening Behavior, 25*(Suppl.) 26–34.

Rotheram-Borus, M., Rebchook, G., Kelly, J., Adams, J., & Neumann, M. (2000). Bridging research and practice: Community-researcher partnerships for replicating effective interventions. *AIDS Education and Prevention, 12*(Suppl. A), 49–61.

Roussos, S. T. & Fawcett, S. B. (2000). A review of collaborative partnerships as a strategy for improving community health. *Annual Review of Public Health, 21*, 369–402.

Sarason, S. (1972). *Creation of settings and the future of societies.* San Francisco: Jossey-Bass.

Sarason, S. B. (1981) *Psychology misdirected.* New York: Free Press.

Seibt, A. C., Ross, M. W., Freeman, A., Krepcho, M., Hedrich, A., McAlister, A., et al. (1995). Relationship between safe sex and acculturation into the gay subculture. *AIDS Care, 7*(Suppl. 1), s85–s88.

Sengupta, S., Strauss, R., DeVellis, R., Quinn, S., DeVellis, B., & Ware, W. (2000). Factors affecting African-American participation in AIDS research. *Journal of Acquired Immune Deficiency Syndrome, 24*, 275–284.

Shweder, R. A. (1990). Cultural psychology: What is it? In J. Stigler, R. Shweder, & G. Herdt (Eds.), *Cultural Psychology: Essays on comparative human development* (pp. 1–43). Cambridge: Cambridge University Press.

Singer, M. (1993). Knowledge for use: Anthropology and community-centered substance abuse research. *Social Science Medicine, 37*(1), 15–25.

Singer, M. & Marxauch-Rodriquez, L. (1996). Applying anthropology to the pre-
    vention of AIDS: The Latino Gay Men's Mental Health Project. *Human Organiz-
    ation*, *55*(2), 141–148.
Singer, M. & Weeks, M. (1996). Preventing AIDS in communities of color: Anthro-
    pology and social prevention. *Human Organization*, *55*(4), 488–492.
Stevenson, H. C. & White, J. J. (1994). AIDS prevention struggles in ethnocultural
    neighborhoods: Why research partnerships with community based organiza-
    tions can't wait. *AIDS Education and Prevention*, *6*(2), 126–139.
Swindle, R. & Moos, R. H. (1992). Life domains in stressors, coping, and adjust-
    ment. In W. B. Walsh, K. H. Craik, & R. H. Price (Eds.), *Person-Environment Psy-
    chology* (pp. 1–34). Hillsdale, NJ: Lawrence Erlbaum Associates, Inc.
Tawil, O., Verster, A., & O'Reilly, K. R. (1995). Enabling approaches for HIV/AIDS
    prevention: Can we modify the environment and minimize the risk? *AIDS, 9*,
    291–306.
Treadway, L. & Yoakam., J. (1992). Creating a safer school environment for lesbian
    and gay students. *Journal of School Health*, *62*(7), 352–357.
Treichler, P. (1987). AIDS, homophobia, and biomedical discourse: An epidemic of
    signification. *Cultural Studies, 1*, 32–70.
Treichler, P. (1992). AIDS, HIV, and the cultural construction of reality. In G. Herdt &
    S. Lindenbaum (Eds.), *The time of AIDS: Social analysis, theory, and method.* (pp.
    65–98). Newbury Park, CA: Sage Publications.
Trickett, E. J. (1996). A future for community psychology: The contexts of diversity
    and the diversity of contexts. *American Journal of Community Psychology*, *24*(2),
    209–234.
Trickett, E. J. (2002). Culture, context, and collaboration in AIDS interventions:
    Ecological ideas for enhancing community impact. *Journal of Primary Preven-
    tion*, *23*(2), 157–174.
Trickett, E. J. (2003). Community collaboration and ethics: New wine in new Bot-
    tles. *Leadership in Public Health*, *6*(3), 11–16.
Trickett, E. J. & Birman, D. (1989). Taking ecology seriously: A community devel-
    opment approach to individually based interventions. In L. Bond & B. Compas
    (Eds.), *Primary prevention in the schools.* Hanover, NH: University of New En-
    gland Press.
Trickett, E. J. & Espino, S. (2004). Collaboration and social inquiry: The multiple
    roles of relationships in creating useful and valid knowledge. *American Journal
    of Community Psychology*, *34*(1-2), 1–69.
Trickett, E. J., Kelly, J. G., & Todd, D. M. (1972). The social environment of the high
    school: Guidelines for individual change and organizational development. In
    S. Golann & C. Eisdorfer (Eds.), *Handbook of community mental health* (pp.
    331–406). New York: Appleton-Century-Crofts.
Trickett, E. J., Kelly, J. G., & Vincent, T. A. (1985). The spirit of ecological inquiry in
    community research. In D. Klein & E. Susskind (Ed.), *Knowledge building in com-
    munity psychology* (pp. 283–333). New York: Praeger.
Trickett, E. J. & Schmid, K. (1993). The social context of the school: An ecological
    perspective on school, adolescents in schools, and intervention in schools. In
    P. Tolan & B. Cohler (Eds.) *Handbook of Clinical Research and Practice with Adoles-
    cents.* New York: Wiley & Sons.
Valdiserri, R. O., Ogden, L. L., & McCray, E. (2003). Accomplishments in HIV pre-
    vention science: Implications for stemming the epidemic. *Nature Medicine*, *9*(7),
    881–886.

van Empelen, P., Kok, G., van Kesteren, N. M. C., van den Borne, B., Bos, A. E. R., & Schaalma, H. P. (2003). Effective methods to change sex-risk among drug users: a review of psychosocial interventions. *Social Science and Medicine, 57*(9), 1593–1608.

Wallerstein, N. (1999). Power between evaluator and "community" research relationships within New Mexico's healthier communities. *Social Science and Medicine, 49*, 39–53.

Weeks, M. R., Schensul, J. J., Williams, S. S., Singer, M., & Grier, M. (1995). AIDS prevention for African-American and Latina women: Building culturally and gender-appropriate intervention. *AIDS Education and Prevention, 7*(3), 251–263.

Weiss, C. H. (1977). Survey researchers and minority communities. *Journal of Social Issues, 33*(4), 20–35.

Whyte, W. (1964). The slum: On the evolution of street corner society. In A. Vidich, J. Benshan, & M. Stein (Eds.), *Reflections on community studies* (pp. 3–71). New York: Harper & Row.

2

Multiple Pathways to Community-Level Impacts in HIV Prevention: Implications for Conceptualization, Implementation, and Evaluation of Interventions

Hirokazu Yoshikawa, Patrick A. Wilson,
John L. Peterson, & Marybeth Shinn

In recent years, researchers, community-based organizations, activists, and policy makers have called increasingly for community-level change in HIV prevention. Behavioral interventions to prevent HIV infection in the United States, particularly those evaluated by researchers, were most commonly directed toward the individual or small-group levels of behavior change in the 1980s and early 1990s. The two most glaring shortcomings of this approach have been pointed out many times: neglect of efforts to change contextual and structural influences on HIV infection, and lack of attention to culturally specific influences omitted from most individual-level theories of behavior change (Diaz, 1998; Friedman, Des Jarlais, & Ward, 1994; Hays & Peterson, 1994; Ickovics & Yoshikawa, 1998; Kelly, 1999; National Institutes of Health [NIH] Consensus Panel, 1997; Sobo, 1995; Trickett, this volume). More importantly, these shortcomings limited evidence-based efforts to bring about community-level reductions in HIV infection. In the past decade, funding agencies, researchers, and activists have engaged in multiple efforts to implement and evaluate community-level HIV prevention across the United States with populations such as injection drug users (IDUs), men who have sex with men (MSM), women, and youth. These interventions have been based on theories that bring much needed extraindividual levels of analysis—whether at the social network, organizational, or community levels—to the behavioral science base of HIV prevention.

This chapter outlines the multiple pathways that may lead to community-level reductions in the incidence of HIV/AIDS. Change in communities, like change in other complex social systems, can operate in multiple ways—that is, a variety of causal processes involving multiple subsystems within communities can lead to the common goal of reduction of HIV infection. We believe that the field of HIV prevention has only begun to consider the many ways in which prevention can occur at the community level. By expanding the scope of such efforts, we hope to inform the conceptualization, implementation, and evaluation of community-level interventions.

SOCIAL CAPITAL AND SOCIAL BARRIERS AS CHARACTERISTICS
OF COMMUNITIES AND TARGETS FOR COMMUNITY-LEVEL HIV PREVENTION

We begin with two questions: What is a community? What is a community-level effect in HIV prevention? It is particularly important to establish clear definitions of community and community-level prevention, as they differ from the public-health notion of a population and populationwide prevention. At first glance, a community and a population may seem like identical terms. Both can define a group of individuals through geographic characteristics (e.g., natural boundaries, resident-perceived boundaries, or political boundaries; Heller, 1989), demographic characteristics (e.g., race, ethnicity, sexual orientation, or a particular minority or majority status), or a combination of the two. Then what makes a community distinct from a population? For our purposes, we define a community as a geographically and/or demographically defined population with 1) a social identity, and 2) some evidence of social capital. Bourdieu (1986, p. 248) defined social capital as "the aggregate of the actual or potential resources which are linked to possession of a durable network of more or less institutionalized relationships of mutual acquaintance and recognition—or in other words, to membership in a group." Putnam (1995) described it as "features of social organization such as networks, norms, and social trust that facilitate coordination and cooperation for mutual benefit." Dimensions of social capital are regularly cited as important characteristics of communities in surveys of community residents (MacQueen, McLellan, Metzger, & Kegeles, 2001; McMillan & Chavis, 1986; Sarason, 1974).

This definition of community already begins to suggest how community-level prevention may differ from what we view as the more encompassing term, populationwide prevention. That is, communities in this definition are distinguished from populations through patterns of care, support, social norms, communication, and resources across individuals who are nested within multiple kinds of networks (e.g., family, social, and organizational) and linked by a common social identity. These aspects of social capital represent particularly important targets for change, or resources that can be used to create change that, by definition, goes beyond the individual level of analysis.

At the same time, the challenges of community-level HIV prevention often stem from social barriers that obstruct the levels of care, support, social norms, communication, and resources that may lead to HIV risk reduction. These barriers include class-based stratification; discrimination and power imbalances across social categories such as gender, race, ethnicity, age, or sexual orientation; and taboos and stigmas regarding particular behaviors, such as drug use or particular forms of sexual behavior.

We argue, then, that successful community-level HIV prevention not only targets particular dimensions of social capital for change but also addresses social barriers in the relevant community in its intervention strategies. This approach is consistent with the tenets of community psychology, which examine influences on behavior that cross multiple levels of analysis (e.g., individuals, small groups, organizations, and community; Peterson, 1998; Revenson & Seidman, 2002).

What are the multiple pathways through which community-level impacts in HIV prevention may be achieved? Which appear to be underutilized, whether for particular populations, community contexts, or modes of transmission? How have programs that successfully reduced HIV risk or incidence changed levels of social capital or social barriers in communities? The remainder of this chapter will address these questions. Our discussion differs from prior ones in this area; they typically focus on contextual or structural factors that predict HIV risk, or summarize successful community-level prevention programs. In contrast, we have chosen to organize the chapter according to different pathways that lead to community-level impacts. We discuss: (1) grassroots community mobilization, (2) the aggregation of subgroup-level change, (3) the aggregation of setting-level change, (4) organizational and institutional change, (5) change in public policy, and (6) the adoption and replication of interventions involving any of these pathways. For each, we offer exemplars and then note challenges they pose for evaluation and next steps in research.

Pathways to Community-Level Change

Grassroots Community Mobilization   Grassroots community mobilization, through processes of community organizing and social action, has led to some of the largest community-level changes in health behavior on record (Hays & Peterson, 1994; Revenson & Schiaffino, 2000; Ross & Kelley, 2000). The response of the White gay communities in large urban centers to the AIDS epidemic in the 1980's, in the absence of government action, is a stunning example. The rise in both service provision and radical activism that occurred in those years among members of the mainstream gay community has been well-documented (Kramer, 1989; Rofes, 1996; Shilts, 1987). These efforts involved the mobilization of social capital, the actual and potential social and organizational resources, of the gay community. They led to the creation of new settings (e.g., advocacy organizations), changes in policy (e.g., speeding up the federal approval process for AIDS treatments), and the mobilization of natural opinion leaders to diffuse new norms in the community. For example, over a 3-year period from 1984 to 1987, the proportion of episodes of anal intercourse in which a condom was used rose from approximately 25% to 70% in a primarily White longitudinal sample of 624 gay men in New York City (Martin, Dean, Garcia, & Hall, 1989).

As early as 1990, however, it was clear that the enormous reduction in HIV risk behavior among White gay men was not paralleled among

African-American gay and bisexual men. In 1990, African-American gay and bisexual men in San Francisco, Berkeley, and Oakland reported rates of unprotected anal intercourse (UAI) of more than 50% in the past 6 months, compared to rates among White gay men in San Francisco of 15%–20% (Peterson et al., 1992). Although rates of UAI among all groups of gay men increased in the late 1990's, particularly after introduction of highly active antiretroviral treatments (HAART), racial disparities have persisted. A seven-city study of young men who have sex with men showed that Latino and especially African-American MSM had substantially higher rates of seroprevalence than White gay men in 1999 (Valleroy et al., 2000). There is evidence that social barriers, particularly multiple experiences of discrimination (e.g., racism, homophobia, and economic hardship), are predictive of the high rates of UAI among Latino gay men (Diaz, Ayala, & Marin, 2000) and therefore may be contributing to the racial disparity. Levels of economic resources and social capital among the White, middle-class gay community who responded most strongly to the HIV epidemic were quite high; communities who experienced discrimination, and who in addition were more likely to lack economic resources and income, appear to have been less able to mobilize effectively in response to the HIV/AIDS epidemic.

An important question is whether such activism, which accompanied the huge reductions in risk behavior among White gay men in the 1980's, may be associated with reduced risk among gay men of color. Recent studies among gay men of color have found that, after controlling for indicators of income and education, African-American men who engage in community activism appear to show lower rates of UAI than men who do not (Wilson, Yoshikawa, & Peterson, 2003). Positive associations between community activism and self-esteem have been demonstrated among Latino gay men, controlling for a variety of demographic factors; associations with HIV risk, however, have yet to be investigated (Ramirez-Valles, in press; Ramirez-Valles & Diaz, 2002). Nonetheless, community-level HIV prevention programs have begun to incorporate community mobilization as a central intervention strategy with young, gay-community men (Kegeles, Hays, Pollack, & Coates, 1999), African-American adolescents (McCormick et al., 2000), and low-income women (Sikkema et al., 2000). Such evidence strongly supports the promise of grassroots community mobilization as an important pathway to community-level effects, including effects on activists and on the community at large.

Continuing questions and challenges for evaluation   Many questions remain unanswered that are critical to mobilization approaches to HIV prevention. Some focus on the process of within-community or researcher-community collaborations. For example, what are the most-effective ways to recruit community members into community involvement and activism? What are the different challenges involved when community mobilization efforts are initiated by particular CBOs vs. by community members vs. mixed coalitions? How can outside researchers or public-health advocates stimulate mobilization of communities, including involvement of institutions that have sometimes been aloof regarding community-based organizations?

Identifying the conditions under which change is most likely to occur is a major challenge. The hypothesis that communities with higher levels of social and economic capital are more likely to engage in community mobilization has not been investigated across communities. The assessment of community characteristics associated with effective mobilization concerning HIV prevention could be linked to ongoing surveillance data to explore such hypotheses. For example, the growth or decline of community-based organizations serving a particular population, as one indicator of the levels of resources and social capital of that population, could be linked to surveillance data across time. Moreover, how can some level of community activism be achieved across diverse social settings that differ in levels of social capital and types of social structure? Research is needed regarding the effects of organizers, settings, type of issues, communicator characteristics, format of communication, and message content on community organizing (Berkowitz, 2000).

Aggregation of Subgroup-Level Change

The fact that grass-roots community organization has differential impact in different subgroups suggests the salient influence of group differences. Community-level impact on HIV infection can be attained by aggregating impacts across most or all high-risk subgroups in the community. The HIV epidemic has not occurred equally in all segments of the American population. Different groups have access to different levels of social capital and are exposed to different barriers and risk contexts. And cultural differences among groups may mean that there are different mediators of HIV risk that should be targeted in different groups or that different types of interventions may be more or less acceptable.

We suggest that type of subgroup should be considered in the design of interventions if there is nontrivial variation in levels or predictors of HIV risk across the relevant groups. Candidate subgroup definitions are important social categories such as race, ethnicity, immigration status, class, and gender; individual characteristics such as mental health or severity of drug use; or characteristics of settings within the community. The definition of subgroups in a particular community-level intervention depends, of course, on what boundaries are set around the original definition of community. Formative and prior research about the structure of social capital in a community, along with social barriers, contexts of risk, and cultural preferences, are vital in determining which subgroups may be most important to consider.

Whatever the definition of subgroups in a community, variation across them in HIV risk and factors associated with risk may indicate how interventions need to differ for various subgroups. Social barriers and discrimination, for example, may represent an important source of such variation. Research on gay men of color in the United States shows that experiences of discrimination, their associations with HIV risk, and levels of HIV risk themselves may differ for African-American, Latino, and Asian/Pacific Islander gay men (Carballo-Diéguez, 1998; Diazet al., 2000; Peterson, Bakeman, & Stokes, 2001; Stokes & Peterson, 1998; Valleroy et al., 2000). A community-level program targeting the overall population of gay men may need to address these different patterns in theory and strategies of intervention to maximize impact across racial/ethnic groups. The tension between a uniform program model and tailoring to specific populations has been recently explored regarding the need to tailor the program across cultural subgroups within the originally targeted population (Miller, Klotz, & Eckholdt, 1997).

Research on injection drug users (IDUs) in urban communities illustrates two important types of subgroup differences with implications for interventions: demographic factors (e.g., race, gender, and age) and the distance between one's risk network and the risk network "core" in a given community. Drug risk networks in the United States are often racially structured. In other words, there is an assortative mixing pattern among IDUs in which Caucasians are most likely to share needles with other Caucasians, Latinos with other Latinos, etc. (Neaigus, Friedman, Kottori, & Des Jarlais, 2001). Similarly, IDU networks are also structured by age and gender (Somlai, Kelly, Otto-Salaj, & Nelson, 1999), with older IDUs avoiding younger ones, and men injecting in venues with few women. These assortative risk networks are likely to have specific group/cultural norms regarding needle sharing and HIV risk (Des Jarlais et al., 1995; Somlai et al., 1999) and are unlikely to overlap. Such evidence of social barriers presents a challenge to programs targeting needle sharing in a community that encompasses such subgroups. Research by Friedman et al. (1994) showed that "core" members of IDU risk networks (defined as those with links to at least two other networks aside from their primary one) were at significantly higher risk for HIV infection than IDUs in other risk network locations.

Variation in subgroups is important to consider not only in conceptualization but also in implementation of community-level interventions. Differential coverage or penetration of the program across different subgroups may reduce the overall efficacy of the program. For example, a recent community-level randomized trial testing the impact of increased STD treatment in Ugandan villages (via universal delivery of home-based mass antibiotics) found significant effects in reducing non-HIV STD incidence but no significant overall effects in reducing HIV incidence (Wawer, 1999). A prior trial in Tanzania, similar in approach, had been successful in reducing both disease outcomes (Grosskurth et al., 1995). Boily, Lowndes, and Alary (2000) hypothesized that differential coverage of high- and low-risk populations may have been responsible for the lower impact in Uganda. In a simulation analysis they showed that coverage of 80% of both high- and low-risk groups by the intervention would have resulted in a significant community-level impact on HIV incidence; however, if only

40% of the high-risk group were treated, the impact would not have reached statistical significance. No community-level program evaluations to date have examined differential exposure among subgroups as an explanation for variation in program impacts across subgroups.

Continuing questions and challenges for evaluation Producing community-level change through aggregation of impacts across subgroups presents particular challenges to evaluation in defining relevant subgroups and mapping differential risks, barriers, contexts, and resources. Different mechanisms of change must also be considered. Many community-level HIV prevention efforts incorporate theories of behavior change that are tailored to particular subgroups in the target community, whether on the basis of race/ethnicity, immigration status, sexuality, SES, etc. (Yoshikawa et al., in press). This suggests that impacts of the overall package of prevention approaches in a community may differ by subgroup, and that the mediators of such impacts may differ by subgroup. Questions have remained unexplored in the field regarding whether impacts of community-level HIV prevention differ systematically by important subgroups, and if so, why? Given the surge in community-level programs evaluated in the past decade in the United States, many of which occurred across multiple sites, a synthesis (preferably meta-analytic) is now possible and needed across sites and evaluations to explore how impacts on risk behavior and hypothesized mediators differ by subgroups of interest, as well as by intervention approach.

Aggregation of Setting-Level Change

Another approach to preventing HIV infection focuses on settings or social networks. Successful interventions of this type use opinion leaders to influence social norms for sexual behavior or injection drug use in existing settings or social networks, or create new settings where peer networks develop that can keep friends safe. Community change comes about by the aggregation of change in norms across settings within the community. For example, the well-known interventions to reduce HIV risk among gay men in small cities in the United States used diffusion of innovation theory (Rogers, 1995), recruiting opinion leaders to diffuse safer sex norms in bars in which opinion leaders were identified and trained to endorse safer sex and other risk-reduction activities in conversations. The intervention successfully reduced mean frequency of unprotected anal intercourse (UAI) at the city level among non-transient patrons of the bars who were not in exclusive relationships (Kelly et al., 1997). In addition, there was an increase, relative to baseline, in the number of condoms taken by men from the bars during the follow-up periods in the intervention cities, but not in the control cities.

Researchers have also endorsed enlisting opinion leaders of IDU networks to act as "agents of change" for other members as a pathway to community-level HIV-risk reduction among IDUs (Hutchinson, Taylor,

Goldberg, & Gruer, 2000; Neaigus, Friedman, & Hopkins, 1994; Neaigus et al., 2001). For example, research conducted in Scotland revealed that the reach of a needle exchange program (NEP) was limited by the geographic range frequented by IDUs who could be potential clients (Des Jarlais, 1995). Study participants (IDUs) who lived within 1 mile of a needle exchange site were less likely to engage in needle sharing than those living farther away. Valente, Foreman, Junge, and Vlahov (1998) found that "satellite exchangers," or individuals who were high-volume exchangers at the programs and who redistributed sterile syringes to other IDUs, were instrumental in extending the reach of another NEP, and thus helped reduce HIV infection through injecting drug use in the community (however, reach was defined in this study simply as the number of target population members who exchanged needles, not geographically).

Creating new settings that serve as gathering places for social networks (and sources of social capital) appears promising in bringing about community-level change in HIV risk behaviors among both IDU and MSM populations. For example, the AIDS Community Demonstration Projects in Dallas, Denver, Long Beach, New York, and Seattle coupled an opinion-leader intervention with the creation of new social settings, an approach that has been central to community psychology (Cherniss & Deegan, 2000; Sarason, 1972). The created settings (storefronts) served as training and networking spaces and drop-in centers for community members (Simons et al., 1996). Networkers and interested individuals could also pick up health supplies (condoms and bleach kits) and other materials at the storefronts. Thus, by creating a setting within the community, and by building peer networks of friends keeping other friends "safe," the programs were able to distribute the intervention message to at-risk populations. The intervention produced significant movement, on a stage-of-change scale based on the transtheoretical model, toward consistent condom use with primary and secondary partners (Center for Disease Control [CDC] AIDS Community Demonstration Projects Research Group, 1999).

The Mpowerment Project, a community-level intervention targeting young gay men's HIV risk behaviors, also rented meeting space in the small cities targeted. These spaces (for example, a house with multiple rooms for meetings and socializing) served as community centers for populations that had no such gathering place, aside from bars. As in the AIDS Community Demonstration Projects, the centers served multiple purposes: as the base for outreach to other settings, and as the site for small-group workshops and social events. The Mpowerment Project has shown positive impacts at the community level on consistency of condom use with primary and secondary partners in the short term, in comparison with a matched community (Kegeles, Hays, & Coates, 1996). Thus, these programs show the efficacy of not only targeting social networks for behavior change but also creating settings that are both attractive to the networks and facilitate risk reduction. The programs provide space for increasing the social capital for risk reduction in their respective communities.

Continuing questions and challenges for evaluation Additional theoretical
and empirical work is needed to clarify when and how effects at the setting level aggregate to produce effects at the community level. The aggregation of setting-level effects needs to be modeled as a dynamic process.
Are there threshold effects, such that relatively small increases in numbers of settings targeted bring about discontinuously large cumulative impacts? What effect size is required per setting in order to achieve overall
community-level impacts? Does aggregation of setting-level effects depend
on the structure of social capital in communities? Relevant dimensions
may include the number of settings and the degree to which clientele are
stable or individuals circulate among a small number of settings, or
whether different settings serve nonoverlapping subgroups. This kind of
information may prove useful in the relatively common situation in which
organizations build community-level prevention in the context of a range
of already existing settings and social activities.

It is also critical to elaborate our understanding of the relationship between social networks and physical settings, which are often targeted simultaneously in approaches based on diffusion of innovation. It is unclear
to what extent change in networks is related to changes in settings. The
distinction here is between social networks, which may function across
multiple settings, and the settings themselves. Diffusion of innovation
theory does not pay much attention to this distinction; however, it may be
important when making decisions about how to implement community-
level prevention. Prevention efforts focused on networks in addition to settings may be beneficial for communities in which settings have high
percentages of transient individuals, or in which a target population fre-
quents a large array of formal and informal settings (common in large
cities).

The aggregation of setting-level changes also poses several challenges
to evaluation. Difficulties arise in modeling "saturation" of a community
through setting-level impacts. Strategic sampling of settings and individuals within settings can clarify interdependencies within and across levels
of analysis (Linney, 2000). Settings differ in frequency of occurrence, size,
and the characteristics and risk levels of people who attend them. Methods have recently been refined for sampling day-time-venue units in a
way that takes into account such variation (Muhib et al., 2001). In evaluation of the process of aggregation across settings, independence of observations, an assumption for most individual-level impact analyses, is
unlikely to hold, given that members in a community may frequent multiple settings (in fact, an aim of community-level intervention is to reach the
same group of target individuals across multiple settings). The cumulative
impact of multiple components of a community-level intervention, each
targeting a different setting, is likely to be key to a community-level impact, yet is very difficult to model when each component is "contami-
nated" by the others. Planned variation still represents the best way to
evaluate the active components in a multiple-component program; all

possible combinations need not be tested in separate conditions to do this (West, Aiken, & Todd, 1993).

Organizational and Institutional Change

Some prevention programs have built upon the social capital of their communities by recruiting formal and informal organizations or institutions as part of their intervention strategies. A wide variety of settings are available in the organizational life of American society to promote community-level change in HIV risks. Private and public sector organizations and institutions include those related to work (e.g., corporations, labor unions), education (e.g., public schools), religion, health care, human services, and voluntary organizations (e.g., self-help groups). Organizations are typically somewhat broader than settings, with more internal structure, and may comprise multiple settings. Institutions may be systems of organizations (e.g., a public school system, the Catholic Church), and typically embody a set of values and norms that may facilitate or impede HIV prevention. Service systems interventions are sometimes considered representative of institutional change (Sumartojo, 2000).

Zimmerman (2000) distinguishes between empowering and empowered organizations in what they provide to members and what they achieve in the community. Empowering organizations provide opportunities for people to gain control over their lives, whereas empowered organizations influence policy decisions or provide effective alternative services. A community achieves empowerment to the extent that it has a sufficient coalition of both empowered and empowering organizations and has accessible resources for all community residents. Changes in organizational or institutional structure and culture can thus facilitate wider processes of community mobilization and change (Shinn & Perkins, 2000) or create barriers to community change. Also, organizations can contribute to HIV prevention through diffusion of innovations and social marketing or provide direct services or serve as the locus for individual and small-group interventions. A single intervention may include multiple such components.

Lauby, Smith, Stark, Person, and Adams (2000) implemented a multipronged program to create change in HIV risk among women at the level of neighborhoods and housing developments. This program—the Women and Infants Demonstration Project—was based on the intervention model of a prior five-city demonstration (CDC AIDS Community Demonstration Projects Research Group, 1999). One component of the program involved recruiting neighborhood organizations, small businesses, and social agencies to distribute intervention materials and host workshops. Demographically similar, but geographically distant, neighborhoods and projects within the same cities were used as comparison sites. After 2 years of the intervention, women in the intervention communities showed increases in attempts to influence partners to use condoms, decreases in reports of never talking to partners about condoms, and a trend toward decreased reports of never using condoms.

Social marketing initiatives often require working with multiple organizations in order to reach a large proportion of their intended audience (Holtgrave, 1997). The few rigorously evaluated social marketing initiatives in HIV prevention that involve multiple organizations used a coalition-building process. For example, the Project Action demonstration in Portland, Oregon aimed to reduce sexual transmission of HIV risk among adolescents by placing condom vending machines throughout the city. Prior to such placement, presentations were made to local community groups who then approved placement of the machines in settings frequented by large numbers of adolescents. In a replication of this project, the Prevention Marketing Initiative, multiple organizations (e.g., radio stations, highs schools, retail outlets, community centers, and local transit systems) were asked to sponsor particular components of the intervention and recruited into a similar coalition. The number of channels through which adolescents were exposed to the intervention was associated with condom use during their most recent sexual encounter with their main partners (Kennedy, Mizuno, Seals, Myllyluoma, & Weeks-Norton, 2000).

School systems may be expected to provide opportunities to produce community-level changes in HIV risk reduction among the nation's youth. Schools represent the single institution in America regularly attended by 95% of youth between 5 and 17 years of age (National Center for Education Statistics, 1993). Given the threat of AIDS and other STDs, some school systems have begun to make condoms available. For example, New York City high schools distributed condoms as part of a broader HIV/AIDS prevention program guided by a school-based team of teachers, parents, school administration, students, and health resource staff. Compared to students without a program in Chicago, New York students reported higher use of condoms during their most-recent intercourse, but no higher levels of sexual activity. Results controlled for demographic, psychosocial, and behavioral variables. Benefits were most pronounced, but still modest, for students at highest risk (Guttmacher et al., 1997). However, less-elaborate programs show fewer results, which prompted Kirby (2000) to conclude that these programs add little to the extensive availability of condoms in stores, and hence are unlikely to dramatically impact STD or HIV transmission without the more comprehensive initiatives warranted.

Religious institutions represent an underutilized resource for community-level HIV prevention efforts. Putnam (1995) notes that American's most common associational membership is religious, and the prominent influence of religious institutions on American life has been well-described (Pargament & Maton, 2000). With nearly 150 million members in the United States, religious institutions have been accessible to wide segments of society, especially the poor and ethnic minorities, for whom the church is central to the community. Religious settings have the resources to provide contact with their congregational members and outreach to the community through a variety of interventions, such as drug abuse prevention, youth academic mentoring, and community revitalization. However, there are limited data on the involvement of religious institutions in the prevention of HIV, and religious leaders have often opposed prevention programs such as condom distribution in schools or needle exchange programs on moral grounds. Ayres (1995) describes homosexuality, illicit drug use, prostitution and marital infidelity as contentious issues for clergy and congregations that limit the involvement of religious institutions in HIV/AIDS prevention. Studies have documented the wide perceptions of stigma toward homosexuality among some religious congregations (Woodyard, Peterson, & Stokes, 2000). Social scientists have tended to ignore the potential of religious institutions while working more closely with other organizations and institutions.

Health care systems have also been targets of prevention efforts, for example, in a program that aimed to increase HIV-related risk assessment and counseling by primary care providers within a health maintenance organization (HMO) (Dodge et al., 2001). The program used a combination of diffusion of innovation methods (providing one provider on each practice team with 6 hours of training), a workshop for other team members, training of support staff, and on-site team resource staff to encourage HIV and other STD screening. In a single-group time series analysis, the intervention produced consistent increases in recall of discussions of HIV and other STDs, discussions of HIV prevention, provider inquiries about sexual behaviors and risk factors, and discussions of ways for the patient to reduce risk. However, the intervention was not successful in increasing rates of counseling about negotiation of condom use.

In areas with little public-health infrastructure (such as in much of the developing world), the creation of a coordinated service system may have communitywide impacts on HIV infection. For example, a well-known STD counseling and treatment intervention in Tanzania created such an infrastructure for STD treatment in the rural region of Mwanza. An STD clinic and laboratory were first established in Mwanza to monitor the implementation of diagnosis and treatment regimens, and the incidence of STDs. Then, staff from health centers and dispensaries across the region were trained to diagnose and treat STDs in villages and to provide information about STDs and inform residents about the availability of effective treatment. Twelve communities in the region were randomized in matched pairs, with six assigned to an intervention condition and six to a delayed-intervention condition. At the 2-year follow-up assessment, HIV incidence was lower in the intervention communities in all six pairs, with overall incidence rates of 1.2% in intervention communities and 1.9% in comparison communities (Grosskurth et al., 1995).

Using a coordinated service delivery system to create community-level change has received much attention in the research literature on HIV transmission among IDUs in drug treatment programs (O'Conner, Selwyn, & Schottenfeld, 1994; Knowlton et al., 2001). However, very little empirical research has examined the impact of such interventions on HIV risk. Programs in the United States that have effectively created service infrastructures similar to those described in the Mwanza study target mostly HIV-infected IDUs and serve as a tertiary prevention, or treatment intervention. For example, Selwyn, Budner, Wasserman, & Arno (1993) examined the feasibility of on-site primary care services and their use by both HIV-positive and HIV-negative IDUs within an outpatient methadone maintenance program. By examining service usage rates, diagnoses, and prophylaxis (e.g., prescription drugs to combat HIV, condom distribution), the researchers concluded that interventions that integrate medical services into drug treatment programs may decrease HIV transmission, promote access to AIDS-related medical services, and lower the costs of acute medical care among HIV-infected IDUs. Thus, preliminary research highlights the importance of broadening the scope of interventions from HIV-risk reduction needs to overall health.

Continuing questions and challenges for evaluation   There are many unanswered questions in the area of organizational and institutional change. We consider organizations first. To what extent are organizations themselves the targets of change or simply the loci for other sorts of prevention? If the former, what dimensions of organizations are important mediators of effects on HIV risk (e.g., changes in organizational structures, norms, or roles)? Does it matter whether the central mission of the organization is related to HIV, health, or a completely unrelated area? The evaluations to date have not disentangled organizational change processes from the impacts of particular services the organizations offered.

The type of organization may be important in influencing the success of community-level prevention. In what types of organizations are intervention efforts most likely to be sustained so that changes in communication patterns and norms are incorporated in the social capital of the community? Do different organizations reach different population subgroups? In multisite community-level programs, is success related to the proportion of target organizations that are involved? When the services and intervention components in multisite evaluations are similar, one might investigate how differences in organizational structure and processes lead to site-level differences in effects.

Important issues in institutional change include how social scientists can best work with institutions to mobilize their potential for sustained prevention efforts and to overcome barriers reflected in values and norms, so that social capital is mobilized for, rather than against, HIV risk reduction. As for smaller-scale organizations, other questions concern the extent to which institutions should be a locus for other sorts of change efforts, or themselves the target of changes, and how change efforts may be sustained. The role of institutions in influencing public policy and both lending authority to, and shaping the approach of, larger coalitions is also critical. The effects of increasing institutional capacity to affect local, state, and federal policy relevant to HIV prevention has been explored in multiple case-study designs (Holtgrave, Harrison, Gerber, Autlman, & Scarlett, 1996; Johnson-Masotti, Pinkerton, Holtgrave, Valdiserri, & Willingham, 2000), but has yet to be extended to effects on prevalence or incidence.

An additional issue for evaluation of organizational and institutional change efforts is the relationship of both implementation of the intervention and exposure of individuals to intervention components to community-level impacts. Both implementation and exposure are crucial mediators of the effects of community-level prevention on individual-level risk behavior. But the fact that they are distinct processes is usually ignored. Many of the community-level programs discussed in this chapter examined exposure of individuals to the intervention as a single continuous dimension, and conducted (usually nonexperimental) analyses showing that exposure was associated with improvements in risk behavior (CDC AIDS Community Demonstration Projects, 1999; Lauby et al., 2000). However, no evaluations that we are aware of have linked features of implementation of community-level HIV prevention to risk behavior.

In addition, both exposure and implementation are potentially multidimensional; individuals may be exposed to components of a community-level intervention at different levels of intensity (Yoshikawa, Rosman, & Hsueh, 2001). Most evaluations conducting exposure analyses simply use an index of exposure when patterns of exposure are likely to be complex. Similarly, when implementation in social intervention research is assessed, it is often reduced to a single index; community-level programs may vary in the quality of implementation, by component or by level of hierarchy in a complex organization or institution. In addition to quantitative methods of investigating such questions, comparative ethnography (across organizations or across levels within organizations) may be productive in exploring links to the risk behavior of community members.

Change in Public Policy

Intervention strategies in HIV prevention often require public policy change, such as needle exchange, partner notification, HIV testing and notification of pregnant women, and the regulation of settings deemed to be high risk, such as bathhouses or commercial sex establishments. Public policy represents a specific instance of institutional change, in that government decisions are involved. Some of the most successful efforts at community-level HIV prevention have occurred in the policy arena. For example, Thailand's model 100% Condom Use program for sex establishments (in which condoms were required in all sexual encounters) resulted in spectacular increases in condom usage among sex workers in that country. An initial pilot implementation of the 100% condom use policy was conducted in the Ratchaburi province in 1989. Following promising evidence of the impact of that program on condom usage among sex workers, the policy was expanded to cover the entire country in following years. Between 1989 and 1993 the use of condoms in commercial sex increased from 14% to 94%, in a series of surveys of sex workers (Hanenberg,

Rojanapithayakorn, Kunasol, & Sokal, 1994). The number of cases of the five most common STD's declined by 79% during those years among Thai men.

For IDU populations, needle exchange programs (NEPs) represent a central policy intervention for the prevention of HIV. The successful implementation of an NEP in the United States requires policy change. Though NEPs have proven successful through reducing risk behavior and HIV transmission in domestic and international contexts and across demographic subgroups of IDUs (Servegev et al., 2000; Singer, Himmelgreen, Weeks, Radda, & Martinez, 1997; Strenski, Marshall, Gacki, & Sanchez, 2000; Weiker, Edgington, & Kipke, 1999), only five states in the United States have laws allowing for needle exchange programs. Most state and local laws prohibit the manufacture, sale, distribution, possession, and advertisement of drug paraphernalia. Similarly, statutes are put into place to restrict syringe or needle use to those with a medical prescription to use such injection equipment (Gostin, Lazzarini, Jones, & Flaherty, 1997).

Gostin et al. (1997) found three types of evidence that federal, state, and local policies are a contributing factor in the multiperson use of needles used for injecting drugs: 1) IDUs report that legal restrictions are a primary reason for sharing needles; 2) IDUs who receive syringes from pharmacists rather than street sellers are less likely to share needles or to go to "shooting galleries;" and 3) IDUs with a history of diabetes (and hence legal access to needles) have significantly lower HIV seroprevalence than nondiabetic IDUs (who lack legal access to needles). Ethnographic studies have shown that IDUs, fearing detection of needles and the fines, incarceration, and increased surveillance that accompany detection, often fail to carry sterile syringes (Grund, Heckathorn, Broadhead, & Anthony, 1995; Koester, 1994).

The successful implementation of policies that promote sterile needle distribution and exchange of needles among IDUs and/or repeal of regulations that hinder access to sterile needles among drug users may require change in public opinion. A common misperception in communities across the United States is that increased access to needles will promote drug use among nonusers and/or increase drug use among current IDUs, though research has shown that no such relationships exist (Buning, 1991; Lurie, Gorsky, Jones, & Shompe, 1998; Normand, Vlahov, & Moses, 1995). Such misperceptions may foil attempts to establish NEPs needed in a community. Many people see the establishment of local needle exchange services as an invitation for open drug use, or a "lure" for drug users to take up residence in one's neighborhood, potentially decreasing social capital and neighborhood cohesion. Although NEPs or repeal of restrictions on needle distribution and possession may have social costs (in terms of societal values and beliefs), cost-benefit research has shown that the benefits of NEPs outweigh the fiscal costs (Buning, 1991; Lurie et al., 1998).

Continuing questions and challenges for evaluation What are the conditions necessary to adopt and successfully implement such policies? With respect to adoption, Phillips (2000) has noted that the "culture of policy" can involve significant conflicts among competing interests groups and stakeholders. The positions policymakers adopt are constrained by factors that range from assumptions about government involvement to the policy structures and personnel that frame choices. For research findings to be considered, persistence, and attention to timing, dissemination, and audience are critical (Phillips, 2000). Public opinion also exerts a powerful influence on the likelihood of consideration of particular policies. The examination and fostering of change in public opinion is an emerging area in policy research in the behavioral sciences (Gilliam & Iyengar, in press) but has yet to be applied to HIV/AIDS-related public policy in the United States.

Implementation of policy changes depends on behavior change across multiple layers of institutional and organizational hierarchies, where even changes at the top can be subverted at other levels (Yoshikawa & Hsueh, 2001). In the case of a condom-use policy for sex establishments, for example, change may be required at the levels of government, local health departments, sex establishment networks, sex establishment managers, and sex workers. Discretion often increases as one goes down this hierarchy toward the level of actual interactions with affected populations (Elmore, 1980). Unfortunately, there has been little study of implementation processes in HIV-prevention policy at any of these levels of policy-driven change.

One exception is work on the role of pharmacies in the implementation of NEPs. Though only 10 states in the United States have specific regulations that require a prescription for the purchase of syringes, pharmacists have considerable discretion in deciding whether, and to whom, to sell syringes (Gostin, et al., 1997). This discretion yields wide variation in the willingness to sell needles to IDUs. Biases against racial minorities, homeless persons, and/or young people appear to limit opportunities for pharmacy customers to purchase sterile needles (Compton, Cottler, Decker, Mager, & Stringfellow, 1992). As a result, virtually no pharmacies sell needles to persons without a prescription, regardless of whether policy prohibits them from doing so. Similarly, local police may hinder the effectiveness of NEPs through targeting and harassing potential exchangers. Blumenthal, Kral, Lorvick, and Watters (1997), in evaluating the effectiveness of "underground" (not legally sanctioned) and "tolerated" NEPs in California, found that police action and the threat of action inhibited the operation and expansion of NEPs, decreased their use by IDUs, and limited the number of volunteers. Thus, successful implementation of policies to create structural change is contingent upon complex, dynamic processes across institutions and organizations. And because the jurisdictions covered by public policies are usually wider than a single community, it is important to investigate inequalities in coverage by geographic area, as well as other kinds of subgroups already discussed.

Techniques of policy analysis, which often rely on econometric techniques, have not often been applied to community-level HIV prevention, with the exception of cost-benefit analysis. Some of the community-level programs discussed earlier have reported cost-benefit analyses, with most finding that the programs did prove to save costs, when extrapolating lifetime medical care costs averted from number of estimated infections averted during the follow-up period (Kahn, Kegeles, Hays, & Beltzer, 2001; Pinkerton, Holtgrave, DiFranceisco, Stevenson, & Kelly, 1998). However, researchers often assume that HIV risk reduction across the follow-up period represents infections averted, rather than delayed (Pinkerton, Chesson, Holtgrave, Kassler, & Layde, 2000). Thus, economic benefits may have been overestimated, if participants who reduced their risk behavior during the follow-up nevertheless continue to engage in some degree of risk behavior thereafter. Future cost-benefit work in this area should incorporate different scenarios of length of delay of infection in their sensitivity analyses.

Adoption and Replication of Interventions

Our final change pathway, the adoption and replication of successful interventions in new contexts, can involve interventions at any level, involving individual, small-group, and community-level approaches. Questions of how interventions are marketed and adopted are potentially more complicated in community-level prevention than in other interventions, in that they are more likely to involve multiple organizations and multiple types of organizations (e.g., community-based organizations, governmental and private funders, and "intermediary" organizations providing technical assistance). The choice of interventions to adopt—a process that occurs "before the beginning"—is also often a community-level effort.

Recent work in HIV prevention has begun to consider the complex processes involved in adoption of preventive interventions by organizations. One study applied Rogers' diffusion of innovation theory (Rogers, 1995) to examine how 38 AIDS service organizations (ASOs) in Illinois chose externally developed prevention programs for use (Miller, 2001). Organizations reported using five criteria for adoption most often: compatibility with the mission, relevance to local populations, evidence regarding acceptability of the program by the populations, feasibility, and extent to which the program fills a gap in existing services. There is also evidence from this sample of organizations that external funding pressures and cross-organizational learning and modeling play important roles in "technology transfer" (Miller, Bedney, & Garcia, 2002).

Another approach to examining the transfer of evidence-based programs to AIDS service organizations is to manipulate the process. A recent randomized trial examined rates of adoption of a social-cognitive, small-group HIV-prevention program (in versions for gay men and for women) that was presented in one of three ways to a sample of 74 ASOs: through intervention manuals; through the manuals and an intensive, on-site 2-day workshop; and through the manuals, workshop, and six monthly telephone calls to provide technical assistance (Kelly, Somlai, DiFranceisco, et al., 2000). The most intensive approach, with follow-up technical assistance, resulted in significantly greater percentages of ASOs adopting the program than the manual-only approach, at both 6-month and 12-month follow-up assessments.

Since 1995, the CDC has required health departments that receive funding from the federal agency to engage in community planning processes to determine effective ways to spend HIV prevention funds. The processes that community planning groups use to prioritize interventions and populations have begun to be studied (Holtgrave et al., 1996; Johnson-Masotti et al., 2000). Community planning groups have found the prioritization of populations (e.g., by race/ethnicity) particularly difficult, with a variety of methods used to develop group consensus. However, by the fifth year of implementation, a majority of the planning groups were using local needs assessments, epidemiology, and behavioral sciences to prioritize interventions and populations (Davis et al., 2000).

The question of whether usual technology transfer mechanisms encourage community-level prevention strategies has been rarely examined. Studies of AIDS service organizations in the United States often show that the majority of ongoing prevention work consists of strategies that rely mainly on individual, rather than community-level change: street outreach and small-group interventions, for example (Wong, Chng, & Lo, 1998; Yoshikawa et al., in press). Community-level prevention may require the "transfer" of what organizations view as multiple types of interventions (e.g., social marketing, small-group, coalition-building). Each type or component may present a different profile regarding feasibility, suitability to the organization and its target population, and fundability (funding requirements often do not permit multiple modalities of intervention). In addition, it may not be within the capacity of a single organization to implement all components; a coalition-building process, for example, may result in multiple organizations working together, with each responsible for one element of a community-level prevention effort. This complexity of funding and transfer issues, from the point of view of AIDS service organizations, may be one reason why community-level prevention is relatively rare.

Successful community-level interventions have begun to be replicated systematically, with guidance from the CDC (Neumann & Sogolow, 2000). The Replicating Effective Programs (REP) project of the CDC supports evidence-based programs for guided replication, using criteria of success in a controlled (though not necessarily randomized) trial. The project funds the researchers who developed the original model interventions to create intervention packages for dissemination to community-based organizations, and evaluates the success of a pilot dissemination to an organization unfamiliar with the intervention (Kegeles et al., 2000). The implementation of the program within that organization is then evaluated, with attention to needs for both fidelity to the original model and adaptation to local conditions (Kelly, Heckman, Stevenson, et al., 2000).

Continuing questions and challenges for evaluation Altman (1995) provides an excellent discussion of the conflicts that community researchers experience in the transfer of innovations to community systems, such as fostering effective long-term relationships between researchers and communities, and implementing interventions that are useful to community systems after the research ends. Many of these issues, which in the language of this chapter involve fostering social capital for prevention, should be examined in the HIV context.

Another important area for investigation in the replication of interventions is the match between the target population's behavioral norms and preferences and community-level prevention programs (Somlai et al., 1999; Trickett, in press). Though several kinds of community interventions may in theory solve a problem, the effectiveness of a given program may vary depending on how acceptable it is to a target population. For example, researchers have shown that the typical "one-for-one, once a day" exchange method used by NEPs in the United States does not give IDUs the freedom to use clean needles within their drug use networks (Des Jarlais et al., 1995; Valente et al., 1998), where needle sharing is most prevalent. Similarly, studies failed to show any relationship between self-reported use of bleach to disinfect injection equipment and protection from HIV (Vlahov, Astemborski, & Solomon, 1994; Titus, Marmor, & Des Jarlais, 1994); nonetheless, interventions aimed at training IDUs to clean their needles persist. Ethnography, observation of persons in the population, interviews, the organization of community groups, and the use of "town hall" meetings, as well as careful attention to other aspects of community entry and collaboration, can all help to ensure that the goals of a CBO's intervention are in accord with the perceived needs of the target population and the perspectives of the wider community (McCormick et al., 2000; Rotheram-Borus, Rebchook, Kelly, Adams, & Neumann, 2000; Trickett, this volume).

Much of the evaluation of technology transfer processes, with some important exceptions, has been conducted using single or multiple case-study approaches. Quantitative approaches using CBOs or staff as the unit of analysis and aiming to test hypotheses concerning such processes are underutilized. Given data on a sufficient number of organizations, prevention planning groups, etc., such research is certainly feasible, but requires analyses beyond the descriptive statistics most commonly used to explore research questions regarding both intra- and interorganizational variation. For example, what characteristics of intermediary organizations, community-based organizations, and the relationships between them are most effective in bringing about high-quality implementation of

HIV prevention programs? How does variation in site-level population, fidelity, adaptation, and implementation affect local program quality and
impacts on HIV risk behaviors? Research on processes of technology
transfer (e.g., Valdiserri, 2000) could be integrated with process, outcome,
and impact evaluation research.

CONCLUSION

The ultimate goal of HIV prevention is to change HIV incidence levels in
populations and communities. The evidence reviewed in this chapter supports the argument that HIV incidence is amenable to change through
community-level interventions, including grass-roots mobilization, aggregation of changes across subgroups and settings, organizational and institutional interventions, changes in public policy, and the adoption and
replication of these processes in new locations. Such interventions emphasize ways that social capital, embedded in social settings, networks, organizations, and institutions, including public policy, can be mobilized to
change the social ecology of risk in communities. They also focus on social
barriers that may obstruct efforts to reduce risk. In this conclusion we describe underexplored areas for research and action in community-level
HIV prevention.

First, it appears that certain approaches to community-level prevention
are rarely explored or evaluated. Some of the largest reductions in HIV
risk on record have come from two type of interventions—policy and
grassroots mobilization—that are among the least evaluated in HIV prevention science. Policy interventions, such as Thailand's 100% Condom
Use program, and community mobilization efforts organized not by social
scientists or public-health practitioners, but by the (White) gay community in U.S. cities in the 1980's, appear to have had enormous effects. Both
cut levels of risk behavior among high-risk populations by more than half.
Behavioral interventions that aspire to equivalent community-level impact, typically those that employ multiple components and modalities of
intervention, have been successful but have not achieved change of that
magnitude.

Public policy interventions appear to be underutilized in the United
States, especially for IDUs. Changes in policies to promote NEPs and to
reduce barriers to obtaining syringes from pharmacies and carrying them
could have a major impact for this group. Allowing high-volume exchanges so that individuals can redistribute needles to their networks
would build on existing social capital to extend the reach of such programs. Similarly, community mobilization has rarely been evaluated in
community-level prevention research. Multicomponent prevention programs may benefit from adding to their media, small-group, and outreach
components greater emphasis on community mobilization to enhance social capital for HIV prevention. Although many of them engaged in some
level of coalition building, that work did not often include the full range of

community mobilization efforts that appear to have produced the enormous reductions in risk among urban, White gay men in the 1980s.

For example, political activism and advocacy, widespread recruitment of community residents to become intervention change agents, and organizational and institutional change have rarely been integrated into these multicomponent interventions. Attending to barriers to change, especially for high-risk subgroups that are often subjected to stigma, and targeting institutions that are important sources of social capital in minority communities may yield additional benefits. By incorporating such mobilization efforts and tracking resultant change processes across settings, sub- groups, organizations, and institutions, evaluators and program change agents alike could ensure that community-level initiatives reach as high a proportion as possible of individuals at risk.

Second, research is sorely lacking that links implementation processes to impacts. Such research is needed at multiple levels of analysis: at the level of organizational and institutional change, at the level of social networks, and at the level of social settings. We have argued that successful community-level prevention may result from the aggregation of effects across settings or networks in a particular community.

Third, the question of threshold effects is urgent to guide questions about the intensity (and expense) required in community-level prevention to achieve an effect of public health, social, or economic significance. What levels of intensity of intervention components, targeting of particular subgroups, and quality and duration of implementation are enough for detectable effects? How do such thresholds differ depending on the mode of transmission that is being prevented and other characteristics of a community?

Fourth, how does the success of community-level HIV prevention depend on the existing structure, loci, and levels of social capital in communities? Are there ways to foster increases in the kinds of social capital that represent "readiness" for community-level intervention? Social change efforts with broader goals (e.g., antipoverty goals, community development goals) have not often been examined as interventions that may influence the success of HIV prevention efforts, or affect HIV risk directly.

Finally, research on all of these factors in community-level HIV prevention may benefit from the application of multiple research methods and techniques, including ecological assessments of community settings; multilevel quantitative analyses taking into account within- and across-setting variation; ethnographic and other qualitative methods; policy analytic methods, such as cost-benefit analysis; and most importantly, collaborative approaches to working with community residents, institutions, and organizations. Are training institutions in the health, social, and behavioral sciences providing adequate training across the full range of these approaches? Improving the science of community-level HIV prevention challenges our research models and may require new approaches to educational and community collaboration.

During the first two decades of the HIV/AIDS epidemic, prevention research in the United States was too often preoccupied with an emphasis on individual-level changes for HIV prevention. One consequence of this focus was neglect of favorable effects that can be achieved through community-level interventions for the promotion of both healthy individuals and healthy communities. Fortunately, calls to target community-level change in HIV prevention have become more frequent and insistent. The arguments offered in this chapter represent our attempt to answer the question, What are the multiple ways in which activists, program developers, and researchers can bring about community-level reductions in HIV incidence?

REFERENCES

Altman, D. G. (1995). Sustaining interventions in community systems: On the relationship between researchers and communities. *Health Psychology, 14*, 526–536.

Ayres, J. R. (1995). The quagmire of HIV/AIDS-related issues which haunt the church. *Journal of Pastoral Care, 2*, 201–219.

Berkowitz, B. (2000). Community and neighborhood organization. In J. Rappaport & E. Seidman (Eds.), *Handbook of community psychology*. (pp. 331–358). New York: Kluwer Academic/Plenum.

Blumenthal, R. N., Kral, A. H., Lorvick, J., & Watters, J. K. (1997). Impact of law enforcement on syringe exchange programs: A look at Oakland and San Francisco. *Medical Anthropology, 18*(1), 61–83.

Boily, M., Lowndes, C. M., & Alary, M. (2000). Complementary hypothesis concerning the community sexually transmitted disease mass treatment puzzle in Rakai, Uganda. *AIDS, 14*, 2583–2592.

Bourdieu, P. (1986). Forms of capital. In J. G. Richardson (Ed.), *The handbook of theory and research for the sociology of education*. Westport, CT: Greenwood Press.

Buning, E. C. (1991). Effects of Amsterdam needle and syringe exchange. *The International Journal of the Addictions, 26*(12), 1303–1311.

Carballo-Diéguez, A. (1998). Latinos. In R. Smith (Ed.), *Encyclopedia of AIDS* (pp. 321–323), New York: Garland Publishing.

Centers for Disease Control AIDS Community Demonstration Projects Research Group (1999). Community-level HIV intervention in 5 cities: Final outcome data from the CDC AIDS Community Demonstration Projects. *American Journal of Public Health, 89*, 336–345.

Cherniss, C. & Deegan, G. (2000). The creation of alternative settings. In J. Rappaport & E. Seidman (Eds.), *Handbook of Community Psychology* (pp. 359–377). New York: Kluwer Academic/Plenum.

Compton, W. M. III, Cottler, L. B., Decker, S. H., Mager, D., & Stringfellow, R. (1992). Legal needle buying in St. Louis. *American Journal of Public Health, 82*, 595–596.

Davis, D., Barrington, T., Pheonix, U., Gilliam, A., Collins, C., Cotton, D., et al. (2000). Evaluation and technical assistance for successful HIV program delivery. *AIDS Education and Prevention, 12*(Suppl. A), 115–125.

Des Jarlais, D. C., Friedman, S. R., Friedmann, P., Wenston, J., Sotheran, J. L., Choopanya, K., et al. (1995). HIV/AIDS-related behavior change among injecting drug users in different national settings. *AIDS, 9*, 611–617.

Diaz, R. M. (1998). *Latino gay men and HIV: Culture, sexuality and risk behavior.* New York: Routledge.

Diaz, R. M., Ayala, G., & Marin, B. V. (2000). Latino gay men and HIV: Risk behavior as a sign of oppression. *Focus: A Guide to AIDS Research and Counseling, 15*(7), 1–4.

Dodge, W. T., Blue, S., Spruce, J., Grothaus, L., Rebolledo, V., McAfee, T. A., Carey, J. W., & Thompson, R. S. (2001). Enhancing primary care HIV prevention: A comprehensive clinical intervention. *American Journal of Preventive Medicine, 20,* 177–183.

Elmore, R. (1980). Backward mapping: Implementation research and policy decisions. *Political Science Quarterly, 94,* 601–616.

Friedman, S. R., Des Jarlais, D. C., & Ward, T. P. (1994). Social models for changing health-relevant behavior. In R. DiClemente & J. L. Peterson (Eds.), *Preventing AIDS: Theories and methods of behavioral interventions* (pp. 95–116). New York: Plenum.

Gilliam, F. & Iyengar, S. (in press). *Race, television news, and American politics.* Princeton, NJ: Princeton University Press.

Gostin, L. O., Lazzarini, Z., Jones, T. S., & Flaherty, K. (1997). Prevention of HIV/AIDS and other blood-borne diseases among injection drug users: A national survey on the regulation of syringes and needles. *Journal of the American Medical Association, 277*(1), 53–62.

Grosskurth, H., Mosha, F., Todd, J., Mwijarubi, E., Klokke, A., Senkoro, K., Mayaud, P., et al. (1995). Impact of improved treatment of sexually transmitted diseases on HIV infection in rural Tanzania: Randomised controlled trial. *Lancet, 346,* 540–546.

Grund, J. P. C., Heckathorn, D. D., Broadhead, R. S., & Anthony, D. L. (1995). In eastern Connecticut, IDUs purchase syringes from pharmacies but don't carry syringes. *Journal of Acquired Immune Deficiency Syndromes and Human Retrovirology, 10,* 104–105.

Guttmacher, S., Lieberman, L., Ward, D., Freudenberg, N., Radosh, A., & Des Jarlais, D. (1997). Condom availability in New York City public schools: Relationships to condom use and sexual behavior. *American Journal of Public Health, 87,* 1427–1433.

Hanenberg, R. S., Rojanapithayakorn, W., Kunasol, P., & Sokal, D. C. (1994). Impact of Thailand's HIV-control programme as indicated by the decline of sexually transmitted diseases. *The Lancet, 344,* 243–245.

Hayes, R. & Peterson, J. L. (1994). HIV prevention for gay and bisexual men in metropolitan cities. In R. DiClemente & J. Peterson (Eds.), *Preventing AIDS: Theories and methods of behavioral interventions* (pp. 61–78). New York: Plenum.

Heller, K. (1989). The return to community. *American Journal of Community Psychology, 17,* 1–16.

Holtgrave, D. R. (1997). Public health communication strategies for HIV prevention: Past and emerging roles. *AIDS, 11*(Suppl. A), S183–S190.

Holtgrave, D. R., Harrison, J., Gerber, R. A., Aultman, T. V., & Scarlett, M. (1996). Methodological issues in evaluating HIV prevention community planning. *Public Health Reports, 111*(Suppl. 1), 108–114.

Hutchinson, S. J., Taylor, A., Goldberg, D. J., & Gruer, L. (2000). Factors associated with injecting risk behavior among serial community wide samples of injecting drug users in Glasgow 1990–94: Implications for control and prevention of blood borne viruses. *Addiction, 95*(6), 931–940.

Ickovics, J. R. & Yoshikawa, H. (1998). Preventive interventions to reduce hetero-sexual HIV risk for women: Current perspectives, future directions. *AIDS, 12*(Suppl. A), S197–S207.

Johnson-Masotti, A. P., Pinkerton, S. D., Holtgrave, D. R., Valdiserri, R. O., & Willingham, M. (2000). Decision-making in HIV prevention community plan-ning: An integrative review. *Journal of Community Health, 25*, 95–112.

Kahn, J. G., Kegeles, S. M., Hays, R. B., & Beltzer, N. (2001). Cost-effectiveness of the Mpowerment Project, a community-level intervention for young gay men. *Journal of Acquired Immune Deficiency Syndrome, 27*, 482–491.

Kegeles, S. M., Hays, R. B., & Coates, T. J. (1996). The Mpowerment Project: A community-level HIV prevention intervention for young gay men. *American Journal of Public Health, 86*, 1129–1136.

Kegeles, S. M., Hays, R. B., Pollack, L. M., & Coates, T. J. (1999). Mobilizing young gay and bisexual men for HIV prevention: A two-community study. *AIDS, 13*, 1753–1762.

Kegeles, S. M., Rebchook, G. M., Hays, R. B., Terry, M. A., O'Donnell, L., Lenoard, N. R., Kelly, J. A., & Neumann, M. S. (2000). From science to application: The development of an intervention package. *AIDS Education and Prevention, 12*(Suppl. A), 62–74.

Kelly, J. A. (1999). Community-level interventions are needed to prevent new HIV infections. *American Journal of Public Health, 89*, 299–301.

Kelly, J. A., Heckman, T. G., Stevenson, L. Y., Williams, P. N., Ertl, T., Hays, R. B., Leonard, N. R., et al. (2000). Transfer of research-based HIV prevention inter-ventions to community service providers: Fidelity and adaptation. *AIDS Educa-tion and Prevention, 12*(Suppl. A), 87–98.

Kelly, J. A., Murphy, D. A., Sikkema, K. J., McAuliffe, T. L., Roffman, R. A., Solomon, L. J., et al. (1997). Randomized, controlled, community-level HIV-prevention intervention for sexual-risk behavior among homosexual men in U.S. cities. *Lancet, 350*, 1500–1505.

Kelly, J. A., Somlai, A. M., DiFranceisco, W. J., Otto-Salaj, L. L., McAuliffe, T. L., Hackl, K., et al. (2000). Bridging the gap between the science and service of HIV prevention: Transferring effective research-based HIV prevention interventions to community AIDS service providers. *American Journal of Public Health, 90*, 1082–1088.

Kennedy, M. G., Mizuno, Y., Seals, B. F., Myllyluoma, J., & Weeks-Norton, K. (2000). Increasing condom use among adolescents with coalition-based social marketing. *AIDS, 14*, 1809–1818.

Kirby, D. (2000). School-based interventions to prevent unprotected sex and HIV among adolescents. In J. L. Peterson & R. J. DiClemente (Eds.), *Handbook of HIV Prevention* (pp. 83–101). New York: Kluwer Academic/Plenum.

Knowlton, A. R., Hoover, D. R., Chung, S., Celantano, D. D., Vlahov, D., & Latkin, C. A. (2001). Access to medical care and service utilization among in-jection drug users with HIV/AIDS. *Drug and Alcohol Dependence, 64*, 55–62.

Koester, S. K. (1994). Copping, running, and paraphernalia laws: contextual vari-ables and needle risk behavior among injection drug users in Denver. *Human Organization, 53*, 287–295.

Kramer, L. (1989). *Reports from the holocaust: The making of an AIDS activist.* New York: St. Martin's Press.

Lauby, J. L., Smith, P. J., Stark, M., Person, B., & Adams, J. (2000). A community-level HIV prevention intervention for inner-city women: Results of the Women and Infants Demonstration Projects. *American Journal of Public Health, 90,* 216–222.

Linney, J. A. (2000). Assessing ecological constructs and community context. In J. Rappaport & E. Seidman (Eds.), *Handbook of community psychology.* New York: Kluwer Academic/Plenum.

Lurie, P., Gorsky, R., Jones, T. S., & Shomphe, L. (1998). An economic analysis of needle exchange and pharmacy-based programs to increase sterile syringe availability for injection drug users. *Journal of Acquired Immune Deficiency Syndromes and Human Retrovirology, 18*(Suppl. 1), S126–S132.

Lurie, P., Reingold, A. L, Bowser, B., et al. (1993). *The Public Health Impact of Needle Exchange Programs in the United States and Abroad* (Vol. 1). San Francisco: University of California, Institute for Health Policy Studies.

MacQueen, K. M., McLellan, E., Metzger, D. S., & Kegeles, S. M. (2001). What is community? An evidence-based definition for participatory public health. *American Journal of Public Health, 91,* 1929–1938.

Martin, J. L., Dean, L., Garcia, M. A., & Hall, W. (1989). The impact of AIDS on a gay community: Changes in sexual behavior, substance use, and mental health. *American Journal of Community Psychology, 17,* 269–293.

McCormick, A., McKay, M. M., Wilson, M., McKinney, L., Paikoff, R., Bell, C., et al. (2000). Involving families in an urban HIV preventive intervention: How community collaboration addresses barriers to participation. *AIDS Education and Prevention, 12,* 299–307.

McMillan, D. W. & Chavis, D. M. (1986). Sense of community: Definition and theory. *Journal of Community Psychology, 14,* 6–23.

Miller, R. L. (2001). Innovation in HIV prevention: Organizational and intervention characteristics affecting program adoption. *American Journal of Community Psychology, 29,* 621–647.

Miller, R. L., Bedney, B. J., & Garcia, D. I. (2002*). Isomorphic processes in AIDS organizations: A model of technology transfer.* Chicago: University of Illinois at Chicago. Manuscript under review.

Miller, R. L., Klotz, D., & Eckholdt, H. (1997). HIV prevention with male prostitutes and patrons of hustler bars: Replication of an HIV prevention intervention. *American Journal of Community Psychology, 26,* 97–131.

Muhib, F. B., Lin, L. S., Stueve, A., Miller, R. L., Ford, W. L., Johnson, W. D., et al. (2001). A venue-based method for sampling hard-to-reach populations. *Public Health Reports, 116*(Suppl. 1), 216–222.

National Center for Education Statistics. (1993). *Digest of Education Statistics.* Washington, DC: U.S. Department of Education, Office of Educational Research and Improvement.

National Institutes of Health Consensus Panel (1997). *Interventions to prevent HIV risk behaviors: Consensus panel report.* Rockville, MD: National Institutes of Health.

Neaigus, A., Friedman, S. R., & Hopkins, W. (1994). The relevance of drug injectors' social networks and risk networks for understanding and preventing HIV infection. *Social Science Medicine, 38,* 97–78.

Neaigus, A., Friedman, S. R., Kottiri, B. J., & Des Jarlais, D. C. (2001). HIV risk networks and HIV transmission among injecting drug users. *Evaluation and Program Planning, 24,* 221–226.

Neumann, M. S. & Sogolow, E. D. (2000). Replicating effective programs: HIV/AIDS prevention technology transfer. *AIDS Education and Prevention, 12*(Suppl. A), 35–48.

Normand, J., Vlahov, D., & Moses, L. E. (1995). *Preventing HIV Transmission: The Role of Sterile Needles and Bleach.* Washington, DC: National Academy Press.

O'Conner, P. G., Selwyn, P. A., & Schottenfeld, R. S. (1994). Medical progress: Medical care for injection-drug users with human immunodeficiency virus infection. *New England Journal of Medicine, 331*(7), 450–459.

Pargament, K. & Maton, K. (2000). Religion in American life: A community perspective. In J. Rappaport & E. Seidman (Eds.), *Handbook of Community Psychology.* (pp. 495–522). New York: Kluwer Academic/Plenum.

Peterson, J. L. (Ed.). (1998). HIV/AIDS prevention through community psychology [Special issue]. *American Journal of Community Psychology, 26,* 1–144.

Peterson, J. L., Bakeman, R., & Stokes, J. (2001). Racial/ethnic patterns of HIV sexual risk behaviors among young men who have sex with men. *Journal of the Gay and Lesbian Medical Association, 5,* 155–162.

Peterson, J. L., Coates, T. J., Catania, J. A., Middleton, L., Hilliard, B., & Hearst, N. (1992). High-risk sexual behavior and condom use among gay and bisexual African-American men. *American Journal of Public Health, 82,* 1490–1494.

Phillips, D. A. (2000). Social policy and community psychology. In J. Rappaport, & E. Seidman, (Eds.), *Handbook of community psychology.* (pp. 397–419). New York: Kluwer Academic/Plenum.

Pinkerton, S. D., Chesson, H. W., Holtgrave, D. R., Kassler, W., & Layde, P. M. (2000). When is an HIV infection prevented and when is it merely delayed? *Evaluation Review, 24,* 251–271.

Pinkerton, S. D., Holtgrave, D. R., DiFranceisco, W. J., Stevenson, L. Y., & Kelly, J. A. (1998). Cost-effectiveness of a community-level HIV risk reduction intervention. *American Journal of Public Health, 88,* 1239–1242.

Putnam, R. D. (1995). Bowling alone: America's declining social capital. *Journal of Democracy, 6*(1), 65–78.

Ramirez-Valles, J. (in press). The protective effects of community involvement for HIV/AIDS risk behavior. *Health Education Research.*

Ramirez-Valles, J. & Diaz, R. M. (2002). *Public health, race, and the AIDS movement: Antecedents and consequences of Latino gay men's movement participation.* Paper presented at the 19th Annual Claremont Symposium on Applied Social Psychology: Processes of community change and social action, The Claremont Colleges.

Revenson, T. A. & Schiaffino, K. M. (2000). Community-based health interventions. In J. Rappaport & E. Seidman (Eds.), Handbook of community psychology. (pp. 471–493). New York: Kluwer Academic/Plenum.

Revenson, T. A. & Seidman, E. (2002). Looking back and moving forward: Reflections on a quarter century of community psychology. In T. A. Revenson, A. D'Augelli, S. E. French, D. Hughes, D. Livert, E. Seidman, M. Shinn, & H. Yoshikawa (Eds.), *Community psychology: A quarter century of theory, research, and action in social and historical context* (pp. 3–31). New York: Kluwer Academic/Plenum.

Rofes, E. (1996). *Reviving the tribe: Regenerating gay men's sexuality and culture in the ongoing epidemic.* New York: Harrington Park Press.

Rogers, E. M. (1995). *Diffusion of innovation* (4th ed. New York: Free Press.

Ross, M. W. & Kelly, J. A. (2000). Interventions to reduce HIV transmission in homosexual men. In J. L. Peterson & R. J. DiClemente (Eds.), *Handbook of HIV Prevention* (pp. 201–216). New York: Kluwer Academic/Plenum.

Rotheram-Borus, M. J., Rebchook, G. M., Kelly, J. A., Adams, J., & Neumann, M. S. (2000). Bridging research and practice: Community-researcher partnerships for replicating effective interventions. *AIDS Education and Prevention, 12*(Suppl. A), 49–61.

Sarason, S. B. (1972). *The creation of settings and the future societies.* San Francisco: Jossey Bass.

Sarason, S. B. (1974). *The psychological sense of community: Prospects for a community psychology.* San Francisco: Jossey Bass.

Selwyn, P. A., Budner, N. S., Wasserman, W. C., & Arno, P. S. (1993). Utilization of on-site primary care services by HIV-seropositive and seronegative drug users in a methadone maintenance program. *Public Health Reports, 108,* 492–500.

Servegev, B., Oparina, T., Rumyantseva, T. P., Volkanevskii, V. L., Broadhead, R. S., Heckathorn, et al. (2000). HIV prevention in Yaroslavl, Russia: A peer-driven intervention and needle exchange. *Journal of Drug Issues, 29*(4), 777–804.

Shilts, R. (1987). *And the band played on: Politics, people and the AIDS epidemic.* New York: St. Martin's Press.

Shinn, M. & Perkins, D. N. T. (2000). Contributions from organizational psychology. In J. Rappaport & E. Seidman. (Eds.), *Handbook of community psychology* (pp. 615–641). New York: Kluwer Academic/Plenum.

Sikkema, K. J., Kelly, J. A., Winett, R. A., Solomon, L. J., Cargill, V. A., Roffman, R. A., et al. (2000). Outcomes of a randomized community-level HIV prevention intervention for women living in 18 low-income housing developments. *American Journal of Public Health, 90,* 57–63.

Simmons, P. Z., Rietmeijer, C. A., Kane, M. S., Guenther-Grey, C., Higgins, D. L., & Cohn, D. L. (1996). Building a peer network for a community level HIV prevention program among injecting drug users in Denver. *Public Health Reports, 111*(Suppl.), 50–53.

Singer, M., Himmelgreen, D., Weeks, M. R., Radda, K. E., & Martinez, R. (1997). Changing the environment of AIDS risk: findings on syringe exchange and pharmacy sales of syringes in Hartford, CT. *Medical Anthropology, 18*(1), 107–130.

Sobo, E. J. (1995). *Choosing unsafe sex: AIDS-risk denial among disadvantaged women.* Philadelphia: University of Pennsylvania Press.

Somlai, A. M., Kelly, J. A., Otto-Salaj, L., & Nelson, D. (1999). "Lifepoint:" A case study in using social science community identification data to guide the implementation of a needle exchange program. *AIDS Education and Prevention, 11*(3), 187–202.

Stokes, J. P. & Peterson, J. L. (1998). Homophobia, self-esteem, and risk for HIV among African American men who have sex with men. *AIDS Education and Prevention, 10,* 278–292.

Strenski, T. A., Marshall, P. A., Gacki, J. K., & Sanchez, C. W. (2000). The emergent impact of syringe exchange programs on shooting galleries and injection behaviors in three ethnically diverse Chicago neighborhoods. *Medical Anthropology, 18*(4), 415–438.

Sumartojo, E. (2000). Structural factors in HIV prevention: Concepts, examples, and implications for research. *AIDS, 14*(Suppl. 1), S3–S10.

Titus, S., Marmor, M., & Des Jarlais, D. C. (1994). Bleach use and HIV seroconversion among New York City injection drug users. *Journal of Acquired Immunodeficiency Syndrome, 7,* 700–704.

Valdiserri, R. O. (2000). Technology transfer: Achieving the promise of HIV prevention. In J. L. Peterson & R. J. DiClemente (Eds.), *Handbook of HIV* (pp. 267–283). New York: Kluwer Academic/Plenum.

Valente, T. W., Foreman, R. K., Junge, B., & Vlahov, D. (1988). Satellite exchange in the Baltimore needle exchange program. *Public Health Reports, 113*(Suppl.), 90–96.

Valleroy, L. A., MacKellar, D. A., Karon, J. M., Rosen, D. H., McFarland, W., Shehan, D. A., et al. (2000). HIV prevalence and associated risks in young men who have sex with men. *Journal of the American Medical Association, 284,* 198–204.

Vlahov, D., Astemborski, J., & Solomon, L. (1994). Field effectiveness of needle disinfection among injecting drug users. *Journal of Acquired Immunodeficiency Syndrome, 7,* 760–766.

Wawer M. J., Sewankambo N. K., Serwadda D., Quinn T. C., Paxton L. A., Kiwanuka N., et al. (1999). Control of sexually transmitted diseases for AIDS prevention in Uganda: A randomised community trial. Rakai Project Study Group. *Lancet, 353,* 525–35.

Weiker, R. L., Edington, R., & Kipke, M. D. (1999). A collaborative evaluation of a needle exchange program for youth. *Health Education and Behavior, 26*(2), 213–224.

West, S. G., Aiken, L. S., & Todd, M. (1993). Probing the effects of individual components in multiple-component prevention programs. *American Journal of Community Psychology, 21,* 571–606.

Wong, F. Y., Chng, C. L., & Lo, W. (1998). A profile of six community-based HIV prevention programs targeting Asian and Pacific Islander Americans. *AIDS Education and Prevention, 10*(Suppl A), 61–76.

Woodyard, J., Peterson, J. L., & Stokes, J. (2000). Let us go into the house of the Lord: Participation in African American churches by African American men who have sex with men (MSM). *Journal of Pastoral Care, 54,* 451–460.

Yoshikawa, H. & Hsueh, J. (2001). Child development and public policy: Toward a dynamic systems perspective. *Child Development, 72,* 1887–1903.

Yoshikawa, H., Rosman, E. A., & Hsueh, J. (2001). Variation in teenage mothers' experiences of child care and other components of welfare reform: Selection processes and developmental consequences. *Child Development, 72,* 299–317.

Yoshikawa, H., Wilson, P. A., Hsueh, J., Rosman, E. A., Kim, J., & Chin, J. (2003). What frontline CBO staff can tell us about culturally anchored theories of change in HIV prevention for Asian/Pacific Islanders. *American Journal of Community Psychology. 32,* 143–158.

Zimmerman, M. A. (2000). Empowerment theory: Psychological, organizational, and community levels of analysis. In J. Rappaport & E. Seidman (Eds.), *Handbook of community psychology.* (pp. 43–63). New York: Kluwer Academic/Plenum.

3

Narrative Insurrections:
HIV, Circulating Knowledges,
and Local Resistances

Eric Stewart & Julian Rappaport

> The [turn of the century] quivers with the extreme microscopic and
> the extreme macroscopic; imaging and communication technologies
> and the metaphoric frames they place on daily experience leave us
> more knowledgeable about the distant and the tiny than we seem to
> be about the proximate and the palpable. The notion that there may
> also be such a thing as medium-range experience seems prosaic, yet
> it is precisely in the medium range that class, race, and gender are in-
> scribed on the body through the micro- and macro-politics of occupa-
> tion and surveillance. Radically different metaphors of power, of
> community, of resistance are deployed across different sites in the
> class war surrounding AIDS.
>
> (Patton, 1990, p. 2)

In the United States, the number of new cases of AIDS, as of 2004, is on
the rise. The rate of new HIV infection has been on the rise—even in
those communities that had previously shown remarkable declines—
for a decade or more (Odets, 1995; Treichler, 1999; Wohlfeiler, 2002). Despite the success of earlier community-based and focused prevention
efforts, in urban gay communities, for instance, the Centers for Disease
Control and Prevention (CDC) has officially declared that prevention
efforts have "stalled." Furthermore, the CDC now recommends (and
funds) an emphasis on counseling or case-management for those already infected (Wohlfeiler, 2002). In this chapter, we suggest that the
narrative framework is a useful conceptual and methodological tool for
examining why prevention has "stalled," and how its engine could be
restarted.

We begin with a brief overview of the contested meanings and representations of HIV/AIDS in United States culture: the surrounding and
sometimes suffocating atmosphere of "circulating knowledges" about HIV.
We then provide some definitional specifics for narrative and community
narrative, and argue for their special relevance to HIV prevention and activism. We make a case for viewing HIV prevention as a matter of fostering
local resistances and helping to excavate and proliferate "subjugated
knowledges" (Foucault, 1980, p. 81). We provide illustration of this strategy

by presenting and analyzing two critical examples of narrating prevention and resistance—in fact, of making prevention a matter of resistance or "counter-practices" (Trend, 1989, 1995). Finally, we discuss some options and implications for a narrative approach, particularly for understanding, telling, and acting from the "inside out." If the chapter seems critical, it is. We try to be positively critical, in a constructive, constituting sense, but we find the narrative landscape of HIV/AIDS to be so overbuilt that some negative, deconstructive criticism seems necessary. We hope, however, that we have made or at least left some room for readers to draw their own moral to this story.

CONTESTS OF MEANING: CULTURE AND HIV

HIV as holocaust, HIV as CIA biomedical experiment, HIV as vaccine testing gone wrong, HIV as divine retribution, HIV as a medico-scientific problem, HIV as a personal/behavioral problem, HIV as a socio-political problem, HIV as something unprecedented, HIV as more of the same old story, HIV as a boon to organizing and unity in marginalized communities, HIV as having fractured unity and derailed progressive social movements in marginalized communities. Each of the stories so indexed reflects a different relationship to the historical and existing order of things and each justifies particular personal, community, and policy responses (Patton, 1990; Treichler, 1999). These narratives, and the preceding list is far from exhaustive, also bear complex and equivocal meanings for those who hold them, in part because they refer to complex, overdetermined forms of power relations.

The perspective we take here is that the community context produces and is produced by meaning-making and meaning-ascribing accounts, the histories and experiences that inform them, and their relationships to broader and narrower cultural narratives. The response to HIV/AIDS and accessory medical and social scientific statements and strategies will be determined largely by these local narrative transactions that bind lived experience to particular social institutions and relations (Aggleton, Hart, & Davies, 1989; Altman, 1993; Hammond, 1988; Patton, 1996; Triechler, 1988, 1991; Weeks, 1993).

From this perspective, HIV/AIDS is not a "thing-in-itself" (Rorty, 1982). HIV/AIDS has long, dense, fringe entangled in almost every other aspect of personal and cultural life and history. Its meanings, and relationships to those meanings, shift, mutate, evolve, and devolve over time and across contexts. In contrast to many other approaches (e.g., public health), narrative does not try to look past or through these polysemous temporal, epistemic, and contextual complexities; rather, a narrative approach aims to engage and perhaps mobilize them. We believe that narrative, particularly community narrative, is an especially useful means to understanding, cultivating, and/or mobilizing shared experience and conceptualizations in response to HIV/AIDS.

But, as the examples we provide demonstrate, understanding and mobilizing community narratives—creating "insurrection of subjugated knowledges" (Foucault, 1980, p. 81)—requires attention to the effects of dominant cultural narratives, because they compete with, infect, and disqualify local knowledges. The effects of dominant cultural narratives can be identified in the ways questions are predetermined, the null hypothesis already claimed, binarisms preset, and center and margins marked off; they circumscribe that which goes without saying and that which is unspeakable (Champagne, 1995; Foucault, 1980, 1981; Garber, 2000; Mills, 1997; Shepard & Hayduk, 2002).

Foucault (1980, 1981) argued that the effects and techniques of this discursive power are most available to observation and challenge at the local level—"the extremities of society"—because this is where they are least "concealed." These "extremities" are also where exceptions or countereffects are most observable, and where domination is confronted by the alienation it engenders (cf., bell hooks's "marginality as site of resistance"; 1990). We interpret this to imply a strategy of identifying and cultivating local resistances, of sparking narrative insurrections.

NARRATIVE MEANS

The narrative literature is broad, multidisciplinary, and far from unitary. There are, however, many good reviews relevant to social science application that discuss narrative as an object of analysis or as a methodological approach (Bruner, 1986; Bruner & Gorfain, 1984; Bruner, 1990; Crosseley, 2000; Denzin, 1996, 1997; Fair, 1995; Howard, 1991; Maines, 1993; Polkinghorne, 1988; Rappaport, 1998; Reissman, 1993; Wyer, 1995). There is also exemplary work examining narrative in relation to medicine and public health (Crosseley, 1997, 2001; Patton, 1996; Treichler, 1999). The definition we employ here is Jerome Bruner's (1990, pp. 43–52, et passim), which we believe addresses critical features without being overly narrow or uselessly broad.

First, narrative is a means for emphasizing human *"agentivity,"* or goal directed action, generally in the form of characters or actors. Second, there is a *plot*, composed of a particular sequence of events and mental states, that establishes a temporality and helps define a developing context. Third, narrative observes *"canonality"*; that is, stories must observe certain rules or conventions, recognize, and draw from, existing cultural forms or genres. Narrative must be sensible to be viable. But crucial to our interests here, narrative also offers the means to make the *"noncanonical"*—the unusual, the transgressive, paradoxical, or seemingly irrational—comprehensible. Highly relevant to matters related to sex, sexuality, drugs, identity, and power, narrative has the capacity to provide "a logic of illogic," a rationale for the apparently irrational. Fourth, narrative always implies a *perspective*. Even when that perspective belongs to a definite or imagined "we," as in cultural or communal narratives, the presentation includes both the shared perspective and that of whoever is invoking it in that instance. It is this point of view that distinguishes narrative from scripts or schemas. Fifth, narrative is *epistemic and rhetorical*, and therefore dramatic. Narratives construct, convey, and aim to persuade others of particular meanings and interpretations. Narrative, then, offers an account both of circumstances and what these *mean* to the actor (and narrator), as well as how to interpret the actor's actions in the context of events. When narratives are being told or invoked, the teller's selection of a particular narrative in particular circumstances conveys additional meaning and implies an interpretation of the situation at hand (Miller, 1995). Sixth, narrative is most often characterized by a *"subjunctiveness,"* or an openness to readings and interpretations that allows for a certain amount of experimentation with experience and meaning among narrative participants. All of these characteristics make narrative particularly useful for social negotiation and for managing apparently incommensurate experiences and interpretations.

In these qualities, narrative offers a transcendence of the private/ public and individual/social dichotomies that have been problematic for the conception and study of persons and culture and, glaringly, the practices associated with HIV/AIDS and HIV prevention. In emphasizing intentional, participating agents constrained by but negotiating a cultural canonality and prefigured set of meanings, narrative provides a way out of the dilemma of cultural determinism versus unencumbered agency. People are both constituted by and participants in constituting social meaning, including personal and community identities (de Certeau, 1984; Miller & Goodnow, 1995). Narratives are political negotiations. Their authoring and performance are always surrounded and defined by a multidimensional social and cultural context. They implicate communicative practices and codes, institutional structure, complex forms and presentations of agency, and the relations of power to knowledge (Denzin, 1997; Frow & Morris, 1993). To employ the terms of Bakhtin (1981, 1986) and Gramsci (1971), narratives of identity and community are social practices, "deployed across the institutionalized terrain of social formation because the genres through which such 'authorship' takes place are institutionally bound" (Yudice, 1990, p. 137). Thus, identity and community narratives are never entirely the property or sole creation of a particular group of people because identity and community are always "populated—over populated—with the intentions of others" (Bakhtin, 1981, p. 294).

For example, gay or bisexual men, African Americans, youth, or IV drug users do not "freely" author or reauthor their own narratives of community or of HIV, but must negotiate, resist, manage, subvert, or appropriate from the existing repertoire of stories or genres through which people (and disease, sex, drugs, gender, "race," health, safety) are represented. All persons have to do this, but in discussing marginalized and/or oppressed communities and problem-saturated identities, the repertoire tends to be more limited, less varied, and the institutional constraints more overdetermined. Furthermore, differences in "storytelling rights" and resources, as in White narratives about Blacks or "straight" narratives about gay men or drug use, mean that communities not only have the task of self-authoring positive, meaningful narratives *for* themselves, but also often of "disauthoring" or divesting themselves of dominant narratives *about* them.

The value of community narratives for constructing, negotiating, and communicating meaning, agency, plot, and context for sexual and drug use practices is potentially great for social scientists willing to engage in dialogical and collaborative inquiry and intervention with community members. They also offer social scientists an important role in helping to analyze and deconstruct problem-saturated personal and community narratives and to excavate, re-author, and perform preferred and empowering accounts of "I" and "we" (Denzin, 1989, 1997; Fair, 1995; Giroux, Lankshire, McClaren, & Peters, 1996; Rappaport, 1993, 1998; Salzer, 1998, 2000; Stewart, 2002; Tessman, 1995; Trend, 1989, 1995). As social scientists, we can assist in narrative insurrection; we can help in proliferating "subjugated knowledges."

In the section that follows, we provide two examples of community and cross-community narratives of HIV/AIDS and its prevention that not only took notice of the political nature of speaking to and about HIV/AIDS, but also made it foundational. These two examples also point to different ways of working with community identity and community difference.

Narrating Resistance

Example 1: Safe Sex Positive

> Limit what sex acts you choose to perform to ones which interrupt disease transmission. The advantage of this approach is that if you avoid taking in your partner(s)' body fluids, you will better protect yourself from most serious diseases but also from many of the merely inconvenient ones. The key to this approach is modifying what you do—not how often you do it nor with how many different partners . . . As you read on, we hope we make at least one point clear: Sex doesn't make you sick—diseases do. Once you understand how diseases are transmitted, you can begin to explore medically safe sex. Our challenge is to figure out how we can have gay, life-affirming sex, satisfy emotional needs, and stay alive! (Callen & Berkowitz, 1983, pp. 1–2)

The above is an excerpt from the first published safer sex guidelines: *How to Have Sex in an Epidemic. How to Have Sex* was developed by and for the gay community and published at very low cost by News from the Front, a political, gay press. It is remarkable for several reasons, the first of which is that 20 years later it still stands as one of the best and most comprehensive sets of guidelines available. These guidelines were produced by a group of gay men, all of whom had AIDS, who culled through extant research, weeding out the merely fantastic and simply useless, to arrive at a set of relatively simple and accurate guidelines in 40 pages. The guidelines include theories of transmission, sexual techniques, and a psychosocial guide to coping with behavioral changes and the fear of AIDS.

How to Have Sex is also remarkable because it was written *before* the cause of AIDS had been identified, while medicine and public health were still pondering such possibilities as "excessive semen deposit" and amyl nitrate usage, and medico-scientific camps were divided between "lifestyle hypothesis" immunology and virology perspectives on etiology (hence the awkward nomenclature of HIV/AIDS) (Patton, 1990; Treichler, 1999). At the time, public health officials were informing hospital pediatricians in the Bronx that it was *impossible* that AIDS was responsible for a rash of mysterious infant deaths (Shilts, 1987).

How to Have Sex in an Epidemic is also important as an index of a particular community narrative that mobilized an extremely effective community-based and community-wide prevention strategy years before government, the media, and many areas of the medical and social sciences, began to pay serious attention. HIV was present in the gay community, at least in "front line" cities, as early as 1978. (It was also present among IV drug users at least as early, though it went unidentified or misidentified as "junky pneumonia" for many years).

Some statistics serve as an index of the success of the first, community-based, and community-developed prevention effort. In San Francisco, rates of incidence rose as high as 18.4% by 1982 then fell to 1% by 1987. In terms of numbers, San Francisco estimates were 8,000 new cases in 1982, 1200 in 1985, and 500 in 1987 (Hessol, Lifson, O'Malley, Doll, Jaffe, et al., 1989; Katz, 1997). Given that it takes from six weeks to several months from infection to the production of antibodies (seroconversion), a 1% incidence rate in early 1987 indicates normative changes taking place perhaps years earlier (Patton, 1990). In addition, the prevalence in San Francisco of receptive anal intercourse with two or more partners in a month declined from 15% in the first half of 1984 to 5% in the second half of the same year, and remained low through 1987 (Winkelstein, Wiley, & Padian, 1988). These are remarkable declines by any comparable standards, but are all the more so as much of this change occurred with little support or resources from government.

Safe sex organizing between 1980 and 1985 grew out of urban gay communities' understanding of the social organization of sexuality and from extrapolations of information hidden in poorly designed epidemiological research (Altman, 1986; Epstein, 1991; Patton, 1985, 1990). Initial efforts were based on a self-help model, informed by the women's health movement and its critiques of health care (Morgan, 2002; Patton, 1985). The model was also strongly shaped by the gay liberation movement of the preceding decades, and that movement's analyses and frank discussions of sex and sexuality. For early AIDS activists, safe sex was not something to be imposed upon the reluctant or recalcitrant, but was rather a form of political resistance, of community building and preservation (Altman, 1986; Patton, 1985). There were two fronts of resistance: preventing new infections and preventing gay men and gay sex from being driven back into the closet and self-loathing. These two goals, or battles, were viewed as inseparable and interdependent (Champagne, 1995; Crimp, 1988; Epstein, 1991; Patton, 1985, 1990, 1996; Shepard & Hayduk, 2002; Yudice, 1990).

These early projects and their narratives were developed before the identification of HIV, and before the development and implementation of an antibody test. This point is critical because, with no testing, there was no possibility of sorting people in the community into categories of "safe" and "unsafe", including oneself. This fact, combined with the politicization of sexual behavior and the glow of a unified political liberation movement, helped to form an ethos of caring in safe sex activism and practices. Rather than the self-preservation that became the ethos of later, professional, safe sex education, early activists fostered a story of community preservation, of protecting one's partner(s) and one's community by observing precautions.

There are important ramifications to this narrative. One is that restricting sexual practices—using a condom or asking one's partner(s) to use condoms—was taken as much as a sign of protecting them as oneself. Opting for safe sex practices did not send a message that one believed one's partner to be a risk in himself (or herself). Risk or threat was not personalized or internalized, but shared and externalized. Another ramification was that it put a fully developed community narrative behind sexual negotiations; the burden and persuasive responsibility did not fall on one or both partners in the (heat of the) moment. One was not alone in the negotiation of safer sex practices, or in authoring the meaning of such negotiations. And, for those inclined to think in such ways, safe sex was an act of community solidarity. The ethos of this narrative also neatly transcended any legitimacy/liberation divides in a community because there was no prescription as to whether one opted for chastity or licentiousness; number or location of partners was not relevant.

In framing the narrative in this way, we do not mean to imply extra capacity for altruism and virtue among gay men. The emergent ethos was partly authored by committed activists and volunteers, and was cemented by a sense of siege and of the general indifference—if not hostility—on the part of government, medicine, and the larger society. It also has to be acknowledged that these gay urban communities were largely White, middle class, and educated and had access to resources. Nonetheless, the narrative of gay men protecting one another was unique in public health, and impressive in its success (Altman, 1986; Crimp, 1988; Patton, 1985; Shepard & Hayduk, 2002; Treichler, 1999).

In a similar vein, gay community-based organizations early on developed a participatory, dialogical method of safe sex education, avoiding the individual behavioral or rational health behavior models of many later professional programs. Early programs intentionally avoided one-on-one interventions, focusing instead on two-way communication with their communities. Here, for example, is an excerpt from an executive memo to the San Francisco AIDS Foundation and the San Francisco Department of Public Health (note the date):

> Given the urgency of behavior change, the educational strategy would focus more on changing community norms and on developing peer support for lower risk behaviors than on changing individual behavior. All educational interventions would be designed as two-way communication devices where possible so that information would be obtained from the audience, as well as being transmitted to the audience, providing a feedback loop that keeps the foundation in touch with the audience's current opinions, beliefs and needs. Marketing and selling, rather than more traditional academic models, would be used. (Research and Decisions Corporation, 1984, p. 27; quoted in Wohlfeiler, 2002)

Whatever one might feel about "marketing and selling" in the context of an epidemic, the method advocated here has a clear participatory edge over most professional prevention methods of the mid '80s and later. It is also plausible to exchange the terms marketing and selling for narrating and storytelling. What is germane is the emphasis on dialogic communications with the community, the "narrative conjunctions" (Miller & Moore, 1989) of community and preventionists, and the conarration of safety and of community. What seems to have shifted over the course of the epidemic's first decade is the nature of the dialog and the parties involved. Government funders and large AIDS Service Organizations (ASOs; often acting as distributors of government funding to smaller projects), rather than community members or activists, became the key narrators and the definers of plot and canon (Edwards, 1997; Labonte, 1997; Patton, 1996; Wohlfeiler, 2002).

TESTING LIMITS Patton (1990) argues that it was the introduction of widespread HIV-antibody testing, surrounded by a consolidating, professionalized AIDS industry and discourse around 1985–86, that directly undermined the ethos of community preservation and community mobilization by making HIV testing central to prevention efforts. It remains a genuine question whether the Counseling, Testing, Referral and Partner Notification programs (CTRPN; now the thrust of the CDC's "prevention" policies) ever truly constitute prevention, at least in the sense of serostatus knowledge showing any correlation to sexual or drug use behaviors (Ekstrand, Stall, Paul, Osmond, & Coates, 1999; Hagar, 1995; Odets, 1995; Ostrow, 1987; Patton, 1996). These programs emphasize self-protection over community well-being, and implement different protocols and advice depending on determined "risk categories." For example, the common practice of adjusting the type and content of pre- and post-test counseling— about the meaning of the results, future retesting, monogamous relationships, and sexual practices—is quickly pegged by many gay and bisexual men as homophobic or at least heterosexist, and by others as classist or racist (Hagar, 1995; Odets, 1995; Patton, 1996; Wohlfeiler, 2002).

Furthermore, even though the lines of safety and risk had not changed since the first safe sex advice, professional prevention programs and safe sex education in the mid '80s helped displace authority for understanding and enacting safe sex from the people who engage in sex and put it in the hands of "experts." Instead of the activists and experts that members of gay and other hard-hit communities had been, the emergent professional AIDS discourse reauthored them as "victims," clients, or volunteers (Epstein, 1991). These are just the kinds of flooding that would "stall" engines of prevention.

We are inclined to agree with the critiques of professionalized prevention and health education efforts offered by Epstein (1991), Odets (1995), Hagar (1995), Patton (1996), Treichler (1999), Wohlfeiler (2002), and others, particularly how they contributed to the shift from truly community-based organizations to ASOs, and from a community-preservation to an individual behavior and case management prevention approach. It has to be conceded that many things contributed to the loss of community involvement in HIV prevention, the concurrent declines in volunteerism and prevention activism, and increases in risky sexual practices in gay communities (Ekstrand et al., 1999; Katz, 1997; Stewart & Weinstein, 1997; Weeks, Aggleton, McKevitt, Parkinson, & Taylor-Linbourn, 1996; Wohlfeiler, 2002). However, it is worth reviewing some of the events and changes accompanying the rise of the AIDS industry, because they also provide a context for the emergence of new narrative and resistance strategies.

Part of what occurred in urban gay communities was a level of complacency (or exhaustion) that came with the slowing of the epidemic among White gay men in front line cities. Another contributor was that while incidence ebbed, because HIV is a "slow virus", the prevalence of people living with HIV/AIDS remained high, requiring a certain level of professionalism to provide and coordinate services, along with extensive financial and volunteer resources, both of which seem to have been diverted from prevention efforts (Wohlfeiler, 2002).

Also, the perceived "face of the epidemic" was changing. On the one hand, a whole new generation of young men was coming into urban gay communities that had not taken part in the gay liberation activism of the '60s and '70s or the early years of AIDS organizing. This generation may have needed not only a "second-wave" of conscientization (Freire, 1970/1998), but also narratives of their own (Odets, 1995; Patton, 1991; 1996; Shepard & Hayduk, 2002). On the other hand, from the beginning, the epidemic had disproportionately affected gay and bisexual men of color, many of whom were not being reached by prevention efforts of the White gay community. Added to this was the increasing visibility of the intravenous drug use (IVDU) epidemic, growing awareness of IVDU-related infections among women—also, disproportionately, people of color—and an epidemic beginning to define itself along lines of class rather than sexuality.

Given these "developments," the limitations of an urban, mostly White, gay community-based narrative, and a libertarian, circle-the-wagons approach, become readily apparent. It certainly did not help, however, that government funding policies: (1) restricted frank discussion of sexuality or drug use for many years (e.g., the Helms Amendment, 1987–1992, or ongoing struggles over condom "promotion" by government-funded programs and agencies); (2) demanded new language and forms of accountability from community based organizations (CBOs) accustomed to responding only to their communities (Cain, 1995; Labonte, 1997; Platoni, 2002); and, (3) tended to favor an individual behavior model of prevention education targeted at (but not particularly reflective of) identified risk groups (Altman, 1993, 1994; Epstein, 1991; Patton, 1990, 1996; Wohlfeiler, 2002). Enter ACT UP.

Example 2: ACT UP and Stepping Over the Lines   It was in this climate, around 1987, that AIDS Coalition To Unleash Power (ACT UP) came to national prominence through a number of well-planned and attention-grabbing performances (the term generally preferred to protest) (Gamson, 1989; Patton, 1990; Shepard & Hayduk, 2002; Treichler, 1991, 1999; Yudice, 1990). ACT UP was formed, in part, as a conscious response to a number of identified problems: (1) the perceived apathy about HIV and AIDS in gay communities; (2) what was seen as the immorality and/or nonresponsiveness of pharmaceutical companies and government agencies; (3) the absence or invisibility of women, the poor, IVDUs, and people of color from most current HIV efforts; (4) the need for new stories and strategies for analyzing HIV/AIDS and its relationships to other "social formations," for disrupting certain "discursive regimes," and ways of organizing that were not reliant on identity politics (ACT UP/NY Women and AIDS Book Group, 1992; Eigo, 2002; Gamson, 1989; Morgan, 2002; Patton, 1990; Shepard, 2002c; Treichler, 1999; Yudice, 1990).

For our purposes, ACT UP offers effective and differently performed examples of community narrative construction. ACT UP made cultural analysis, art, performance, and aesthetics important parts of HIV activism. Art, performance, and style are also key ways of conveying or referencing community (Art and Revolution, 2001; Clifford, 1988; Fair, 1995; Patton, 1996; Rappaport, 2000; Thomas & Rappaport, 1996; Yudice, 1990). As one now iconic example, think of ACT UP's graphically smart and arresting "Silence=Death" posters, buttons, and stickers with an upward pointing pink triangle on a black background. For many people, the density of referenced narratives may be only partly penetrable, but the central message is hard to miss (Crimp & Rolston, 1990). First, there is the obvious reference to the holocaust, but it is not as straightforward as that. The pink triangle, as mentioned, is pointed *upward* in contrast to the downward pointed triangles of the Third Reich, symbolically referencing action or resurgence. The in-your-face quality of the design and referents, along with strategic placement (often illegally and unavoidably posted), were meant to speak to a growing complacency, particularly in that segment of urban gay communities loathe to make waves, but willing to hand the problem over to a new professional AIDS industry. On an insider level, "silence" also refers to closets, passing, and good behavior, with the promise of invisibility/safety these seem to offer, but which in fact only serve to perpetuate oppression and the epidemic.

Furthermore, the appropriation of Nazi symbolism can be read as a comment on the CDC's epidemiological classifications and "risk groups." Haitians, homosexuals, hemophiliacs and IV drug (heroin) users were the initial, identified high-risk categories (so-dubbed the "4H Club"). Haitians, originally the only overtly marked racial category, were tied to AIDS on the basis of public health's beliefs about voodoo practices, not on the basis of race, sexual, or drug use practices (Patton, 1990). Because of the way HIV/AIDS statistics were compiled and reported, the public perception became that homosexuals were White and drug users were poor people of color (Patton, 1990). That non-White men were overrepresented in *every* risk category was not realized or politicized until 1985, when the gay press reported that men of color were disproportionately represented in the CDC category "homosexual/bisexual." Moreover, women were erased from the epidemic for almost a decade (Treichler, 1999). This system of epidemiological classification, unreal and incoherent from the perspective of people most affected by the epidemic, helped to short-circuit possibilities of meaningful, responsive narration in affected communities for many years. In addition, it has been argued that the AIDS=gay and, secondarily, AIDS=junky equations helped foster or maintain a nonmilitant silence in these communities (e.g., ACT UP/NY Women and AIDS Book Group, 1992; Dalton, 1989; Henthoff, 1990; Patton, 1990, 1996).

This brings us to a final point about "Silence=Death." Reflecting ACT UP's anarchic structure, contingent agendas, and ambitions for crossing the borders of defined "risk communities," the terms of *Silence Equaling Death* could be read and defined differently according to local community history and experience. However, the equation was equivalently relevant for women, people of color, IV drug users, the poor in general, and bisexuals, gay men and lesbians—particularly in relation to science and medicine (Crimp & Rolston, 1990; Patton, 1990). Cindy Patton (1990) tells a story about the first time she saw a "Silence=Death" poster. She believed it read "*Science*=Death":

> When the poster became a button, a T-shirt, a key symbol of the anarchic resistance to a pogrom masquerading as disease, I was sure that the slogan had been changed. It was only when I went back to Manhattan that I saw that I had misread the original poster, now tattered and nearly lost under layers of newer posters. But the dyad silence/science was no mistake. Straight people find this slip funny. Gay people do not. Silence/science has dogged our very existence— once the closet, now media blackouts; once psychiatry, now internal medicine. The twin threats are oblivion and diagnosis." (p. 127)

Many African Americans do not find the slip funny either. Most of the communities affected by HIV/AIDS have histories of medicalized or criminalized identities. For many of these same people, brutal or dehumanizing encounters with medical and psychiatric science are part of their collective narratives. Many African Americans are influenced by memory of the Tuskegee syphilis studies, as one example among many, many others (Jones, 1981; Junod, 1993; Quinn, 1997; *San Francisco Chronicle*, 1990, October 30). Women, too, have their own antagonistic history with medicine and psychiatry. And, in the interests of always saying what goes without saying, gay men and lesbians are only a generation or two removed from incarceration or forced hospitalizations and "treatment," which may have included castration, insulin and electroshock therapy, or even psychoanalysis.

All of these people, along with the poor and non-White in general, have good reasons to be apprehensive about visibility and speaking up, especially in the "wrong places." And sex and drugs are, in varying but precise ways, tropes of stigma and stereotype by which these groups have been disqualified, watched, and controlled. ACT UP directly confronted the invisibility = safety narratives generated by these histories and circumstances and turned them on their heads. Lack of restraint was reframed as a solution, not a cultural, genetic, or characterological flaw.

The strategy of coalition building and of a more complex and multivocal storytelling met with varying degrees of success and commitment, depending in part on local demographics of the epidemic and variance in local political strength of various communities. But ACT UP members were instrumental in, and arrested for, developing the earliest needle exchange programs and in mounting legal challenges to restrictions on such programs. ACT UP also early on joined others in pointing to the War on Drugs and draconian penalties for possession as accelerating—not slowing—the spread of HIV among IV drug users. It worked to keep or make sex clubs and other "public" sex venues "safer sex zones" (Eigo, 2002; Saalfield, Chris, Lurie, & Pearl, 1990; Saalfield & Navarro, 1991). For the most part, ACT UP kept racism and classism central in their analyses and actions. ACT UP also maintained active women's participation, both in general and in more gender-specific activities (ACT UP/NY Women and AIDS Book Group, 1992; Morgan, 2002; Shepard, 2002c). It may be that a certain degree of involvement had more to do with "radical chic" and a limited politics of style, but ACT UP strove to maintain a narrative of HIV/AIDS as explicitly a political, rather than personal or medical, matter, one of community building and preservation. And, ACT UP revived an insistence on involvement in decision- and policy-making by those most affected by decisions and policies. This represented a radically different kind of public health.

In these ways, ACT UP built upon, but also diverged sharply from, the earlier, identity-based and single-issue focused model of gay community mobilization against HIV/AIDS. In the late 1980s, the politics, demographics and the economics of the epidemic were becoming increasingly complicated. ACT UP, along with other mobilization efforts, faced navigating collisions within and between the identity and community politics of the period. These collisions included heightening class and ethnic tensions around the epidemic, an official discourse that was "de-gaying" and de-politicizing HIV/AIDS, and the relentless professionalization of and government influence on formerly community-based organizations (Altman, 1993; Epstein, 1996; Gamson, 1989; Henthoff, 1990; Patton, 1990; Treichler, 1991, 1992, 1999; Weeks, 1993; Weeks et al., 1996).

Anarchic and deconstructive by design in both tactics and structure, ACT UP responded by bracketing identity politics and by remaining relatively decentralized and contingent in its organization. In many ways this was its genius. Local chapters developed out of and acted on local concerns and politics, and ACT UP looked and performed differently in different places and situations. Furthermore, despite a general perception of ACT UP as a "gay" activism group, ACT UP in many locales was quite involved with communities of color, IVDUs, and women. It always intended to create and maintain *coalitions*, even if provisional, rather than reifying an identity politics that was read as an impediment to effective AIDS treatment and prevention activism, and too much resembled public-health categorizations (Butler, 1990; Crimp & Rolston, 1990; Duggan, 1992; Foucault, 1980; Fuss, 1989; Gamson, 1989; Patton, 1990; Saalfield et al., 1990; Shepard, 2002a,b,c; Treichler, 1991).

Where is ACT UP now? We think the answers to that question say some important things about the ACT UP narrative, the one about it, and those it put forward about the epidemic. First, ACT UP did not *die*. In many places it did, however, disperse into many local community-based efforts and narratives, or atomize into various component interest groups and strategy factions (Gamson, 1989; Greig & Kershnar, 2002; Eigo, 2002; Patton, 1996; Shepard, 2002a,b,c). As examples, people committed to keeping HIV/AIDS activism part of a broader social change agenda moved in different directions from those who were invested in and highly self-educated in treatment research, development, and availability (e.g., San Francisco's ACT UP split; Gamson, 1989). The artists, academics, and intellectuals interested in creating new kinds of resistance strategies or "transversal power" and emphasizing local resistances, diverged from those seeking a broader, "unified," identity-derived or -constructing political strategy (Patton, 1990).

This "dispersal" can be storied either as a positive and coherent set of developments or as a failure, depending on one's perspective. The significance of the emergence of ACT UP and the narratives of "Silence=Death" remains the "sparks given off through attempts to 'unleash power' within the discourse/power gap" (Patton, 1990, p. 163). Action and change in diverse locales may be "ignited" by these sparks, but this ignition must occur out of local situations, local narratives of relations between silence and death.

Except in relation to scientific breakthroughs in vaccine or treatment research (and, on astoundingly few occasions, the pandemic in the rest of the world), in recent years HIV/AIDS has generally dropped below the media horizon. Although no current narrative or collective action captures the media attention that ACT UP did in its visibility heyday, the narratives and local resistances of ACT UP do persist within and across many communities. A large number of local or specialized groups and organizations grew directly out of, include members of, or borrowed theory and strategies from, ACT UP. We offer here just four examples from among dozens: (1) Fed Up Queers (FUQ), who among other things initiated civil disobedience in response to the Diallo shooting in NYC and organized AIDS Drugs for Africa (Sawyer, 2002; Shepard, 2002b). (2) Church Ladies for Choice, a direct action reproductive rights organization of men and women (in appropriate dress) (Church Ladies for Choice, 1993a, b; Cohen-Cruz, 2002). (3) Housing Works, a coalition of homeless and formerly homeless people living with HIV or AIDS, current and former IV drug users, current and former social workers, and former ACT UP members that advocate for the homeless—particularly HIV+, IV drug users of color—against police harassment and for access to services and safe housing (Shepard, 2002a). (4) *Fuerza Latina*, a Boston-area coalition of Latino men, all self-identified current and former drug users, who formed a harm-reduction support group to mobilize for needle cleaning and needle exchange, and to unite their larger community for social, economic and drug policy change (Greig & Kershnar, 2002).

What these projects share is the ACT UP legacy of local resistances—based in the particular moment and the particular experiences, histories, and narrative of a specific, located set of individuals—and fluid, nontotalizing coalitional strategies. They also share ACT UP's understanding of local concerns and resistances as inextricably tied into a broader web of dominant narratives and structures of gender, class, race or ethnicity, sexuality, place, age and "truth."

"AN INSURRECTION OF SUBJUGATED KNOWLEDGES"

Our aim in presenting these examples is not to romanticize the "clarity and camaraderie of the years before AIDS became an acceptable issue" (Patton, 1990, p. 129). Rather, we want to demonstrate the importance and challenges of "authoring" community preservation, community building, and community action in response to and in spite of HIV/AIDS. This authoring is important because a community narrative approach addresses the fact that HIV/AIDS is inextricably tied into a host of social, structural, and poststructural problems and concerns that cannot be met or even fully conceived within a strictly individual or an abstract universal framework. It is important as well because for both theoretical and empirical reasons (well-explicated throughout this volume), we believe that being "part" of a community relates to better prognoses on many levels (Aggleton, Hart, & Davies, 1989, 1990; Altman, 1993, 1994; Centers for Disease Control and Prevention [CDC] AIDS Community Demonstration Projects

Research Group, 1999; Minkler, 1997; Dowsett, 1989a,b; hooks, 1989, 1990; Kraft, Beeker, Stokes, & Peterson, 2000; Labonte, 1997; Quimby & Friedman, 1989; Shepard & Hayduk, 2002; Sibthorpe, Fleming, & Gould, 1994; Wohlfeiler, 2002; Yudice, 1990).

But community—as concept and as experience—also presents a number of challenges. Not least of these is a difficulty of stable definition and the fluidity of changing experience. Many of us are aware of the complexities presented by the experience of inhabiting multiple communities, particularly when these community memberships and the identities implied by them are in one or more senses incompatible. Perhaps the most obvious example in relation to HIV/AIDS is gay or bisexual men of color, and the liminality they may experience both in gay communities and in their "cultural communities." Except in those cities with populations large enough to support, say, a Black gay and lesbian or a gay Latino community, there are few sites and little cultural space for creating and performing such "hyphenated identities," and those that do exist may offer a restricted range of roles and stories (Fine, 1994; Flores & Yudice, 1990; Moraga & Anzaldua, 1981; Socialist Review Collective, 1995).

On the other hand, we would also point out that the homophobia ascribed to, say, Black communities glosses a much more complex set of relationships than is implied by that easy characterization (Champagne, 1995; Dalton, 1989; Hemphill, 1991; hooks, 1989; Kraft et al., 2000; National Coalition of Black Lesbians and Gays, 1986; Patton, 1990, 1996; Porter, 1988; Woodyard, Peterson, & Stokes, 2000). In fact, it is hard for us to interpret this ascribed homophobia apart from Whiteist, class-based, and/or Western readings of different constructions of community and sexuality, or minimizations of the effects of history and oppression (Beam, 1996; Champagne, 1995; Dyson, 1999; Garber, 1996; Hemphill, 1991; hooks, 1989). We do not deny the usefulness and effect that organizing around identity has had in the United States, but that does not prohibit a critical analysis of, for example, the difference between thinking of homo-, bi-, or hetero-sexual as *adjectives* describing behaviors, versus *nouns* inscribing identities. The first can apply anywhere or to anyone, the second is a fairly recent, localized and evolving development; in fact, something similar could be argued for many identity and community categories (Butler, 1990; Flores & Yudice, 1990; Foucault, 1981; Garber, 1996; Omi & Winant, 1986; Tessman, 1995; Weeks, 1985). It is, for example, not possible to mobilize a constructed category like "MSMs" (men who have sex with men).

Community may present special problems in relation to HIV prevention because, as Patton (1990) argues, "the meanings of sexuality and drug use are engendered within networks of face-to-face communications and within cultural productions (counter-cultural practices, the media, art, rituals of partnering, styles of dress) which *cut across* the 'communities' articulated for the purpose of engaging in the political languages of civil rights and claims for the apportionment of social resources" (p. 8, emphasis in original; see also West, 1989). Community, as it is commonly understood, may also present difficulties for those at the margins of margins. For example, IV drug users, like those "captured" by the category of "MSM," frequently do not develop community or even identity around their risk behaviors except perhaps, though not inconsequentially, in very specialized and provisional senses of those terms.

This makes the use of risk categories doubly problematic. Whole communities already stigmatized in one or more ways are saddled with the designation of "risky" (e.g., youth, poor people, non-Whites, gay, and bisexual men), yet the actual risk behaviors may not bear any relation (or even an inverse relation) to "actual" community per se, or to community membership (CDC AIDS Community Demonstration Projects Research Group, 1999; Patton, 1990, 1996). Furthermore, HIV/AIDS activists are often concerned to *un*couple practices and identity, so that, for instance, "MSMs" can recognize risks involved in particular practices without having to identify as gay or with a gay community (Garber, 1996; Patton, 1996).

Finally, many communities share common experiences and difficulties that span community boundaries and may be better addressed in coalitions. For instance, the women's health movement created a kind of community of women that crossed (or attempted to cross) borders of class, ethnicity or nationality, and sexuality, even as "the women's community," as concept or location, seems to present practical and analytical problems. There are also many historical and many currently shared reasons for African Americans, women, lesbians and gay men, and poor people in general to have ambivalent or aversive relationships to the medical and social sciences. These experiences and relationships could potentially offer bases for powerful coalition, particularly as these community memberships overlap frequently.

Our point is not to question or diminish the importance of the concept, practice, or study of community and community identification; we believe it is the most appropriate site or "level of analysis" for HIV/AIDS prevention. Rather, we have tried to offer ways to qualify and expand conceptualizations by demonstrating the value of a narrative approach to community and identity. Community *narratives*, we believe, are critical because narratives are flexible, expansive, and subjunctive and so are able to accommodate the vicissitudes of this epidemic and a social and political environment that is continually shifting and changing. Narrative communities allow for a certain permeability of boundaries, for the negotiation of simultaneous and often circumstantial membership in multiple communities and, importantly, for an authoring of shared community depending on the particular problem or experience at hand. In this regard, it is worth remembering that for many people their experience of community membership is primarily or only narrative in nature, for instance nonheterosexuals living in rural communities or otherwise removed from a physical gay or lesbian community.

A narrative approach allows and provides a vocabulary for community as self-contained and self-referential, in some ways exclusive (e.g., urban gay male communities and the libertarian, circle-the-wagons approach of the early community preservation models of HIV prevention). But narrative is "subjunctive" enough to accommodate nonessentializing and nontotalizing experiences, as well as definitions of community as dynamic, open to reworkings and reauthorings, permeable, and with "conjunctive clauses" that allow for coalition formation and inclusion without loss of identities. A narrative approach also can accommodate recognition that not all aspects of community or community identity are positive or even especially "native," that they may reflect the distortions of dominant, problem-saturated or -saturating narratives, and can provide means for analyzing and reauthoring those effects. And, because the narrative metaphor suggests an understanding of "truth" as more or other than "fact" based knowledge, you do not have to be a scientist to participate in the storytelling and story-making (Dyson, 1999).

We furthermore believe that alienation is itself an important epistemological source (Bakhtin, 1981; Foucault, 1980; Gadamer, 1975; Kögler, 1997), particularly in regard to the culture that alienates. HIV/AIDS for the most part takes us to the "extremities of society," where exceptional or counter-cultural practices and experiences are most available, where the alienating effects of the "order of things" are most observable. This is why, Foucault argues, the strategy of change or action is not to impose a new "truth regime" (however well-intended), but to facilitate "an insurrection of subjugated knowledges" (1980, p. 81).

DIALOGIC NARRATION: METHODOLOGIES

> For those of us living and working in the various constituencies most devastated by HIV it seems as if the rest of the population were tourists, casually wandering through at the very height of a blitz of which they are totally unaware.
>
> (Watney, 1994, p. 47)

Let us not be tourists. Many symptoms of science—objectivity, control, generalization, pathologies and taxonomies, acontextualism and ahistoricism, and the impulse to begin with, rather than question, "higher-order constructs"—have impeded progress. Many social science and public-health efforts have distanced not just *us* from the problems, but also alienated the people we aim to help from their own experience and from their capacities to respond. Interpretations of *empirical* seem to have been hijacked by the "empire" part of the term, and allowed us to forget what it should mean: Why assume or make up what we can actually find out?

The reason we offer that short polemic here is to keep in focus the fact that there are at least several narrative streams of potential or simultaneous concern, including our own. More people than those designated "at risk" express symptoms of the epidemic. When we talk about community narratives, we include such communities as medical and social scientists, health educators, policy makers and legislators, social philosophers, media, activists, communities designated "at risk," and those designated as the "general population." HIV/AIDS is a "dialogic narrative" (Bruner & Gorfain, 1984).

In this respect, it is telling that the term "resistance" should be so ubiquitous in HIV/AIDS discourses. The usage-in-context highlights different meanings of resistance: political/cultural resistance; immunological resistance; and the resistance to behavior change or abstinence of certain "hard to reach" or "recalcitrant" populations, so lamented by medical and social scientists. There is, too, the resistance in many affected communities to associating themselves with or publicly discussing particular sexual practices or partnering styles, or with drug use. Often this is because these communities are already trying to manage marginalization and a host of stereotypes relating to wantonness, irresponsibility, decadence or criminality (Weeks & Holland, 1996). In many "minority" communities concerned with maintaining unity and culture—which often extends to family structure and gender roles—homosexuality or drugs may be understood as opportunistic infections by dominant culture. But resistance can also be read as either a response to or as a failure of *seduction*: The seductive powers held by sex and drugs or certain stories, but also the seductive power or failure of community interventions. HIV prevention always implicates both resistance and seduction. If we are encountering resistance to our prevention efforts, perhaps we should examine our strategies of seduction. Instead of being tourists, we should offer an attraction.

On Not Being A Tourist

Narrative, as theory, unit of analysis, and method is useful because it spans levels of analysis. It emphasizes the ways in which these levels are not distinct but are inhabited simultaneously and are seamlessly transactional. These are some advantages of a narrative approach, but these characteristics also make it difficult to delineate specific methods of or a priori decisions about what the best focus for research and intervention ought to be. In many communities, HIV/AIDS prevention per se will not seen as a problem apart from more general problems of health care access or disaffected youth. It is often overlooked that urban gay communities were unique in being positioned to identify HIV/AIDS as a central concern tied to community identity. In other communities, it is more likely to be understood as another symptom of more long-standing, systemic problems. In fact, HIV/AIDS does not need to be our priority or only interest, particularly if it is not so for communities we wish to assist or mobilize. Preventing Hepatitis C or cervical cancer will have effects on HIV transmission. Organizing for access to health care and preventive medicine for high blood pressure, diabetes, and other epidemic problems is quite likely to energize impulses to community preservation that will translate to sex and drug use practices. It will not make for elegant evaluation data, but these kinds of indirect or "full plate" approaches may be ultimately more effective strategies for generating the narrative insurrections we are advocating (Minkler, 1997).

So, targets of change and units of analysis, like a particular specification of context or community, may be broad and distributed (e.g., AIDS discourse, arrangements of identity, or federal drug policy) or extremely local and ideographic (e.g., negotiating sexual encounters or a specific social network of IV drug users), and points in between. We assume that these choices will depend on one's training, immediate goals and interests, or intended audience. Similarly, the range of methods and analyses is defined only by one's inclinations, training and questions. Narrative strategies can encompass everything from analysis of particular "speech actions" or conversations (Labov, 1972; Mishler, 1987) to a cultural analysis of "AIDS discourse" (Crimp, 1988; Patton, 1996; Treichler, 1999), and intersections of the two (Trew, 1979). Narrative can also serve as an extremely useful framework for or component of community studies, neighborhood or setting ethnography, needs/resources assessments, program evaluation, network analyses, or for assessing the resonant effectiveness of prevention messages.

We tend to favor a focus on local, community narratives, in part because we believe this is the most promising level at which to identify and facilitate change strategies. But this is also because we have found the community level to be the site of key transactions between the individual, the institutional, and the cultural. We do not want to prescribe or proscribe particular methodologies for identifying, understanding, and mobilizing community narratives, anymore than we would predefine what community might mean in particular circumstances. However, we will suggest some considerations that might be indispensable for understanding and mobilizing narrative and narrative insurrections: language, collaboration, contextualism and exemplars.

Language In the current climate of government funding and review, when many concerns central to HIV/AIDS prevention dare not speak their names (Waxman, 2003), the importance (and dangers) of language may already be obvious. It is a concern not only in grant proposals and research reports, but also in the terms of ascribing and deriving meaning, persuasion and motivation, how to converse with and represent constituencies, and the naming of problems. Language shapes experience, and language is shaped by experience (Bakhtin, 1981, 1986; Bruner, 1986; Bruner, 1990; Denzin, 1989; Goffman, 1981; Heath, 1983; Miller & Hoogstra, 1992; Mishler, 1987; Rorty, 1982; Treichler, 1999). Language practices are critical for many reasons, but one is that language moderates and mediates relationships between individuals and settings, communities, and culture. Language is also how we determine and ascribe meaning, for example, the meaning of safer sex practices, of Black or homosexual, or of risk. Because prevention of HIV is always in part about *persuading* people to think and behave in particular ways, we had better be speaking a persuasive, resonant language. Because we are often working with and writing about people already saddled with negative, pathological or objectifying representations, we have to be careful about the language of our representations and of interactions with our constituencies.

We expect that many readers work in disciplines in which quantification is the ultimate goal and the coin of the realm. We are much less frequently trained to think about and analyze language and language practices. But language determines what and how we quantify, especially the form of the questions we ask and how we define problems. Consider Trew's (1979) now classic analysis of the effects of passive voice and subject/object arrangements in apartheid era, South African newspaper headlines: "RIOTING BLACKS SHOT DEAD BY POLICE AS ANC LEADERS MEET," an actual and typical headline, versus the effect of the "not said": "WHITE POLICE SHOOT BLACKS AGAIN." Each tells, and derives from, a different story of events. How are we storying HIV/AIDS, its transmission and its prevention? Are people and communities represented as sensible agents, or as victims and rudderless ciphers? In another vein, consider the difference in effects and utility of "bodily fluids" versus "blood, semen and vaginal fluids". When is it preferable or allowable to use one or the other? Should we say condoms, caps, or jimmy hats?

The language of science often obliterates the language and voice of people's lived experience, and it is that voice that needs to inflect both prevention strategies and our writings about them. The importance of amplifying and of "deploying" the voice of our constituencies also underscores the importance of working with, rather than on, and of talking with, rather than about, our "persons of interest."

Collaboration Much has already been written about the values and difficulties of collaboration, and we will not attempt to recapitulate it (Bond, 1990). Collaboration is not vital to all examinations of HIV prevention or narratives. The kinds of discourse or policy analysis referenced throughout this chapter, for example, may benefit from a variety of perspectives but are not reliant on it. For examining community narratives, however, or for inciting the kinds of insurrections we advocate, collaboration is sine qua non. One reason is that we believe that a useful objectivity is not achieved through distance from our "subject." If objectivity is what we are after (and that is an "If"), it is better reached through the inclusion of as many perspectives as possible. Another reason is that we more than likely do not know anything about the intricacies of needle sharing, for example, or the negotiation of anonymous sexual encounters, or what it is to be 17 in a mortality-saturated environment. The scientific information necessary for interrupting HIV transmission can fit in a pocket—remember *How to Have Sex in an Epidemic*. Most everything else is a matter of social negotiations, persuasion, and resource availability; matters about which science and scientists have something to contribute, but not enough to monopolize story-telling rights.

Collaborative work can prevent us from remaining tourists, but we have to look beyond the usual suspects in identifying collaborators. Social service agencies, quasi-governmental AIDS organizations, or community "leaders" may not do much to expand our perspectives or bring us in contact with really "local knowledge." These people may already think like we do (no gain), but they are also often susceptible to problem-saturated, "these people" views of those they claim to serve (Labonte, 1997).

Also, it is desirable to expand our range in considering potential professional collaborators. Here, too, it is worthwhile looking past the usual lineup of medical, public health, and social science professionals. The examples we offered above point to the broad array of expertise relevant to community-level change. These include, but are not limited to, the arts, media and discourse analysis, literature and literary criticism, theology, gender and queer studies, African American studies, history and oral history, linguistics, marketing, communications, political science, and party planning (yes, really). Finally, in forming these kinds of community and professional collaborations, the ways in which HIV is not, or cannot be approached as, a stand-alone problem will become apparent, and ways of addressing symbiotic or accessory problems, health care disparities or homophobia for examples, can be identified.

Contextualism   A community narrative approach implies at least a partial ethnography of local culture and how HIV figures into it. Narratives are constructions and interpretations of experience; they represent constructions of particular people in particular social contexts and positions. The social contexts that provide the forum, resources, and constraints for narratives also provide or limit the range of interpretive possibilities; and narratives say quite a bit about social contexts and their practices. In terms of understanding and interpretation, Denzin (1989) has emphasized spending as much time as possible in the context of the subjects (the term used here in the artistic sense, as in literature or portraiture). The aim is a kind of "objective hermeneutics," which can be taken to mean that the human conduct of interest will be studied and understood, to the extent possible, from the perspective of the persons involved. This perspective will be related to "definitions and meanings that are lodged in social relationships and social groups" (Denzin, 1989, p. 183). Attention to the context and positions of the narrators, their interpretive communities and referents, is requisite for interpreting behavior and accounts of behavior.

The practices and stories associated with HIV transmission or prevention are probably not "readable" without a relatively full contextualization. For example, it may be legal to distribute clean needles or syringes, but in most places you can still be arrested for possessing them if stopped by police, making the trip from needle exchange to the place you use a risky one. In some communities, especially for youth, expectations of a long and healthy life are not high, HIV or not; combined with an impression that infection is inevitable, "safe sex" takes on a new meaning or meaninglessness. Practicing safe sex or using clean needles restoried as being a matter of protecting one's partner, brother or sister, parents, children, or neighbors, gives safer practices meaning.

A fully contextualized narrative approach will reduce the likelihood of seeing and portraying people or communities *as* problems in themselves; it will also enable us to understand problem behavior and problematic responses as the *effects* of recruitment into particular, problem-saturated positions and narratives. As researchers, consultants, or interventionists we can try to cast or recast problems as external to people and community, and position ourselves as allies in resistance to those problems. Thinking contextually can act as an antidote to the kinds of myopia and perseveration that prevent us from understanding HIV or other problems the same way community members do.

Although not be a necessary component of every evaluation, research plan, or intervention design, we think it is ultimately important that local narratives, projects and outcomes be linked to, analyzed, or placed in relation to broader cultural regularities and discourses, positionings, and representations. We take it as a qualified given that there are a number of social, structural, practical, and historical regularities and constraints in place for storying and managing sexuality and sexual practice, drug use, and HIV/AIDS. It is therefore important to position our work in relation to the narrative transactions between this larger or dominant social terrain, the local community or context, and individuals' negotiations of meaning and identity. For example, instead of focusing on IV drug users, more energy might be generated by interrogating the War on Drugs and the ways it shapes context, creates certain plots that support the spread and power of HIV (and incarceration) in a community, and restricts community resources to respond (Greig & Kershnar, 2002).

Wherever we have staked the boundaries of context for our particular purposes, they are to an extent always arbitrary, because these boundaries are permeable to the larger cultural context. To really make sense of individuals' stories, strategies, choices and behaviors, however, it is necessary to see them in relation to the options and restrictions, resources and distortions, of broader cultural institutions and discourses. Finally, from a contextualist perspective, some features of these narrative interactions may be generalizable or amenable to translation into "higher-order" constructs, but exactly how cannot be prespecified, as we may not know exactly what we have an example *of* until it can be understood in relation to other contexts, cultures, or accounts (Psathas, 1995).

Exemplars If there are no a priori restrictions on the range of analytic or measurement perspectives for a narrative approach to community interventions, it should be no surprise that there is no "how to" guide available for excavating and deploying local narratives for HIV prevention. This is so partly because HIV prevention necessarily involves crossing disciplinary and cultural borders and partly because some of the best examples are situated and context-specific, so applicability is a matter of some inter-pretation or translation. As with ethnographic work, we have found that in a community narrative approach the most important training, insight, and decision-making occur in the process of engagement. But elaborating questions and sensitizing oneself to the pitfalls of tacit assumption and rigid methodolatry will still be critical "advance work" (Shweder, 1991, 1996; Shweder & Sullivan, 1993).

We believe that a very good way of orienting oneself, and of developing appropriate guidelines for validity, is by exploiting *exemplars*—concrete models of actual, situated research and intervention practice in one's or others' field or fields of inquiry (Becker, 1996; Cronbach, 1988; Denzin, 1996, 1989; Kuhn, 1970; Mishler, 1990; Rappaport, 1998; Stewart, 2000). Beyond showing up, listening, looking, and asking questions (especially stupid ones), we do not know of mandatory methods. In fact, we have found that the best work involves a responsive *bricolage*, the employment of a variety of adapted and adaptable tools and methods of inquiry and assistance (Clifford, 1988; Denzin, 1996; Denzin & Lincoln, 2000; Lévi-Strauss, 1966; Weinstein & Weinstein, 1991).

Ethnographic and participatory methods seem to recommend them-selves because they may provide the best means for identifying, under-standing, and deploying narratives and narrative contestations in the context of local culture and concerns, and for relating them to the options and constraints determined by the "institutionalized terrain of social for-mations" (Clifford & Marcus, 1986; Denzin, 1997; Sullivan, 1996; Yudice, 1990). Also, ethnographic strategies bring attention to and some means for reading local cultural artifacts like art, architecture and public spaces, music, texts, and performance that not only provide data and enhance understanding, but also provide forms and forums for intervention or re-sistance (Clifford, 1988; Clifford & Marcus, 1986; Denzin & Lincoln, 2000; Geertz, 1973; Gran Fury, 1990; Shepard & Hayduk, 2002; Shweder & LeVine, 1984; Treichler, 1999). Ethnography, however, is not the alpha and omega of methods for community understanding and change (Cham-pagne, 1995; Derrida, 1976; Hammersley, 1992), and narratives can be employed as part, object of, or point of departure for many different types and methods of study and intervention (Maines, 1993; Miller, 1996; Rappaport, 1998; Treichler, 1999; Wyer, 1995).

CODA

> There's a possibility that even an invisible man has a socially respon-sible role to play.
>
> (Ellison, 1952/1989, p. 581)

We have left out any direct mention of what may be the primary subtex-tual specter in most HIV/AIDS narratives: individual responsibility. It was not because we are in any way opposed to the idea of "individual responsibility"; on the contrary, we support any move or environment that allows this to be more than a fiction. We do, however, think it is a relatively fragile foundation on which to build HIV prevention efforts. Aside from the questions that arise immediately—"responsibility to whom and for what?"—the idea of individual responsibility is open to interpretations, and indexes a wide array of stories and assumptions that may or may not be useful or effective (in much the same way that "independence" functions in discourses about disability or serious mental illness). Furthermore, it is an idea subject to devolution into all of the fallacies and rationalizations encountered in doing prevention work—many of which can be framed as HIV as a matter of *self*-protection. And, because we are talking about drug use and sex, two domains where self-destructive or self-sacrificing behavior is not particularly rare, the limitations of self-preservation or even of self-responsibility as key construct or first assumption should be obvious. Throw in power inequities based on age, gender, addiction and lucidity, economic need, whether one is in the "active" or "receptive" role in intercourse, even physical attractiveness, and one runs into real problems with the idea of individual responsibility.

Because we suspect it is neither effective nor fair to place responsibility for what Wilkinson (1996) called "afflictions of inequality" on individuals, we prefer community preservation—an ethos of mutual protection—as an orientation. So conceived, safer behaviors and the resources to support them would be matters of collective authoring and audiencing, acts of local, but not lone, resistance. HIV/AIDS could then be authored and reauthored as neither a stand-alone, self obvious "thing-in-itself," nor as a problem so global and complex in its scope that it defies optimistic action. Rather, communities can determine how HIV/AIDS is (or is not) related to the range of other problems they must contend with (or need not contend with). The extent to which HIV is or is not a *class* thing, a *gay* or a *homophobia* thing, a *race* or *racism* thing, a *sex* or a *sexism* thing, a *drug* or a *drug policy* thing, can be a matter of situated conarrations. HIV/AIDS "is" all of these things, and more—especially if we can take an international perspective—but it is not all of these things to everybody.

We end where we began, with Cindy Patton making a point about *our* narratives and purpose in relationship to those of the people we are "trying to reach." If we encounter resistance in our efforts, maybe it is what we are trying to perpetrate:

> People have more than a responsibility to know, more than right to choose. People have the right to understand the ideologies of science and of education: HIV/AIDS education must always be political. HIV/AIDS education either reinscribes the sexual, class, and racial ideologies that are propped up by moralism and science, or disrupts the hierarchical formations of knowledge and opens up space for groups and communities to work out their interrelationships with information *they* have decided is relevant. (Patton, 1990, p. 105)

REFERENCES

ACT UP/NY Women and AIDS Book Group. (1992). *Women, AIDS & activism.* Boston: South End Press.

Aggleton, P., Hart, G., & Davies, P. (Eds.). (1989). *AIDS: Social representations, social practices.* Philadelphia: Falmer Press.

Aggleton, P., Hart, G., & Davies, P. (Eds.). (1990). *AIDS: Individual, cultural, and policy dimensions.* Philadelphia: Falmer Press.

Altman, D. (1986). *AIDS in the mind of America.* New York: Doubleday.

Altman, D. (1993). Expertise, legitimacy and the centrality of community. In P. Aggleton, P. Davies, & G. Hart (Eds.), *AIDS: Facing the second decade.* London: Falmer Press.

Altman, D. (1994). *Power and community: Organizational and cultural responses to AIDS.* Bristol, PA: Taylor & Francis.

Art and Revolution. (2001). *Introduction.* Retrieved May 21, 2002, from http://www.artandrevolution.org.

Bahktin, M. (1981). *The dialogic imagination.* Austin: University of Texas Press.

Bahktin, M. (1986). *Speech genres and other late essays.* Austin: University of Texas Press.

Beam, J. (Ed.). (1986). *In the life: A Black gay anthology.* Boston: Alyson.

Becker, H. S. (1996). The epistemology of qualitative research. In R. Jessor, A. Colby, & R. A. Shweder (Eds.), *Ethnography and human development: Context and meaning in social inquiry* (pp. 53–72). Chicago: University of Chicago Press.

Bond, M. (1990). Collaboration and action. In P. Tolan, C. Keys, F. Chertok, & L. Jason (Eds.), *Researching community psychology: Issues of theories and methods* (pp. 183–186). Washington, DC: American Psychological Association.

Bruner, E. & Gorfain, P. (1984). Dialogic narration and the paradoxes of Masada. In E. Bruner (Ed.), *Text, play, and story: The construction and reconstruction of self and society* (pp. 56–79). Washington, DC: The American Ethnological Society.

Bruner, J. (1990). *Acts of meaning.* Cambridge, MA: Harvard University Press.

Butler, J. (1990). *Gender trouble: Feminism and the subversion of identity.* New York: Routledge.

Cain, R. (1995). Community-based AIDS organizations and the state: Dilemmas of dependence. *AIDS and Public Policy Journal, 10,* 83–93.

Callen, M. & Berkowitz, R. (1983). *How to have sex in an epidemic.* New York: News From the Front.

Centers for Disease Control and Prevention AIDS Community Demonstration Projects Research Group. (1999). Community-level HIV intervention in five cities: Final outcome data from the CDC AIDS community demonstration projects. *American Journal of Public Health, 89,* 336–345.

Champagne, J. (1995). *The ethics of marginality: A new approach to gay studies.* Minneapolis: University of Minnesota Press.

Church Ladies for Choice. (1993a). *In your face with amazing grace (video).* New York: Land of Fire Productions.

Church Ladies for Choice. (1993b). *Starter kit.* New York: Church Ladies for Choice.

Clifford, J. (1988). *The predicament of culture: Twentieth-century ethnography, literature, and art.* Cambridge, MA: Harvard University Press.

Clifford, J. & Marcus, G. E. (Eds.). (1986). *Writing culture: The poetics and politics of ethnography.* Berkeley: University of California Press.

Cohen-Cruz, J. (2002). At cross purposes: The Church Ladies for Choice. In B. Shepard & R. Hayduk (Eds.), *From ACT UP to the WTO: Urban protest and community building in the era of globalization* (pp. 234–241). New York: Verso.

Crimp, D. (Ed.). (1988). *AIDS: Cultural analysis, cultural activism.* Cambridge, MA: MIT Press.

Crimp, D. & Rolston, A. (1990). *AIDS Demo Graphics.* Seattle: Bay Press.

Cronbach, L. J. (1988). Five perspectives on the validity argument. In H. Wainer & H. I. Braun (Eds.), *Test validity* (pp. 67–116). Hillsdale, NJ: Lawrence Erlbaum.

Crosseley, M. (1997). "Survivors" and "victims": Long-term HIV positive individuals and the ethos of self-empowerment. *Social Science and Medicine, 45*(12), 1863–1873.

Crosseley, M. (2000). *Introducing narrative psychology: Self, trauma, and the construction of meaning.* Buckingham, UK: Open University Press.

Crosseley, M. (2001). Commentary: How to use a condom: Narratives, sexualities and moralities in safer sex health promotion literature. *Culture, Health and Sexuality, 3*(3), 363–370.

Dalton, H. (1989). AIDS in blackface. *Daedalus, 118*(3), 3–25.

de Certeau, M. (1984). *The practice of everyday life.* (S. Rendall, Trans.). Berkeley: University of California Press.

Denzin, N. K. (1989). *Interpretive interactionism.* Newbury Park, CA: Sage.

Denzin, N. K. (1996). The epistemological crisis in the human disciplines: Letting the old do the work of the new. In R. Jessor, A. Colby, & R. A. Shweder (Eds.), *Ethnography and human development: Context and meaning in social inquiry* (pp. 127–152). Chicago: University of Chicago Press.

Denzin, N. K. (1997). *Interpretive ethnography: Ethnographic practices for the twenty-first century.* Thousand Oaks, CA: Sage.

Denzin, N. K. & Lincoln, Y. S. (Eds.). (2000). *The handbook of qualitative research* (2nd ed.). Thousand Oaks, CA: Sage.

Derrida, J. (1976). *Of Grammatology.* Baltimore: Johns Hopkins University Press.

Dowsett, G. (1989a). *Reaching men who have sex with men in Australia.* Plenary paper presented at the Second International AIDS Information and Education Conference, Yaounde, Cameroon.

Dowsett, G. (1989b). *You'll never forget the feeling of safe sex! AIDS prevention strategies for gay and bisexual men in Sydney, Australia.* Paper presented at the World Health Organization Workshop on AIDS Health Promotion Activities Directed Toward Gay and Bisexual Men, Geneva, Switzerland.

Duggan, L. (1992). Making it perfectly queer. *Socialist Review, 22*(1), 11–31.

Dyson, M. E. (1999). What's Derrida got to do with Jesus? Rhetoric, Black religion, and theory. In M. Garber & R. L. Walkowitz (Eds.), *One nation under God? Religion and American culture* (pp. 76–97). New York: Routledge.

Edwards, M. (1997). AIDS policy communities in Australia. In P. Aggleton, P. Davies, & G. Hart (Eds.), *AIDS activism and alliances* (pp. 41–58). London: Taylor and Francis.

Eigo, J. (2002). The city as body politic/The body as city unto itself. In B. Shepard & R. Hayduk (Eds.), *From ACT UP to the WTO: Urban protest and community building in the era of globalization* (pp. 178–195). New York: Verso.

Ekstrand, M. L., Stall, R. D., Paul, J. P., Osmond, D. H., & Coates, T. J. (1999). Gay men report high rates of unprotected anal sex with partners of unknown or discordant HIV status. *AIDS, 13*(12), 1525–1533.

Ellison, R. (1952/1989). *Invisible man.* New York: Vintage.

Epstein, S. (1991). Democratic science? AIDS activism and the contested construction of knowledge. *Socialist Review, 21*(2), 35–64.

Epstein, S. (1996). *Impure science: AIDS, activism, and the politics of knowledge*. Berkeley: University of California Press.

Fair, G. A. (1995). Public narration and group culture. In H. Johnson & B. Klandermans (Eds.), *Social Movements and Culture* (233–244). Minneapolis: University of Minnesota Press.

Fine, M. (1994). Working the hyphens: Reinventing self and other in qualitative research. In N. K. Denzin & Y. S. Lincoln (Eds.), *Handbook of qualitative research* (pp. 70–82). Thousand Oaks, CA: Sage.

Flores, J. & Yudice, G. (1990). Living borders/Buscando America: Languages of Latino self-formation. *Social Text, 24*(Spring), 98–112.

Foucault, M. (1980). *Power/Knowledge: Selected interviews and other writings* (C. Gordon, Ed.). New York: Pantheon.

Foucault, M. (1981). *The history of sexuality. Vol. I: An introduction*. New York: Vintage/Random House.

Freire, P. (1970/1998). *Pedagogy of the oppressed*. New York: Continuum.

Fuss, D. (Ed.). (1989). *Essentially speaking*. New York: Routledge.

Gadamer, H. G. (1975). *Truth and method*. New York: Continuum.

Gamson, J. (1989). Silence, death, and the invisible enemy: AIDS activism and social movement newness. *Social Problems, 36*(4), 351–369.

Garber, M. (1996). *Vice versa: Bisexuality and the eroticism of everyday life*. New York: Touchstone.

Garber, M. (2000). *Symptoms of culture*. New York: Routledge.

Geertz, C. (1973). *The interpretation of culture*. New York: Basic Books.

Giroux, H., Lankshire, C., McClaren, P., & Peters, M. (Eds.). (1996). *Counternarratives: Cultural studies and critical pedagogy in postmodern spaces*. New York: Routledge.

Gramsci, A. (1971). *Selections from the prison notebooks* (Q. Hoare & G. N. Smith, Eds.). New York: International Publishers.

Gran Fury. (1990). International AIDS information. *The Act, 2*(1), 5–9.

Greig, A. & Kershnar, S. (2002). Harm reduction in the USA: A movement toward social justice. In B. Shepard & R. Hayduk (Eds.), *From ACT UP to the WTO: Urban protest in the era of globalization* (pp. 360–369). New York: Verso.

Grmek, M. D. (1990). *History of AIDS: Emergence and origin of a modern pandemic* (R. C. Maulitz & J. Duffin, Trans.). Princeton: Princeton University Press.

Hagar, L. (1995). Why has AIDS education failed: Interview with Walt Odets. *East Bay Express, 17*(37), 1, 10–16.

Hammersley, M. (1992). *What's wrong with ethnography?* London: Routledge.

Heath, S. B. (1983). *Ways with words: Language, life, and work in communities and classrooms*. Cambridge, UK: Cambridge University Press.

Hemphill, E. (Ed.). (1991). *Brother to brother: New writings by Black gay men*. Boston: Alyson.

Henthoff, N. (1990, February 27). Silence=Black and Hispanic deaths. *Village Voice*, p. 22.

Hessol, N. A., Lifson, A. R., O'Malley, P. M., Doll, L. S., Jaffe, H. W., & Rutherford, G. W. (1989). Prevalence, incidence and progression of Human Immunodeficiency Virus in homosexual and bisexual men in Hepatitis B vaccine trials, 1978–1988. *American Journal of Epidemiology, 130*(6), 1167–1175.

hooks, b. (1989). Homophobia in Black communities. In b. hooks (Ed.), *Talking back: Thinking feminist, thinking Black* (pp. 120–126). Boston: South End Press.

hooks, b. (1990). Marginality as a site of resistance. In R. Ferguson, M. Gever, T. T. Minh-ha, & C. West (Eds.), *Out there: Marginalization and contemporary culture* (pp. 341–343). New York & Cambridge: New Museum of Contemporary Art & MIT Press.

Howard, G. S. (1991). Culture Tales: A narrative approach to thinking, cross-cultural psychology, and psychotherapy. *American Psychologist, 46*(3), 187–197.

Jones, J. H. (1981). *Bad blood: The Tuskegee syphilis experiment—A tragedy of race and medicine.* New York: Free Press.

Junod, T. (1993). Deadly medicine. *Gentlemen's Quarterly, 6,* 164.

Katz, M. H. (1997). AIDS epidemic in San Francisco among men who report sex with men: Successes and challenges of HIV prevention. *Journal of Acquired Immune Deficiency Syndrome and Human Retrovirology, 14*(Suppl. 2), 38–46.

Kögler, H. H. (1997). Alienation as epistemological source: Reflexivity and social background after Mannheim and Bourdieu. *Social Epistemology, 11*(2), 141–165.

Kraft, J. M., Beeker, C., Stokes, J. P., & Peterson, J. L. (2000). Finding the "community" in community-level HIV/AIDS interventions: Formative research with young African American men who have sex with men. *Health Education and Behavior, 27*(4), 430–441.

Kuhn, T. S. (1970). *The structure of scientific revolutions* (2nd ed.). Chicago: University of Chicago Press.

Labonte, R. (1997). Community, community development, and the forming of authentic partnerships. In M. Minkler (Ed.), *Community organizing and community organizing for health* (pp. 88–102). New Brunswick, NJ: Rutgers University Press.

Labov, W. (1972). *Language in the inner city: Studies in the Black English vernacular.* Philadelphia: University of Pennsylvania Press.

Lévi-Strauss, C. (1966). *The savage mind.* Chicago: University of Chicago Press.

Maines, D. R. (1993). Narrative's moment and Sociology's phenomena: Toward a narrative sociology. *Sociological Quarterly, 34,* 17–38.

Miller, P. J. (1995). Personal storytelling in everyday life: Social and cultural perspectives. In R. S. Wyer (Ed.), *Advances in Social Cognition* (pp. 177–184). Hillsdale, NJ: Lawrence Erlbaum.

Miller, P. J. (1996). Instantiating culture through discourse practices: Some personal reflections on socialization and how to study it. In R. Jessor, A. Colby, & R. A. Shweder (Eds.), *Ethnography and human development: Context and meaning in social inquiry* (pp. 183–204). Chicago: University of Chicago Press.

Miller, P. J. & Goodnow, J. J. (1995). Cultural practices: Toward an integration of culture and development. *New Directions in Child Development, 67,* 5–16.

Miller, P. J. & Moore, B. B. (1989). Narrative conjunctions of caregiver and child: A comparative perspective on socialization through stories. *Ethos, 17,* 428–449.

Miller, P. J. & Hoogstra, L. (1992). Language as tool in the socialization and apprehension of cultural meanings. In T. Schwartz, G. White, & C. Lutz (Eds.), *New directions in psychological anthropology* (pp. 83–101). Cambridge: Cambridge University Press.

Mills, S. (1997). *Discourse.* New York: Routledge.

Minkler, M. (Ed.). (1997). *Community organizing and community building for health.* New Brunswick, NJ: Rutgers University Press.

Mishler, E. G. (1987). *Research interviewing: Context and narrative.* Cambridge, MA: Harvard University Press.

Mishler, E. G. (1990). Validation in inquiry-guided research: The role of exemplars in narrative studies. *Harvard Educational Review, 60*(4), 415–442.

Moraga, C. & Anzaldua, G. (Eds.). (1981). *This bridge called my back: Writings by radical women of color.* Latham, NY: Kitchen Table Press.

Morgan, T. (2002). From WHAM! to ACT UP. In B. Shepard & H. Hayduk (Eds.), *From ACT UP to the WTO: Urban protest and community building in the era of globalization* (pp. 141–149). New York: Verso.

National Coalition of Black Lesbians and Gays. (Eds.). (1986). *Special Issue:Homecoming. Black/Out, II*(1).

Odets, W. (1995). Why we stopped doing HIV prevention for gay men in 1985. *AIDS and Public Policy, 10*(1).

Omi, M. & Winant, H. (1986). *Racial formations in the United States: From the 1960s to the 1980s.* New York: Routledge & Kegan Paul.

Ostrow, D. (1987). Antibody testing won't cut risky behavior. *American Medical Association News, June,* 34–39.

Patton, C. (1985). *Sex and germs: The politics of AIDS.* Boston: South End Press.

Patton, C. (1990). *Inventing AIDS.* New York: Routledge.

Patton, C. (1991). Visualizing safe sex: When pedagogy and pornography collide. In D. Fuss (Ed.), *Inside/out: Lesbian theories, gay theories* (pp. 373–386). New York: Routledge.

Patton, C. (1996). *Fatal advice: How safe-sex education went wrong.* Durham, NC: Duke University Press.

Platoni, K. (2002, August 28). Racing for funding, fuming about race. *East Bay Express,* 9–11.

Polkinghorne, D. E. (1988). *Narrative knowing and the human sciences.* Albany: State University of New York Press.

Porter, V. (1988). Minorities and HIV infection. In P. O'Malley (Ed.), *The AIDS epidemic: Private rights and the public interest.* Boston: Beacon Press.

Psathas, G. (1995). *Conversation analysis: The study of talk-in-interaction.* Thousand Oaks, CA: Sage.

Quimby, E. & Friedman, S. R. (1989). Dynamics of Black mobilization against AIDS in New York City. *Social Problems, 36*(4), 403–415.

Quinn, S. C. (1997). Belief in AIDS as a form of genocide: Implications for HIV prevention programs for African Americans. *Journal of Health Education, 28*(6), 417–419.

Rappaport, J. (1993). Narrative studies, personal stories, and identity transformation in the mutual help context. *The Journal of Applied Behavioral Science, 29*(2), 239–256.

Rappaport, J. (1998). The art of social change: Community narratives as resources for individual and collective identity. In X. B. Arriaga & S. Oskamp (Eds.), *Addressing community problems: Research and intervention* (pp. 225–246). Thousand Oaks, CA: Sage.

Rappaport, J. (2000). Community Narratives: Tales of terror and joy. *American Journal of Community Psychology, 28*(1), 1–24.

Reissman, C. K. (1993). *Narrative analysis.* Newbury Park, CA: Sage.

Research and Decisions Corporation. (1984). *Memo to San Francisco AIDS Foundation and San Francisco Department of Public Health.* San Francisco AIDS Foundation.

Rorty, R. (1982). *Consequences of Pragmatism.* Minneapolis: University of Minnesota Press.

Saalfield, C., Chris, C., Lurie, R., & Pearl, M. (1990). Intravenous drug use, women, and HIV. In ACT UP/NY Women & AIDS Book Group (Eds.), *Women, AIDS and Activism* (pp. 123–129). Boston: South End Press.

Saalfield, C. & Navarro, R. (1991). Shocking pink praxis: Race and gender on the ACT UP frontlines. In D. Fuss (Ed.), *Inside/out: Lesbian theories, gay theories* (pp. 341–369). New York: Routledge.

Salzer, M. (1998). Narrative approach to assessing interactions between society, community, and person. *Journal of Community Psychology, 26*(6), 569–580.

Salzer, M. (2000). Toward a narrative conceptualization of stereotypes: Contextualizing perceptions of public housing residents. *Journal of Community and Applied Social Psychology, 10,* 123–137.

San Francisco Chronicle. (1990, Oct 30). *Twenty-nine percent of Blacks in poll see AIDS as racist plot*, p. A-12.

Shepard, B. (2002a). Building a healing community from ACT UP to Housing Works: Benjamin Shepard interviews Keith Cyler. In B. Shepard & R. Hayduk (Eds.), From *ACT UP to the WTO: Urban protest and community building in the era of globalization* (pp. 351–360). New York: Verso.

Shepard, B. (2002b). From Stonewall to Diallo: Benjamin Shepard interviews Bob Kohler. In B. Shepard & R. Hayduk (Eds.), *From ACT UP to the WTO: Urban protest and community building in the era of globalization* (pp. 126–132). New York: Verso.

Shepard, B. (2002c). The reproductive rights movement, ACT UP, and the Lesbian Avengers: Benjamin Shepard interviews Sarah Schulman. In B. Shepard & R. Hayduk (Eds.), *From ACT UP to the WTO: Urban protest and community building in the era of globalization* (pp. 133–140). New York: Verso.

Shepard, B. & Hayduk, R. (Eds.). (2002). *From ACT UP to the WTO: Urban protest and community building in the era of globalization.* New York: Verso.

Shilts, R. (1987). *And the band played on: Politics, people, and the AIDS epidemic.* New York: St. Martin's Press.

Shweder, R. A. (1991). *Thinking through cultures: Expeditions in Cultural Psychology.* Cambridge, MA: Harvard University Press.

Shweder, R. A. (1996). True ethnography: The lore, the law, and the lure. In R. Jessor, A. Colby, & R. A. Shweder (Eds.), *Ethnography and human development: Context and meaning in social inquiry* (pp. 15–52). Chicago: University of Chicago Press.

Shweder, R. A. & LeVine, R. A. (Eds.). (1984). *Culture theory: Essays on mind, self and emotion.* Cambridge, UK: Cambridge University Press.

Shweder, R. A. & Sullivan, M. L. (1993). Cultural psychology: Who needs it? *Annual Review of Psychology, 44,* 497–523.

Sibthorpe, B., Fleming, D., & Gould, J. (1994). Self-help groups: A key to HIV risk reduction for high-risk injection drug users? *Journal of Acquired Immune Deficiency Syndrome, 7,* 592–598.

Socialist Review Collective (Eds.). (1995). Arranging identities: Constructions of race, ethnicity and nation. *Socialist Review, 94*(1&2), 1–265.

Stewart, E. (2000). Thinking through others: Qualitative research and Community Psychology. In E. Seidman & J. Rappaport (Eds.), *Handbook of Community Psychology* (pp. 725–736). New York: Kluwer Academic/Plenum Publishers.

Stewart, E. & Weinstein, R. S. (1997). Volunteer participation in context: Motivations and political efficacy within three AIDS organizations. *American Journal of Community Psychology, 25*(6), 809–837.

Sullivan, M. L. (1996). Neighborhood social organization: A forgotten object of ethnographic study? In R. Jessor, A. Colby, & R. A. Shweder (Eds.), *Ethnography and human development: Context and meaning in social inquiry* (pp. 205–224). Chicago: University of Chicago Press.

Tessman, L. (1995). Beyond communitarian unity in the politics of identity. *Socialist Review, 94*(1&2), 129–164.

Thomas, R. E. & Rappaport, J. (1996). Art as community narrative: A resource for social change. In M. B. Lykes, R. Liem, A. Banuazizi, & M. Morris (Eds.), *Myths about the powerless: Contesting social inequalities* (pp. 317–336). Philadelphia: Temple University Press.

Treichler, P. (1988). AIDS, homophobia and biomedical discourse: An epidemic of signification. In D. Crimp (Ed.), *AIDS: Cultural analysis, cultural activism.* London: MIT Press.

Treichler, P. (1991). How to have theory in an epidemic: The evolution of AIDS treatment activism. In C. Penley & A. Ross (Eds.), *Technoculture* (pp. 57–105). Minneapolis: University of Minnesota Press.

Treichler, P. (1992). Beyond Cosmo: AIDS, identity, and inscriptions of gender. *Camera Obscura, 28*, 22–76.

Treichler, P. (1999). *How to have theory in an epidemic: Cultural chronicles of AIDS.* Durham, NC: Duke University Press.

Trend, D. (1989). Beyond resistance: Notes on community counter-practice. *Afterimage, 4*, 2–21.

Trend, D. (1995). Representation and resistance: An interview with bell hooks. *Socialist Review, 94*(1&2), 115–128.

Trew, T. (1979). Theory and ideology at work. In R. Fowler, R. Hodge, G. Kress, & T. Trew (Eds.), *Language and control* (pp. 94–116). London: Routledge & Kegan Paul.

Watney, S. (1994). *Practices of freedom: Selected writings on HIV/AIDS.* Durham, NC: Duke University Press.

Waxman, H. A. (2003). *Politics and science in the Bush adminstration.* U.S. House of Representatives Committee on Government Reform, Minority Staff Special Investigations Division. Retrieved March 10, 2004, from www.reform.house. gov/min.

Weeks, J. (1985). *Sexuality and its discontents.* London: Routledge & Kegan Paul.

Weeks, J. (1993). AIDS and the regulation of sexuality. In V. Berridge & P. Strong (Eds.), *AIDS and contemporary history.* Cambridge, UK: Cambridge University Press.

Weeks, J., Aggleton, P., McKevitt, C., Parknison, K., & Taylor-Linbourn, A. (1996). Community responses to HIV and AIDS: The "de-gaying" and "re-gaying" of AIDS. In J. Weeks & J. Holland (Eds.), *Sexual cultures: Communities, values and intimacy* (pp. 161–179). New York: St. Martin's Press.

Weeks, J. & Holland, J. (Eds.) (1996). *Sexual cultures: Communities, values and intimacy.* New York: St. Martin's Press.

Weinstein, D. & Weinstein, M. A. (1991). Georg Simmel: Sociological flaneur bricoleur. *Theory, Culture, and Society, 8*, 151–168.

West, C. (1989). *The American evasion of philosophy: A geneology of Pragmatism.* Madison: University of Wisconsin Press.

Wilkinson, R. G. (1996). *Unhealthy societies: The afflictions of inequality.* London: Routledge.

Winkelstein, W., Wiley, J. A., & Padian, N. S. (1988). The San Francisco men's health study: Continued decline in HIV seroconversion rate among homosexual/ bisexual men. *American Journal of Public Health, 78*(11), 1472–1474.

Wohlfeiler, D. (2002). From community to clients: The professionalization of HIV prevention among gay men and its implication for intervention selection. *Sexually Transmitted Infections, 78*(1), 176–182.

Woodyard, J. L., Peterson, J. L., & Stokes, J. P. (2000). "Let us go into the house of the Lord": Participation in African American churches among young African American men who have sex with men. *The Journal of Pastoral Care, 54*(4), 451–460.

Wyer, R. S. (Ed.). (1995). *Advances in Social Cognition,* (pp. 1–243). Hillsdale, NJ: Lawrence Erlbaum.

Yudice, G. (1990). For a practical aesthetics. *Social Text, 25,* 129–145.

4

The State of the Art in Community HIV Prevention Interventions

Jeffrey A. Kelly

HIV infection is contracted through behavior practices, and primary prevention of the disease rests upon helping vulnerable persons to make and sustain changes in those practices that confer risk. Because the vast majority of HIV transmission occurs through unprotected sexual behaviors or needle sharing, sexual and drug injection risk practices are the major targets for change in most HIV prevention programs.

For more than two decades, behavior and public scientists have developed and studied the effectiveness of interventions designed to assist persons in reducing their risk for contracting HIV infection by making changes in their behavior. Most of the approaches studied in the HIV prevention research field have been based on individual and small-group counseling models. These counseling approaches are offered to clients face-to-face, and typically combine risk- reduction education with attention to such psychosocial factors as skills training in how to enact behavior change (for example, through correct condom use and sexual negotiation skills); the development of positive attitudes, beliefs, intentions, and outcome expectancies concerning risk reduction; planning and setting goals to lessen risk behavior; and reinforcing the efforts of the person being counseled to make change. A well-established research literature has shown that individual and small-group interventions based on cognitive-behavioral or social-cognitive theoretical principles can—when culturally tailored—bring about reductions in sexual risk behaviors among gay or bisexual men (Kelly, St. Lawrence, Hood, & Brasfield, 1989; Peterson et al., 1996; Valdiserri et al., 1989); women (DiClemente & Wingood, 1995; Ehrhardt et al., 2002; Kelly, Murphy, Washington et al., 1994); adolescents (Jemmott, Jemmott, & Fong, 1992); patients seen in STD and urban health clinics (Kamb et al., 1998; National Institute of Mental Health [NIMH] Multisite HIV Prevention Trial Group, 1998); and other at-risk populations.

Face-to-face interventions like these are an important part of the repertoire of HIV prevention strategies needed by clinicians and service providers who counsel clients at risk for the disease. However, these models alone are insufficient in the fight against AIDS. On a practical level—unless carried out with persons in "captive" settings—these approaches require that people perceive their behavior to be problematic and seek out risk-reduction counseling or are at least willing to accept it. Counseling-based approaches require the time of trained counselors, therapists, or skilled facilitators, and thus are relatively expensive to carry out on a large scale. Even if assigned high public-health priority, it is difficult to foresee how—on a practical level—all persons at risk for HIV infection could be reached with intensive, effective face-to-face risk-reduction counseling. Finally, while interventions of this kind can produce significant reductions in sexual risk behavior in the short term, the magnitude of behavior-change effects is not always large and may not be maintained well over time (Kalichman, Carey, & Johnson, 1996).

The counseling approaches that have dominated the research literature on HIV prevention for many years are based on models of "intraindividual" change. These approaches presume that if one changes an individual's internal psychological characteristics—such as by improving AIDS-related knowledge, attitudes, beliefs, and skills—that person will then be able to successfully and durably avoid or more safely handle situations that formerly conferred risk. This is certainly part of the picture, but is insufficient because it attributes too much importance to counseling as a vehicle responsible for behavior change and does not adequately take into account how social, community, and interpersonal factors influence whether persons initiate behavior change and how successfully they sustain change over time. Although "change-the-individual" counseling approaches can help people enact initial risk reduction steps and develop motivations to make short-term risk-behavior changes, successful long-term maintenance of HIV-protective behavior is likely only when peer group social norms, relationships, the environment, and public-health policies also support persons' behavior-change efforts. This requires that we change communities, the social environment, and social norms, not just counsel individuals.

In this chapter, we will consider five aspects of community intervention approaches for HIV prevention: (1) examples that illustrate community responses to the threat of AIDS early in the epidemic's history; (2) the rationale for community-level interventions and characteristics of effective programs; (3) several examples of these interventions and their outcomes; (4) factors that influence the success of community-level HIV prevention interventions; and (5) the way in which partnerships between researchers and community agencies are essential to the development of effective programs.

Early Community Responses to the Threat of AIDS

Although what would later become known as AIDS had long and without notice been taking a toll on human life in Africa, the first cases of the disease were diagnosed in 1979 among gay men in New York, San Francisco, and Los Angeles. Even before the putative viral agent responsible for the disease was identified and its specific epidemiology became known, there was rapid awareness of the danger in gay communities of major cities throughout the United States. Within a very short period of time, there was also wide understanding that the disease (known initially as "gay-related infectious disease" [GRID] or as "Kaposi's Sarcoma Syndrome" for the form of opportunistic cancer that was then often diagnosed in patients with it) was sexually transmitted, related to having large numbers of partners, and probably contracted during unprotected anal intercourse between men.

Apart from case surveillance and epidemiological monitoring, there was little immediate response with respect to prevention programs from federal government agencies in the United States when AIDS cases first appeared. Traditional public-health systems had little experience and limited understanding of gay communities, and the political era at the time was socially conservative. However, gay communities in large cities already had organizational infrastructures that were long active in political, social, and rights advocacy. Cities such as New York, Los Angeles, San Francisco, and Chicago also had both relatively well-defined gay residential neighborhoods and social gathering venues, permitting community programs to be targeted. Almost immediately after the threat of AIDS became known, these organizations rapidly mounted grassroots community prevention programs emphasizing AIDS education and awareness, soon followed by wide-scale campaigns promoting condom use and safer sex. Organizations such as "Stop AIDS," which originated in San Francisco and shortly expanded to other cities, the Gay Men's Health Crisis (GMHC) in New York City, and AIDS Project Los Angeles (APLA) carried out extensive AIDS outreach information dissemination programs in bars, clubs, and sexually oriented venues; sponsored risk-reduction workshops for men who have sex with men (MSM); and initiated volunteer-based "friends educating friends" house parties to enhance AIDS awareness, encourage safer sex practices, and create normative support for risk-reduction behavior change. Similar programs were quickly replicated by gay community organizations and the AIDS community-based organizations (CBOs) that grew from them in cities throughout the United States.

Gay and AIDS CBOs were well-suited for these important roles early in the epidemic because they were indigenous to the communities they served, understood well the culture of the community, had credibility, had extensive volunteer networks, and were nonbureaucratic and able to quickly initiate innovative programs. As entities with deep roots in the communities they served, the organizations could draw upon volunteers and could function as vanguards for mobilizing the larger gay community against AIDS. While governmental public-health agencies were—and remain—reluctant to provide explicit information and recommendations concerning sensitive sexual behavior, autonomy allowed AIDS CBOs to candidly and openly discuss risk behaviors and advocate for safer sex practices in terms relevant, comprehensible, and credible to the populations they sought to reach. We know now that HIV infection rates declined among gay or bisexual men in large urban areas in the United States by the mid-1980s. It is likely that the community programs quickly initiated by gay and AIDS CBOs contributed substantially to that decline.

Rationale for Community-Level Interventions and Characteristics of Effective Programs

Community-level HIV prevention approaches differ from individual counseling-based models because they attempt to reach entire community populations (or population segments) and because they seek to lower the prevalence of risk behavior or the incidence of disease at a population level. Community-based HIV prevention approaches that change the norms, collective self-efficacy, and risk-behavior practices in populations vulnerable to AIDS are essential for a variety of reasons. People contract HIV infection as a result of sexual or drug use activities that take place in settings and in relationships that exist in their day-to-day lives in the community. Changing communities to make them safer places is a logical direction for HIV prevention efforts. Approaches that strengthen risk-reduction social norms in one's peer reference group, that create and support expectancies for the positive outcomes of safer behavior, and that strengthen social and environmental structures that support risk avoidance are critical objectives in community-level HIV prevention. Population-focused interventions have the potential to reach large numbers of people, create social environments that help persons maintain safety, and be cost-effective by virtue of their scope, especially when targeting populations that would otherwise have high HIV incidence.

The importance of changing the social milieu rather than just the individual is not unique to HIV prevention. Smoking rates in some segments of the American population have declined, not because smokers in mass numbers enrolled in intensive "quit smoking" counseling workshop programs, but primarily because social norms concerning smoking have changed. In a similar sense, the HIV prevention research field should acknowledge past successes in developing intensive face-to-face interventions that can help individuals make risk-reduction behavior changes, and press forward to improve our understanding of how to create and carry out broader community-level models that will reach more people and help them better maintain behavior change (Kelly, 1999). Both research and applied experience in community-level HIV prevention programs suggest that four domains are critical to successful outcomes. They involve the content of a program, the source of prevention messages delivered to population members, the ability of the intervention to reach and adequately expose population members to effective messages, and the program's sustainability in the community.

Program Content and Focus   A first question of both theoretical and practical significance is what factors community interventions should target in order to have their greatest public-health impact. Fortunately, a large body of behavioral and social science literature has identified psychosocial determinants of high-risk behavior and also of persons' success in enacting behavior change. Consistent with the principles of contemporary theoretical formulations such as social-cognitive theory (Bandura, 1986), the theory of reasoned action (Fishbein & Azjen, 1975), and variations of these theories specifically applied to AIDS prevention (Catania, Kegeles, & Coates, 1990; Fisher & Fisher, 1992), lower levels of sexual risk behavior are associated in many populations not only with accurate knowledge about risk-reduction steps but also with positive condom use beliefs and attitudes, the perception that peer norms favor safer sex, strong intentions or readiness to enact behavior change, and high perceived self-efficacy or confidence in one's ability to avoid or reduce risk (Catania et al., 1991; Jemmott, Jemmott, Spears, Hewitt, & Cruz-Collins, 1991; Kelly, St. Lawrence, Stevenson, et al., 1992; McKusick, Hortsman, & Coates, 1985; Sikkema et al., 1996). Programs that target these multiple domains are therefore likely to have the greatest impact. It is important to note that knowledge about AIDS was a much stronger predictor of risk-behavior avoidance early in the epidemic than it is at present. This is probably because basic information levels about AIDS, risk behaviors, and risk-reduction steps are now quite high in most populations in the United States and other western countries. Consequently, programs that focus primarily on risk education alone are likely to have much less effect than those that also directly target risk-reduction attitudes, beliefs, intentions, normative perceptions, and self-efficacy.

Apart from psychosocial constructs, HIV risk is situationally influenced, and effective community interventions must be tailored to relevant situational risk determinants in the population. For example, condom use is typically higher during first sex with a new partner than during subsequent meetings with the same partner in both same-sex and heterosexual relationships, and unprotected behavior is more likely to occur in primary than in casual relationships even when the primary relationship is brief and is not exclusive (Fortenberry, Tu, Harczzlak, Katz, & Orr, 2002; Ku, Sonnenstein, & Pleck, 1994). Knowing, liking, or loving a partner are strong predictors of unprotected behavior and represent situational relationship factors that must be better addressed in HIV prevention interventions. Other situational influences or risk behavior that require special program targeting include associations between alcohol and other substance use with risky sex, barriers posed by lack of access to condoms and clean syringes, the belief that new antiretrovial medication now makes AIDS a less serious problem, and handling coercive risk pressures in power-imbalanced relationships, an issue of particular relevance to women.

The Sources of Prevention Messages   There is a long history of research on the use of media and other mass-scale health promotion community campaigns for such public-health problems as cigarette smoking, problem drinking, and cardiovascular risk. These campaigns have primarily used "impersonal" channels of communication from external sources such as mass- and micro-media. However, these campaigns have often been disappointing and have produced only very small reductions in population-level health risk behavior (Carleton, Lasater, Assaf, Feldman, & McKinay, 1995; Wagenaar et al., 2000; Winkleby, Taylor, Jatulis, & Formann, 1996). Such findings illustrate the limitations of mass media effects on changing certain forms of high-risk behavior and also suggest that the source of behavior-change recommendations, advice, and modeling may greatly influence the impact of intervention programs on population-level risk practices. As we will discuss in more detail later, community-level HIV prevention interventions that have produced substantial effects are those which identified, mobilized, and engaged persons already known, liked, trusted, and credible within the high-risk target community to actively communicate and personally endorse HIV prevention steps to others in the same population. This principle has been well-established in research-based community intervention trials that identified and trained popular opinion leaders (POLs) to disseminate to others risk-reduction messages (Kelly et al., 1997; Kelly, et al., 1991; Kelly, St. Lawrence, Stevenson et al., 1992) that identified influential members of social networks and then engaged them to take on HIV prevention advocacy roles with other network members (Amirkhanian, Kelly, Kabakchieva, McAuliffe, & Vassileva, 2003; Latkin, 1998), or that trained indigenous members of the injection drug user (IDU) community to serve as informal outreach works to other IDUs (Trotter, Bowen, Baldwin & Price, 1996, Weibel et al., 1989). Collectively, these findings suggest that who delivers prevention messages influences their impact on others, and that behavior-change recommendations coming from personally known and trusted sources are likely to have greater impact than those coming only from impersonal sources.

Sufficient Population Exposure to Intervention   Behavioral interventions can have an effect only if the intended recipients of the intervention are adequately exposed to it. In the case of community-level interventions, a particular challenge is ensuring that community populations receive high levels of exposure. Some community-level public-health interventions have proven unsuccessful in producing behavior-change effects both in the AIDS field (Elford, Bolding, & Scherr, 2001; Flowers, Hart, Williamson, Frankis, & Der, 2002) and for other health risk behaviors (Carleton et al., 1995; Wagenaar et al., 2000; Winkleby et al., 1996). In all of these cases, a major problem was that the interventions were too weak and a high proportion of population members received little or no exposure to the intervention. If an intervention is not "received" in adequate dosage, it cannot have an effect.

Community HIV prevention interventions that fail to produce positive outcomes are often not sufficiently intensive, do not reach a sufficient

number of population members with enough effective program components, or are too limited in scope relative to the overly large size of a target
community population (Kelly, 2004). There is also very little reason to believe that brief or occasional passive exposure to HIV prevention messages
will produce significant population-level behavior change; this is especially true because HIV risk reduction involves making changes in strong,
biologically driven motives related to sex and substance addiction. Community interventions that have proven effective in the HIV prevention
field have been intensive, have repeatedly exposed a high proportion of
population members to multiple prevention messages delivered by credible sources, and have worked with well-defined target populations small
enough in size so that all members could receive a high "dosage" of the
intervention.

Sustaining Intervention Over Time   Brief community interventions are
likely to produce, at best, brief effects. The process of making and then
sustaining changes in sexual or substance use risk behavior requires ongoing reinforcement, and behavior change is best maintained when social
norms, the environment, and relationships are durably altered to support
safer practices. This requires that one conceptualize community interventions not as brief or "one-shot" programs but rather as an ongoing series
of activities that are sustainable, can grow, and can evolve and expand
over long periods of time. In the case of time-limited interventions that are
developed by entities outside of a community, such as research interventions or programs that are carried out by outside agencies, important objectives are to develop mechanisms that ensure joint initial community
ownership of the intervention, to assist in the development of community
structures that can sustain it in the long term, and to ensure that control of
the intervention ultimately rests with community stakeholders, members,
and organizations.

Examples and Outcomes of Community-Level HIV Prevention Interventions

Several studies reported in the research literature have evaluated the effectiveness of community-level HIV prevention interventions using randomized trial designs. These studies have produced positive outcomes
and can be used to illustrate some of the principles already discussed.
Successful interventions include the "Popular Opinion Leader" intervention and the "M-Powerment" intervention, both carried out to reach gay
or bisexual men in the community, and a community-level intervention
developed for at-risk women living in low income, inner-city housing
developments.

*Engaging Popular Opinion Leaders (POLs) to Serve as Risk Reduction Advo-
cates*   If the prevalence of sexual risk behavior in a community population is influenced by social norms concerning safer sex, it should be
possible to reduce population-level risk by intervening to strengthen
norms that emphasize the acceptability and desirability of safer practices.

One means to do this is by identifying, recruiting, training, and engaging cadres of key POLs from within the target population to actively and systematically communicate effective HIV prevention messages and to personally endorse the benefits of risk-reduction steps to other members of the same population.

The conceptual basis of this intervention model rests upon principles of "diffusion of innovation" theory (Rogers, 1983). Diffusion theory postulates that innovative new trends in population behavior are often instigated when enough of the population's opinion leaders—those population members who are naturally liked, popular, and likely to be emulated by others—establish, are seen, and are known to endorse a behavioral innovation. New trends first modeled and endorsed by opinion leaders are observed, may then be adopted by others, and—as more and more population members also adopt the same innovation—the new trend diffuses and becomes normative within the population. In the case of HIV prevention in a vulnerable population where unprotected sex is prevalent, less unprotected behavior, greater condom use, and increased safe sex practices are the innovations that one seeks to promote.

The POL community intervention model was initially tested with populations of men attending gay bars in small southern U.S. cities (Kelly, St. Lawrence, Diaz et al., 1991; Kelly, St. Lawrence, Stevenson et al., 1992); the model was subsequently evaluated in a true randomized community-level trial in eight additional small cities (Kelly et al., 1997). Each city in the randomized outcome trial had between one and three gay bars. The clubs functioned not only as drinking places but also as communities where MSM in each small city could meet, socialize, and freely congregate. Preliminary ethnographic work established that the crowds attending the gay bars were quite stable and nontransient and that social interactions were frequent. In this sense, the crowd of persons regularly present in a city's club was defined as a community population. Anonymous assessment surveys were administered to all men entering each city's bars (over 1,100 respondents) in order to ascertain baseline levels of population risk behavior. Following baseline data collection, four cities were randomly assigned to a control condition in which AIDS educational awareness posters and brochures were prominently and continuously displayed. In the other four cities, the same awareness materials were displayed and a community intervention based on the POL model was also implemented.

Working closely with club managers, key informants, and other gatekeepers, bartenders in each club were taught to observe the crowds present in the venues and to identify those persons who were observed to be most popular with others. Efforts were made to characterize the different segments or strata in each club (such as younger men, older men, and men of different ethnicities and races) and to identify opinion leaders influential within each segment. Because diffusion theory postulates that approximately 15% of a population members are its opinion leaders and early innovation adopters, 10% to 15% of the total number of different people present in a city's clubs were identified and recruited. Reflecting community interest, concern about AIDS, and altruism, nearly all persons nominated as opinion leaders agreed to participate in the project when it was explained.

Groups of opinion leaders attended a series of five 2-hour weekly sessions that first encouraged attendees to think of themselves as social leaders with the ability to reduce the threat of HIV/AIDS in their own community by talking with others. Over the course of the training sessions, POLs were taught how to communicate effective, theory-based HIV prevention messages to friends, acquaintances, and even strangers during the course of everyday conversation. Instruction, modeling, and role-playing exercises were used to teach opinion leaders to initiate and deliver messages about behavior change, such as the importance of carrying condoms at all times, discussion of risk-reduction precautions with partners before sex, avoiding sex when intoxicated, and handling coercion to engage in unprotected acts. Leaders were taught to communicate about the positive benefits of change, to personally endorse safer behavior, and to identify it to others as a socially acceptable norm. Conversational messages emphasized the positive and desirable consequences of making changes in behavior. In these ways, POLs learned to expand their communications beyond risk education alone and to target attitude, belief, self-efficacy, and normative views in others. During each group meeting, all POLs specified goals for the number of conversations with others each would have before the next session, and outcomes of these conversations were reviewed—and continued conversation goals were established—during each subsequent meeting. In order to reach momentum, achieve a "critical mass" of risk-reduction endorsers, and ensure not only high but also repeated exposure of population members to multiple HIV prevention messages coming from different well-liked people, successive waves of new POLs were identified and sequentially trained in each intervention city.

Follow-up risk assessment surveys were administered to all men entering gay bars in all eight cities 1 year after the POL intervention had been carried out. Comparisons between baseline and follow-up revealed no evidence of population-level risk-behavior change in the control cities where educational materials alone had been present in the clubs. By contrast, there were substantial reductions in the prevalence and frequency of high-risk sexual practices—as well as increased condom use—in populations of men attending intervention city bars. At follow-up, the mean frequency of unprotected anal intercourse decreased from 1.68 acts during the past 2 months at baseline to 0.59, and the mean percentage of condom use during sex increased from 44.7% to 66.8%; these reported behavior changes were corroborated by increased condom taking in intervention city bars (Kelly et al., 1997). The study showed that reductions in the risk level of a community population can be achieved when enough popular and well-liked members of that population systemically are mobilized on a large scale to endorse and recommend behavior change to others.

"M-Powerment": A Multicomponent Community Intervention   Kegeles, Hays, and Coates (1996) examined the effectiveness of a community-level intervention for young gay or bisexual men that employed the same type of message dissemination elements just described with several additional components. This work, carried out in two midsized cities on the West coast, utilized one city population as a control and implemented in the other city a multielement intervention. It included two forms of peer outreach. In formal outreach, teams of young gay men visited locations frequented by other young MSM where they communicated safer sex encouragement messages, distributed project safer sex materials, and invited other men to join their outreach team. During informal outreach, young MSM in the community were invited to attend sessions, similar to those used in the POL intervention described by Kelly et al. (1991; Kelly, St. Lawrence, & Stevenson, 1992; 1997), in which they learned to diffuse safer sex endorsement messages to their friends. In addition to these outreach activities, the project also carried out 3-hour risk-reduction workshop sessions in community venues that corrected misconceptions about risk, encouraged correct condom use, taught skills for enacting risk-reduction steps, and—if participants were willing—enlisted their efforts to serve as informal HIV prevention outreach workers to their own friends. The overall project, as well as other community AIDS awareness activities, was jointly orchestrated by the research team; a core group of young MSM that developed project materials, logos, and themes; and a community advisory board.

In contrast to the Kelly et al. (1997) study, which evaluated program effectiveness by surveying large cross-sections of over 1,000 population members at baseline and 1 year after the POL intervention, Kegeles, Hays, and Coates (1996) longitudinally followed a smaller cohort of gay men (N = 191) drawn from the intervention and control cities. However, the pattern and approximate magnitude of behavior changes were similar in the two studies. Kegeles, Hays, and Coates. found that, among members of the longitudinal cohort, no significant changes in risk behavior were present in the control city. In contrast, cohort members in the intervention city had become less likely to engage in unprotected anal intercourse during the past 2 months (41.0% to 30.0%). Thus, both of these community-level interventions produced substantial reductions in the presence and frequency of high-risk sexual behaviors among MSM, the population most affected by HIV/AIDS in the United States.

A Community-Level Intervention for Inner-City Women   One might make the argument that gay or bisexual men constitute a population that is highly sensitized to AIDS and therefore highly ready for change, and that this population faces comparatively fewer change barriers related to impoverishment, social disadvantage, and gender than do inner-city women. An important question is whether community risk-reduction interventions can also prove successful with disadvantaged inner-city populations. Sikkema et al. (2000) studied this question in a randomized trial with women living in 18 low-income housing developments located in five American cities. Residents of the developments were predominantly racial and ethnic minority women, and most were unemployed.

In a study design similar to the trial of the POL model in gay bars (Kelly et al., 1997), baseline assessment surveys were first administered to nearly 1,800 women living in the 18 housing developments to ascertain initial levels of population risk behavior. AIDS educational materials were distributed in all developments, and condoms were made available at no cost to all women requesting them. Housing developments were then randomized to intervention and comparison group conditions. The intervention tested in the study involved three components: (1) risk-reduction workshops for women; (2) the identification and training of POLs among women in each housing development to disseminate risk-reduction endorsement messages to other women in the same development; and (3) periodic AIDS awareness social events that brought together women and families living in the development and that provided an opportunity for POLs to have more intensive risk-reduction endorsement conversations with their neighbors.

In contrast to gay men, inner-city women were found in pilot work to have less information about HIV/AIDS, sexual health issues, and HIV risk reduction and sexual communication skills. For this reason, the community intervention began by inviting women to attend four-session group workshops held in common meeting rooms in each housing development. Approximately half of all women in intervention-condition developments attended the workshops. Workshop content areas included HIV/STD risk education, women's reproductive health, male and female condom use, sexual assertiveness and condom negotiation skills, and skills training in how to talk with friends and family members about HIV and sexual behavior. The workshops were intended to provide a basic foundation in areas needed to successfully enact behavior change.

Questions imbedded in the baseline risk-assessment survey asked each woman in a housing development to identify which other women, from among those living in the same development, were the most liked and trusted for advice. Responses were cross-tabulated to determine who received the greatest number of nominations. POLs were identified and invited to serve on the development's "Women's Health Council." Approximately 12% of the total number of women residents in each development functioned in these roles. In addition to being the first women to attend the community risk-reduction workshops, Health Council members assumed the roles of both disseminating risk-reduction endorsement messages in conversations with neighbors and inviting other women to attend successive waves of workshops. Each housing development's Health

Council planned and organized periodic social events such as potluck dinners, family game activities, and women's discussion groups that brought
neighbors together and always included an AIDS awareness component,
providing an opportunity for POL/Health Council women to discuss AIDS
concerns and visibly endorse protective steps. Ethnography carried out during the project's preliminary phase had revealed that women were less comfortable than gay men in discussing explicit aspects of their sexual behavior,
often had to deal with men's negative attitudes toward condom use, and
were motivated to learn about AIDS not only for self-protection but also to
become able to discuss it with their family members. These themes received
particular attention during all subsequent phases of the intervention.

The same risk-assessment survey used at baseline was readministered
to all women living in all 18 housing developments 12 months following the
completion of the community risk-reduction workshops. The proportion
of women in intervention-condition developments who had any unprotected intercourse in the past 2 months declined from 50% to 37.6%, and
the percentage of women's intercourse acts that were protected by condoms increased from 30.2% to 47.2%. There was an approximately one-
third reduction in the mean frequency of unprotected acts among women
who reported exposure to intervention activities.

Factors Influencing the Success of Community-Level
HIV Prevention Interventions

These examples provide compelling evidence—often using rigorous, "gold
standard" randomized control group designs—that community HIV prevention interventions can produce substantial reductions in sexual risk
behavior at a population level. At the same time, some evaluations of
community-level HIV prevention interventions with gay men have not
yielded positive findings (cf. Elford et al., 2001; Flowers et al., 2002), and
community outreach programs for IDUs have sometimes found large
secular trends for decline in injection-related risk practices even in
standard-care conditions (Stephens, Simpson, Coyle, & McCoy, 1993). It is
important to identify and understand factors that have been responsible for
the success of some interventions and the reasons that others have not produced positive outcomes. Although little or no research has empirically and
directly examined these questions, several characteristics distinguish community intervention studies that produced convincing behavior-change
outcomes from those that did not (Kelly, 2004). These include the following:

(1) Successful projects have been grounded in theory-based models
    and have been implemented with fidelity to their key theoretical
    foundations. For example, the successful diffusion-based inter-
    ventions discussed earlier all identified and trained sufficiently
    large cadres of POLs to deliver to others messages that targeted
    not only the recipient's knowledge about AIDS but also normative

beliefs, attitudes, intentions, skills, and self-efficacy. Interventions producing positive effects have focused on factors known to influence risk behavior.

(2) Successful interventions have relied on intensive field ethnography and on eliciting community input, support, and involvement during intervention development. These steps are critical for ensuring that HIV prevention interventions direct attention to relevant risk-producing situations, are culturally relevant and appropriate, and are accepted in the population one seeks to reach.

(3) Successful interventions have produced among population members high levels of exposure to key elements and "active ingredients" responsible for behavior change. Programs that have been able to deliver only a small level of intervention exposure— either because the intervention was itself too weak or because the target population was too large in relation to program scope— have generally been unsuccessful (Kelly, 2004). Programs that have produced population-level behavior change have generally ensured the potential for high exposure by working with smaller population units and venues (such as gay men present in a small city's gay bars or venues, or women living in identifiable inner-city housing developments) than do those directed to diffuse, broad, hard-to-target, or transient populations (such as all gay men or women in a large city).

(4) Most successful community HIV prevention interventions have employed multiple program components that directly reached most members of the target population. The Sikkema et al. (2000) housing development project, which combined community-setting risk-reduction workshops, sustained message delivery by POLs among women living in the developments, and AIDS-themed social events that brought together neighbors and families, illustrated such a multifaceted approach.

(5) Successful community-level interventions have been sustained and ongoing. As discussed earlier, programs that produced evidence of change have had active intervention components sustained over relatively long periods of time, commonly 6 to 12 months. The activities also often changed, evolved, and built momentum by drawing new community members into the intervention process.

(6) Successful community interventions have not only delivered prevention messages but have also created social movements against AIDS. Each of the intervention examples described earlier in this chapter included programs that went far beyond providing AIDS education. Each also illustrated a process in which community members' altruism, support, concern about AIDS, and desire to do

something to help fight the disease became critical components of the intervention. To a large extent, project personnel functioned not as staff who delivered a program to a "passive" community but as staff who facilitated, mobilized, and channeled the volunteer efforts of community members themselves, whether as POLs, Women's Health Council members, or informal outreach workers. Interventions that successfully mobilize community effort and structures carry the potential for durably changing the social fabric to reduce risk.

The Role of Partnerships Between Researchers and Community Agencies

Whether carried out in the context of a research trial or purely as a community service, effective HIV prevention interventions must be informed by both behavioral and social science research findings and—equally—by the experience, cultural understanding, and credibility of CBOs. It is theoretically possible for researchers to be sufficiently community savvy—or for CBOs to be sufficiently research savvy—to bring both research and community perspectives to these endeavors. However, the challenges of conceptualizing, designing, implementing, and evaluating effective community-level HIV prevention interventions are great, and efforts in this area are most likely to prove successful when they can benefit from the combined expertise of applied behavioral or social scientists and service agency partners with a deep understanding of the communities they serve. Intervention models that arise from researcher/provider collaborations can then rest on a foundation of both sound science and community understanding.

ACKNOWLEDGMENTS Support for the preparation of this chapter was provided by Center Grant P30-MH52776 from the National Institute of Mental Health (NIMH).

REFERENCES

Amirkhanian, Y. A., Kelly, J. A., Kabakchieva, E., McAuliffe, T. L., Vassileva, S. (2003). Evaluation of a social network HIV prevention intervention program for young men who have sex with men in Russia and Bulgaria. *AIDS Education and Prevention, 15,* 205–221.

Bandura, A. (1986). *Social foundation of thought and action: A social-cognitive theory.* Englewood Cliffs, NJ: Prentice Hall.

Carleton, R. A., Lasater, T. M., Assaf, A. R., Feldman, H. A., & McKinlay, S. (1995). The Pawtucket Heart Health Program: Community changes in cardiovascular risk factors and projected disease risk. *American Journal of Public Health, 85,* 777–785.

Catania, J. A., Coates, T. J., Stall, R., Bye, L., Kegeles, S. M., Capell, F., et al. (1991). Changes in condom use among homosexual men in San Francisco. *Health Psychology, 10,* 190–199.

Catania, J. A., Kegeles, S. M., & Coates, T. J. (1990). Towards an understanding of risk behavior. An AIDS risk reduction model (ARRM). *Health Education Quarterly, 17,* 53–72.

DiClemente, R. J. & Wingood, G. M. (1995). A randomized, controlled trial of an HIV sexual risk reduction intervention for young African American women. *Journal of the American Medical Association, 274,* 1271–1276.

Ehrhardt, A. A., Exner, T. M., Hoffman, S., Silberman, I., Leu, C. S., Miller, S., et al. (2002). A gender-specific HIV/STD risk reduction intervention for women in a health care setting: Short-and long-term results of a randomized clinical trial. *AIDS Care, 14,* 147–161.

Elford, J., Bolding, G., & Sherr, L. (2001). Peer education has no significant impact on HIV risk behaviours among gay men in London (letter). *AIDS, 15,* 535–537.

Fishbein, M. & Ajzen, I. (1975). *Belief, attitude, intention and behavior: An introduction to theory and research.* Reading, MA: Addison-Wesley.

Fisher, J. D. & Fisher, W. A. (1992). Changing AIDS-risk behavior. *Psychological Bulletin, 111,* 455–474.

Flowers, P., Hart, G. J., Williamson, L. M., Frankis, J. S., & Der, G. J. (2002). Does bar-based, peer-led health promotion have a community-level effect amongst gay men in Scotland? *International Journal of STD and AIDS, 13,* 102–108.

Fortenberry, J. D., Tu, W., Harczzlak, J., Katz, B. P., & Orr, D. P. (2002). Condom use as a function of time in new and established adolescent sexual relationships. *American Journal of Public Health, 92,* 211–213.

Jemmott, J. B., Jemmott, L. S., & Fong, G. T. (1992). Reductions in HIV risk-associated sexual behavior among Black male adolescents: Effects of an AIDS prevention intervention. *American Journal of Public Health, 82,* 372–377.

Jemmott, J. B., Jemmott, L. W., Spears, H., Hewitt, N., & Cruz-Collins, M. (1991). Self-efficacy, hedonistic expectancies, and condom use intentions among inner-city Black adolescent women: A social-cognitive approach to AIDS risk behavior. *Journal of Adolescent Health, 13,* 512–519.

Kalichman, S. C., Carey, M. P., & Johnson, B. T. (1996). Prevention of sexually transmitted HIV infection: A meta-analytic review of the behavioral outcome literature. *Annals of Behavioral Medicine, 18,* 6–15.

Kamb, M. L., Fishbein, M., Douglas, J. M., Rhodes, F., Rogers, J., Bolan, G., et al. (1998). Efficacy of risk reduction counseling to prevent HIV and STDs. *Journal of the American Medical Association, 280,* 1161–1167.

Kegeles, S. M., Hays, R. B., & Coates, T. J. (1996). The Mpowerment Project: A community-level HIV prevention intervention for young gay men. *American Journal of Public Health, 86,* 1129–1136.

Kelly, J. A. (1999). Community-level interventions are needed to prevent new HIV infections (Editorial). *American Journal of Public Health, 89,* 299–301.

Kelly, J. A. (2004). Popular opinion leaders and HIV prevention peer education: Resolving discrepant findings and implications for the development of effective community programmes. *AIDS Care, 16,* 139–150.

Kelly, J. A., Murphy, D. A., Roffman, R. E., Solomon, L. J., Winett, R. A., Stevenson, L. Y., et al. (1992). AIDS/HIV risk behavior among gay men in small cities: Findings of a 16-city sample. *Archives of Internal Medicine, 152,* 2293–2297.

Kelly, J. A., Murphy, D. A., Sikkema, K. J., McAuliffe, T. L., Roffman, R. A., Solomon, L. J., et al. (1997). Randomized, controlled, community-level HIV prevention intervention for sexual risk behaviour among homosexual men in U.S. cities. *The Lancet, 350,* 1500–1505.

Kelly, J. A., Murphy, D. G., Washington, C. D., Wilson, T. S., Koob, J. J., David, D. R., et al. (1994). The effects of HIV/AIDS intervention groups for high-risk women in urban clinics. *American Journal of Public Health, 84,* 1918–1922.

Kelly, J. A., St. Lawrence, J. S., Diaz, Y. E., Stevenson, L. Y., Hauth, A. C., Brasfield, T. L., et al. (1991). HIV risk behavior reduction following intervention with key opinion leaders of a population: An experimental analysis. *American Journal of Public Health, 81,* 168–171.

Kelly, J. A., St. Lawrence, J. S., Hood, H. V., & Brasfield, T. L. (1989). Behavioral intervention to reduce AIDS risk activities. *Journal of Consulting and Clinical Psychology, 57,* 60–67.

Kelly, J. A., St. Lawrence, J. S., Stevenson, L. Y., Hauth, A. C., Kalichman, S. C., Diaz, et al. (1992). Community AIDS/HIV risk reduction: The effects of endorsements by popular people in three cities. *American Journal of Public Health, 82,* 1483–1489.

Ku, L., Sonnenstein, F. L., & Pleck, H. H. (1994). The dynamics of young men's condom use during and across relationships. *Family Planning Perspectives, 26,* 246–251.

Latkin, C. A. (1998). Outreach in natural settings: The use of peer leaders for HIV prevention among injecting drug users' networks. *Public Health Reports, 113*(Suppl. 1), 151–159.

McKusick, L., Horstman, W., & Coates, T. J. (1985). AIDS and sexual behavior reported by gay men in San Francisco. *American Journal of Public Health, 75,* 493–496.

National Institute of Mental Health Multisite HIV Prevention Trial Group. (1998). The NIMH multisite HIV prevention trial: Reducing HIV sexual risk behavior. *Science, 280,* 1889–1894.

Peterson, J. L., Coates, T. J., Catania, J. A., Hauck, W. W., Acree, M., Daigle, D., et al. (1996). Evaluation of an HIV risk reduction intervention among African American homosexual and bisexual men. *AIDS, 10,* 319–325.

Rogers, E. M. (1983). *Diffusion of innovations,* 2nd edition. New York: Free Press.

Sikkema, J. A., Heckman, T. G., Kelly, J. A., Anderson, E. S., Winett, R. A., Solomon, L., et al. (1996). HIV risk behaviors among women living in low-income, inner-city housing developments. *American Journal of Public Health, 86,* 1123–1128.

Sikkema, K. J., Kelly, J. A., Winett, R. A., Solomon, L. J., Cargill, V. A., Roffman, R. A., et al. (2000). Outcomes of a randomized community-level HIV prevention intervention for women living in 18 low-income housing developments. *American Journal of Public Health, 90,* 57–63.

Stephens, R. C., Simpson, D. D., Coyle, S. C., McCoy, C. B., & National AIDS Research Consortium (1993). Comparative effectiveness of NADR interventions. In B. S. Brown & G. M. Beschner (Eds.), *Handbook on Risk of AIDS* (pp. 519–556). Westport, CT: Greenwood Press.

Trotter, R. T., Bowen, A. M., Baldwin, J. A., & Price, L. J. (1996). The efficacy of network-based HIV/AIDS risk reduction programs in midsized towns in the United States. *Journal of Drug Issues, 26,* 591–605.

Valdiserri, R. O., Lyter, D., Leviton, L., Callahan, C., Kingsley, L., & Rinaldo, C. R. (1989). AIDS prevention in homosexual and bisexual men: Results of a randomized trial evaluating two risk reduction interventions. *AIDS, 3,* 21–26.

Wagenaar, A. C., Murray, D. M., Gehan, J. P., Wolfson, J. P., Forster, M., Toomey, et al. (2000). Communities mobilizing for change on alcohol: Outcomes from a randomized community trial. *Journal of Studies on Alcohol, 61,* 85–94.

Weibel, W., Lampinen, T., Chene, D., Jimenez, D., Johnson, W., & Ouellet, L. (1989). *Risk for HIV infection among homeless IV drug users (IVDUs) in Chicago.* Paper presented to International Conference on AIDS, 5:86. Abstract No. M.A.P. 50.

Winkelby, M. A., Taylor, C. B., Jatulis, D., & Formann, S. P. (1996). The long-term effects of a cardiovascular disease prevention trial: The Stanford Five-City Project. *American Journal of Public Health, 12,* 1773–1779.

5

Social Network Approaches to HIV Prevention: Implications to Community Impact and Sustainability

Carl A. Latkin & Amy R. Knowlton

THEORIES OF BEHAVIOR CHANGE

The first two decades of HIV prevention research demonstrate the limitations of individual-oriented approaches to behavior change and the need for understanding alternative, social-level approaches to behavior change. Predominant individual-oriented, psychoeducational approaches to intervention are insufficient to alter the course of HIV epidemics (Kalichman, Kelly, & Stevenson, 1997). Models of behavior change employed in HIV prevention intervention tend to be highly cognitive, emphasizing such factors as risk perceptions, attitudes, and beliefs, diverting attention from the social and economic contexts that help shape these cognitions. Moreover, individual-level approaches also present challenges to identifying and recruiting hard-to-reach, socially and economically marginalized populations often at highest risk for HIV. Furthermore, individual-oriented interventions tend to lack sustainability, with most HIV behavioral change decaying over 3 to 6 months after intervention.

New intervention approaches are needed to address the social nature of HIV risk behaviors within their community contexts. Research suggests that social-oriented compared to individual-oriented approaches to behavior change can potentially be more effective, affect a greater number of individuals, and have more sustainable effects on behavior change. Yet, while there has been increasing recognition of the need for a social-level HIV intervention agenda, the underlying theories and methodologies of intervention have largely remained individual-oriented, limiting the potential of social avenues of intervention for behavior change. Pursuing promising social-oriented avenues to HIV intervention requires social theories of behavior and social-oriented methodologies of behavioral assessment.

Classic social psychology studies by Sheriff, Latene and Darley, and Zimbardo among others, have demonstrated the immense power of social situations to define and influence behavior. Research indicates the importance of social environmental factors in HIV risk behaviors as well (Des Jarlais et al., 1995; Friedman et al., 1987). Of particular importance are more recent social theories of behavior that have elucidated the structural, that is, network, basis of the dynamic interactions between individuals and their social and economic environments (Bourdieu & Delsaut, 1981; Coleman, 1990), linkages between microsocial and macrosocial patterns of behavior (Giddens, 1987), and relationships between social statuses, identities, and behavior (White, 1992). Increasingly, research is illuminating the structural basis of contextual influences on health behaviors and resultant health disparities (Berkman, Glass, Brissette, & Seeman, 2000).

While great strides have been made in developing social theories of behavior, far less attention has been given to applying these theories to behavioral intervention (Rogers, 2003). A major challenge to developing an agenda of social-oriented HIV behavioral intervention remains the systematic delineation and measurement of social factors that affect HIV risk behaviors. We propose that analyses of social networks and social behavioral settings may help contribute to the systematic measurement of social environmental influences on HIV-related behaviors and help elucidate the role of environment on behavior and behavior change. The analyses of networks within risk behavior settings can also be used to identify social roles and identities and their attendant behavioral norms, which may aid in the development of social-oriented interventions that capitalize on social influence processes. Furthermore, network-based sampling and assessment can be used to empirically assess the efficacy of interventions to alter social norms and the potential social diffusion of intervention effects within a community.

In the present chapter we propose social theory–based strategies to a network approach to HIV prevention that capitalize on social influence processes. We discuss how such concepts as referent others, social identities, social roles, norms, behavioral settings, and social diffusion of innovation can be operationalized in network terms and applied to the development of HIV prevention intervention tailored to social environmental influences on HIV risk within a given community. We propose that greater attention to networks as not only channels of disease transmission but also as channels of resource exchange, information dissemination, and potential social influence may contribute to the development of more powerful approaches to HIV prevention. Furthermore, we propose that greater attention to the influence of behavioral settings on HIV risk, and common venue attendance as network may also improve the success of our targeting and intervention outcomes.

NETWORKS AS COMMUNITY

A network can be defined as individuals linked by a certain behavior or interaction of interest. A *personal network* can be defined as an individual, termed ego or index, and those linked directly, that is, first degree contacts, to her by a particular behavior or interaction. *Social networks* are sets of individuals that are linked together by one or more specific types of relations between them. They can be a set of linked personal networks.

Networks have been used in conceptualizing a systemic model of community as a dynamic system of kin, friends, and weaker ties (Kasarda & Janowitz, 1974). As such, social networks have been considered a contemporary form of community and an alternative to traditional (geography- or clan-based) notions of community that may no longer hold validity (Bott, 1957; Mitchell, 1969; Wellman, 1981).

Personal network members are typically nominated by the ego through name-generating questions that elicit names of individuals with whom the respondent has engaged in specific behaviors or interactions. For example, a network inventory may include such name-generating questions as with whom one eats or sleeps, or sources and recipients of the respondent's support, termed her support network. Modes of social support queried often include emotional, financial, instrumental or tangible, informational, and social participation. Support-network name-eliciting questions may include: Who can you talk to about something private or personal? (emotional support); Who would give you $25 or something of value? (instrumental or material support); and Who could you ask for advice or help about health problems, like infections, birth control, or HIV or AIDS? (informational support). In HIV research, additional interactions of interest may include sexual behavior or drug sharing; such nominated individuals are termed the ego's sex and drug networks, respectively, or collectively, ego's risk network.

After delineating names, attributions of network members are elicited through a series of additional questions. Attributions queried may include age, gender, employment status, frequency of contact, residential propinquity, HIV status, illicit drug use, reciprocity of support, emotional closeness, trust, interpersonal conflict, HIV risk behaviors, and knowledge of ego's HIV status.

Network inventories differ from traditional survey instruments in that the major goal is to elicit from the respondent a set of names and attributes of those individuals. Respondents vary on both the size of their networks and their abilities to recall the names of their network members. Probes have been found to assist in the recall process (Brewer, 2000), necessitating detailed training and supervision of interviewers. Network measures have been demonstrated to have predictive, concurrent, and discriminative validity (Latkin, Mandell, Vlahov, Oziemkowska, & Celentano, 1996a). Social networks can be visually modeled as sociograms (Figure 5.1). Computer technology, for example, UCINET, Pajek, and NetDraw, has enhanced the ease of visualization and analyses of social network data.

Network Structure

Networks are comprised of functional, relational, and structural components (Hall & Wellman, 1985; House, Umberson, & Landis, 1988). Functional components may include modes of support (emotional, financial, informational, instrumental, and social participation, and interpersonal conflict) and other interactions of interest such as sex or drug-sharing

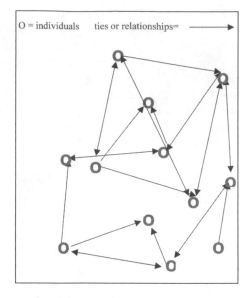

Figure 5.1 Sociogram of social network.

ties. Relational components are usually described in terms of institution-alized social roles such as kin, coworkers, and friends. Social network structural components include *network size*, (i.e., number of network members); *direction of the relationship* (unidirectional or bidirectional); *multiplexity* (i.e., the number of relationships between the ego and a net-work member, which can be indexed by the number of network members named in two or more functional or relational network domains); *durabil-ity, or* duration of network ties; *density*, (e.g., the proportion of individuals within a network who are linked to each other divided by the number of possible links); and *centrality* (i.e., individuals within a network with the highest numbers of direct and indirect ties).

Network members tend to be homophilous not only with regard to race, ethnicity, and social class, but also with regard to beliefs, attitudes, and behaviors (Marsden, 1990). That is, similar others tend to affiliate, and affiliates tend to reciprocally support, influence, and perpetuate each oth-ers' attitudes and behaviors. As high-risk individuals tend to affiliate with each other, network analysis can be used to delineate potential routes of HIV transmission, key support exchange ties, and potential sources of so-cial influence on HIV risk behaviors.

Behavioral Settings and Social Networks

Behavioral settings can have profound implications to HIV because re-search indicates that behaviors can be influenced by social settings (Barker, 1978; Barker & Wright, 1955). Theories of the influence of set-tings on behaviors (Wicker, 1987) emphasize the social construction (Berger & Luckmann, 1967) of social interactions and the importance of motives and social cognitions, such as scripts (Abelson, 1981) and social episodes (Forgas, 1979), in this construction. Behavior settings are of particular importance for network analysis and intervention because they provide a venue in which individuals at risk of disease transmission may be linked by various forms of social interaction. Indeed, common settings for meeting sexual partners and the concomitant risk profiles of those who frequent these settings have been delineated by key informants (Weir et al., 2003). Common attendance at social settings can also be used to define social networks.

Bars are one type of behavioral setting that has been studied in detail. Bars tend to attract heavy drinkers, and individuals who frequent bars tend to increase their drinking over time (Curran, Muthen, & Harford, 1998). Further, bars are a site for the development of social norms that influence risk conditions. In observational studies of bars, Aitken found that bar patrons reported social pressures to conform to norms of round buying and that the group norm of buying rounds of drinks for drinking partners predicted the amount of alcohol consumed (Aitken, 1985). Bar attendance has also been found to be associated with transmission of infectious diseases. In a study of STIs in Colorado Springs, six bars accounted for half of the social venues attended. In a tuberculosis study, Klovdahl et al., found that common attendance at specific social settings was linked to a genetic strain of tuberculosis infection (Klovdahl et al., 2001), suggesting a causal link between setting attendance and infection. Some prior successful HIV prevention studies that targeted gay men were located in bars because they were the nexus of gay networks within the communities studied (Kelly et al., 1992).

Shooting galleries, crack houses, bus stops, and truck stops have also been observed as settings associated with HIV risk behaviors (Celetano, Vlahov, Cohn, & Anthony, 1991; Latkin & Knowlton, 2000). Some of these settings contain stable networks, whereas others are places to meet new partners. In addition, potentially unexpected settings may also emerge as important sites for network formation and interaction. In an outbreak investigation of syphilis in St. Louis, Stoner et al. found that a doughnut shop was the central meeting place for infected individuals (Stoner, Whittington, Hughes, Aral, & Holmes, 2000).

Settings may also have independent effects on risk behaviors. The physical attributes of settings, such as the lack of running water for cleaning needles, and the social norms, such as exchanging sex for drugs in crack houses, may have profound effects on HIV transmission. Given the influences of both settings and networks on risk behaviors, it may be useful to consider both attributes of social environments when designing HIV prevention programs.

Network- and Setting-Based Sampling

Delineation of networks and behavioral settings also has important applications to targeted sampling of high-risk, hard-to-reach populations. Because those at highest risk of HIV are often socially and economically marginalized, they are often not accessible by traditional sampling strategies. Venue- and network-delineated sampling has been used to recruit such high-risk and hard-to-reach populations as injection drug users, sex workers, and other hidden populations (Broadhead & Heckathorn, 1994; Carlson, Siegal, & Falck, 1994; Simpson, Camacho, Vogtsberger, & Williams ML, 1994).

There are several approaches to network sampling. The simplest is to collect personal network data on the sample without actually sampling network members. To assess sampling biases, one can then compare the attributes of the recruited sample to those of the sample's network members. The second approach is to recruit the actual network members of the initial sample. If the investigators wish to reduce statistical biases of systematic sampling, they can randomly choose network members to recruit. This approach, called a *random walk*, has been successfully utilized to parsimoniously estimate the sample's characteristics (Klovdahl, 1989).

Another method is *network delineated sampling*. Using this method, network members are recruited based on specific attributes. For example, investigators may want to recruit network members who are most difficult to enroll. If it is difficult to recruit young injection drug users, then the youngest injectors listed on a network may be targeted for enrollment. Once these individuals are enrolled, their network can be also delineated and their youngest injection partners can be targeted from enrollment. To reduce respondent bias of only recruiting certain types of network members, parameters such as age and residential location can be placed on the type of network members respondents are asked to recruit. By first delineating their networks, the investigators can guide the participants as to the type of networks members requested to participate.

Setting- or venue-based sampling is another method of recruiting hidden populations. In venue sampling, venues known to be frequented by the target group are enumerated and then random or quota samples are recruited from these venues. This method has been effective in recruiting young men who have sex with men (MSM) (Valleroy et al., 2000). One of the disadvantages to venue sampling is that some individuals in the target group do not frequent the venues.

To deal with this and other issues, venue- and network-delineated sampling can be combined. For some groups it may be most effective to initially recruit from a venue, such as bars. Then network members not represented in the venue could be recruited in the second stage of sampling, targeting participants' risk network members who do not go to the bars. This approach of network-delineated sampling allows investigators to bridge their recruitment between networks and can be used with venue-based, for example, street- or clinic-based, recruitment strategies. This avoids some of the systemic selection biases in venue-based recruitment. Moreover, it presents a viable approach to recruitment of high-risk groups that may not easily be identified through either approach alone, such as those who frequent a computer chat room that serves as a high-risk MSM network and as a forum for advertising the changing venues of their rave parties.

Networks and HIV/STIs: Networks as Channels of Disease Transmission

Because of its emphasis on social interactions, social network analysis is well-suited to the study of infectious diseases and their transmission through a population. Research on networks and HIV has delineated structural components of networks and emphasized conceptualizations of networks as channels of infectious disease transmission. This research has emphasized that HIV, like other infectious diseases, is not randomly dispersed within a population but rather located and transmitted within networks of linked individuals.

There is ample evidence that personal network factors are associated with HIV and sexually transmitted infection (STI) risk behaviors (Klovdahl et al., 1994; McManus & Coxon, 1995; Morris & Kretzschmar, 1995; Rothenberg et al., 1998; Woodhouse et al., 1994). Needle sharing, cessation of drug use, and relapse have been found to be associated with personal network characteristics of density and size of drug networks (Latkin, Mandell, & Vlahov, 1996; Trotter, 2nd, Bowen, & Potter, 1995).

Several structural network characteristics have been found to be useful in understanding HIV transmission and informing the development of social interventions. The structural network factors that may be associated with HIV transmission include bridge groups, centrality, multiplexity, and network turnover. Bridge groups are categories of individuals who bridge HIV infection from high-risk groups to other social groups and are, therefore, important targets of HIV intervention. Similarly, individuals with high *centrality* (i.e., greatest numbers of ties) may be important transmitters of infection. For example, small, isolated networks not connected to each other by ties among them, present a much lower probability of HIV/STI transmission compared to large, highly interconnected networks. In a social network study of drug users in New York City, Friedman and et al. (1997) found that HIV positive serostatus was associated with a greater likelihood of links to a large highly interconnected core network component. Findings that women injection drug users more so than men had greater multiplexity of ties, as reflected in greater overlap between drug and sex partners (Latkin et al., 1998; Pivnick, Jacobson, Eric, Doll, & Drucker, 1994), help to explain women's greater HIV risk and need for interventions that focus on interpersonal negotiation of both safer sex and drug behaviors. Network turnover, a measure of network stability, has been reported to be associated with increased HIV seropositivity (Friedman, DeJong, & Wodak, 1993).

Network analysis has also been used to identify the contribution of sexual mixing or sex pairing patterns to the transmission of HIV. Sexual mixing is the degree to which people have sexual partners from inside (assortative mixing) and outside (disassortative mixing) their own networks.

Selective sexual mixing can have a profound effect on the speed and direction of HIV/STI transmission. Renton, Whitaker, Ison, Wadsworth, and Harris (1995) found that individuals with high rates of STIs tend to select as sex partners others with high rates of STIs, which may be explained by tendencies of assortative mixing, that is, selecting sexual partners from inside one's network. This pattern of sex partner selection may lead to isolated pockets of infection within the community, which should be prime targets of intervention to reduce the potential of transmission to individuals outside the network. In other examples, age mixing patterns have helped to explain HIV seroprevalence patterns of young gay men in San Francisco (Service & Blower, 1995) and young African women (Ford, Sohn, & Lepkowski, 2002) One study found that age mixing was strongly associated with STI infection even after adjusting for number of sex partners (Catania, Binson, & Stone, 1996). Age mixing has also been found to be associated with lower condom use (Diclemente et al., 2002; Ford et al., 2002).

Network analysis can also be used to identify specific sources and forms of social support associated with health outcomes. For example, multiplexity of drug users' ties, for example, financial support, exchange support and sexual interaction, or economic interdependence in sex partner ties, has been found to be associated with riskier sexual practices (Sherman & Latkin, 2001), particularly for women. Disadvantaged populations' reliance on support exchange with network members may also help explain the resistance to adopt safer sex and safer drug practices, especially within their main sex-partner and main drug-sharing ties. Introducing new behaviors may threaten their access to valued resources.

Networks and Social Support: Networks as Channels of Resource Exchange

While networks clearly function as channels of disease transmission, they also serve as channels of resource exchange. Thus, a comprehensive conceptualization of networks incorporates their functional and relational components as well. More specifically, network inventories can be used to elicit information on individuals to whom the ego provides and from whom the ego receives informational, emotional, and material support. The social support literature has traditionally distinguished between perceived support and enacted support. Perceived contingent support, or global appraisals of perceived support, has been consistently found in prior studies to be associated with morbidity and mortality (Berkman et al., 2000). Research suggests that perceived support reflects support expectations or norms about the availability and potential value of such support. Enacted support, on the other hand, reflects instances in which support has been utilized (Dunkel-Schetter & Bennett, 1990). Each, however, represents a potential resource that can be enlisted in network-oriented preventive interventions.

Prior studies indicate that individuals of lower socioeconomic status, having fewer personal reserves of resources, are more likely to utilize network support (Hobfoll, 2001). Those of very low socioeconomic status tend to rely on their networks for support exchange for basic subsistence needs (Stack, 1974). As HIV disproportionately affects such disadvantaged populations, attention to support availability, and the resources exchanged among these ties, provides insights into microsocial processes that affect HIV risk. In addition, individuals of lower socioeconomic status and greater HIV risk tend to have greater degrees of homophily within their network, or less access to individuals with greater resources (including financial) than themselves. This social and economic marginalization implies that they tend to be reliant on resource exchange with similarly marginalized, high-risk others; exigencies to engage in resource exchange within their networks leaves them vulnerable to resource depletion and distress (Stack, 1974). By focusing on the transactional components of these networks, network analysis can be used to emphasize the structural basis of the unequal opportunities for social ties through which individuals access resources that affect their individual and collective health (Wellman, 1981).

Interpersonal Conflict

Many studies of social ties and health focus on prosocial functions of ties and ignore disruptive or conflictive qualities of ties. Interpersonal conflict in network ties may indicate threats to main ties and their potential instability and dissolution. The importance of such conflict is shown in research suggesting that conflictive qualities of relationships may be more consequential to health than supportive qualities (Fiore, Becker, & Copple, 1983; Rook, 1984). Conflictive compared to supportive qualities of ties have also been found to have greater associations with stability and duration of relationships. Violations of norms of support exchange, or reciprocity of support, contribute to interpersonal conflict and potential dissolution of supportive ties (Turner, Pearlin, & Mullan, 1998). Thus, network-based preventive interventions need to be mindful of potential conflict in existing networks, as well as the potential of the intervention to introduce additional conflict as a function of information conveyed, changing norms, or threat to a predictable though potentially maladaptive lifestyle.

Networks as Channels of Support Exchange

Viewing networks as channels of resource exchange also provides some conceptual benefits for the design of interventions. The resource exchange perspective focuses on naturally occurring relationships contributing to risk and on behaviors and network-level resource exchange. In so doing, the network conceptual framework avoids the limitations of perspectives that suggest that networks are static and imply a specific social role. Further, it does not presume that risk group labels connote personal identity. Some risk ties, particularly among marginalized populations, may not conform to institutionalized social roles. Moreover, these role categories may not neatly fit into the categories of sex partner ties commonly referred to in HIV research, that is, main, casual, and exchange sex partners. Further, in many settings, it may be difficult to distinguish exchange sex from other types of sex. Understanding patterns of support exchange as a dynamic and reciprocal process within a population seeking to meet basic subsistence needs such as food, shelter, clothing, and education, may contribute to a greater understanding of HIV risk and, in the process, introduce real-world complexity into interventions intended to affect the lives of these individuals.

Networks as Referent Others: Networks and Social Influence

Besides conceptualizations of networks as channels of disease transmission and of resource exchange, networks can also be conceptualized as comprised of referent others who may serve as important sources of social influence. Interpersonal ties can have a powerful influence on individuals' risk behaviors through processes of social comparison, fear of social sanctions, information or other resource exchanges, and through social interactions that provide opportunities to meet new sex partners or drug-using ties (Edwards, Tindale, Heath, & Posavac, 1990; Fisher, 1988; Hall & Wellman, 1985).

Networks as Referent Others

Research on the power of referent others has greatly influenced interventions in HIV/AIDS. For example, this work suggests that similar individuals, compared to individuals who are perceived as different, have stronger influences on individuals' behavior. Thus, many intervention approaches have targeted "peers" as potential sources of social influence on behavioral risk reduction. Social cognitive approaches to intervention in particular often include social process components, such as use of peers for modeling and providing social rewards such as affirmative feedback for public statements of intentions to engage in risk reduction.

Social influence theories also propose that above and beyond similar others, social influence is greater among those with whom one identifies or compares oneself, termed referent others, compared to those outside one's referent group. Studies of social influence processes have drawn attention to comparative self-assessments (Hyman & Singer, 1968; Merton & Kitt, 1950), proposing that individuals are influenced by their continual engagement in comparing themselves with others and through their identification with a referent group and the norms of the group (Festinger, 1954; Newcomb, 1958).

As naturally occurring groups, social networks may comprise a referent group. Compared to community members outside one's network, network members may exert greater influence on each other through social comparison and social control processes, for example, social rewards and censure, resource exchange, and socialization of new members. Bourgois' (1998) ethnography of networks of homeless drug injectors demonstrates their high reliance on each other for basic subsistence needs, and the strong influences network members exert on each other's risk behaviors.

Social ties may also influence risk behaviors through the labeling of a situation as "high risk." Other people's perceptions and behaviors are a critical component of labeling a situation as requiring intervention (Myers, 1985). Social cognitions are also influenced by where one is situated in a network. Network location is related to information received and patterns of social interaction (Pattison, 1994). As network members help to define situations as high risk and whether and how risk behaviors may be mutable, interventions must consider these influences on risk perceptions and behavior change.

Social Norms and Networks

One mechanism through which networks as referent others affect individual behavior involves the social norms generated among network members. Empirical research in a number of countries indicates that social norms are strongly associated with HIV risk behaviors (Latkin, Forman, Knowlton, & Sherman, 2003a; Organista, Organista, Bola, Garcia de Alba, & Castillo Moran, 2000). Indeed, predominant models of behavior change posit that social norms are important determinants of behavior change, and propose altering social norms of risk behaviors as a strategy of HIV prevention.

Network analysis has been used to examine social norms and processes of norm formation, as well as opinion formation (Galaskiewicz & Marsella, 1978; Friedkin, 1990; Marsden, 1990), decision making (Laumann & Franzoi, 1976), and social diffusion of innovation (Dearing, Meyer, & Rogers, 1994). In one study, drug injectors' network-level behavior norms at baseline, defined as mean level of risk behaviors reported among their respective drug-sharing ties, predicted their risk behaviors at 18-month follow-up, even after controlling for their own risk behaviors at baseline (Latkin et al., 1996a). Indeed, countervailing social norms are thought to contribute to the resistance of many individuals to adopt HIV risk protection (Fisher, Goff, Nadler, & Chinsky, 1988).

Yet little progress has been made in developing interventions that effectively alter social norms of HIV risk behaviors. One important reason for this may be that the predominant emphasis of most such interventions focus on changing individuals' perceptions of their referent group norms, termed proscriptive norms, rather than altering social norms of existing groups, termed descriptive norms, or actual behaviors shared among a group (Latkin et al., 2003a). Thus, possible countervailing norms among participants' referent groups may help explain the limited effectiveness and sustainability of behavior change of predominant individual-oriented approaches to behavior change (Fisher, 1988).

Social Identities and Social Roles

Networks also provide a source of social identities and social roles that have powerful influences on behavior. Social identity theories, based on the work of Tajfel (1981) and Turner (1978), suggest that when individuals identify with a group, the collective group concept becomes part of their self-concepts. In this process, a redefinition of self emerges and the individual's behaviors tend to become congruent with the group's goals and actions. Threats to social identity can be utilized to motivate individuals to protect their identity. They can also be used to enhance community solidarity. Enhancing a current social identity or providing a new identity can motivate individuals to engage in HIV prevention behaviors and advocacy among network members. It can also be used as a method of social influence. People are more strongly influenced by those with whom they have a shared social identity than by those with whom there is no shared social identity.

Within a given community there are many culturally recognized social roles. In network analysis, social roles can be defined post facto by shared relational attributes, or substitutability of position within a network (Lorrain & White, 1971). By identifying individuals who interact in similar ways to one another, or, in network terms, are "structurally equivalent," network analysis allows for identifying culturally recognized or institutionalized social roles, as well as emergent social roles relevant to health. Conversely, by engaging structurally similar individuals in similar behaviors, and making salient their shared behaviors, it is possible that new social roles and identities may be developed to promote HIV risk reduction.

Through network analysis, social roles that have a high degree of contact with high-risk groups may be identified and targeted for developing HIV interventions. Some of these roles may be a function of social status, local culture or economy, or geographic area. For example, many U.S. inner-city drug users may be involved in the local drug economy (Sherman & Latkin, 2002). These social roles may include needle sellers, touts, drug dealers, lookouts, hit doctors, shooting gallery proprietors, and individuals who hold money or drugs. In other contexts, indigenous healers may be important social roles to target for intervention. As roles vary in social status, popularity, and network centrality, some role types may be more influential in promoting risk reduction than others.

NETWORK-FOCUSED INTERVENTIONS: SELECT EXAMPLES

Using network resource and setting approaches allows one to gather information for developing interventions specific to a particular population and setting. Through network analysis, potential influences on specific risk behaviors of a population can be identified. This information can be used to develop an intervention targeting particular types of individuals to promote risk reduction among certain types of their network ties. While many different intervention implications have been previously mentioned, it is useful to provide select concrete examples representing network-oriented approaches to intervention. These examples, in turn, demonstrate ways to approach the issue of community impact of interventions through interpersonal and normative change and the diffusion of intervention effects.

Altering Network Norms

Social network-oriented approaches to intervention appear to be a promising approach to assessing and altering social norms of HIV risk behaviors. Targeting risk networks for preventive intervention, and focusing on altering their norms of risk behaviors, emphasizes the role of descriptive norms of risk ties in behavior change. Assessment of intervention participants' perceived norms and network members' risk behaviors are methods of assessing change in interventions' effectiveness in altering both proscriptive and descriptive norms, respectively.

The Stop AIDS for Everyone (SAFE) study was a psychoeducational HIV prevention intervention for inner-city African-American injection drug–sharing networks (Latkin, Mandell, Vlahov, Oziemkowska, & Celentano, 1996b). The study used former injection drug users as facilitators of one of two randomly assigned conditions: a six-session, network-focused cognitive-behavioral intervention or a two-session control group consisting of HIV education. The intervention goal was to change the norms of the group. Specifically, the intervention was designed to promote both risk-reduction discussion within the networks and lower the networks' risk behaviors. Results indicated that experimental indexes were significantly more likely than control indexes at the three-month follow-up to report reduction in drug-related HIV risk behaviors. At the 18-month follow-up, HIV-negative index participants in the experimental condition reported significantly less-frequent needle sharing compared to those in the control condition, and less-frequent injecting of heroin and cocaine than in the control condition. The findings suggest that drug risk networks are sufficiently stable to be identified and be the focus of a clinic-based network intervention. The intervention had long-term effectiveness for modifying drug risk behaviors among HIV-negative individuals, and was effective for both clinic- and street-recruited participants.

Network-Oriented Interventions Involving Peers

Peer education approaches and peer outreach advocacy strategies to prevention are based on theories of social influence and have been successfully used with MSM, commercial sex workers, students, drug users, and others at risk for HIV (Agha, 2002; Campbella & MacPhail, 2002; Ford, Wirawan, Suastina, Reed, & Muliawan, 2000; Khoat, West, Valdiserri, & Phan, 2003; Pearlman, Camberg, Wallace, Symons, & Finison, 2002; Smith, Dane, Archer, Devereaux, & Katner, 2000).

Use of peers as agents of intervention may depend on the particular context. For example, where there is little organizational support for behavior change or where there is a lack of clear authority structure with which one can readily intervene, peers may be the most readily available avenue for intervention. Such was the case in our work in an inner-city African-American drug-using community (Latkin, Sherman, & Knowlton, 2003b). Here, formative network research suggested that religious leaders and drug dealers were major authority figures and potential influential others but that these leaders had little influence over risk behaviors. Moreover, there was a lack of consensus among drug users regarding informal leaders in their drug networks. Given the lack of consensus, we used a network-oriented intervention approach to develop a health-advocate role credible to these major authority figures.

The SHIELD (Self Help to Intervene in Eliminating Lethal Diseases) study was a network-oriented intervention that trained individuals in a drug-using community to promote HIV prevention messages and behaviors through their existing networks (Latkin et al., 2003b). Based on social identity and dissonance theories, the training emphasized the social role of health outreach workers. Formative qualitative research suggested that the role of outreach workers was meaningful in religious and drug treatment institutions within the community, and that the role of worker was highly valued in this mostly unemployed population. Participants were randomly assigned to the experimental condition, a multisession, small-group behavioral training in peer HIV prevention outreach, or to the equal attention control condition that focused on family psychodynamics associated with addictions. Those in the outreach condition were encouraged to conduct outreach with family, friends, risk network members, and community contacts. The psychoeducational training emphasized social influence techniques, such as interpersonal communication skills, and sought to maximize potential social rewards for the performance of this role. At the 6-month follow-up, participants in the experimental groups, regardless of HIV serostatus, were more likely to report reduction of injection risk behaviors, increased condom use with casual sex partners, and more frequent HIV prevention conversations with network members compared to individuals in the control group (Latkin et al., 2003b).

While such results are encouraging, not all peer advocacy interventions have been successful (Warwick, Douglas, Aggleton, & Boyce, 2003). One potential reason for this mixed success may be that in designing prevention interventions far greater attention has been paid to questions of who appropriate *peers* are than on questions of who are most *influential* with respect to the particular behaviors among a specific group. In prior interventions, "peer" educators are often defined as those who share one or more attributes with the target population, such as risk behaviors, race or ethnicity, socioeconomic background, gender, or age. Few studies have assessed characteristics of effective peer educators, or specifically, which attributes of "peers" similarity with the target population are associated with effective HIV risk reduction. Network research suggests that to capitalize on social influence processes, it is important to select as health advocates those who are influential from the perspective of the target group. Attributes of influential others may be based on risk behavior, demographic characteristics, or on social role or role relation to the target group. Moreover, this may vary by the social status of the targeted group. For example, among brothel-based commercial sex workers, it may be far more effective to promote risk reduction by intervening with the brothel owner than by targeting sex workers in the absence of the brothel owner's support of risk reduction.

Attention to the role of networks and major sources of social influence within a particular network may improve peer advocacy interventions' ability to capitalize on social influence processes in affecting behavior change. Indeed, many prior peer advocacy interventions, though not designated as network interventions, may incorporate network members and their influential others. For example, school-based interventions targeting youths may include groups of influential peers (Agha, 2002; Kirby, 2002; Smith et al., 2000).

Network Analysis and Identification of Community Change Agents or Opinion Leaders

One strength of network analysis is its potential for empirically identifying influential others. These may be opinion leaders based on the number of ties with other, key individuals who bridge network components, and/or individuals who have ties to influential others. Networks analysis can assist in delineating cliques and subgroups within a community, school or other setting, and the potentially influential members who may serve as "change agents" for facilitating behavior change within the group. This focus on key change agents or opinion leaders has served as a conceptual basis for diffusing promising interventions among members of a specified community.

An opinion leader approach to behavior change has been used for HIV prevention intervention in natural social environments. For example, an opinion leader approach to educating peers on HIV and risk reduction has been successfully applied in an intervention for gay men attending bars in small towns (Kelly et al., 1992). Here, gays bars were selected in urban U.S. settings and bartenders identified as popular and credible sources of information were trained to provide relevant AIDS-related information to customers (Kelly et al., 1992). In these settings, opinion leaders promoted condom use with their peers though discussions of their perceptions of the importance of safer sex.

Kincaid (2000) reported on a family-planning intervention in Bangladesh in which a network-focused intervention was compared to a field peer health worker intervention. In the network condition, family health workers held discussion groups in homes hosted by women who had been identified as the individuals community members sought out for health advice. One of the goals of the meetings was to increase discussion of family planning among women, family members, and spouses. In the comparison condition, the health workers visited the women's individual homes. Results indicated that women in the network intervention were almost twice as likely to report using modern contraceptives compared to those in the control condition (Kincaid, 2000).

Community Impact and Sustainability of Prevention Interventions

The above examples from Kelly and Kincaid draw attention to a central issue related to the community impact of AIDS interventions: sustainability. Sustainability can be thought of in network terms as social diffusion of an innovation or behavior. Social diffusion refers to the spread of an innovation, such as a newly adopted behavior, from individuals to their social network members and the larger networks to which they are linked (Rogers et al., 1999). Diffusion of intervention effects refers to the ability of the intervention to affect behaviors of participants' community members not directly involved in the intervention. In network analysis, social diffusion or participants' potential influence on network members' behaviors can be assessed by recruiting intervention participants' network members and measuring changes in their self-reported risk behaviors and familiarity with intervention messages.

In the field of diffusion of innovation there are well-established methods of introducing behaviors into a community (Kincaid, 2000; Rogers, 1993; Rogers et al., 1999), and such methods have been extensively used in medical, pharmaceutical, and other business sales. New ideas and behaviors have been found to diffuse through existing personal networks by individuals who may be referred to as "innovators," or early adopters of a new behavior. Diffusion of innovation interventions often attempt to identify innovators by their network structure. For example, individuals with high centrality, that is, a high number of ties, within a network, or those rated by many networks members as sources of health information or advice, may be important targets of intervention not only because of their greater potential exposure of their ties but also because they may be important sources of social influence on network members. Highly central individuals have been termed "opinion leaders."

Other aspects of network structure are also thought to influence diffusion and sustainability of interventions. Highly dense or isolated networks are more likely to sustain behavior change; however, there is likely to be less diffusion of behavior change from these networks to other networks. In addition to network density, network stability may mediate intervention impact and sustainability. For example, in networks that are less stable, new behaviors that are introduced may quickly dissipate. Network interventions may also work to alter the structure of the network by shifting the ties of individuals who may be bridges between groups. Altering the network structure may reduce the possibility of HIV transmission between network components. Another approach is to form new networks that are less prone to transmission due to their norms and structures.

Future research is needed to investigate not only who in the network to target but also how many network members should be targeted for intervention, that is, the critical mass for sustaining behavior change. Once these network members are identified, interventionists also need to consider the relative value of altering social roles, risk perceptions, skills, network structure, and network function.

Sustainability and Social Roles

Sustainability of intervention effects can also be promoted by designing interventions that develop or promote social roles that are sustainable by the community. Sustainability of social roles may be promoted through institutionalizing targeted social roles, for example through labeling, rewarding, and making salient a desired social role. HIV prevention may also be promoted by introducing social roles that may potentially be reinforced through incurring social rewards from community members. Roles are more likely to be sustained if they are meaningful and include positive aspects of self-identity that are congruent with the role. Individuals actively work to maintain positive self-identities. Therefore, one approach to sustaining interventions is to enhance individuals' self-concepts in ways that are congruent with health promoting behaviors. If the identity is congruent with individual- or group-level risk reduction, then individuals with this identity will work to maintain the identity and the risk reduction associated with it.

Social identities are identities linked to a group. The group's behavior and activities are perceived as important to individuals' self-concepts. Thus, for example, successes by the group are seen as individual achievements. If HIV prevention is seen as an important component of a group identity, then individuals may promote risk reduction in an effort to maintain this social identity. For example, if HIV prevention is seen as vital to the group's survival or if being a peer health advocate is perceived as a valued group role then the social identify provided by group membership may result is risk reduction.

The diffusion of innovation literature also suggests that certain types of innovations or behaviors are more readily adopted and spread than others. Behaviors readily adopted tend to be those that are public, easy to perform, and the benefits of which are quickly realized. With HIV prevention, the behaviors of interest often are not public, safer practices may require resources (e.g., condoms, clean needles) often not available, and the outcome of not becoming infected is abstract and not quickly realized. The modeling of safer behaviors that are public, such as refusing to share needles, may diffuse through networks and lead to community-level risk reduction. But more private behaviors, such as condom use among drug users, are unlikely to be diffused through modeling. These behaviors are often changed through interpersonal communication.

Diffusion as Discourse

In linguistic terms, networks can be considered the channels through which intervention messages diffuse and mutate. Network structures, therefore, may promote or inhibit the diffusion and mutation of messages. In small-group interventions, stories may be told as examples of the application of skills or information to behavior change. Assessing which stories may die out, which quickly spread, and how they may mutate in their telling through a network may provide insight into stories or myths that may help sustain behavior change through their promotion of new self-concepts or identities.

To effectively diffuse stories through networks, research suggests it is important to utilize images, phrases, metaphors, and stories that can be easily told to network members. Gossip has intrinsic proprieties that promote rapid diffusion, but it may be distorted as it passes among individuals (Rosnow, 1998). The use of metaphors and similes, on the other hand, offers the advantage of allowing for the introduction of new concepts that can be linked to images that are easily accessible and have common understandings within a certain community. For example, statements such as "needle sharing is like sharing tooth brushes" or "condoms are sexy" can be used to change the meanings of risk and risk reduction behaviors.

In developing new discourses for HIV prevention, network analysis can assist in deciding who is the most appropriate audience for a certain type of message and which network members would be most receptive to a new discourse. For example, a goal of discourse on condoms is to alter the meaning of condoms to overcome barriers to their use. It is usually easier to alter commonly ascribed meanings with new network members or one with whom the meaning is not already deeply circumscribed.

Discourses are also a function of role relationship. Condom use in a long-term primary relationship may require a completely different discourse compared to introducing condoms into a new relationship. Yet, a focus on discourse is important because these discourses or stories may become diffused within networks and through the community and become commonly shared stories and meanings. The stories and meanings then become available for individuals to utilize in their own HIV prevention activities.

Virtual Networks

The Internet is now a common venue for meeting new sex partners, acquiring information about HIV/STIs, and potentially for risk-behavior change (Hospers, Harterink, Van Den Hoek, & Veenstra, 2002). There are several potential approaches to Internet HIV prevention. One approach would be to identify and train key individuals as measured by network centrality, betweenness, and group affiliation. Such identifications could be made in chat rooms. A second approach would be to use the Internet to assist in altering the structure of risk networks. Among Internet sites that serve as sexual matching services, high-risk individuals could be dissuaded from joining low-risk networks. Moreover, health education materials could be tailored to individuals' risk behaviors and their network characteristics.

There are ethical issues that may arise from such interventions. For example, matching partners on risk level may reduce the network-level risk and lead to lower HIV/STI incidence, but for some network members it may increase individual-level risk. The growth in the use of the Internet for partner selection highlights the importance of HIV prevention programs adapting to a changing social environment. Sustainability is not just a result of picking the right intervention but also adapting interventions to changing social conditions.

CONCLUSIONS

We must redouble our prevention efforts by utilizing more-appropriate theories and methods to alter the essentially social behaviors that drive the HIV pandemic. Our social interactions are the sea of our existence, defining who we are and what we do. Because our social world is all encompassing and because of our individualistic bias in Western societies, we tend to overlook or discount the role of social ties in influencing behavior change. Moreover, in research, our implicitly static models of community and social structure lead us to assume that social structural factors are not amenable to intervention.

Network and behavioral setting analyses offer dynamic, culturally specific models of community that may contribute to a deeper understanding of the role of social ties in HIV risk and prevention. Application of network analysis and operationalization of concepts of referent others, social identities, social roles, norms, behavioral settings, and social diffusion of innovation, may be used to develop effective HIV prevention intervention tailored to a population's context. Such approaches to HIV intervention draw attention to the everyday social interactions that imbue the meanings and ends to which sex and drug risk behaviors are engaged, and that form the structural basis of HIV risk and transmission.

Network- and behavioral-setting analyses allows for delineation of interactions, sampling risk groups, community social structures and sources of influence, and networks that can be harnessed for changing behaviors. Greater attention to networks not only as channels of disease transmission but also as channels of resource exchange, information dissemination, and potential social influence may contribute to the development of more powerful approaches to HIV prevention that affect individuals, as well as communities of individuals.

Systematic, longitudinal analysis of naturally occurring personal and social networks, beyond just risk networks, are important for contributing to our understanding of how networks within a particular culture or subculture change over time, how ties form and dissolve, and how these individual-level changes lead to changes in the structure of the larger network. Such information may inform appropriate strategies of network-oriented HIV prevention intervention in several ways. For example, they may explain how some populations are able to successfully adapt to health risks, develop new social roles, alter the cultural value of a particular resource, or redefine norms of resource exchange in response to HIV in ways that do not compromise their ability to obtain resources to meet basic needs. Further research is needed to understand how behavioral settings interact with networks, how to identify appropriate settings for network interventions, how to identify key structural elements and social roles within networks for interventions, and the scope and duration of network interventions necessary to achieve norm change and sustained risk reduction at the community level.

ACKNOWLEDGMENTS This chapter was supported Grants from NIDA and NIMH. We thank Melissa Davey for her assistance in writing this chapter.

REFERENCES

Abelson, R. (1981). Psychological status of the script concept. *American Psychologist, 36*, 715–729.

Agha, S. (2002). An evaluation of the effectiveness of a peer sexual health intervention among secondary-school students in Zambia. *AIDS Education and Prevention, 14*, 269–281.

Aitken, P. P. (1985). An observational study of young adults' drinking groups–2. Drink purchasing procedures, group pressures and alcohol consumption by companions as predictors of alcohol consumption. *Alcohol, 20*, 445–457.

Barker, R. (1978). *Habits, environments, and human behavior.* San Francisco: Jossey-Bass.

Barker, R. & Wright, H. F. (1955). *Midwest and its children.* New York: Harper and Row.

Berger, P. & Luckmann, T. (1967). *The social construction of reality.* Garden City, NY: Anchor.

Berkman, L. F., Glass, T., Brissette, I., & Seeman, T. E. (2000). From social integration to health: Durkheim in the new millennium. *Social Science and Medicine, 51*, 843–857.

Bott, E. (1957). Urban families: Conjugal roles and social networks. *Human Relations, 8*, 345–384.

Bourdieu, P., & Delsaut, Y. (1981). Towards a sociology of the perception. *Actes De La Recherche En Sciences Sociales, 40*, 3–9.

Bourgois, P. I. (1998). The moral economies of homeless heroin addicts: Confronting ethnography, HIV risk, and everyday violence in San Francisco shooting encampments. *Substance Use and Misuse, 33*, 2323–2351.

Brewer, D. D. (2000). Forgetting in the recall-based elicitation of personal and social networks. *Social Networks, 22*, 29–43.

Broadhead, R. S. & Heckathorn, D. D. (1994). AIDS prevention outreach among injection drug users; agency problems and new approaches. *Social Problems, 41*, 472–495.

Campbella, C. & MacPhail, C. (2002). Peer education, gender and the development of critical consciousness: Participatory HIV prevention by South African youth. *Social Science and Medicine, 55*, 331–345.

Carlson, R. G., Siegal, H. A., & Falck, R. S. (1994). Ethnography, epidemiology, and public policy: Needle-use practices and HIV-1 risk reduction among injecting drug users in the Midwest. In D. A. Feldman (Ed.), *Global AIDS policy* (pp. 185–214). Westport, CT: Bergin & Garvey/Greenwood.

Catania, J. A., Binson, D., & Stone, V. (1996). Relationship of sexual mixing across age and ethnic groups to herpes simplex virus-2 among unmarried heterosexual adults with multiple sexual partners. *Health Psychology, 15,* 362–370.

Celetano, D., Vlahov, D., Cohn, S., & Anthony, J. C. (1991). Risk factors for shooting gallery use and cessation among intravenous drug users. *American Journal of Public Health, 81,* 1291–1295.

Coleman, J. S. (1990). *Foundations of Social Theory.* Chicago, IL: University of Chicago Press.

Curran, P. J., Muthen, B. O., & Harford, T. C. (1998). The influence of changes in marital status on developmental trajectories of alcohol use in young adults. *Journal of Studies on Alcohol, 59,* 647–658.

Dearing, J. W., Meyer, G., & Rogers, E. M. (1994). Diffusion theory and HIV risk behavior change. In R. J. Diclemente & J. Peterson (Eds.), *Preventing AIDS: Theories and methods of behavioral interventions.* (pp. 79–93). New York: Plenum Press.

Des Jarlais, D. C., Friedman, S. R., Friedmann, P., Wenston, J., Sotheran, J. L., Choopanya, K., et al. (1995). HIV/AIDS-related behavior change among injecting drug users in different national settings. *AIDS, 9,* 611–617.

Diclemente, R. J., Wingood, G. M., Crosby, R. A., Sionean, C., Cobb, B., Harrington, K., et al. (2002). Sexual risk behaviors associated with having older sex partners: A study of black adolescent females. *Sexually Transmitted Diseases, 29,* 20–24.

Dunkel-Schetter, C. & Bennett, T. L. (1990). Differentiating the cognitive and behavioral aspects of social support. In B. R. Sarason, I. G. Sarason, & G. R. Pierce (Eds.), *Social support: An interactional view* (pp. 267–296). New York: Wiley.

Edwards, J., Tindale, R. S., Heath, L., & Posavac, E. J. (1990). Applying Social influence processes in preventing social problems. New York: Plenum Press.

Festinger, L. (1954). A theory of social comparison processes. *Human Relations, 7,* 117–140.

Fiore, J., Becker, J., & Copple, D. (1983). Social network interactions: A buffer or a stress. *American Journal of Community Psychology, 11,* 423–439.

Fisher, J. D. (1988). Possible effects of reference group-based social influence on AIDS-risk behavior and AIDS-prevention. Special Issue: Psychology and AIDS. *American Psychologist, 43,* 914–920.

Fisher, J. D., Goff, B. A., Nadler, A., & Chinsky, J. M. (1988). Social psychological influences on help seeking and support from peers. In B. H. Gottlieb (Ed.), *Marshaling social support: Formats, processes, and effects* (pp. 267–304). Thousand Oaks, CA: Sage.

Ford, K., Sohn, W., & Lepkowski, J. (2002). American adolescents: Sexual mixing patterns, bridge partners, concurrency. *Sexually Transmitted Diseases, 29,* 13–19.

Ford, K., Wirawan, D., Suastina, S., Reed, B., & Muliawan, P. (2000). Evaluation of a peer education programme for female sex workers in Bali, Indonesia. *International Journal of STDs and AIDS, 11,* 731–733.

Forgas, J. (1979). *Social episodes: The study of interaction routines.* New York: Academic.

Friedkin, N. E. (1990). Social networks in structural equation models. *Social Psychology Quarterly, 53,* 316–328.

Friedman, S. R., DeJong, W., & Wodak, A. (1993). Community Development as a response to HIV among drug injectors. *AIDS, 7,* S263–S269.

Friedman, S. R., Des Jarlais, D. C., Sotheran, J. L., Garber, J., Cohen, H., & Smith, D. (1987). AIDS and self-organization among intravenous drug users. *International Journal of the Addictions, 22,* 201–219.

Friedman, S. R., Neaigus, A., Jose, B., Curtis, R., Goldstein, M., Ildefonso, G., et al. (1997). Sociometric risk networks and risk for HIV infection. *American Journal of Public Health, 87,* 1289–1296.

Galaskiewicz, J. & Marsella, A. (1978). Interorganizational Resource Networks: Formal Patterns of Overlap. *Social Work Research and Abstracts, 7,* 89–107.

Giddens, A. (1987). Time and space in social theory. *Social Science, 72,* 99–103.

Hall, A. & Wellman, B. (1985). Social networks and social support. In S. Cohen & L. Syme (Eds.), *Social support and health.* New York, NY: Academic Press.

Hobfoll, S. E. (2001). The influence of culture, community, and the nested-self in the stress process: Advancing conservation of resources theory. *Applied Psychology: An International Review, 50,* 337–421.

Hospers, H. J., Harterink, P., Van Den Hoek, K., & Veenstra, J. (2002). Chatters on the Internet: A special target group for HIV prevention. *AIDS Care, 14,* 539–544.

House, J. S., Umberson, D., & Landis, K. R. (1988). Structures and Processes of Social Support. *Annual Review of Sociology, 14,* 293–318.

Hyman, H. H. & Singer, E. (1968). Introduction. In H. H. Hyman & E. Singer (Eds.), *Readings in reference group theory and research* (pp. 3–20). New York: Free Press.

Kalichman, S. C., Kelly, J. A., & Stevenson, L. Y. (1997). Priming effects of HIV risk assessments on related perceptions and behavior: An experimental field study. *AIDS and Behavior, 1,* 3–8.

Kasarda, J. & Janowitz, M. (1974). Community Attachment in Mass Society. *American Sociological Review, 39,* 328–339.

Kelly, J. A., St. Lawrence, J. S., Stevenson, L. Y., Hauth, A. C., Kalichman, S. C., Diaz, Y. E., et al. (1992). Community AIDS/HIV risk reduction: The effects of endorsements by popular people in three cities. *American Journal of Public Health, 82,* 1483–1489.

Khoat, D., West, G., Valdiserri, R. O., & Phan, N. (2003). Peer education for HIV prevention in the socialist republic of Vietnam: A national assessment. *Journal of Community Health, 28,* 1–17.

Kincaid, D. L. (2000). Social networks, ideation, and contraceptive behavior in Bangladesh: A longitudinal analysis. *Social Science and Medicine, 50,* 215–231.

Kirby, D. (2002). The impact of schools and school programs upon adolescent sexual behaviors. *Journal of Sex Research, 39,* 27–33.

Klovdahl, A. S. (1989). Urban social networks: Some methodological problems and possibilities. In M. Kochen (Ed.), *The small world* (pp. 176–210). Norwood, NJ: ABLEX.

Klovdahl, S., Graviss, E. A., Yaganehdoost, A., Ross, M. W., Wanger, A., Adams, G. J., et al. (2001). Networks and tuberculosis: An undetected community outbreak involving public places. *Social Science and Medicine, 52,* 681–694.

Klovdahl, A. S., Potterat, J. J., Woodhouse, D. E., Muth, J. B., Muth, S. Q., & Darrow, W. W. (1994). Social networks and infectious disease: The Colorado Springs Study. *Social Science and Medicine, 38,* 79–88.

Latkin, C. A., Forman, V., Knowlton, A., & Sherman, S. (2003a). Norms, social networks, and HIV-related risk behaviors among urban disadvantages drug users. *Social Science and Medicine, 56,* 465–476.

Latkin, C. A. & Knowlton, A. R. (2000). New directions in HIV prevention among drug users: Settings, norms, and network approaches to AIDS prevention (SNNAAP): A social influence approach. *Advances in Medical Sociology, 7,* 261–287.

Latkin, C. A., Mandell, W., Knowlton, A. R., Doherty, M. C., Vlahov, D., Suh, T., et al. (1998). Gender differences in injection-related behaviors among injection drug users in Baltimore, Maryland. *AIDS Education and Prevention, 10,* 257–263.

Latkin, C. A., Mandell, W., & Vlahov, D. (1996). The relationship between risk network patterns of crack cocaine and alcohol consumption and HIV-related sexual behaviors among adult injection drug users: A prospective study. *Drug and Alcohol Dependence, 42,* 175–181.

Latkin, C. A., Mandell, W., Vlahov, D., Oziemkowska, M., & Celentano, D. A. (1996a). People and places: Behavioral settings and personal network characteristics as correlates of needle sharing. *Journal of Acquired Immunodeficiency Syndromes and Human Retrovirology, 13,* 273–280.

Latkin, C. A., Mandell, W., Vlahov, D., Oziemkowska, M., & Celentano, D. A. (1996b). The long-term outcomes of a personal network-oriented HIV prevention intervention for injection drug users: The SAFE study. *American Journal of Community Psychology, 24,* 109–121.

Latkin, C. A., Sherman, S., & Knowlton, A. (2003b). HIV prevention among drug users: outcome of a network-oriented peer outreach intervention. *Health Psychology, 22,* 332–339.

Laumann, E. & Franzoi, S. L. (1976). *Networks of collective action: A perspective on community influence systems.* New York: Academic.

Lorrain, F. & White, H. (1971). Structural equivalence of individuals in social networks. *Journal of Mathematical Sociology, 1,* 49–80.

Marsden, P. V. (1990). Network data and measurement. *Annual Review of Sociology, 16,* 435–463.

McManus, T. J. & Coxon, A. P. (1995). Sexual behaviour of men. Review mis-stated prevalence of anal intercourse [letter]. *British Medical Journal, 311,* 1163.

Merton, R. K. & Kitt, A. S. (1950). Contributions to the theory of reference group behavior. In R. Merton & P. F. Lazarsfeld (Eds.), *Continuities in social research: Studies in the scope and method of the "The American Soldier"* (pp. 40–105). Glencoe, IL: Free Press.

Mitchell, J. (1969). *Social networks in urban situations.* Manchester Press: University Press.

Morris, M. & Kretzschmar, M. (1995). Concurrent partnerships and transmission dynamics in networks. *Social Networks, 17,* 299–318.

Myers, G. P. (1985). *Social Psychology.* New York: McGraw-Hill.

Newcomb, T. M. (1958). Attitude development as a function of reference groups: The Bennington study. In E. Maccoby, T. Newcomb, & E. Hartley (Eds.), *Readings in social psychology* (pp. 265–275). New York: Holt.

Organista, K. C., Organista, P. B., Bola, J. R., Garcia de Alba, J. E., & Castillo Moran, M. A. (2000). Predictors of condom use in Mexican migrant laborers. *American Journal of Community Psychology, 28,* 245–265.

Pattison, P. (1994). Social cognition in context: Some applications of social network analysis. J. Galaskiewicz & S. Wasserman (Eds.), *Advances in social network analysis: Research in the social and behavioral sciences* (pp. 79–109). Thousand Oaks, CA: Sage.

Pearlman, D., Camberg, L., Wallace, LJ., Symons, P., & Finison, L. (2002). Tapping youths as agents for change: Evaluation of a peer leadership HIV/AIDS intervention. *Journal of Adolescent Health, 31,* 31–39.

Pivnick, A., Jacobson, A., Eric, K., Doll, L., & Drucker, E. (1994). AIDS, HIV infection, and illicit drug use within inner-city families and social networks. *American Journal of Public Health, 84,* 271–274.

Renton, A., Whitaker, L., Ison, C., Wadsworth, J., & Harris, J. (1995). Estimating the sexual mixing patterns in the general population from those in people acquiring gonorrhea infection: Theoretical foundation and empirical findings. *Journal of Epidemiology and Community Health, 49*(2), 205–213.

Rogers, E. M. (1993). Diffusion and re-invention of Project D.A.R.E. In T. Backer & E. Rogers (Eds.), *Organizational aspects of health communication campaigns: What works?* (pp. 139–162). Thousand Oaks, CA: Sage.

Rogers, E. M. (2003). *Diffusion of innovations* (5th ed.). New York: Free Press.

Rogers, E. M., Vaughan, P. W., Swalehe, R. M., Rao, N., Svenkerud, P., & Sood, S. (1999). Effects of an entertainment-education radio soap opera on family planning behavior in Tanzania. *Studies in Family Planning, 30,* 193–211.

Rook, K. S. (1984). The negative side of social interaction: Impact on psychological well-being. *Journal of Personality and Social Psychology, 46,* 1097–1108.

Rosnow, R. (1998). Rumor as communication: A contextualist approach. *Journal of Communication, 38,* 12–28.

Rothenberg, R. B., Potterat, J. J., Woodhouse, D. E., Muth, S. Q., Darrow, W. W., & Klovdahl, A. S. (1998). Social network dynamics and HIV transmission. *AIDS, 12,* 1529–1536.

Service, S. K. & Blower, S. M. (1995). HIV transmission in sexual networks: An empirical analysis. *Proceedings of the Royal Society of London, Series A, Containing papers of a mathematical and physical character, 260,* 237–244.

Sherman, S. G. & Latkin, C. A. (2001). Intimate relationship characteristics associated with condom use among drug users and their sex partners: A multilevel analysis. *Drug and Alcohol Dependence, 64,* 97–104.

Sherman, S. & Latkin, C. A. (2002). Drug users' involvement in the drug economy: Implications for harm reduction and HIV prevention programs. *Journal of Urban Health, 79,* 266–277.

Simpson, D., Camacho, L. M., Vogtsberger, K. N., & Williams M. L. (1994). Reducing AIDS risks through community outreach interventions for drug injectors. *Psychology of Addictive Behaviors, 8,* 86–101.

Smith, M., Dane, F., Archer, M., Devereaux, R., & Katner, H. (2000). Students together against negative decisions (STAND): Evaluation of a school-based sexual risk reduction intervention in rural south. *AIDS Education and Prevention, 12,* 49–70.

Stack, C. (1974). *All our kin: Strategies for survival in a black community.* New York: Harper and Row.

Stoner, B. P., Whittington, W. L., Hughes, J. P., Aral, S. O., & Holmes, K. K. (2000). Comparative epidemiology of heterosexual gonococcal and chlamydial networks: Implications for transmission patterns. *Sexually Transmitted Diseases, 27,* 215–223.

Tajfel, H. (1981). *Human groups and social categories: Studies in social psychology.* New York: Cambridge University Press.

Trotter, R. T., 2nd, Bowen, A. M., & Potter, J. M. (1995). Network models for HIV outreach and prevention programs for drug users. *NIDA Research Monograph, 151,* 144–180.

Turner, H. A., Pearlin, L. I., & Mullan, J. T. (1998). Sources and determinants of social support for caregivers of persons with AIDS. *Journal of Health and Social Behavior, 39,* 137–151.

Turner, J. C. (1978). Social comparison and social identity: Some perspectives for intergroup behavior. *European Journal of Social Psychology, 5,* 5–34.

Valleroy, L., MacKellar, D., Karon, J., Rosen, D., McFarland, W., Shehan, D., et al. (2000). HIV prevalence and associated risks in young men who have sex with men. Youth Men's Survey Study Group. *Journal of the American Medical Association, 284,* 198–204.

Warwick, I., Douglas, N., Aggleton, P., & Boyce, P. (2003). Context matters: The educational potential of gay bars revisited. *AIDS Education and Prevention, 14,* 320–333.

Weir, S., Pailman, C., Mahlalela, X., Coetzee, N., Meidany, F., & Boerma, J. (2003). From people to places: Focusing AIDS prevention efforts where it matters most. *AIDS, 17,* 895–903.

Wellman, B. (1981). Applying network analysis to the study of support. In B. H. Gottlieb (Ed.), *Social networks and social support* (pp. 171–200). Beverly Hills, CA: Sage.

White, H. (1992). Strategy and Choice. *Contemporary Sociology, 21,* 838–840.

Wicker, A. (1987). Temporal stages, resources, internal dynamics, and context. In D. Stokols & I. Altman (Eds.), *Handbook of environmental psychology.* New York: Wiley.

Woodhouse, D. E., Rothenberg, R. B., Potterat, J. J., Darrow, W. W., Muth, S. Q., Klovdahl, A. S., et al. (1994). Mapping a social network of heterosexuals at high risk for HIV infection. *AIDS, 8,* 1331–1336.

6

Rapid Assessment Strategies for Public Health: Promise and Problems

Robert T. Trotter, II & Merrill Singer

INTRODUCTION

We are going through a period of increased institutional enthusiasm for rapid ethnographic assessment in both the national and international public health arenas. Rapid assessment is being actively promoted as a direct, fast, easy, and community-controlled process that will solve crucial time sensitive problems for HIV and AIDS programs in both developing countries and hard-to-reach populations in the developed world. This chapter discusses rapid ethnographic assessment in HIV research. Nearly 15 years of application have produced successes along with concerns and some partial-to-complete failures. The chapter takes a critical look at the most recent design and application of HIV related rapid ethnographic assessment and provides a model and examples of the key points of failure of rapid-assessment programs. The perspective developed in the chapter is that rapid assessment offers a potentially valuable approach for effective, community/researcher collaboration in applied AIDS research.

THE EMERGENCE OF RAPID ASSESSMENT

Rapid ethnographic assessment is a logical extension of broader, more traditional ethnographic research, utilizing advances in theory, systematic methods, and a growing enthusiasm for the involvement of local communities in public health research, planning, intervention, and action. Rapid assessment was first formally named and described in the mid '80s (Scrimshaw et al., 1987, 1991; Scrimshaw, Nevin, and Gleason, 1992; Bentley et al., 1988), along with other rapid-assessment and evaluation models, such as rural rapid appraisal and participatory action research, developed at about the same time (Bebe, 1995; Chambers, 1992; Heaver, 1991; Kachondham, 1992; Park, 1999; Price, 1990; Whyte, 1995). Rapid-assessment techniques rely on targeted ethnographic data collection and analysis (qualitative interviewing and direct observation), complemented by survey information and secondary data analysis. From inception, it has utilized anthropological theory coupled with extensive local cultural knowledge and involvement. (Scrimshaw, Carballo, and Hurtado, 1987; Bentley et al., 1988).

Rapid assessment is amenable to exploring the cultural epidemiology of single diseases, as well as broad community health profiles. It is used both as a substitute for survey and other quantitative data collection processes and as a compliment to existing data sets and data systems. It is valuable in targeting conditions and contexts that are more highly concentrated than those identified by normal surveillance and epidemiological efforts. It provides information for spotting emerging conditions that are not yet visible in other data sets (e.g., new epidemics) and allows for the development of interventions successfully adapted for local contexts, especially where local cultural conditions and values differ from the dominant cultural system. In addition, rapid assessment is designed to shorten the gap between research for specific programmatic purposes and the implementation of sound intervention strategies, emphasizing the adaptation of interventions to local cultures and conditions (Scrimshaw, Nevin, and Gleason, 1992; Trotter and Needle, 1999).

An additional strength is that rapid assessment and response strategies are organized around the involvement of the community in planning and conducting the assessment, accessing the data, and interpreting and using it for planning interventions. The purpose of combining rapid assessment with community response development has been to improve both the methods and the linkage of those methods to community-based interventions and program developments (Trotter and Needle, 1999; Needle et al., 2003). Properly used, this approach helps to address some of the distrust and resistance to participating in public health programs encountered in racial and ethnic minority communities. This distrust is a legacy of the ethical failures of earlier research in those communities. These failures include the Tuskegee Syphilis Study and the labeling and stigmatizing of Haitians as a "risk group" in 1983-1984, both of which remain a critical part of the collective consciousness in many communities of color. Designating Haitians as a risk group on the basis of national origin rather than focusing on risk behavior was very harmful to the Haitian community and was subsequently stopped by the Centers for Disease Control (CDC) in 1985. By being conducted in the community, by community members, and for purposes that are acceptable to the local community, rapid assessment represents one possible antidote to these historical sources of community distrust and suspicion.

In general, rapid ethnographic assessment offers an intervention rational that is simultaneously scientific, logistical and political. The process is relatively inexpensive in comparison with survey research, is responsive to collecting locally relevant data about emerging patterns of risk behaviors, provides a philosophical and ethical rationale for local control of research and findings, offers a practical model for research/community collaboration, and can be done relatively rapidly when compared to other forms of social science policy and planning research.

Scope of Rapid Assessment

In recent years, rapid-assessment projects have produced data directed at addressing a wide range of social problems and issues. These include family planning, malaria, diarrheal disease, dengue fever, and water sanitation, (Almedon, Blumenthal, and Manderson, 1997; Askew et al., 1993; Ayepong, Bertha, Dzikunu, and Manderson, 1995) disaster intervention (Malilay, Flanders, and Brogan, 1997), disabilities research (Trotter, Needle, et al., 2001), pregnant women and sexually transmitted disease in Thailand (Kilmarx et al., 1996), family planning in Burkina Faso (Askew et al., 1993) preschool children exposed to pesticides in Mexico (Guillette, Mercedes, Guadalupe, Soto, and Enedina, 1998), and injection drug use in Vietnam (Power, 1996).

Rapid-assessment strategies are increasingly employed to design community level responses to HIV/AIDS around the world. They have been employed to design community level responses to deal with STD and HIV prevention in Turkey (Aral and Fransen, 1995) and HIV research among young people in Cambodia (Tarr and Aggleton, 1999).[1] In addition, the World Health Organization (WHO), Joint United Nations Programme on HIV/AIDS (UNAIDS) (WHO 1998), and Doctors Without Borders (Medicins sans frontiers) recently conducted rapid assessments in Eastern Europe, Russia, and the newly independent states (WHO 1998; Rhodes, Ball, et al., 1999; Rhodes, Stimson, Fitch, Ball, and Renton, 1999). Their focus was the cooccurring and explosive epidemics of injection drug use and HIV that affect noninjection users, commercial sex workers, and their clients as well. In resource poor countries in particular, WHO and other authorities have often chosen rapid-assessment methodologies to create critical data bases, in part because the process is responsive to collecting locally relevant data about emerging patterns of risk behaviors quickly and relatively inexpensively.

In the United States and Western Europe, rapid-assessment strategies have complemented ongoing national and regional epidemiological data and surveillance systems focused on identifying, enumerating, and monitoring "risk or exposure groups", transmission routes, and determinants and distribution of risk behaviors, by developing data that are more time and micro-epidemic sensitive than conventional systems alone. Scrimshaw et al. (Scrimshaw et al., 1991) provided an early design model for HIV/AIDS rapid-assessment studies directed at health education needs in hard-to-reach communities. Following that lead, an extensive qualitative or ethnographic research tradition in the United States grew in response to AIDS, primarily focused on conducting ethnographic studies on hidden populations (Trotter, 1996; Marshall, Singer, and Clatts, 1999; Singer, 1999). More recently, both the National Institutes of Health and the Department of Health and Human Services have either recommended or actually implemented rapid ethnographic assessment projects in the United States (Needle et al., 2000; Trotter, Needle, et al., 2001) to address emerging or changing health problems in more broadly based community efforts.

Overall, then, rapid-assessment strategies have the potential to lead to early identification and understanding of rapidly emerging risk behavior patterns and the changing dynamics of epidemics, particularly in hidden, hard-to-reach, marginalized and stigmatized populations. In addition, they shorten the gap between research for specific programmatic purposes and the implementation of sound intervention strategies, emphasizing the adaptation of practical, feasible, low-cost interventions to local cultures and conditions (Manderson and Aaby, 1992). This combined national and locally responsive approach enhances the capacity of resource-challenged countries (at the international level), or highly impacted communities, (nationally) to respond to increasing numbers of HIV/AIDS cases and persons living with HIV/ AIDS, regardless of the limitations on their existing infrastructures.

Critiques and Responses

While rapid assessment is growing as a community level intervention methodology, it is also consistently controversial and consistently revitalized. Some social scientists, including traditional ethnographers, attack this paradigm with reasonable critiques of the methodological underpinnings of rapid assessment. These critiques generally focus on the limited time (hasty research, hasty conclusions), limited or biased qualitative samples (incomplete data leading to incorrect conclusions), or poorly constructed questions showing researcher bias. However, many more attacks are thinly reasoned polemics by researchers who are opposed to qualitative research in general, or rapid assessment in particular. The well-constructed critiques have produced a number of healthy and beneficial methodological discussions (Harris, Jerome, and Fawcett, 1997; Kachondham, 1992; Nordberg et al., 1993; Manderson and Aaby, 1992; Lambert, 1998; Schwartz, Molnar, and Lovshin, 1988; Vakil, 1994) and consistent improvement in project design and analytical procedures, such as improved sampling procedures. The poorly reasoned attacks have mostly wasted valuable journal space.

THE NEW RAPID-ASSESSMENT METHODS MIXES

The current synthetic view of rapid assessment promulgates six key design elements that address both types of critique mentioned above. These include (1) using appropriate qualitative and quantitative sampling frames and sample sizes to provide valid and reliable data; (2) using an integrated suite of methods to provide appropriate triangulation of data (i.e., confirmation from multiple methods, and multiple informants that identify all critical cultural viewpoints and confirm identified themes, patterns, or relationships across data collection methods); (3) sound and systematic qualitative data analysis; (4) appropriate community participation; (5) an evaluation component to determine the impact of the project; and (6) a built-in collaborative mechanism for the translation of findings into community responses. Each of these areas is bolstered by strong and steady methodological progress appearing in the ethnographic methods literature (Bernard, 1998; Schensul and Schensul, 1998).

The core rapid-assessment methods include ethnographic qualitative interviews (predominantly focus group and cultural expert interviews), direct observations, mapping, and some form of rapid-assessment surveys (from household surveys to street intercepts) containing both qualitative and quantitative questions (cf. Stimson et al., 1999; Rhodes, Stimson, et al., 1999; Trotter and Needle, 1999). The high-quality rapid-assessment projects also include supplemental methods where needed. The most common are systematic data collection techniques focused on knowledge and beliefs (Weller and Romney, 1988), life history analysis (Woodhouse, 1990), advanced elicitation and audiovisual methods (Schensul and LeCompte, 1999), and social network data collection (Trotter and Needle, 1999; Trotter and Schensul, 1998). The mix varies somewhat in response to the question that is being explored, the cultural context of the issue, and the types of applications that are expected from the project (Trotter and Schensul, 1998; Trotter, 1997).

The core rapid-assessment methods achieved their status for three reasons. First, they cover all of the primary data needs for most rapid-assessment projects, allowing for quick turn around of intervention recommendations for the community decision-making process. Second, they produce data that are summarized in the form of high impact quotes, maps, pictures, and summaries in clear language that can be understood by all of the parties involved. There is no obfuscation by professional jargon or concern over statistical sophistication. Third, they allow for clear triangulation using multiple methods that provide complimentary data for each domain, within a scientifically defensible framework.

These methods focus the data collection on a basic set of questions (cultural domains) that need to be explored to establish appropriate public health interventions (Trotter and Schensul, 1998). Salient domains include community beliefs and knowledge about the specific health or other issues of primary concern, risk taking and health seeking behaviors within vulnerable groups and the community, and cultural and physical contexts in which risk and other behaviors of interest unfold. These are supplemented by information on language use, cultural symbolism, and communication, to establish culturally appropriate interventions. The following methods and cultural domains matrix (Table 6.1) identifies the ways in which the core methods provide triangulation of information within this paradigm.

DESTRUCTION POINTS FOR RAPID-ASSESSMENT PROGRAMS

When the combination of design elements, appropriate methods mixes, and well-trained/experienced personnel come together, the result is a successful rapid-assessment project. Failure in one of these elements produces partial to complete disaster. There are seven primary destruction points for rapid assessment. These are conditions that potentially degrade the quality or defensibility of the rapid-assessment data that constitute the evidence

Table 6.1 Domains and Methods Matrix

	Domains			
Methods	Beliefs, Knowledge Values	Activities and Actions	Physical Context and Structure	Symbols, Language and Communication
Key Informant Interviews	Yes	Yes	Yes	Yes
Focus Groups	Yes	Yes	Yes	Yes
Mapping		Yes	Yes	
Direct Observation	Yes	Yes	Yes	Yes
Rapid Surveys and Short Street Interviews	Yes	Yes	Yes	Yes
Natural Language and communication exploration	Yes	Yes		Yes

for recommendations and programmatic changes. The points include 1) poor design; 2) incorrect qualitative sampling; 3) an inappropriate methods mixture; 4) inadequate personnel; 5) critical failures in the model for or use of community participation; 6) implementation issues; and 7) logistics and administrative support.

(1) Design Choices and Threats

There are several primary dangers to sound rapid-assessment design. They include poor initial targeting of the rapid-assessment research, local agendas overwhelming the research design, too broad a research agenda that makes the research goals impossible to accomplish, and inadequate resources and support infrastructure. In addition, the ethnographic emphasis in rapid assessment limits design generalizablity.

The first destruction point is to pursue a poorly thought out question or need as the focus of a rapid-assessment project. This destruction point is often related to the political process through which the rapid-assessment goals are defined. The community is normally involved in identifying the primary area where there is inadequate data. Since this is a political process, "stakeholders" such as health officials, community representatives, service providers, community based organization staff, local political officials, and community leaders (often clergy) come together to decide what the target of a rapid-assessment project should be (Trotter and Needle, 1999; WHO, 1998). Nearly everyone in these groups has a clear and urgent agenda, whether it is youth, drug use, men who have sex with men, women, or any other group that has strong advocacy representation (or lack of representation) in the community. Concerted lobbying for a target group of special concern or the presence of one outspoken stake holder can sometimes turn the rapid-assessment into a project designed to satisfy the most insistent voice, rather than the greatest emerging problem or need. Consequently, strategies have been developed in focus group research to ensure that all voices are heard and that no single individual dominates the floor. One technique that has proven successful is to allow a neutral or outsider individual or team to guide the community based group in determining the focus of a local rapid-assessment project. This can create a "balance of power" condition that allows a more consensual approach to the key decisions in a rapid-assessment project.

Rapid assessment works best when it is targeted, relatively narrow in scope, and reasonably geographically bounded. Most of the failed projects that we have information on became problematic at the start, because either the local advocacy agenda had to be accommodated, even when there were more significant needs to be addressed, or because the initial problem identification was either too fuzzy or too broad. Targeting all drug use in a community is a good example of poor design, as there is already sufficient information to indicate that injection drug use has different epidemiological and prevention implications at the local level than do crack use or other forms of drug use. Targeting all of the hard-to-reach populations in a community, as opposed to one or two populations, is another example of design failure unless—which is rarely the case—resources are available for separate rapid assessments of the varied groups involved. This specific design failure can be avoided by consulting secondary data sets that allow some clear description of the populations that are potential foci for rapid assessment. If the groups are reasonably definable as a community (i.e. in contact with each other, relatively geographically bounded, and living reasonably similar lifestyles), then the targeting will be successful. Outsider, rather than insider, definitions of a group (based on risk, based on stereotype, or based on incorrect theory) are common causes for poor targeting, as is the pressure of advocacy groups.

Inadequate resources (often people's time, rather than dollars) and missing or incomplete support infrastructure (administrative support, transcription services) are other common sources of design failure in rapid-assessment projects. This is accompanied by the problem of not budgeting adequate time to complete tasks at the appropriate level.

Finally, in addition to the political constraints, the ethnographic basis for rapid assessment places some key design constraints on rapid-assessment projects. Unlike surveys, rapid ethnographic assessment must be strongly localized. The localization is a significant strength at the action end of the assessment, since the solutions to problems of concern are clearly bounded, culturally sensitive, and politically feasible. However, it also means that the design cannot be geographically diffuse. This is not a great weakness, since the results are not supposed to be generalizable, but any design that tries to go beyond the boundaries of a clear geographic base (such as a neighborhood, a culturally salient site, a key community locale) will put the project at some risk that is proportionate to the fuzziness or expansiveness of the boundaries of the project.

(2) Sampling Issues

One of the key elements that must be tied directly to the methods is the use of appropriate sampling procedures for these approaches. Failure to sample appropriately provides incomplete or inaccurate information about core issues and cultural beliefs relevant on which action recommendations are based. Most rapid-assessment projects combine qualitative and quantitative sampling procedures appropriate to the specific method employed (cf. Trotter and Needle, 1999). General qualitative sampling has been presented in several texts (Johnson, 1990; Kuzel, 1992; Luborsky and Rubinstein, 1995; Nickel et al., 1995). These designs can be supplemented by works that describe how to combine qualitative and quantitative sampling (cf. Miller and Payne, 1993; Johnson, 1990), and by general quantitative sample design features (cf. Fink, 1995).

The ideal procedure for assuring adequate sample size in qualitative research is to interview to redundancy (i.e., until no new or unexplained elements or conditions of the cultural domain have been exposed in a new interview), using nominated and/or targeted samples (see Trotter and

Needle, 1999 for full methodological exploration). However, practical applications of rapid assessment have demonstrated that "pragmatic redundancy," that is, sufficient information to provide confidence in the data, can
be achieved long before total redundancy occurs if a representative sample
of cultural experts is achieved. Thus, sampling strategies are designed to
provide a representative sample of cultural, rather than individual, variability within the population. They are drawn from nominated sample
frames constructed of individuals who are representative of the range of
views, values, beliefs, and risk behaviors found in the target neighborhoods, city as a whole, or other geographically bounded unit of analysis
(e.g., a rural postal zone, reservation). Complimentary sampling strategies
are used to target populations (Singer, 1999; Watters and Biernacki, 1989)
and to conduct observations, interviews, and rapid-assessment surveys of
hidden populations, specifically at-risk populations.

The number of people interviewed is generally tied to specific methods.
However, since qualitative samples in rapid assessment are normally expert samples selected to be representative of the primary knowledge about
a single cultural domain, most cultural domains can be adequately explored with fifteen to thirty in-depth cultural expert interviews. This empirically based approach produces a strong cultural consensus description
and the majority of variation in views within the culture, since expert interviews provide evidence of both the experts' beliefs and knowledge of
competing or complimentary beliefs or information about the cultural domain of interest (Johnson, 1990; Romney, Weller, and Batchelder, 1986);
The cultural expert interviews thus focus on the core cultural beliefs, values and contextual information that is available in the overall population.

(3) Inappropriate Methods Mixture: Multiple Methods, Timing, and Sequencing

The data collected in rapid assessment have to meet key qualitative reliability and validity standards, including the need to triangulate all data. It
is impossible to draw a triangle based on a single point (or point of view).
Since we know that sometimes what people say they do is not what they
do, and since we know that sometimes people tell us what they think we
want to know (or should know) rather than what we need to know, rapid-
assessment projects need a combination of methods, including direct observation, to produce defensible information. A poor methods mix is thus
a guarantee of inadequate information being promoted as scientific evidence for some political action. This is the "we only have limited resources, so we will get the information we need from a couple of focus
groups" syndrome. This is usually accompanied by the "I know I can call
some people who can tell us everything we need to know" approach to sampling. The most common failure for the methods mixes in rapid assessment is where there is no mix (only one method, such as focus groups, is
used), and consequently no ability to meet the reliability and validity standards of good qualitative research.

The second most common failure point is where the methods mix is imbalanced (in terms of quality, as well as quantity) because of a lack of skills or because of a misuse of the time needed to organize, conduct, and process the data for one of the methods. There are examples of studies where the community became enamored with observations but ran out of time to conduct interviews to fill out the data needs generated by the observations.[2] The opposite is also possible, where interviewing was comfortable and emphasized, but no other methods were conducted. There are also examples where data were collected but not analyzed because of misuse of time or lack of adequate resources.

Rapid-assessment methods are often organized in two basic clusters, one an interview cluster, the other an observational and mapping cluster. The effective timing and sequencing of methods allows a project to be run with very little down time for the field research teams by utilizing methodological time to mix and match methods. This, in turn, makes the overall process efficient and shorter in duration than otherwise possible. The most common methods failures for rapid-assessment projects occur when the original design and theory configurations built into the project are somehow either ignored, partially missed, or misused.

(4) Community Participation: A Two-Edged Sword

The most notable and consequent change in rapid assessment in recent years has been the deliberate increase in community involvement in planning, designing, and conducting the research, as well as assisting in, or conducting, the analysis. Community involvement is helpful for two scientific features of rapid assessment, and a couple of methodological issues as well. In design, community involvement improves the validity of the questions being asked, as well as the expert sampling process being used. Community involvement also acts as both a validity and cultural reliability check at the analysis stage. The scientific compliment to community involvement ensures that, once targeted, both design and sampling become scientifically sound, and do not rely on cronyism or the pursuit of local agendas (especially oligarchic networks). This allows data to be collected beyond the normal limits of the political sphere, while taking community politics into account throughout the data collection process.

However, community participation in rapid assessment is a double-edged sword. On the one hand, without a reasonable level of participation and buy-in, it is both unethical and virtually impossible to conduct research in communities. Still, there are many cases in which community involvement in providing input and approval for the research has been kept to a minimum. In such cases, the research tends to reflect the concerns and career needs of the researcher rather than the concerns and needs of the community. At the other extreme, community participation can become a threat to the integrity of the data collection process, resulting in polemics, rather than honest discovery and recommendations.

Thus, community involvement requires a strong set of both scientific and political checks and balances, or the project will founder from too much or too little of either or both. If local cultural and political agendas dominate, the information may take on a bias that destroys both the potential and the direction of the assessment. If the scientific agenda dominates, the project may not address crucial community needs or may not have the community buy-in that is necessary for action. A balance can be struck between the unethical and the polemic in a wide variety of ways, all of which work in specific local circumstances. Balance is, however, hard to achieve or maintain, and remains a potential destruction point in rapid assessment.

Stages of Community Involvement   There seem to be three stages in which community involvement is important, and different in content, in rapid-assessment projects. The start up stage is dominated by the need to get both permission for field teams to work in the community, even if they are from the community, and the need to get key elements (leadership, institutional support, etc.) to help structure or target the project, to provide the most salient focus for the rapid assessment (buy-in on design strengths and weaknesses). Most projects accomplish this stage by creating representative community advisory or oversight groups that include many of the key stakeholders concerned with the target of the study who can identify the needs of the community. This process institutionalizes and systematizes the input needed by the field team, and provides a forum for discussion and reaction to the design of the project and the data collected. This stage usually includes a training program that thoroughly familiarizes the group with the theory, methods, and best practices of rapid assessment, sets goals for the project, and provides a framework for judging the quality of the project and the data collected. The more sophisticated the oversight group is about the methods and processes, the more likely they are to support the findings and move them toward action.

The second stage normally occurs during the data collection process. The ideal state is to have at least some of the oversight group participate in data collection (or at least monitor it closely enough to be familiar with it), as part of a project monitoring function (without interfering with the process). The monitoring function also includes presentation of preliminary data and findings to the group to keep them informed about direction and progress. Involving oversight group members in data collection increases the likelihood that the oversight group will understand and validate field team findings and recommendations.

The final stage of community participation begins with involvement in, or understanding of, the analysis of the data. This involves the transformation of the basic data into "findings" (single or grouped elements) that can then be directly translated, usually by the people making up the oversight committee, into policy, policy changes, program and program changes, or specific actions by some group or organization in the community (from law to community-based organization [CBO]). Politics often plays a strong part in stage one, and positive politics and advocacy for change come back strongly in stage three, while being minimized in the middle data collection stages. When participation turns to control, however, control often misfires.

(5) Personnel: Roles, Selection, Attributes, and Training

Careful personnel selection is critical to the rapid-assessment process because if inappropriate staff members are hired there may be inadequate time to hire replacement personnel. Personnel can provide three destruction points for rapid-assessment projects. The roles that people play throughout the project are critical, but inadequate to success unless they are accompanied by key attributes (knowledge and skills) and appropriate training where knowledge and skills are missing.

Key Roles, Selection, and Attributes   There are a number of key roles that are necessary for successful rapid-assessment projects; scientific oversight (maintaining standards and quality control), political oversight, and administrative processes. They also include advocacy and political action roles. If any of these roles are not adequately addressed, the project is weakened. The first critical oversight role is that of project director (often labeled the principal investigator or P.I., for research projects). This person needs the broadest and deepest knowledge, skills, and training in ethnographic methods of all of the individuals on the project, since this person is responsible for translating the community's initial targeting and problem identification into sound rapid-assessment question, design, and field procedure. The P.I. also is responsible for overseeing the data collection process and providing quality control for the data that is collected. This means that the P.I. must supervise staff, assure adherence to project design, and check the completeness of the data assembled by the field team. Finally, the P.I. is the primary individual responsible for the appropriate analysis of the field data and the development from the data of useful recommendations. While some of the routine administrative functions of the project can be done by others, the quality of the P.I. is directly correlated with the quality of the data, the quality of the analysis, and the impact of the recommendations for the project.

This is no place for on the job training as an alternative to the a priori possession of a high level of ethnographic research and analytic skills. Projects are better off with a skilled individual who has to learn to work with a community than a community individual in need of learning the research skills needed to carry out the project. The ideal is an individual from the community who already has the needed skills. However, attempting to substitute an administrator or community leader without the science skills for this role is a good prescription for disaster.

Basic administrative skills are also needed. Field personnel for rapid-assessment projects are commonly recruited from existing agencies and community based organizations for their "street knowledge" of the community and/or target group, as well as because of their positive reputation in the community. Both qualities contribute significantly to project success. However, this diversity of "temporary" or short term personnel creates a significant need for logistical administration (scheduling, payroll, data storage and processing, etc.). The P.I. can take on this role in most cases, but it adds time and stress to the overall project burden on that individual, resulting in other problems.

The choice of field personnel is the third crucial personnel feature of rapid assessment. Ethnographic methods work best when the individuals doing the data collection are familiar with and accepted by the community. Standard ethnographies are often conducted by individuals who begin as strangers to a community but who have the commitment, communication skills, and time to become fairly familiar, accepted, trusted, and integrated into community life. The first third of most classic ethnographies is taken up by rapport building processes. However, the time needed for classic ethnography often exceeds the time available for conducting a rapid assessment. This is the reason that most of the early rapid-assessment projects were conducted by ethnographers who were already grounded in the culture being studied, and were simply doing a focused continuation of their field work to solve a public health problem.

Since there are many communities that do not have trained ethnographers but need rapid assessment, the trend has been to find community members who already have community rapport, and train them to be ethnographers or para-ethnographers supported by a P.I. who has full ethnographic skills. A number of projects have demonstrated that this approach can work, with levels of success varying from outstanding to none at all.[3]

There are several individual personal characteristics that appear to be important for selecting field personnel as well. First, they need to be part of the culture but able to step outside it and see elements of it clearly; a combination of having an insider identity with the ability to adopt outsider viewpoints. Commonly, this versatility is expressed as being able (during the project) to see a familiar culture with new eyes and to hear it with new ears. Curiosity about how things works is another key trait, and the ability to engage people, ask good questions, and spontaneously see and change directions also are excellent traits, since good ethnographic interviews often turn what at first appear to be tangents (but in fact are unexpected discoveries) into central themes.

The other element that appears to be important is to select people who are committed to their community's well-being, but stop short of being so committed to immediate service delivery that they have difficulty assuming a research role. Field personnel have to be capable of adopting new roles rather than simply carrying out their old one in a new context. For example, some of outreach workers from strong and successful community organizations make excellent field workers, while others cannot temporarily vacate their old outreach involvement in teaching people the "way things really are" rather than finding out how people see the world. These individuals are not able to let people speak in their own words, but feel the need to change responses to fit their conception of cultural good. They consistently introduce their own beliefs and biases into the interviews and observations.

The most welcome role mix is to have a balance of analysis roles combined with, or tied to, advocacy and action roles. Rapid-assessment projects are designed to create action, not simply create data. The data have to be defensible (scientific, triangulated, solid), but they do no good sitting silently on a shelf as an unread report or a scientific publication that is inaccessible to the community. Rapid assessment has its greatest impact when information is translated into local action. This is a critical area for successful community involvement. Rapid-assessment projects can be designed to maintain community control and involvement through the analysis stage, linking findings with recommendations, which then have to be transferred into local program and political arenas for effective program, policy, and political change. This normally means that the advocates, leaders, and program people on the community advisory board (or oversight group) move the project from data collection and analysis to action and community change.

Training   Training has become the critical element in creating rapid-assessment projects as a substitute for using previously trained and experienced ethnographers as field personnel. Full project-related training consists of targeted training for several groups. This includes basic information and training for the community oversight group to provide them with the knowledge necessary to understand the entire rapid-assessment process (oversight group responsibilities, strengths and weaknesses of rapid methods, types of data expected, scientific foundations of rapid assessment, processes for reviewing, and moving findings into action). Assuming that the P.I. is experienced and can provide ongoing methods training and quality control, the second area of training is initial field data collection training for the field personnel. The third training focus is analysis training, and the final area is training in translating findings into community action.

The amount of training can vary significantly, based on the experience and expertise of the individuals fulfilling various roles on the project. Because of the potential loss of field team members in midstream (given the fact that they are part-time workers with other work demands, their inexperience in data collection, and the demands place on them by the rapid nature of the methodology), the P.I. or other trainers have to be prepared to do update training for existing staff and start-up training for late-starter new staff.

Data Collection   Rapid-assessment methods training is actually the most straight forward of all of the training processes, and field personnel can rapidly learn how to conduct ethnographic interviews, do observations, and complete mapping and survey data collection. There are a number of new methods texts and journals that provide strong models and rationales, methodological descriptions, and analytical schema for ethnographic and other qualitative research (Bernard, 1998; Miles and Huberman, 1994; Schensul and Schensul, 1998; Mason, 1996; Dey, 1993) that follows high-quality science paradigms. These resources have been distilled into training manuals and training resources for various configurations of rapid-assessment projects.

However, initial training must be followed up with consistent monitoring and quality control, often resulting in the conclusion that retraining or enhanced training is needed to ensure that data are consistent and valid. Key responsibilities of either the P.I. or field director (or both in tandem) include monitoring all data coming into the project, correcting problems in data collection, and reinforcing good practices. Early on, it is useful for the P.I to assess the range of skills of each field team member. While some individuals can do it all, it is much more common for newly trained field teams to exhibit a considerable amount of variation in skills for the field tasks. For example, some individuals who are very good at one-on-one interviews are not very effective in conducting high-quality focus groups, or vice versa. Some people are far better at observation and recording what they see than what they hear. These differences in skill levels directly affect the quality of the information being collected and analyzed, and must be dealt with during any field project. Training is the answer for some of these variations, but careful assignment is also necessary, since no amount of training can replace ability at some levels.

Data analysis is the single greatest weakness for the vast majority of community based rapid-assessment projects. The manuals and training programs for rapid-assessment programs offer thorough description and instruction on data collection; however, only limited resources tend to be provided on approaches for qualitative data analysis. This oversight all too often leaves a local group with the unfortunate condition of having a massive amount of well-collected data that they do not know how to analyze, leading to their failure to complete the project in a defensible format.

There has been a recent expansion of information on the systematic analysis of qualitative data, focusing on sources of variation in interview data (Aunger, 1994), coding (Carley, 1988; MacQueen et al., 1998), model building (Gittelsohn, 1992), explorations of meaning (Manson, 1997), use of computers (Dohan, Sanchez, & Jankowski, 1998), network studies (Mitchell, 1986; Trotter and Schensul, 1998; Page and Trotter, 1999), and life history studies (Woodhouse, 1990). The result is that a significant gap is potentially being filled in the methodological rigor of rapid-assessment projects. Unfortunately, it is not easy to learn how to do these types of analysis from books alone, and consequently there is a need for personnel who are already experienced in this type of analysis to play lead roles in helping the rest of the team through the analysis process.

The analysis is organized according to the general questions asked in the assessment questions or design. Standard qualitative data management and preparation procedures include interviews being transcribed verbatim, coded, reviewed, memoed, and analyzed for both consensus models of key issues and cultural variability across individual or subgroups with reference to behaviors, attitudes, relationships, beliefs, context, or other issues of concern. Observations are recorded on site. Quantitative findings from the rapid-assessment surveys are summarized using descriptive statistics.

While quantitative statements are relatively easy to make and qualitative data readily transcribed, there are relatively few models that provide community based groups with the three elements of analysis that are necessary to complete the rapid-assessment task. These include analytical theory (particularly the kind of midrange theory that may be of greatest utility in an applied, rapid-assessment project), a systematic and defensible protocol for coding (i.e., identifying and marking key elements in the data, including the relationships among elements such as the various subtypes of complex categories within the data), and a model for presenting the data in summary form using direct study participant quotes that express or otherwise support the conclusions that are drawn by the field team (i.e., findings) in the words of the people being studied (Trotter, 1997).

One strategy for making sure that a rapid assessment identifies new information (or new ways of thinking about things that were already known, such as contextualizing behavioral patterns in light of larger structures of social relationships) is the use of a "discovery log." During the course of fieldwork, field team members are constantly encouraged to record any observations, insights, or other information that goes beyond previously known knowledge in the discovery log. At the end of the period of data collection, the discovery log provides a constantly updated record of the uncovering of new knowledge that can be used to gauge the advances achieved by the project in gaining new insight on the issues, groups, and relationships of concern.

A few projects, such as the RARE Brazil project,[4] have incorporated multiple qualitative data management and analysis training workshops for the key personnel, but in most cases participants are expected to intuitively identify the key elements in the data, often causing suspicion that the analysis is either biased toward some existing agenda, or that the data are only partially analyzed and tend to reflect what was known by field team members at the start of the project (leading to the discounting of rapid assessment by the "everyone knows that stuff" criticism). This is one of the greatest areas of need for supporting community based rapid-assessment projects.

(6) Implementation Issues: From Analysis to Recommendation

Most rapid assessments are conducted based on the promise of local, community-controlled action. The changes that occur can be policy changes, program changes, redirection of resources, expansion of services, or other local actions. One of the largest areas of failure of rapid-assessment programs is where this process of community implementation, rather than the rapid-assessment process, fails. There are numerous cases where the rapid assessment was conducted, important findings emerged, the analysis was linked to recommendations, and the recommendations were solidly linked to realistic local actions, yet the community failed to carry through on the recommendations. Some of the conditions that lead to this failure include a poorly selected community group, where there was no buy-in to the process, or where the participants were individually competent and connected but did not have the collective ability to facilitate change. In some cases, the group was outstanding, but the changes were blocked at an institutional level by other political forces. Such bottlenecks can appear because the recommendations do not fit the agendas of key decision-makers.

While community processes can undermine the implementation of rapid-assessment recommendations, it is important to focus on issues in the recommendation development process itself. It cannot be assumed that it is easy to develop recommendations, and there are several pitfalls. If broad cultural forces (poverty, large value systems, culture in general) are identified as findings, rather than specific conditions, issues, beliefs, or processes that can be changed locally, then the rapid-assessment analysis has been misapplied. The outcome of the analysis should fit and support broader cultural issues, but they should be specific enough that some kind of change can be made to improve conditions locally. In addition, at the point of recommendation development, it is very easy for the field team to revert to what it knew (and emotionally embraced) before the initiation of the data collection. At the same time, given the range of problems facing impoverished or otherwise hard hit but underserved communities, it is easy for the field team to stray beyond its area of focus, to develop recommendations that go beyond and are not directly an outgrowth of the data collected, or to formulate recommendations for so many changes that the advisory group has no sense of what should be prioritized.

To counteract these tendencies, it is critical that the field team and P.I. understand the following: 1) overly ambitious recommendations (e.g., "end poverty") that cannot be easily acted upon by the oversight committee are not useful; 2) recommendations flow directly from and can be tied directly to specific research findings; 3) recommendations be achievable in the short run by entities that have buy-in with the project or can be influenced by the project report; and 4) the number of recommendations be limited so as not to overwhelm the oversight committee or trivialize any of the specific recommendations for change developed by the field team.

(7) Logistics and Administrative Support

A final common destructive element in rapid-assessment projects is the process of logistics support and administrative support. If the administration and logistics are unorganized or late, the whole project founders. There are a number of tasks or conditions that directly translate into either a positive or negative project experience. These range from the need for someone to identify and recruit all of the key players in the rapid-assessment process (P.I., community leaders, field workers, etc.), to the necessity of having checks for personnel arrive on time and in the correct amounts. There is also a need for someone to schedule meetings, make sure equipment is available, determine the different forms of support that are needed and provide them, and bring all of the parts of the process together in the right time and right places. A lack of administrative support has resulted in projects using up all of their resources on observations, with no interviews to confirm or explain them, and has created a project in which wonderful data were collected with neither the time nor the personnel available to analyze the data or turn it into action at the local level.

THE FUTURE OF RAPID ASSESSMENT

Rapid-assessment models and programs are likely to continue to be periodically criticized, revitalized, and frequently utilized for community based research into the foreseeable future. It is an opportunity to follow the admonition to think global and to act local. This approach provides a venue for community control, interest, and action backed by scientifically defensible data and information. It is also an arena where social scientists can appropriately test and refine new methods, and meet new challenges to validity and reliability of both qualitative and quantitative data. It is a good venue to test the limits and the creativity of training versus existing expertise, and to identify both the limits and the limitless boundaries for political action within the context of evidence based recommendations. Both the potential and the limitations appear important and manageable for the future. In the end, rapid assessment emerges as an important tool for bridging the gap between science and community concern, for empowering communities to take action on issues of concern, and for forging new bridges for achieving desired community change.

One of the most critical next steps now underway is the extension of rapid-assessment training to include extensive analysis training. Most projects can now accomplish very good quality data collection. However, only recently has it become clear that the links that the most experienced qualitative researchers readily produce, which directly tie patterns in the data to summarized findings to data based recommendations, have not yet been standardized and systematized. It is not yet easy for community based organizations to accomplish the same processes with the same outcomes. The CDC's global AIDS program is undertaking the task of producing greatly improved training programs that focus on analysis, and that provide a much more systematic way of linking findings to locally productive recommendations. This process also sets up both an end point of targeted recommendations producing targeted success, where linear thinking and processes are dominant, and a feedback loop where rapid-assessment and evolutionary problem-solving processes are allowed to be nonlinear instead of strictly straight line. Each incremental success leads to not only a clear reflection of community life as it is, but also leads to improvements in at least part of the conditions that have a direct impact on the community.

Rapid assessment can be viewed as a one-time fix for a simple problem, or as an ongoing tool kit for evolutionary improvement in the overall life of a community. Its role in contributing to the community impact of interventions is tied to the degree to which its considerable promise is critically assessed and elaborated in future work. Attention to its potential destruction points provides a roadmap for systematically attending to its current limitations while capitalizing on its successes thus far.

NOTES

1. Additional examples of these types of rapid-assessment projects include information on the health problems of homeless youth in Baltimore (Ensign and Gittelsohn, 1998; Ensign and Santelli, 1998), methamphetamine studies in Australia (Vincent et al., 1999), identification of priority health issues for healthcare management policy review in France (Lerer, 1999), descriptions of HIV transmission conditions for six ethnocultural communities in Canada (Williams et al., 1997), assessing home based care for people with AIDS in the United States (McDonnell et al., 1994), as well as the RARE project, Rapid Assessment Response and Evaluation, conducted through the U.S. Surgeon General's Office of HIV/AIDS Policy (Trotter and Needle, 1999; Trotter, Needle, et al., 2001).

2. These observations come from experience with a large number of direct experiences assisting community based rapid assessment. The literature tends to ignore some of the difficulties faced by community based research groups and focuses on either successes, or hypothetical and methodological reasons for failure.

3. Specific examples here would potentially violate confidentiality issues, or embarrass specific cities, however, in at least two cases where U.S.-based rapid-assessment projects were being implemented without a local project leader who had ethnographic experience, one succeeded by very carefully following the RARE guidelines step-by-step, and requesting extended assistance from the RARE team, and one basically failed to follow the guidelines, did not request additional support, and produced very mediocre data and recommendations.

4. RARE Brazil is being supported by the Global AIDS Program (GAP) from the Centers for Disease Control and Prevention, in cooperation with the Brazilian Ministry of Health. Multiple projects are underway and will be reported in the literature shortly.

REFERENCES

Almedon, A. M., Blumenthal, U., & Manderson, L. (1997). Hygiene evaluation procedures: Approaches for assessing water and sanitation related hygiene practices. *Boston International Nutrition Foundation for Developing Countries.*

Aral, S. O. & Fransen, L. (1995). STD/HIV prevention in Turkey: Planning a sequence of interventions. *AIDS Education & Prevention, 7*(6), 544–553.

Askew, I., Tapsoba, P., Ouedraogo Y., Viadro, C., Bakouan, D., & Sebgo, P. (1993). Quality of care in family planning programmes: A rapid assessment in Burkina Faso. *Health Policy and Planning, 8*(1), 19–32.

Aunger, R. (1994). Sources of variation in ethnographic interview data: Food avoidances in the Ituri forest. *Zaire Ethnology, 33*(1), 65–99.

Ayepong, I. A., Bertha, A., Dzikunu, H., & Manderson, L. (1995) The malaria manual. Geneva: World Health Organization.

Bebe, J. (1995). Basic concepts and techniques of rapid appraisal. *Human Organiz-ation, 54,* 42–51.

Bentley, M. E., Pelto, G. H., Straus, W. L., Schumann, D. A., Adegboda C., de la Pena, E., et al. (1988). Rapid ethnographic assessment: Applications in a diar-rhea management program. *Social Science and Medicine, 27*(1), 107–116.

Bernard, H. (Ed.). (1998). *Handbook of Methods in Cultural Anthropology.* Walnut Creek, CA: AltaMira Press.

Carley, K. (1998). Formalizing the social expert's knowledge. *Sociological Methods and Research, 17*(2), 165–232.

Chambers, R. (1992). Actual or potential uses of RRA/PRA methods in health and nutrition. *Special issue of applications for health* (pp. 101–106). London: IIED.

Dey, I. (1993). *Qualitative data analysis: A user friendly guide.* New York: Routledge.

Dohan, D. & Sanchez Jankowski, M. (1998). Using computers to analyze ethno-graphic field data: Theoretical and practical considerations. *Annual Review of Sociology, 24,* 477–498.

Ensign, B. J. & Santelli, J. (1998). Health status and access to care: Comparison of adolescents at a school-based health clinic with homeless adolescents. *Archives of Pediatrics and Adolescent Medicine, 152*(1), 20–24.

Ensign, J. & Gittelsohn, J. (1998). Health and access to care: Perspectives of home-less youth in Baltimore city, U.S.A. *Social Science & Medicine, 47*(12), 2087–2099.

Fink, A. (1995). *How to sample in surveys. The survey kit, volume 6.* Thousand Oaks, CA: Sage.

Gittelsohn, J. (1992). Building ethnographic models. *Qualitative Research Methods Newsletter* (pp. 8–15). Bombay: Tata Institute for Social Sciences.

Guillette, E. A., Mercedes, M. M., Guadalupe, A. M., Soto, A. D., & Enedina, G. I. (1998). An anthropological approach to the evaluation of preschool children ex-posed to pesticides in Mexico. *Environmental Health Perspectives, 106*(6), 347–353.

Harris, K. J., Jerome, N. W., & Fawcett, S. B. (1997). Rapid assessment procedures: A review and critique. *Human Organization, 56*(3), 378.

Heaver, R. (1991). Participative rural appraisal. Potential applications to family planning, health and nutrition programs. *Technical Department Asia Region World Bank.*

Johnson, J. C. (1990). *Selecting Ethnographic Informants.* Newbury Park, CA: Sage.

Kachondham, Y. (1992). Rapid rural appraisal and rapid assessment procedures: A comparison. In N. S. Scrimshaw & G. R. Gleason (Eds.), *Qualitative methodolo-gies for planning and evaluation of health-related programmes.* Boston: IFDC.

Kilmarx, P. H., Black, C. M., Limpakarnjanarat, K., Shaffer, N., Yanpaisarn, S., Chaisilwattana, P., et al. (1998). Rapid assessment of sexually transmitted dis-eases in a sentinel population in Thailand: Prevalence of chlamydial infection, gonorrhea, and syphilis among pregnant women. *Sexually Transmitted Infec-tions, 74*(3), 189–193.

Kuzel, A. J. (1992). Sampling in qualitative inquiry. In B. F. Crabtree & W. L. Miller (Eds.), *Doing qualitative research: Research methods for primary care* (pp. 31–44). Newbury Park, CA: Sage.

Lambert, H. (1998). Methods and meanings in anthropological, epidemiological and clinical encounters: The case of sexually transmitted disease and human immunodeficiency virus control and prevention in India. *Tropical Medicine and International Health, 3*(12), 1002–1010.

Lerer, L. (1999). Health impact assessment. *Health Policy and Planning, 14*(2), 198–203.

Luborsky, M. R. & Rubinstein, R. L. (1995). Sampling in qualitative research: Rationale, issues, and methods. *Research on Aging, 17*(1), 89–113.

MacQueen, K., McLellan, E., Kay, K., & Milstein, B. (1998). Codebook development for team-based qualitative analysis. *Cultural Anthropological Methods, 10*(2), 31–36.

Malilay, J., Flanders, W. D., & Brogan, D. A. (1997). Modified cluster sampling method for the rapid assessment of needs after a disaster; Metodo modificado de muestreo por conglomerados para la evaluacion rapida de necesidades despues de un desastre. Revista Panamericana de Salud Publica/*Pan-American Journal of Public Health, 2*(1), 7–12.

Manderson, L. & Aaby, P. (1992). An epidemic in the field? Rapid assessment procedures and health research. *Social Science and Medicine, 35,* 839–850.

Manson, S. M. (1997). Ethnographic methods, cultural context, and mental illness: Bridging different ways of knowing and experience. *Ethos, 25*(2), 249–258.

Marshall, P. L., Singer, M., & Clatts, M. C. (Eds.). (1999). Integrating cultural, observational, and epidemiological approaches in the prevention of drug abuse and HIV/AIDS. USDHHS/National Institute on Drug Abuse, *NIH Publication No. 99,* 4565.

Mason, J. (1996). *Qualitative researching.* Thosand Oaks, CA: Sage.

McDonnell, S., Brennan, M., Burnham, G., & Tarantola, D. (1994). Assessing and planning home-based care for persons with AIDS. *Health Policy and Planning, 9*(4), 429–437.

Miles, M. B. & Humberman, A. M. (1994). *Qualitative data analysis: An expanded sourcebook* (Vol. 338). Thousand Oaks, CA: Sage.

Miller, A. C. & Payne, B. S. (1993). Qualitative versus quantitative sampling to evaluate population and community characteristics at a large river mussel bed. *American Midland Naturalist, 130*(1), 133–145.

Mitchell, J. C. (1986). Ethnography and networks. *Connections, 9*(1), 17–23.

Needle, R. H., Coyle, S. L., Genser, S. G., & Trotter, R. T., II. (1995). (Ed.) Social Networks, Drug Abuse, and HIV Transmission. *NIDA Research Monograph Series, 151.*

Needle, R. H., Trotter, R. T., II, Goosby, E., Bates, C., & von Zinkernagel, D. (2000). Methodologically sound rapid assessment and response: Providing timely data for policy development on drug use interventions and HIV prevention. *International Journal of Drug Policy, 11,* 19–23.

Needle, R. H., Trotter, R. T., II, Singer, M., Bates, C., Page, J. B., Metzger, D., et al. (2003). Rapid assessment of the HIV/AIDS crisis in racial and ethic minority communities: An approach for timely community interventions. *American Journal of Public Health, 93*(6), 970–979.

Nickel, B., Berger, M., Schmidt, P., & Plies, K. (1995). Qualitative sampling in a multi-method survey: Practical problems of method triangulation in sexual behavior research. *Quality and Quantity, 29*(3), 223–240.

Nordberg, E., Oganga, H., Kazibwe, S., & Onyango, J. (1993). Rapid assessment of an African health system: Test of a planning tool. *International Journal of Health Planning and Management, 8,* 219–233.

Page, J. B. & Trotter, R. T. (1999). To theorize or not to theorize: Anthropological research in drugs and AIDS. In P. L. Marshall, M. Singer, & M. C. Clatts (Eds.), *Integrating cultural, observational, and epidemiological approaches in the prevention of drug abuse and HIV/AIDS* (pp. 51–73). Besthesda, MD: NIH.

Park, P. (1999). People, knowledge, and change in participatory research. *Management Learning, 30*(2), 141–157.

Power, R. (1996). Rapid assessment of drug injecting situations at Hanoi and Ho Chi Minh City, Viet Nam. *Bulletin on Narcotics, 1*(3), 35–52.

Price, R. H. (1990). Whither participation and empowerment? *American Journal of Community Psychology, 18*(1), 163–167.

Rhodes, T., Ball A., Stimson, G., Kobyshcha Y., Fitch, C., Pokrovsky, V., et al. (1999). HIV associated with drug injecting in the newly independent states, Eastern Europe: The social and economic context of epidemics. *Addiction, 94,* 1323–1336.

Rhodes, T., Stimson, G. V., Fitch, C., Ball, A., & Renton, A. (1999). Rapid assessment, injecting drug use, and public health. *The Lancet, 354*(9172), 65–68.

Romney, A. K., Weller, S. C., & Batchelder, W. H. (1986). Culture as consensus: A theory of culture and informant accuracy. *American Anthropologist, 88*(2), 313–338.

Schensul, J. J. & LeCompte, M. D. (1999). *Ethnographers Toolkit.* Walnut Creek, CA: AltaMira Press.

Schensul, S. & Schensul, J. J. (1998). *Essential ethnographic methods: Observations, interviews, and questionnaires.* (Ethnographer's toolkit Series: Vol. 2.) Walnut Creek, CA: AltaMira Press.

Schwartz, N. B., Molnar, J. J., & Lovshin, L. L. (1988). Cooperatively managed projects and rapid assessment: Suggestions from a Panamanian case. *Human Organization, 47*(1), 1–14.

Scrimshaw, S., Carballo, M., & Hurtado, E. (1987). Rapid assessment procedures for nutrition and primary health care. *UCLA Latin American Center References Series, 11.*

Scrimshaw, S., Carballo, M., Ramos, L., & Blair, B. A. (1991). The AIDS rapid anthropological assessment procedures: A tool for health education planning and evaluation. *Health Education Quarterly, 18,* 111–123.

Scrimshaw, S., Nevin, S., & Gleason, G. R. (Eds.) (1992). *Rapid assessment procedures: Qualitative methodologies for planning and evaluation of health related programs.* Boston: International Nutrition Foundation for Developing Countries.

Singer, M. (1999). Studying hidden and hard-to-research populations. In J. Schensul, M. LeCompte, R. Trotter, E. Cromley, & M. Singer (Eds.), *Mapping networks, spatial data and hidden populations* (The Ethnographer's Toolkit: Vol. 4). Walnut Creek, CA: AltaMira Press.

Stimson, G. V., Fitch C., Rhodes T., & Ball A. (1999). Rapid assessment and response: Methods for developing public health responses to drug problems. *Drug and Alcohol Review, 18,* 317–325.

Tarr C. M. & Aggleton, P. (1999). Young people and HIV in Cambodia: Meanings, contexts and sexual cultures. *AIDS Care, 11*(3), 375–384.

Trotter, R. T., II (1996). (Ed.) *Multicultural AIDS prevention programs.* New York: The Haworth Press.

Trotter, R. T., II (1997). Anthropological midrange theories in mental health research: Selected theories, methods, and systematic approaches to at-risk populations. *Ethos, 25*(2), 259–274.

Trotter, R. T., II & Needle, R. H. (1999). *Crisis response teams and communities combat HIV/AIDS in racial and ethnic minority populations: Rapid assessment, rapid response, and evaluation field assessment training workbook.* Rockville, MD: National Institutes of Health. Office of HIV/AIDS Policy.

Trotter, T., II, Needle, R. H., Goosby, E., Bates, C., & Singer, M. (2001). A methodological model for rapid assessment, response and evaluation: the RARE program in public health. *Journal of Field Methods, 13*(2), 137–159.

Trotter, T., II & Schenshul, J. J. (1998). Methods in applied anthropology. In H. Russell Bernard (Ed.), *Handbook of methods in cultural anthropology* (pp. 691–736). Walnut Creek, CA: AltaMira Press.

Vakil, A. C. (1994). Of designs and disappointments: Some limits to participatory research in a third world context. *American Sociologist, 25*(3), 4–19.

Vincent, N., Shoobridge, J., Ask, A., Allsop, S., & Ali, R. (1999). Characteristics of amphetamine users seeking information, help and treatment in Adelaide, South Australia. *Drug and Alcohol Review, 18*(1), 63–73.

Watters, J. K. & Biernacki, P. (1989). Targeted sampling: Options for the study of hidden populations. *Social Problems, 36*(4), 416–430.

Weller, S. C. & Romney, A. K. (1988). *Systematic data collection* (Vol. 96). Thousand Oaks, CA: Sage.

Whyte, W. F. (1995). Encounters with participatory action research. *Qualitative Sociology, 18*(3), 289–299.

Williams, D., Singer, M. S., Adrien, A., Godin, G., Maticka-Tyndale, E., & Cappon, P. (1997). Participatory aspects in the qualitative research design of phase II of the ethnocultural communities facing AIDS study. *Canadian Journal of Public Health, 87*(Suppl. 1), S15–S25.

Woodhouse, L. D. (1990). An exploratory study of the use of life history methods to determine treatment needs for female substance abusers. *Response, 13*(3), 12–15.

World Health Organization (WHO). (1998). *Rapid assessment and response guide on injecting drug use.* Geneva: World Health Organization.

7

The Hartford Model of AIDS Practice/Research Collaboration

Merrill Singer & Margaret Weeks

Public-health researchers tend to view research as a "social good," an activity that contributes directly and substantially to better technical understandings, expanded levels of public awareness, and general health and social improvement. In fact, there is remarkably little debate among researchers about the ultimate value of public-health research. While researchers contest the value of particular methodologies or criticize certain lines of inquiry, the basic research enterprise is not in question, nor often up for discussion. To a greater or lesser degree, investigators concerned with public-health issues also assume that this attitude is or at least should be universal, as it is easy to assemble lists of the benefits and contributions of public-health research to society. While it is recognized that some researchers are unethical or that research can, on occasion, lead to dangerous knowledge, in day-to-day practice the only real issue for public-health researchers is how to do better research, not whether to do research at all.

Communities, by contrast, especially those that have been subjected to social disadvantage, poverty, discrimination, and external domination, often have a very different view of research than do those for whom it is both an occupation and an epistemology. In particular, communities may object to being the subjects of scientific examination, including study that is said by the researcher to be in their best interests. Additionally, they may harbor pointed criticism of the way research commonly is conducted, the lack or limited nature of community input into the development of both research questions and design, the failure of researchers to openly and fully share findings, and the inaccessibility or clear utility of the technical, disciplinary-centric, and jargon-filled publications that research generally produces. Even when researchers have attempted to limit tensions with the communities they study, their "paternalist attitudes toward community people have frequently signaled the undoing of any possible partnership based on equality" (Gills, 2001, p. 4). Additionally, as Reback et al. (2002, p. 838) note, "the most common complaint heard from the community is a feeling of powerlessness in relation to the research team".

These issues have led to considerable distrust of research and research institutions in diverse communities. Certain communities (e.g., some Native American nations), in fact, have even banned external research at times or established committees to serve as stern gatekeepers of research access

(LeCompte et al., 1999; Shriver et al., 1998; Singer, 1993). This "research backlash" reflects the fact that communities may feel themselves to be over-researched and underserved. In the final analysis, many community voices have questioned who the real benefactor of community health research is: the communities being studied or the researchers conducting the research. The result is not just community opposition to this or that research project, or to any particular researcher, but criticism of the entire research enterprise as alien, self-serving for researchers, valueless or inaccessible to the communities that are studied, and exploitive of community goodwill.

This sentiment is effectively captured in the biting lyrics of Jimmy Curtis and Floyd Westerman's playful but pointed ballad "Here Comes the Anthros," a musical indictment of the history of relations between both cultural anthropology and archeology researchers and American Indians. While the actual relations between individual anthropologists and specific Indian groups is varied, and ranges from intense support to open hostility, structurally, as an academic discipline within the institutional framework of the dominant society, anthropology is the visible part that can come to represent (and be criticized as an agent of) the wider social order (Asad, 1973; Gough, 1968; Smith, 1999). In this sense, all health, social, and behavioral research with marginalized, exploited, and disadvantaged communities may be suspect, with the burden of proving the community value of any particular research initiative falling squarely on the shoulders of the researchers involved.

At the same time, health and social service providers and practitioners who see the potential value of research have pointed to significant gaps between the everyday needs of community-based programs and the issues addressed by researchers. For example, the Committee on Community-Based Drug Treatment of the Institute of Medicine has argued that community substance abuse treatment providers feel frustrated with the failure of researchers to provide them with relevant answers to important treatment questions (Lamb et al.,1998). Ironically, researchers themselves have expressed frustration that research-based drug and alcohol treatment innovations are not being utilized by treatment providers and that research findings take a long time to impact intervention efforts (Lamb et al.,1998). Assessment by the Committee on Community-Based Treatment concluded that research remains remote from drug treatment and pointed to the need to develop more collaborative approaches. Similarly, observers have expressed concern that AIDS research "is too far removed from the [pressing] needs and concerns of the men and women who are on the front lines of the battle to halt the transmission of HIV, those who design and implement on-the-ground programs of intervention intended to reduce high-risk behaviors" (Bolton & Singer, 1992).

In response to the growing ability and willingness of communities to speak openly and sometimes loudly about their criticisms of research, researchers, and research institutions, as well as a result of the multiple challenges of complex community health and social problems like the AIDS pandemic and substance abuse, researchers have began to recognize the value of community collaboration. As part of this development, researchers have initiated discussions about the need to carefully consider community concerns about research, including past negative experiences with research activities and researchers (White, 2000). Further, they have begun to see the value of working closely with communities at all stages in the research process, starting with gaining approval for and community involvement in new research initiatives (Altman, 1995).

Despite these developments, there continues to be considerable uncertainty among many researchers about how to initiate contact with legitimate community representatives, how to develop and maintain trusting community relations, how to structure research so that it truly strengthens communities in their effort to address their health and social problems, and how to translate findings into a format and language that is accessible to and meaningful for practitioners. As Auerbach and Coates (2000) emphasize, "how best to do this translation, transferal, and collaborative research is an undeveloped scientific question that requires further investigation." The purpose of this chapter is to examine one model for "translation, transferal, and collaborative research" focusing on a long-standing Practice/Research Collaboration (PRC) in HIV/AIDS prevention intervention research.

For the past 15 years, our interdisciplinary, community-based applied research team in Hartford, Connecticut, has been involved in the development, implementation, management, and evaluation of HIV prevention projects targeted to high-risk populations, especially drug users, sex partners of drug users, commercial sex workers, adolescents, farm workers, and gay men and youth. The ecological model that has guided this work, which we refer to as the Hartford Model, developed most immediately out of over 10 years of prior applied research on a range of health issues facing low-income, underserved populations.

The Hartford Model, as developed by researchers and practitioners at the Hispanic Health Council and the Institute for Community Research, emphasizes the following: 1) long-term, community-based partnerships between activist public-health researchers and research-informed community interventionists; 2) highly collaborative team efforts guided by a participatory action orientation to research and the transfer of research skills; 3) closely linked community-based research with research-informed intervention; and 4) an interdisciplinary or blended methodological approach to formative research, needs assessment, and program process and outcomes evaluation. The remainder of this chapter describes the development of the Hartford Model of community-based HIV/AIDS research, reviews its history of development, identifies its core practice/research components and variants, and describes its methodological orientation to community HIV prevention research.

DEVELOPMENT OF THE HARTFORD MODEL

The Hispanic Health Council

Over the last 25 years, the Hispanic Health Council (HHC), and, for the last 15 years, the Institute for Community Research (ICR), of Hartford, Connecticut, have collectively participated in longitudinal initiatives to build community-based practice/research focused on the perilous health and social problems of the inner-city and rural poor. The seeds of this ongoing initiative were sown early in the history of the HHC, when its founders selected an organizational approach that prioritizes experience-near applied ethnographic and qualitative research methods as primary tools in multimethod community-based research and practice efforts to achieve critical health change (Schensul & Borrero, 1982).

This approach seeks to wed ongoing community-centered public-health research with community-based services, training, and advocacy efforts. The approach emphasizes ethnographic methods, but also includes epidemiological and other methods, such as social network approaches. It highlights the importance of social context in three ways: 1) in the selection of research methods that tend to focus on specific behaviors or issues of interest *within their encompassing and generative social and structural environments*; 2) in grounding the research initiative firmly within the community through the use of nongovernment organizations as the primary research institutions; and 3) in using local research and practice/research collaboration to shape local intervention efforts.

The roots of the Hartford Model, which are embedded most deeply in Action and Advocacy Anthropology (Schensul, 1973, 1974; Singer, 1990), date to the end of the Second World War, long before the founding of either the Hispanic Health Council or the Institute for Community Research. Action Anthropology, as developed initially by Sol Tax and his students at the University of Chicago, is a collaborative community-based approach to the application of anthropological methods and concepts to solving real world problems (Gearing, 1960).

In 1948, Tax launched a unique project intended as a field school to train of a number of graduate students at the Fox (also called Mesquawkie) Indian reservation in Iowa. Presaging the far later calls within postmodern anthropology for multivocal texts that give equal say to ethnographers and informants, Tax developed a program in which the Fox participated not as subjects of other people's studies but as coinvestigators and initiators of research-guided social development projects. The emergence of this approach was serendipitous because, at the outset, it was assumed that the students would focus primarily on describing traditional aspects of Fox culture, replicating the prewar anthropological model of salvage ethnographic description of disappearing ways of life.

The initiative for a new approach came from the students who quickly came to realize that the Fox were quite cognizant that they faced numerous problems, including the psycho-social readjustment of war veterans to reservation life and the struggle to maintain a distinct Fox identity in the face of acculturation into mainstream society. Rather than just study these problems, Tax and his students began to work with the Fox to develop potential routes for solving the problems that the Fox themselves defined as the issues of concern. As Tax (1970) realized, this required that researchers remove themselves as much as possible from a position of power, or undue influence. As researchers, we know that knowledge is power and we try hard to reject the power that knowledge gives us. Instead, decision-making power, Tax asserted, should stay within the community, with anthropologists assisting community members to achieve their own vision.

Another action anthropologist, Allan Holmberg, adopted this new orientation to guide a project designed to demonstrate that scientific methods and knowledge could be used to improve the lives and social well-being of oppressed communities. Called the Vicos Project, this initiative, which grew out of a unique set of circumstances, embraced a belief in the right of self-determination. In the project, Holmberg assumed the role of *patrón* (in the name of Cornell University) of a 40,000-acre Peruvian *hacienda*. The residents of the hacienda had been in a feudal-like, serfdom relationship with the previous landowner prior to Cornell's purchase of the property. Working with them over a 5-year period to expand educational, health care, and economic capacity, Holmberg was eventually able to transfer full ownership to the residents. Holmberg (1970) argued that an "interventionist or action approach to the dynamics of culture, applied with proper restraint, may in the long run provide considerable payoff in terms both of more rational policy and better science."

Subsequently, Stephen Schensul (1973, 1974) worked with activists and organizers from the Mexican American community of Chicago for 6 years (1968–1974) to document community needs, identify social problems, and develop and implement over twenty different projects in bilingual education, maternal and child health, mental health, and gang prevention. Reflecting the action orientation of Schensul and his colleagues, these projects were research driven, collaborative, and based in the community, and they reflected a long-term commitment to community health and social development.

Evolution of the Hartford Model   In Hartford, application of the model began in the late 1970s with community efforts to address pressing health problems in the burgeoning Puerto Rican population. Attracted by available work in the nearby tobacco fields, Puerto Ricans had begun migrating to Hartford in growing numbers during the 1960s. In their new home, Puerto Ricans—a group that has had American citizenship since the First World War—faced the triple burden of poverty, discrimination, and cultural and linguistic difference from the dominant population. Health and other social institutions were ill prepared to respond to the needs of this growing community and, as a result, were not particularly inclined initially to become more responsive. Reacting to this mainstream indifference, a core of Puerto Rican community health activists developed and soon found willing partners among a small group of applied anthropologists affiliated with the University of Connecticut, including Stephen Schensul, Jean Schensul, and Perti Pelto.

Receptivity to the action model in the Puerto Rican community of Hartford was driven in part by a tragic incident that occurred in 1976, when a Puerto Rican infant died because of the inability of a Spanish-speaking mother to communicate effectively with English-speaking medical personnel. In response to this and various other incidents that embodied the lack of cultural fit between the Hartford health care system and the city's rapidly growing ethnic minority communities, a grassroots community task force was organized to seek changes in health care service delivery. Maria Borrero, a young Puerto Rican woman working in the Employment Development Division of Hartford Hospital, one of three general hospitals then operating in the city, was appointed to chair the task force. Before long, the task force began picketing Hartford Hospital to protest the cultural incompatibility between the hospital and the Latino community that surrounded it. Conceding some of its shortcomings, the hospital agreed to develop the staff position of "clerk-interpreter," with the objective of improving communication with Spanish-speaking patients. That summer, Stephen Schensul and Maria Borrero met and agreed to work together to push the health care system to be more responsive to the needs of the Puerto Rican community, which was rapidly on its way to constituting more than a third of the city's population and a majority of Hartford's school-age youth.

Eventually, this embryonic partnership led to the preparation and submission of a National Institute of Mental Health research proposal designed to carry out a broad community study of Puerto Rican health beliefs, behaviors, and health care adaptations. Additionally, the task force took on several other education and advocacy projects focused on making the health care system more responsive to and appropriate for serving Puerto Ricans. By the late spring of 1978, with several initiatives in the field, task force members decided to develop a formal organizational structure and to hire an executive director. A grant developed for this purpose was approved and funded by the Hartford Foundation for Public Giving, and the Hispanic Health Council (HHC) became a legally incorporated nonprofit community organization with Maria Borrero as its first executive director. The mission of the new organization was "improving the quality and accessibility of health, mental health and education related services in the Puerto Rican/Hispanic community." Later in the year, another Hartford anthropologist, Jean Schensul, joined the staff of the HHC and eventually became its associate director.

Over the next several decades, the HHC advanced from having offices in a rat-infested store front, a handful of staff, and a budget of several hundred thousand dollars, into the largest Latino community health and social service organization in Connecticut. It had a staff of 75 and had special expertise in culturally sensitive programming, gender-specific drug treatment for inner-city women, AIDS prevention, nutrition promotion, high-risk pregnancy intervention, youth development, environmental health, behavior health, and community health education, among other issues.

In its day-to-day practice, the HHC resembles a typical minority, community-based service agency, in that it works in the trenches addressing many of the most urgent community health problems facing the poor, including AIDS, cancer, substance abuse, and poor nutrition. The HHC provides a wide range of health-related and social services to low income, marginalized, and oppressed populations, with a strong focus on Latinos, but extending to all underserved populations. Its approach is not limited to service delivery, however, but rather emphasizes empowerment, advocacy, and the need for social restructuring to address health quality.

At the same time, the HHC also resembles a multidisciplinary research center, in that it has a strong research portfolio of social science of health and epidemiological studies, participates actively in scientific and scholarly activities, and recognizes research as the foundation for good services and useful social policy.

The Institute for Community Research

The Institute for Community Research (ICR) was established 10 years after the IIIC, when Jean Schensul became executive director of a small organization that conducted evaluations of local service organizations and programs, funding for which was being eliminated. She rebuilt the organization following the principles of community/research partnerships for the development and implementation of research issues of relevance to local communities. The cornerstone principles that guide its projects and programs include the following: (1) collaboration and partnership, (2) action research, (3) intervention and advocacy; and (4) cultural diversity, including cultural conservation and support for the right of cultural expression. Each of these principles is considered in the creation and conduct of all research projects at ICR.

In applying these cornerstone principles, the Institute's mission is to conduct research—in partnership with communities—that promotes justice and equity in access to health, education, and cultural resources in a socially diverse world. Thus, some of the early programs of the Institute included the following: 1) a rapid socio-demographic assessment of Hartford's inner-city neighborhoods, in partnerships with local neighborhood organizations, to identify key neighborhood health, educational, cultural, social, and political concerns and to empower local organizations in methods of inquiry to identify those concerns and seek appropriate responses; 2) a participatory action research (PAR) training program with inner-city women on issues they identified as primary concerns, in which they learned to design questions, collect, manage, and analyze data, and use findings to advocate for their interests; 3) a state-wide program to identify, document, and promote the work of heritage and folk artists representing the cultural heritage and various art forms of Connecticut's numerous nationalities and ethnic groups; and 4) a joint project with the HHC and four other community health and service organizations in Hartford to conduct an AIDS prevention demonstration research project and to develop and test culturally targeted intervention programs for drug users and their sex partners in the primarily African American and Puerto Rican inner city.

Over the past 10 years, ICR has evolved from these initial activities. It has received federal, state, local, and foundation funding for numerous subsequent community/research partnerships programs and projects in the areas of health, education, and cultural heritage and expression in the city and across the state. The Institute collaborates with a wide range of community and institutional partners in research and development designed to improve services, build community capacity, impact public policy, and contribute to social science theory and practice with programs that support social change.

Though ICR programs have primarily been conducted in the city of Hartford and the state of Connecticut, they have also expanded to include partnership projects in other cities in the U. S. and other countries internationally. Linked by their organizational histories, by collaborative projects and contractual relationships, and by personal relationships spanning many years, the HHC and ICR have jointly contributed to the development and implementation of the Hartford Model.

Institutional Similarities and Differences   While similar in many ways, there are notable differences between the HHC and ICR that have contributed to a range of programmatic expressions within the Hartford Model. The Hispanic Health Council, as the name suggests, is specifically rooted in the Latino (or more specifically, Puerto Rican) community of Hartford, even though it has a multicultural staff, serves diverse communities, and even maintains several international projects in non-Latino countries. By contrast, while the ICR is deeply involved in a number of ethnic minority communities and has a multicultural staff, it is not based in a specific ethnic community, and it too maintains an international program. Additionally, while direct service is a primary mission of the Hispanic Health Council, the ICR has emphasized both cultural arts as an expressive, community building, emancipatory domain and community research training initiatives. It should be noted, however, that ICR programs do offer important community services, while the HHC emphasizes the arts in its youth development initiatives.

Characteristics and Variants of the Hartford Model

The initial issues addressed through the Hartford Model were community mental health problems, family health and social crisis events, threats to women's reproductive health, and communication breakdowns in neonatal intensive care hospitalization (Schensul & Borrero, 1982). In the mid '80s, alcohol use and abuse and tobacco smoking also began to be addressed using this approach (Singer et al., 1992). Finally, in 1987, with the devastating emergence of the AIDS epidemic, the HHC and ICR applied the model to issues of drug use, drug related HIV risk, and HIV sexual risk (Singer & Weeks, 1996). The model also has been used by the HHC and ICR (alone and in collaboration) to address the following: barriers to health care access and disease assessment among the elderly, environmental health issues, risk reduction and resiliency among teens, cultural conservation, the development of access to artistic resources, occupational health issues, and a variety of other topics.

Despite the organizational differences between the HHC and ICR mentioned above, HIV/AIDS projects developed within the framework of the Hartford Model tend to be characterized by several key features, including a theoretical orientation toward health and illness, a particular approach to intervention and community capacity building, an organizational plan, and a distinctive practice/research methodology. Each of these will be examined in turn.

THEORETICAL ORIENTATION

The Hartford Model views health as much more than a biological state; in addition to a physical condition, health is understood as a reflection of social structural relations at the global, national, and local levels (e.g., as expressed in conditions like poverty, social inequality, stigmatization, racial or other discrimination) and the quality of the living and working conditions that they produce (Farmer, 1999; Singer, 2001). Notably, the World Health Organization (WHO) has defined health as "not merely the absence of disease and infirmity but complete physical, mental and social well being" (WHO 1978).

Taking this approach a step further, Kelman (1975) has argued for the necessity of viewing health within the context of a system of production. From this broader, critical perspective, health is defined as access to and control over the basic material and nonmaterial resources that sustain and promote life at a high level of satisfaction. With reference to the AIDS epidemic, for example, it has become clear that health is not merely the absence of symptoms but also the absence of social stigma and discrimination, which are often experienced by people living with HIV/AIDS as being more damaging than the direct clinical effects of infection (Parker & Aggleton, 2003; Valdiserri, 2002). Moreover, it means freedom from the oppressive social conditions that have become the breeding grounds of the epidemic.

Flowing from this perspective, two theoretical concepts for health research have emerged from the Hartford Model: *oppression illness* and *syndemic*. The term oppression illness (OI) (Baer, Singer, & Susser, 1997; Singer & Toledo, 1995) is used to label the chronic, traumatic effects of experiencing social bigotry over long periods of time (especially during critical developmental periods of identity formation) combined with the negative emotional effects of internalizing such prejudice. Oppression ill-ness, in other words, is a psychosocial product of the impact of suffering from social mistreatment based on prejudice (i.e., not simply oppression but oppression that is publicly rationalized as fair treatment of inferior or defective beings) and, at some level, accepting blame for one's suffering as just punishment for someone who does not deserve any better treat-ment. Individuals who suffer from OI not only have low or highly con-flicted self-esteem but also tend to embrace, at least to some degree, prevailing negative social stereotypes about their ethnic group, social class, gender, or sexual orientation. As this description implies, OI is a stress disorder, a product of an oppressive social environment of "struc-tural violence" (Farmer, 2003) and reflected in a pattern of oppressive so-cial relationships with multiple reinforcers of devalued individual and group worth.

OI encumbers AIDS prevention because research indicates associations among victimization stress, substance abuse, and AIDS risk. High rates of childhood violence victimization, for example, have been found among women who develop alcohol and drug abuse in adulthood (Miller, Downs, & Testa, 1993; Murphy, 1991). Kilpatrick (NIDA Notes 1992), us-ing a representative national sample of over 4,000 women, found that vio-lent crime victims who met criteria for PTSD were 9.7 times more likely to have major alcohol-related problems and 17 times more likely to have major drug abuse-related problems than nonvictims. The study also found that rape-related PTSD significantly increased a woman's risk for substance abuse. In these cases, substance abuse may represent a form of self-medication for the stress disorder (Hoffer & Cervantes, 1992; Parson, 1985).

The end result, however, is that individuals are put at heightened risk for a range of other health problems, including AIDS. Consequently, respond-ing to the AIDS epidemic in oppressed minority communities requires an acknowledgment of and a confrontation with a range of economic, social, health, and mental health issues. It also requires an awareness that piece-meal approaches that address part, but not the whole, of the intertwined complex social forces that contribute to and complicate the AIDS epidemic, are doomed to have limited, short-term success at best. In this context, OI represents a major challenge to effective community based intervention be-cause target population members suffer not only from numerous indicators of poor physical health and significant structural barriers to effective health access, but also from the inability to effectively respond to the chal-lenges they face because of the trauma of internalized oppression (Singer, Huertas, & Scott, 2000).

A second term introduced through work within the Hartford Model is "syndemic" (Baer, Singer, & Susser, 1997; Singer, 1994, 1996). At its simplest level, syndemic refers to two or more epidemics (i.e., notable increases in the rate of specific diseases in a population), interacting synergistically with each other inside human bodies and contributing to excess burden of disease in a population. As Millstein (2001) notes, "Syndemics occur when health-related problems cluster by person, place or time."

Importantly, the term syndemic refers not only to the temporal or locational cooccurrence of several diseases or health problems, but also to the health consequences of the biological interactions among the health conditions present. For example, researchers have found that coinfection with HIV and tuberculosis (TB) augments the immunopathology of HIV and accelerates the damaging progression of the disease (Ho, 1996). If both of these diseases cluster in the same population, opportunities for individuals to be coinfected spiral upward. Research has shown that patients who are coinfected with HIV and tuberculosis do not survive as long as those infected with solely HIV or tuberculosis, suggesting a synergistic interaction with deadly consequence for coinfected individuals (Singer, 1996).

Beyond the notion of disease clustering in a location or population, the term syndemic points to the importance of social location in the development of intertwined epidemics (Gilbert et al., 2000; Stall & Purcell, 2000). Living in poverty, for example, increases the likelihood of exposure to the bacteria that causes TB because of overcrowding in poorly ventilated dwellings. Once infected, the poor are more likely to develop active TB both because they are more likely to have multiple exposures to the TB bacteria (which may push dormant bacteria into a state of aggressive reproduction) and because they are more likely to have preexistent immune system damage from other infections and malnutrition. Finally, poverty and discrimination place poor individuals and families at disadvantage in terms of access to diagnosis and treatment for TB, effectiveness of available treatments because of weakened immune systems, and ability to adhere to TB treatment plans because of structurally imposed residential instability and the frequency of disruptive economic and social crises in their lives. As this example suggests, diseases do not tend to spread in a social vacuum nor solely within the bodies of those they inflict; thus their transmission and impact are never merely biological. Ultimately, social factors like poverty, racism, sexism, ostracism, stigmatization, disruption of social systems, and structural violence may be of far greater importance than the nature of pathogens or the bodily systems they infect in the transition of the development of epidemics.

Understanding AIDS as a syndemic has been a focal point of research within the Hartford Model, with a special focus on the interactions among drug use, violence, and HIV risk (Singer, 1996; Duke, Teng, Simmons, & Singer, 2003). Recognizing that the target populations in greatest need are subject to both OI and the AIDS syndemic has helped shape the kinds of intervention approaches (see below) that have developed within the Hartford Model. Participants in our research programs standardly are provided with advocated referral to health and mental health service, including HIV/AIDS testing and counseling, at the conclusion of project interviews (including to our own services). Moreover, a strong emphasis is placed on treating participants with respect and dignity.

INTERVENTION STRATEGY

The broad intervention strategy of the Hartford Model emphasizes the following: a) culturally appropriate programming and the linguistic and cultural matching of intervention staff and clients; b) sensitivity to the beliefs, concerns, cultural traditions, and social experiences of the target population; c) respecting the dignity of each participant, including those from socially denigrated groups such as drug users, sexual minorities, and commercial sex workers; d) being keenly sensitive to past insults and injuries associated with prejudice based on class, race, gender, sexual orientation and related social divisions, and e) recognizing that scarce resources limit the capacity of communities to address these concerns and that research provides a powerful tool that can be used to access new community resources.

In other words, the intervention strategy of the Hartford Model pushes for embracing but moving beyond cultural appropriateness, and even beyond essential ethical treatment, to an added level of awareness and solidarity with the target research community. This step involves attention not only to what a community knows, or what it wants or needs, but also to what it feels and the wounds it has suffered at the hands of the dominant society.

While we recognize that it is possible to achieve small but important improvements (e.g., in HIV risk levels) through narrowly focused intervention approaches (e.g., one-on-one or small-group risk-reduction education), the Hartford Model seeks to identify strategies that can achieve broader, sustained, improvements in public-health and community well-being. Consequently, interventions within the model take various shapes depending on the nature of the problem under consideration and the availability of resources. They emphasize the following: (1) assessment of intertwined health and social problems; (2) multidimensional intervention (i.e., interventions that addressed two or more interrelated health and social problems); (3) organizing community consortia with diverse arenas of expertise and resources (see below), and (4) community capacity building, training, and resource sharing to enhance representativeness and community/research partnership. This multifaceted approach is supported by findings showing that interventions are most effective when they are able to address several interrelated levels simultaneously and make enduring improvements in the capacity of communities to respond to future problems (Dryfoos, 1990; Hawkins, Catalano, & Miller 1992; Nastasi & DeZolt, 1994).

For example, Project Recovery, a drug treatment and AIDS prevention program for pregnant and recently postpartum women developed within the framework of the Hartford Model, included program components that addressed the following additive and interdependent goals: (1) ensure citywide community identification of substance abusing women by providing training to existing high-risk pregnancy and other health outreach workers affiliated with community organizations and the city health department; (2) provide a critically needed triaging and advocated referral system to facilitate the rapid entry of identified women into existing or new substance abuse detoxification and treatment; (3) initiate hospital-based substance abuse day treatment with close linkage to hospital departments of obstetrics, pediatrics, social services, psychiatry, and child psychiatry; (4) offer professional day care during treatment hours with attention to the special training and care needs of children of substance abusing parents; (5) make available intensified well-baby pediatric visits with a special focus on alcohol and drug exposure during pregnancy; (6) provide intensive long-term case management to address continuity of care needs, family-level problems, referral needs, and relapse issues among project participants; (7) organize a support group for the partners of women enrolled in the program to increase support for recovery; and (8) address the wide range of survival needs of substance abusing women and their children, including AIDS prevention and treatment, vocational training, housing, life skills acquisition, self-esteem enhancement, family violence prevention, and partner substance abuse. Most of these objectives have been sustained across several community consortia for almost a decade (Singer, 2000).

ORGANIZATIONAL PLAN

The organizational approach of the Hartford Model emphasizes the development of long-term practitioner/researcher collaboration. It is a broad-based and usually multidimensional *community consortia* for applied research and intervention on *community identified* health problems and related social issues. At the HHC and ICR, emphasis is placed on building an approach to research that (1) is developed through a "perpetual discussion" (Gudeman & Rivera, 1989) between experienced researchers and experienced community health educators and activists, and consequently (2) tends to reflect issues, concerns or pressing problems as perceived by members of the community being researched; that (3) is carried out by a multidisciplinary research/practice team and (4) leads to recognition not only for the researchers but also for the community-based institution that sponsors it, as well as (5) transferring research skills to minority researchers, while (6) contributing to the intervention, public education, social development, advocacy, and/or empowerment goals of the sponsoring agency (Parker, 1996; Singer, 1993). This approach corresponds to what Orlando Fals Borda (1990) has termed "participatory-action research" (PAR), in that it emphasizes a highly collaborative, community-driven, demystifying, empowering, and applied research orientation.

Critical to the Hartford Model is the PAR proposition that constructive social change must be driven by an "awareness-building process" (Rahman, 1985). This process entails two main features: (1) using science to produce knowledge and action that is directly useful to a community; and (2) using science to enhance the locus of effectiveness in the community of concern by helping participants identify and build their own knowledge, apply that knowledge, and assess the impact of their efforts. This proposition is derived from the PAR theory that valuing of community knowledge, active community participation, facilitated community discussion of common goals, planning of community efforts, and the sharing of findings from the assessment of outcomes produces effective community-based initiatives (Fals Borda, 1990). Moreover, it fosters a sense of ownership, values and rewards creativity and innovative approaches, pools the collective knowledge and experience base of a diverse set of community experts, and facilitates "resource add-on", in that committed participants tend to identify and access new avenues of direct project support. In addition, it cultivates community appreciation of research as an effective tool for social change and development (Whyte, 1995).

An Example

Exemplary of the participatory approach is the CDC-funded Building Community Responses to Risks of Emergent Drug Use Project. Through the 15 years of our work on drug issues at the HHC and ICR, we have observed that change in drug use behaviors is constant, including the periodic introduction of new drugs, the adoption of new drug combinations, the appearance of new drug use equipment, the discovery of new ways of using existing drugs, the incorporation of new drug use settings, and the emergence of new populations of drug users. These new patterns of drug use, and the changing social and biological environments in which they appear, have potentially significant public-health consequences. All too often, however, the public-health response to emergent drug-related epidemics is slow and fragmented. Too often we are only able to observe changes in drug use behaviors *after* public-health consequences (e.g., the drug-related HIV epidemic) have already become widespread.

Building on a 1-year pilot study initiated by our research team in conjunction with the Connecticut Department of Public Health, the goals of the "Building Community Response" project are to develop current knowledge of the ongoing changes in drug use. This is accomplished through the following: (1) using ethnographic and epidemiological methods (including in-depth key informant interviewing, direct observation, and structured surveys) to identify and track emergent drug use trends across several waves of data collection; (2) analyzing identified emergent drug use trends in terms of several key sociodemographic traits, including age, gender, ethnicity, neighborhood of residence, and drug use; (3) using a PAR model to implement a Participatory Community Response Team (PCRT) made up of researchers, drug treatment providers, health care providers, HIV prevention workers, concerned community members, and public-health officials; and (4) conducting a process and outcome evaluation of the project as a transferable community-based public-health methodology.

The PCRT model provides a means for direct participation by practitioners, policy makers, citizens, and/or lay leaders in defining the research questions, conducting and analyzing the research, and interpreting and applying the research findings. Its specific role is to provide advice on the identification of emergent drug use trends; assess the health risks of the new trends identified in the data collection component; and develop and implement community-based public-health responses (e.g., public education efforts) to the health risks generated by the identified emergent drug use trends. These objectives respond directly to the recognized need for research on new methods for enhancing surveillance, needs assessments, program delivery and evaluation, and the translation of research into effective intervention.

In the first wave of data collection (ongoing), the research team focused on three specific issues voiced at the first meeting of the PCRT: (1) the spread of club drugs like Ecstasy and ketamine to use on the street (sometimes in combination with street drugs like cocaine and heroin); (2) the use of embalming fluid as a recreational drug; and (3) the mixing of street drugs with prescription pharmacy drugs like tranquilizers. Findings from data collection on these issues will be examined to explore the nature and extent of the public-health risk (e.g., the further spread of HIV) produced by the spread of the new drug use patterns under examination.

The Value of Multidisciplinary Work

Beyond the internal perpetual discussion among researchers and practitioners within invested community-based organizations, the Hartford Model emphasizes the value of multidisciplinary, multiorganization practice/research partnerships. Such consortia are hard to sustain, in part because they are often grant-initiated and grants have limited life spans. In addition, however, they also present numerous challenges for organizers, including differing levels of commitment to research, multiple competing organizational demands, and differing personnel policies, philosophies, and contrastive salary and benefit plans. Yet they are critical because of the following: (1) individual researchers or practitioners are limited in their awareness of complex social groups and settings; (2) complex social issues require intersectorial approaches that can address the various aspects of a multifaceted problem; and (3) skills and resources are dispersed across community agencies, disciplines, and social institutions. Sharing tasks, knowledge, skills and resources allows the development of comprehensive responses that are attuned to the complexity of the types of issues resource-poor communities in the AIDS epidemic generally face.

Projects developed within the Hartford Model may include as collaborators researchers from universities, medical institutions, or research centers. However, the emphasis is on community-based organizations (CBOs) and community-centered research. While collaboration with non-community-based institutions provides a means of adding disciplinary skills not often found in CBOs, it is possible to build broad multidisciplinarity within community research organizations like the HHC and ICR. Indeed, collaboration across fields of expertise is easier in a community organization because people of different disciplines (e.g., in HHC, anthropologists, psychologists, epidemiologists, social workers, political scientists) are housed under one roof rather than being spread across departments on a sprawling university or research campus. Collaboration is further enhanced by a shared commitment to community centered applied research and to an ethic of multidisciplinary work that recognizes the value of diverse qualitative and quantitative methods.

The organizational approach of initiatives launched within the Hartford Model is illustrated by a consortium effort called the AIDS Community Research Group. This effort was developed in response to the recognition that AIDS could best be addressed through the adoption of a citywide strategy. In 1987, funding from the CDC provided the opportunity to conduct two AIDS knowledge, attitude, and behavior studies in Hartford with the goal of establishing baseline levels of AIDS knowledge, risk, and prevention in the general community. A multiethnic consortium was formed and six neighborhoods were identified for data collection. Each member organization within the consortium took on a different set of responsibilities to complete project tasks, including project management and coordination, staff training, data collection, data entry and analysis, report preparation, and dissemination of findings. Through two studies implemented in different neighborhoods, 750 household interviews were conducted with respondents between the ages of 18 and 49 (AIDS Community Research Group 1988, 1989; Schensul & Schensul, 2002; Singer et al., 1990). Findings were used to guide the development of a series of early HIV prevention programs within the city (Singer et al., 1990). They also formed the knowledge base upon which a series of specialized demonstration projects were constructed to test culturally appropriate prevention intervention with several highly at risk populations, including injection drug users, crack cocaine users, sex partners of street drug users, youth, women and MSM (Singer et al., 1993; Singer et al., 1994; Singer et al., 1997; Weeks et al., 1992; Weeks et al., 1993; Weeks et al., 1995; Weeks et al., 1996).

METHODOLOGICAL APPROACH

Methodologically, the Hartford Model grounds intervention in long-term epidemiological and ethnographic research on community conditions, beliefs, behaviors, and social structural relations. A number of anthropologists and epidemiologists have pointed out the potential benefits of closer collaboration between the two disciplines (Agar, 1996; Janes,

Stall, & Gifford, 1986). To this union, epidemiology brings a rigorous scientific approach, an emphasis on quantitative data collection, and a specifically applied orientation. Anthropology's contribution includes an emphasis on intensive qualitative investigation of behaviors and social relations in context and a keen awareness of the importance of culture (and hence, meaning) in shaping people's behavior, as well as their willingness to change behaviors to accommodate public-health dictates.

While open to multimethod research designs, anthropology favors immersion-based research methods, such as ethnography, that are conducted in "natural settings" in which the researcher(s) directly observes and, at least to some degree, participates in the everyday life of members of the group under study, records findings, and "writes an account . . . emphasizing descriptive detail" (Marcus & Fischer, 1986). In HIV-related research on drug use, for example, ethnography has provided fine-grained qualitative information on the following: (a) the actual technologies and processes of drug use, (b) the structure of the networks and social relations of drug users, (c) the immediate contexts of street drug consumption, (d) the interrelationship between drug use and a range of health risks, (e) cross-site variation among drug users and focused investigation of various drug user subgroups (e.g., drug injectors, crack users, women, minorities, adolescents, gay men and lesbians), and (f) the political economic structures, policies, and dominant social practices that foster drug use behaviors (Singer, 1999). Depending on the goals of the study, psychological, sociological, or other methods may be added to this mix, reflecting the multidisciplinarity of much contemporary AIDS research.

Over the last several decades of social and behavior AIDS research, blended methods have become increasingly common. For example, anthropologists at the HHC and ICR have worked closely with epidemiologists in assessing social context factors that contribute to HIV risk among injection drug users in different urban settings. This approach combines anthropological emphasis on direct observation of social interactions in actual risk settings, exchanges within social networks, systems of belief and motivation, and routine behavior with an epidemiological focus on careful measurement (e.g., using standardized surveys and the thoughtful structuring of participant sampling). Multidisciplinary teams have been able to identify key local context factors at both the neighborhood and city levels that contribute to differences in HIV risk and infection in different social environments (Singer, Juvalis, & Weeks, 2000; Buchanan et al., 2002; Buchanan et al., 2003).

Findings such as this are important in moving AIDS prevention intervention from a "one-size-fits-all" approach to the tailoring of prevention to fit the specific characteristics of local social environments. At the same time, this approach to community-based HIV research has helped shift the focus from individual beliefs and behaviors to a more balanced orientation that adds concern with group-level processes and the role of structural factors in HIV risk. Additionally, such an approach allows the collection and linkage of qualitative and quantitative data so as to help explicate the nature of human thoughts, behaviors, and relationships in their social contexts of origin.

Within the Hartford Model, we use several different approaches for linking qualitative and quantitative data, including sequential or staged data collection, concurrent parallel data collection, coordinated substudies, and analytic integration (Office of Behavioral and Social Sciences Research, 2001). In sequential integration, qualitative data may be collected during a formative phase and findings are then used to inform the creation of epidemiological survey instruments. In parallel concurrent studies, qualitative and quantitative methods are used simultaneously to address the same research questions. For example, in our initial pilot study of emergent drug trends and health sequelae (Singer, Juvalis, & Weeks, 2000), our project ethnographer remained in the field throughout the period of survey interviewing. Both arms of the study were focused on the same question: What are the emergent drug use behaviors in this population and what are their potential health consequences?

In coordinated substudy research, nested subgroups from a larger survey sample may be drawn for closer qualitative investigation of particular research questions. In our study of drug use, partner violence, and HIV risk (Duke et al., 2002), for example, we surveyed a sample of 524 drug-involved women recruited through street outreach. From this sample, 30 women who had experienced domestic violence were recruited for in-depth qualitative interviews to contextualize the lives of women at risk for violence, clarify the sequence of events leading to violence, and explicate the impact of violence on the women's drug use and HIV risk. Based on initial findings, a second survey was subsequently conducted with a subsample of women to investigate the relationship between adult HIV drug use and risk and early sexual abuse.

Finally, data integration may occur during the analytic phase of a study. Patterns that are suggested through content analysis of narrative data, for example, may be tested through statistical analysis or, conversely, correlations found during quantitative analysis may be clarified and the directionality of causation tested through the analysis of qualitative data on the behaviors in question.

Because of its focus on insider perspectives and behaviors in social and ecological context, ethnography is a core methodology of the Hartford Model. It informs formative research, needs assessment, the investigation of social relationships, the study of marginalized groups, and socially denigrated and hidden behaviors. It is of special use in HIV program evaluation because of its emphasis on understanding the operation and impact of programs that are intended to become normalized as part of regular social practice. A fundamental goal of effective HIV intervention is that it should lead to measurable improvements in health and well-being. To accomplish this, intervention techniques must be found that are socially and culturally acceptable to and practically adaptable by communities at risk.

Consequently, in community intervention design and evaluation, an ethnographic approach has a number of advantages, including comprehensiveness, provision of detail, and offering an approach for addressing threats to program integrity.

CONCLUSION

As Auerbach, Wypijewska, and Brodie (1994) stress, "How the two worlds of researchers and service providers interact is of great concern to all those involved in AIDS activities. . . . To facilitate the exchange of ideas . . . [we] must overcome differences and develop strategies for effective coordination and communication." The "two worlds" conception of research and practice has led to the assumption that the divide between research and intervention is so wide that improvements in coordination and communication cannot be achieved by housing both endeavors under a common roof. A Senate report that rationalized the reorganization of the Alcohol, Drug Abuse and Mental Health Administration (ADAMHA) noted the following:

> It might seem logical to keep research and services under the same roof to facilitate 'technology transfer,' the process by which research findings are applied in the field. In practice, however, the research and services enterprises are so different that they cannot be effectively administered in one agency. (quoted in Auerbach et al., 1994)

Underlying this conclusion is the view that because research "requires objectivity and limited involvement with the subjects of research" and service requires that workers "identify with and . . . advocate for their clients," there are enormous barriers to close collaboration (Auerbach et al., 1994).

The Hartford Model emerged as a "one roof" response to community health needs and provides one antidote for the schism described above. While the challenges noted in the Senate report are real and require regular attention, in Hartford we have found that by centering researchers and research projects in community-based organizations, by fostering a spirit of shared commitment to improving community health and well-being, and by being constantly vigilant about improving both communication and coordination, it is possible to achieve productive integration of the two domains of research and service. This effort has been aided by maintaining ethnography as a guiding discipline. Unlike other research methodologies, ethnography begins with the realization that to gain a full and useful understanding of an issue or group, it is necessary to break the shackles of "limited involvement" and participate in the lives and even in the struggles of the people under study. This orientation toward community participation and to field-based research lends itself to the practice/research collaboration that characterizes the Hartford Model. Finally, the Hartford Model rests on a commitment to advocacy and social change nested in an analysis of the role of structural factors, including structural violence, in the generation of risk, the spread of disease, and the production of social misery.

ACKNOWLEDGMENTS   An earlier version of this chapter was presented at the NIMH Conference on Context and Culture in HIV/STD Interventions: Ecological Strategies for Enhancing Community Impact, Washington, DC, 2000.

REFERENCES

Agar, M. (1996). Recasting the "ethno" in "epidemiology." *Medical Anthropology 16*, 391–403.

AIDS Community Research Group. (1988). *AIDS: Knowledge, attitudes and behavior in an ethnically mixed urban neighborhood.* Special Report to the Connecticut State Department of Health Services, Hartford, CT.

AIDS Community Research Group. (1989). *AIDS: Knowledge, attitudes and behavior in Hartford's neighborhoods.* Special Report to the Connecticut State Department of Health Services, Hartford, CT.

Altman, D. (1995). Sustaining interventions in community systems: On the relationship between researchers and communities. *Health Psychology, 14*(6), 526–536.

Asad, T. (1973). *Anthropology and the colonial encounter.* Atlantic Highlands, NJ: Humanities Press.

Auerbach, J. & Coates, T. (2000). HIV prevention research: Accomplishments and challenges for the third decade of AIDS. *American Journal of Public Health, 90*(7): 1029–1032.

Auerbach, J., Wypijewska, C., & Brodie, K. (1994). *AIDS and behavior: An integrated approach.* Washington, D.C.: National Academy Press.

Baer, H., Singer, M., & Susser, I. (1997). *Medical anthropology and the world system.* Westport, CT: Greenwood Publishing Co.

Bolton, R. & Singer, M. (1992). Introduction. Rethinking HIV prevention: Critical assessments of the content and delivery of AIDS risk reduction messages. In *Rethinking AIDS Prevention: Cultural Approaches.* Ralph Bolton and Merrill Singer (Ed.), pp. 1–5. Philadelphia: Gordon and Breach Science Publishers.

Buchanan, D., Khoshnood, K., Stopka, T., Santelices, C., & Singer, M. (2002). Ethical dilemmas created by the criminalization of status behaviors: Case studies from ethnographic field research with injection drug users. *Health Education and Behavior, 29*(1), 30–42.

Buchanan, D., Shaw, S., Teng, W., Hiser, P., & Singer, M. (2003). Neighborhood differences in patterns of syringe access, use and discard among injection drug users: Implications for HIV outreach and prevention education. *Journal of Urban Health: Bulletin of the New York Academy of Medicine, 80*(3), 438–454.

Dryfoos, J. (1990). *Adolescents at risk: Prevalence and prevention.* New York: Oxford University Press.

Duke, M., Saleheen, H., Teng, W., Wakefield, J., Rohena, L., Murphy, J., et al. (2002). *Examining the effects of domestic violence on HIV risk.* Presented at the CIRA Science Day. Center for Interdisciplinary Research on AIDS, Yale University.

Duke, M., Teng, W., Simmon, J., & Singer, M. (2003). Structural and interpersonal violence among Puerto Rican drug users. *Practicing Anthropology, 25*(3), 28–31.

Fals Borda, O. (1990). The application of participatory-action research in Latin America. In M. Albrow & E. King, *Globalization, Knowledge and Society.* London: Sage Publications.

Farmer, P. (1999). *Infections and inequality: The modern plagues.* Berkeley, CA: University of California Press.

Farmer, P. (2003). *Pathologies of power: Health, human rights, and the new war on the poor.* Berkeley: University of California Press.

Gearing, F. (1960). *Documentary history of the Fox Project.* Frederick Gear (Ed.). Chicago: University of Chicago.

Gilbert, L., El-Bassel, N., Rajah, V. Foleno, A., Fontdevila, J., Fryle, V., et al. (2000). The converging epidemics of mood-altering-drug use, HIV, HCV, and partner violence. *The Mount Sinai Journal of Medicine, 67*(5 & 6), 452–464.

Gills, D. (2001). Unequal and uneven: Critical aspects of community-university partnership. In *Collaborative research: University and community partnership.* Myrtis Sullivan and James Kelly (eds), pp. 3–23. Washington, D.C.: American Public Health Association.

Gough, K. (1968). Anthropology and imperialism. *Monthly Review, 19*(11), 12–27.

Gudeman, S. & Rivera, A. (1989). Colombian conversations: The strength of the earth. *Current Anthropology, 30,* 267–281.

Hawkins, J., Catalano, R., & Miller, J. (1992). Risk and protective factors for alcohol and other drug problems in adolescence and early adulthood: Implications for substance abuse prevention. *Psychological Bulletin, 112,* 64–105.

Ho, J. (1996). The Influence of Coinfections on HIV Transmission and Disease Progression. *The AIDS Reader, 6*(4), 114–116.

Hoffer, T. & Cervantes, R. (1992). Psychological effects of exposure to gang violence. In *Substance abuse and gang violence,* Cervantes, R. (Ed.), pp. 121–135. Newbury Park: Sage.

Holmberg, A. (1970). The research and development approach to the study of change. In *Applied anthropology:Readings in the uses of the science of man,* James Clifton, (Ed.), pp. 83–93. Boston: Houghton Mifflin.

Janes, C., Stall, R., & Gifford, S. (1986). *In anthropology and epidemiology: Interdisciplinary approaches to the study of health and disease.* Dordrecht, Netherlands: D. Reidel.

Kelman, S. (1975). The social nature of the definition problem in health. *International Journal of Health Services, 5,* 625–642.

Lamb, S., Greenlick, M. R., & McCarty, D., (Eds.). (1998). *Bridging the gap between practice and research: Forging partnerships with community-based drug and alcohol treatment.* Washington, D.C.: National Academy Press.

LeCompte, M., Schensul, J., Weeks, M., & Singer, M. (1999). *Research roles and research partnerships.* Walnut Creek, CA: AltaMira Press.

Marcus, G. & Fischer, M. (1986). *Anthropology as cultural critique.* Chicago: The University of Chicago Press.

Miller, B., Downs, W., & Testa, M. (1993). Interrelationship between victimization experiences and women's alcohol use. *Journal of Studies on Alcohol, Suppl. 11,* 109–117.

Millstein, B. (2001). *Introduction to the syndemic prevention network.* Atlanta: Syndemic Prevention Network, Centers for Disease Control and Prevention.

Murphy, J. (1991). Substance abuse and serious child mistreatment. *Child Abuse and Neglect, 15,* 197–211.

NIDA Notes. (1992). Female crime victims with stress disorder more likely to abuse drugs. *NIDA Notes, 7*(5), 12–13.

Office of Behavioral and Social Sciences Research. (2001). *Qualitative methods in health research.* NIH Publication No. 02-5046. Bethesda, MD: National Institutes of Health.

Parker, R. (1996). Empowerment, community mobilization and social change in the face of HIV/AIDS, *AIDS, 10*(Suppl. 3), S27–S31.

Parker, R. & Aggleton, P. (2003). HIV and AIDS-related stigma and discrimination: A conceptual framework and implications for action. *Social Science and Medicine*, 57, 13–24.

Parson, E. (1985). Ethnicity and traumatic stress; the intersecting point in psychotherapy. In *Trauma and its wake: the study and treatment of posttraumatic stress disorder*. New York: Brunner/Mazel.

Rahman, M. (1985). The theory and practice of participatory action research. In *The challenges of social change*, Orlando Fals Borda (Ed.). London: Sage.

Reback, C., Cohen, A., Freese, T., & Shoptaw, S. (2002). Making collaboration work: Key components of practice/research partnerships. *Journal of Drug Issues*, 32(3), 837–848.

Schensul, S. (1973). Action research: The applied anthropologist in a community mental health program. In *Anthropology beyond the university. Southern Anthropology Society Proceedings #7*, A. Redfield (Ed.). Athens, GA: University of Georgia Press.

Schensul, S. (1974). Skills needed in action research: Lessons from El Centro de La Causa. *Human Organization*, 33(2), 203–208.

Schensul, S. & Borrero, M. (1982). Introduction: The Hispanic Health Council. *Urban Anthropology*, 11(1), 1–8.

Schensul, J. J. & Schensul, S. (2002). Collaborative Rresearch: Methods of inquiry for social change. In *Handbook on qualitative research methods in education*, J. Goetz and Margaret Le Compte (Eds.). New York: Academic Press.

Shriver, M. DeBurger, R., Brown, C., Simpson, H., & Myerson, B. (1998). Bridging the gap between science and practice: Insight to researchers from practitioners. *Public Health Reports*, 113, Suppl. 1, 189–193.

Singer, M., (1990). Another perspective on advocacy. *Current Anthropology*, 31(5), 548–549.

Singer, M. (1993). Knowledge for use: Anthropology and community-centered substance abuse research. *Social Science and Medicine*, 37(1), 15–26.

Singer, M. (1996). A dose of drugs, a touch of violence, a case of AIDS: Conceptualizing the SAVA syndemic. *Free Inquiry in Creative Sociology*, 24(2), 99–110.

Singer, M. (1999). The ethnography of street drug use before AIDS: A historic review. In *Cultural, observational, and epidemiological approaches in the prevention of drug abuse and HIV/AIDS*. Patricia Marshall, Merrill Singer, and Michael Clatts, (Eds.)., pp. 228–264. Bethesda, MD: National Institute on Drug Abuse.

Singer, M. (1999). Toward the use of ethnography in health care program evaluation. *High Plains Applied Anthropologist*, 19(2), 144–157.

Singer, M. (2000). Updates on projects recovery and CONNECT. In *Careers in anthropology: Profiles of practitioner anthropologists*. Paula Sabloff (Ed.), pp. 64–66. NAPA Bulletin #20.Washington, D.C.: National Association for the Practice of Anthropology, American Anthropological Association.

Singer, M. (2001). Toward a bio-cultural and political economic integration of alcohol, tobacco and drug studies. *Social Science and Medicine*, 53, 199–213.

Singer, M., Flores, C., Davison, L., Burke, G., Castillo, Z., Scanlon, K., et al. (1990). SIDA: The sociocultural and socioeconomic context of AIDS among Latinos. *Medical Anthropology Quarterly*, 4, 72–114.

Singer, M., Flores, C., Davison, L., & Gonzales, W. (1993). Reaching minority women: AIDS prevention for Latinas. *Practicing Anthropology*, 15(4), 21–24.

Singer, M., Gonzalez, W., Vega, E., Coenteno, I., & Davison, L. (1994). Implementing a community based AIDS prevention program for Puerto Ricans: The

Comunidad y Responsibilidad Project. In *AIDS prevention and services: Community cased research*, Johannes P. Van Vugt (Ed.). South Hadley, MA: Bergin and Garvey Press.

Singer, M., Himmelgreen, D., Weeks, M., Radda, K., & Martinez, R. (1997). Changing the environment of AIDS risk: Findings on syringe exchange and pharmacy sale of syringes in Hartford, CT. *Medical Anthropology, 18*(1), 107–130.

Singer, M., Huertas, E., & Scott, G. (2000). Am I my brother's keeper: A case study of the responsibilities of research. *Human Organization, 59*(4), 389–400.

Singer, M., Jia, Z., Schensul, J. J., Weeks, M., & Page, J. B. (1992). AIDS and the IV drug user: The local context in prevention efforts. *Medical Anthropology, 14*, 285–306.

Singer, M., Juvalis, J. A., & Weeks, M. (2000). High on illy: Monitoring and emergent drug problem in Hartford, CT. *Medical Anthropology, 18*, 365–388.

Singer, M. & Toledo E. (1995). *Oppression illness: Critical theory and intervention with women at risk for AIDS*. American Anthropology Association, Washington, D.C.

Singer, M. & Weeks, M. (1996). Preventing AIDS in communities of color: Anthropology and social prevention. *Human Organization, 55*(4), 488–492.

Smith, L. (1999). *Decolonizing methodologies: Research and indigenous peoples*. London: Zed Books.

Stall, R. & Purcell, D. (2000). Intertwined epidemics: A review of research on substance use among men who have sex with men and its connection to the AIDS epidemic. *AIDS and Behavior 4*(2), 181–192.

Tax, S. (1970). The fox project. In *Applied anthropology: Readings in the uses of the science of man*, James Clifton (Ed.), pp. 106–112. Boston: Houghton, Mifflin.

Valdeserri, R. (2002). HIV/AIDS stigma: An impediment to public health. *American Journal of Public Health, 92*(3), 341–342.

Weeks, M., Grier, M., Hunte-Marrow, J., Perez, W., Sanks, M., & Singer, M. (1992). Working together to make a difference: A consortium model for culturally appropriate AIDS intervention. In *Community-cased AIDS prevention among intravenous drug users and their sexual partners: The many faces of HIV disease*. Bethesda, MD: NOVA Research Company.

Weeks, M., Schensul, J., Williams, S., Singer, M., & Grier, M. (1995). AIDS prevention for African American and Latina women: Building culturally and gender appropriate intervention. *AIDS Education and Prevention, 7*(3), 251–263.

Weeks, M., Singer, M., Grier, M., Hune-Marrow, J., & Haughton, C. (1993). AIDS prevention and the African American injection drug user. *Transforming Anthropology, 4*(1-2), 39–51.

Weeks, M., Singer, M., Grier, M., & Schensul, J. (1996). Gender relations, sexuality, and AIDS risk among African American and Latina women. *In Gender and health: An International perspective*, pp. 338–370. Carol Sargent and Caroline Brettell, (Eds.) NJ: Prentice Hall.

White, R. (2000). Unraveling the Tuskegee Study of Untreated Syphilis. *Archives of Intern Medicine, 160*(5), 585–598.

Whyte, W. F. (1995). Encounters with Participatory Action Research. *Qualitative Sociology, 18*(3), 289–299.

World Health Organization. (1978). *Primary Health Care*. Geneva: World Health Organization.

8

Sustainability in HIV Prevention Research

Jean J. Schensul

> If existing prevention strategies were "brought to scale" we could pre-
> vent as many as 29 million of the 45 million new infections that have
> been projected to occur by 2010. But resource sufficiency is not the
> only condition required for successful HIV prevention. It is also cru-
> cial to support various prevention approaches, to integrate HIV pre-
> vention into treatment and care, to recognize and address the social
> factors that facilitate HIV transmission, and to provide strong, contin-
> uous leadership in support of HIV prevention efforts.
>
> (Valdiserri, Ogden, & McCray, 2003, p. 884)

> ... A community empowerment intervention seeks to increase the
> community's capacity to be self-determining in a specific domain: in
> the case of HIV/AIDS, the ability to integrate effective HIV interven-
> tion into existing community structures; to adapt interventions to
> changing conditions and to apply relevant skills and resources to
> other community health concerns.
>
> (Beeker, Guenther-Grey, & Raj, 1998, p. 833)

This chapter focuses on the problem of sustainability of effect in
community-based HIV prevention research. HIV prevention research is
conducted in local communities, generally those with significantly high
rates of HIV. Reducing HIV rates over time is a priority for these communities. But despite the fact that persistence of effects can satisfy local community needs, and at the same time answer questions of longer term efficacy
central to replication and scaling up (Altman, 1986, 1995; Booysen & Arntz,
2003; Stryker et al., 1995; Winkleby, 1994), prevention science has largely ignored questions of local sustainability. The purpose of this chapter is to address this critical aspect of the community impact of interventions.

We define sustainability as consisting of three dimensions:

- persistence of changes resulting from a preventive intervention
- institutionalization of core intervention components believed to
  contribute to desired outcomes
- capacity to adapt existing intervention components to respond to
  changing circumstances in order to maintain positive effects

These issues have not been properly addressed in prevention science
because the prevailing cultures of experimental social science and preven-

tion science funding and the structures that underpin these sets of ideologies constitute significant barriers to consideration of local intervention sustainability, thus offering little to assist communities in addressing their ongoing prevention needs. On the other hand, emerging research, intervention, and capacity building paradigms such as community-based participatory research (Minkler & Wallerstein, 2003), community-level interventions (cf. Miller & Kelly, 2002; Trickett, 2002; Wohlfeiler, 2002), community empowerment (Beeker et al., 1998; Strawn, 1994), and community organizing strive to address community needs while failing to consider important dimensions of prevention science. Synthesizing these contrasting research paradigms (Burrell & Morgan, 1979; Deetz, 1996; Guba & Lincoln, 1994; LeCompte & Schensul, 1999; Lincoln & Guba, 2000; Schensul & Berg, in press) and concentrating on the development and maintenance of intervention infrastructure can reconcile the contradictions between scientific concerns about generalizability/replication, sustainability of effects, and the necessary and inevitable local adaptations of preventive interventions. Once this is clearly understood, social science researchers, community advocates, and national and international funders can take substantial steps to mediate barriers and promote structural changes that support local sustainability more consistently over time.

We first discuss the clinical trial model that drives prevention science, and its limitations in HIV intervention research. Through examples of current or completed multilevel community studies that have utilized experimental or quasi-experimental designs, we identify elements of intervention research design that, with advance consideration, could lead to local sustainability. The chapter concludes with a summary of the factors that contribute to both replicability and sustainability and why they must coincide in order to produce ethical HIV prevention science.

INQUIRY PARADIGMS AND HIV PREVENTION SCIENCE

The need to develop interventions to address dramatically accelerating rates of HIV in the United States, Europe, and Africa resulted in a rapid increase in HIV prevention programs and research in the late 1980s and 1990s. The first knowledge, attitude, and behavior (KAB) and epidemiological studies were followed by almost two decades of behavioral intervention research targeting the behaviors of a wide range of populations in an equally wide variety of contexts: injection drug users, female sex partners, commercial sex workers of both sexes, youth at risk in and out of school, homeless youth, gay and lesbian young and older men and women, pregnant women, and HIV seropositive men and women at high risk of HIV infection or of infecting others (Becker & Joseph, 1988; Choi & Coates, 1994; Ekstrand & Coates, 1990; Shain et al., 1999; Sikkema et al., 2000; Valdiserri et al., 1989; van Empelen et al., 2003).

Over time, these studies have increased in complexity and sophistication. Following medical research practice, most of them have drawn on social science theories addressing individual behavioral change, using a variety of experimental and quasi-experimental designs (Booth & Watters, 1994; Gibson, McCusker, & Chesney, 1998; Kalichman, Carey, & Johnson, 1996; Oakley, Fullerton, & Holland, 1995; Office of Technology Assessment, 1995; O'Neill et al., 1996; Slonim-Nevo, Auslander, Ozawa, & Jung, 1996; Stanton et al., 1998). Some studies have focused on service providers, with the goal of improving services designed to reduce HIV infection (treatment of STDs or other HIV-related diseases) or improving testing and counseling (Kamali et al., 2003; Kamb et al., 1998; Weinhardt, Carey, Johnson, & Bickham, 1999). Others have evaluated the efficacy of street outreach, site-based interventions, needle exchange programs, and partner notification (Gibson, Flynn, & McCarthy, 1999; Groseclose et al., 1995; Hurley, Jolley, & Kaldor, 1997; Valleroy et al., 1995).

The early stages of HIV prevention research did not take guidance from large-scale, ecologically oriented, multilevel prevention studies in other domains of health such as the Framingham and Minnesota heart health studies. Rather, prevention theories and subsequent interventions were drawn from cognitive behavioral psychology and focused on individual-level changes in attitudes, beliefs, intentions, and knowledge. In terms of research design, these funded studies were driven by the medical model of science research, randomizing participants into treatment and control groups and utilizing a variety of brief individualized interventions.

Over time, the recognition that prevailing concepts and standardized measures did not meet the requirements of multiethnic, international, or new and hidden populations produced renewed interest in the "culture of risk" and risk behavior (Shadish, Cook, & Campbell, 2002). Interpretist paradigms and observational (Bourgois, 1995), narrative (Fisher & Fisher, 1993), and network methods (Needle, Genser, & Trotter, 1995; Trotter, 1999) were introduced to improve community-situated understandings of risk and to develop culturally appropriate instrumentation (Trotter & Schensul, 1998). Even with these new, more culturally targeted or specific intervention approaches, however, the emphasis on individualized outcomes prevailed, and study requirements called for and focused on adequate recruitment, assignment, tracking, and evaluation. In prevention science, collaboration with communities beyond the accomplishment of these study needs was not important.

By the early 1990s, the widespread recognition that the root causes of HIV were situated beyond the individual gave rise to a number of broader approaches to HIV prevention research that utilized culturally targeted group or network diffusion models to influence individual behavioral change (cf. Coyle, Needle, & Normand, 1998; Latkin, Mandell, Vlahov, Oziemkowska, & Celentano, 1996; van Empelen et al., 2003; Weeks, Clair, Borgatti, Radda, & Schensul, 2002). These new approaches required greater collaboration between researchers and local communities because they depended on community willingness to locate intervention activities in sites within the communities, and for community members to participate in recruitment and evaluation efforts. Research partnerships began to influence the science of HIV prevention as community partners provided, and at times insisted upon, input into intervention and evaluation designs. Nevertheless, the dominant research paradigm continued to situate research in but not with communities, and to emphasize individual-level behavioral outcomes.

Bolstered by the infrastructure of funding and review, the culture of experimental science currently calls for a standardized four-stage approach: evaluation for acceptability (local pilot testing), determination of short-term outcomes (Phase 1: "local" efficacy), determination of multisite effectiveness (Phase 2: replicability), and broad-based scaling up (Phase 3: dissemination). In this model, communities constitute the sites where "scientifically validated" interventions can be assessed, replicated, and eventually disseminated.

Sustainability of effect and the development of infrastructure in intervention sites have no place in this model. Phase 1 and Phase 2 clinical trials are managed by researchers trained to maximize intervention fidelity and desired outcomes, not to build infrastructure for continuity of results, or intervention sustainability. Publication guidelines and clinical/experimental research focus on research methods and results. Thus, most articles summarizing the results of intervention research generally do not describe any or many of the processes required for establishing local partnerships and other infrastructure needed to conduct (and to sustain) a successful intervention study. Those few articles that do document the process of forming relationships consider effects of such relationships on recruitment, instrument development, intervention content, and performance and outcomes, but not on longevity (Felix Aaron & Bass, 2002; Kalichman, Rompa, & Cage, 2000; Leonard et al., 2003).

Community/patient consultation in human subjects issues, interpretation of results, and planning for future activities are important contributions with respect to improving the quality of research and ensuring compatibility between research goals and community views, needs, and outcome expectations. However, they do not necessarily lead to, nor are they usually intended to lead to, sustainability of results, institutionalization of practices, or technology transfer.

A second limitation of the current culture of experimental prevention science, funding, and review involves a lack of attention to the duration of effect over time. Most behavioral or mixed behavioral/clinical intervention studies in the literature are limited to the assessment of short- or intermediate-term, rather than longer term outcomes (cf. Coates et al., 2000; Grosskurth et al., 1995; Jemmott, Jemmott, & Fong, 1998; van Empelen et al., 2003; Wiebel et al., 1996). They measure outcomes immediately post intervention and up to 2 years post intervention, an endpoint usually determined not by theoretical considerations but by funding sources that support 3- to 5-year studies. "Booster" sessions have been utilized as a means of strengthening intermediate (up to 2 years) rather than longer term outcome effects.

Only a handful of studies have been able to pursue cohorts for multiple 5-year periods, and most of these cohort studies address health problems other than HIV (cf. Altman, 1986; Winkleby, 1994). Some studies have shown interesting counterintuitive effects over time, such as short-term declines and longer term improvements in desired outcomes. In addition, some interventions may have unanticipated negative effects. For example, Rhodes and Quirk (1995) link drug harm–reduction interventions to increases in sexual risk taking. Such short-term perspectives have both theoretical as well as pragmatic limitations related to sustainability. For example, as yet there is little research on outcome variability and attention to the conditions under which long-term effects of behavior change studies may be achieved (cf. Rapkin, 2002). Why some interventions have immediate positive and long-term negative outcomes, and others have immediate negative and long-term positive outcomes is clearly a subject for further research. Thus, reviews based on short-term outcome assessments that suggest that we have sufficient knowledge to scale up known interventions (Valdeserri, 2003) are misleading; they may be seen as implying both more enduring and more positive intervention effects than may indeed be the case.

From the point of view of sustainability and continuing to use the clinical trials model, the main paradigm guiding prevention science has three major limitations: 1) It emphasizes the individual to the exclusion of the context; 2) it accepts shorter term effects as adequate proof of success; and 3) it overlooks the importance of methods for the formation and maintenance of community-based research partnerships.

INSTITUTIONALIZATION OF INTERVENTIONS IN LOCAL COMMUNITIES

Institutionalization can be defined as building the capacity to continue service or programmatic components of an intervention in order to maintain desired outcomes. Successful institutionalization requires the following:

- committed, informed, and supportive organizational partners
- intervention personnel who understand and can implement the intervention as it was theorized and planned
- the necessary financial resources to conduct the intervention at a level that promises effect
- the capacity to recruit and retain participants
- a system for identifying whether the approach is acceptable in the target community (cf. Altman, 1995).

Citing Jackson (1994), Altman describes technology transfer models that shift project responsibility and technology to the local community. These models focus on building new community infrastructure (similar to the CDC-funded URCs) to continue a project, building community capacity by identifying and working with existing community organizations, developing training for intervention technology transfer and innovation, and promoting mutual respect for needs of both researchers and implementing organizations (cf. Jackson et al., 1994). These approaches assume that local interest exists or can be generated, but they overlook initial and ongoing local community input into the process; that is, they ignore partner reciprocity.

New research technologies supporting quasi-experimental design (Shadish et al., 2002), Group Control Trials, and multilevel or ecological approaches to HIV prevention are beginning to appear in the prevention science literature (Nastasi, Moore, & Varjas, 2003; Trickett, 2002). Implementation of these community wide–intervention research designs demands good local partnerships that could be instrumental in ensuring intervention continuity after a study is completed. However, most of these models are incomplete in their lack of specification about how to couple local partnerships with sustainability. With some additional effort, however, these partnerships could be activated in such a way as to sustain an intervention in place over time. Some examples of multilevel HIV intervention firmly rooted in local communities illustrate ways that advance consideration of the institutionalization process could contribute to maintenance when the research phase is over. They also illustrate obstacles in translating intervention research to sustainable, long-term practice.

Roberta Paikoff and colleagues implemented a community-based AIDS prevention partnership that began with a strong relationship with a community activist committed to reducing sexual risk. Through this relationship, parents, schools and other sectors of the school community became involved in formative research identifying behaviors, sites, and scripts surrounding sexual risk opportunities for elementary school African-American children. They then joined in putting this research into practice in a successful multilevel school- and community-based intervention with the participation of all the partners. The intervention approach was replicated in the United States and internationally, and it became widely recognized as a model program (Madison, McKernan McKay, Paikoff, & Bell, 2000; McCormick et al., 2000; Paikoff, 1996; Paikoff, Parfenoff, Williams, & McCormick, 1997; Sagrestano & Paikoff, 1997). Thus, from the standpoint of the current paradigm of intervention research, this project was extremely successful. It demonstrated results in one community and was replicated elsewhere.

Local institutionalization, however, was never one of its goals and was certainly never intended to be one of its measurable outcomes. Thus, it was not initially structured to attend to this concern. Community involvement and project success had earned the commitment of local community residents and activists, who wanted to continue it. But community activists and families associated with the intervention were not linked to any organizational base, nor did they have independent capacity for fundraising, two critical factors in ensuring local institutionalization. Thus, despite the strong partnerships and community support critical to the success of the project, the end of the study marked the end of the project.

The work of Susan Kegeles and colleagues with young gay and bisexual men provides an example of multilevel HIV preventions that built and depended on local support and volunteerism for its success (Hays, Rebchook, & Kegeles, 2003; Kegeles, Hays, & Coates, 1996). The project promotes norms for safer sex through a variety of social, outreach, and small-group activities conducted in four matched study communities in different parts of the country using a staged crossover design. It was designed to be run by a "Core Group" of 12–15 young gay and bisexual men who, along with volunteers, designed and carried out multilevel project activities that diffused messages about safer sex through informal conversations, small-group discussions, and small media. Outcomes were measured by examining changes in percentages of risk behavior using cross-sectional surveys at several time points (Kegeles & Hart, 1998; Kegeles et al., 1996).

From the point of view of potential sustainability, the Mpowerment intervention model offers many strengths. Unlike the previous project, Mpowerment was a community-wide intervention designed to change local structures for HIV prevention, local culture (beliefs and practices), and group norms regarding sexual risk taking. To do so, it engaged members of the community as peer educators and opinion leaders who participated in developing and carrying out the project. The intervention was deemed sustainable because of its low cost (Kahn, Kegeles, Hays, & Beltzer, 2001), voluntary nature, and the way in which it embedded new norms, beliefs, and behaviors in local community networks of practice. It was located in communities where few opportunities existed for young gay men to socialize, so it offered a hidden population new and desirable means of socializing. Project volunteers used low-level technology in a setting in which the supply of young men was continually replenished. These conditions fulfilled several requirements of local institutionalization: continuous recruitment, training and engagement of committed new project managers to maintain the flow of communication through risk networks, and maintaining new and existing sites and activities where prevention activities took place.

Though the researchers noted these advantages as contributing to the intervention's potential for local institutionalization, it did not happen. Researchers did not describe the reasons for noninstitutionalization except for noting funding gaps. Nor did they indicate whether they believed they had any responsibilities for institutionalization of the intervention.

Kelly and colleagues' Opinion Leader approach, another multilevel community intervention, shared some of the same elements: the presence of a large gay constituency in a small community, the presence of "high-risk sites" (gay bars) where young gay and bisexual men gathered who could partner with the researchers, and volunteer (or quasi-volunteer) opinion leaders who could diffuse the messages easily through bar client networks. A community-level pre-post design showed short-term efficacy, and the project has been replicated in the United States and elsewhere (Kelly et al., 1997; Kelly et al., 1991; Kelly et al., 1992). Despite widespread acceptance, however, no longer term evaluation of outcome duration beyond the standard 2-year period has ever been carried out in study sites. Indeed, none of the published articles on this well-established intervention has described efforts to institutionalize the project in gay bars in the study communities even though substantial infrastructure for local continuity existed even prior to the initiation of the study.

Another multilevel, communitywide intervention study, now in its 2nd year of implementation in India, has structural features that support high potential for institutionalization. Designed to reduce HIV risk through culturally appropriate STD testing and sexuality counseling, the intervention delivers risk reduction at the community-wide, provider, and individual levels. Counseling through informational campaigns is conducted by local NGOs (community wide), and allopathic and traditional health practitioners are trained to counsel men on causes of sexual dysfunction and STD protection (provider level). In addition, the project treats sexually active men for STDs and sexual dysfunction problems that lead to high-risk sexual behavior in a newly initiated, publicly funded, male health clinic (individual level).

Like the other studies, the design is an GRT (Group Randomized Trial) that involves three matched communities, two treatment communities where allopathic and traditional providers are trained in STD management and sexual dysfunction prevention, and one control community (standard treatment). Outcomes are assessed through structural changes in provider treatment, changes in male beliefs about sexual dysfunction, risk behavior, and reduction in STD rates.

Several aspects of the structure of this project support its potential for sustainability. The inclusion of male health components in standard NGO-delivered health promotion campaigns is cost effective. Providers, when trained, should readily be able to incorporate new intervention components into their standard practice at no extra cost. Some may be trained to continue training others through local medical centers granting degrees and certificates in Ayurvedic, Unani, allopathic, and homeopathic medicine. The male health clinic model can thus be institutionalized as part of the public-health service structure. For scaling up purposes, the close association with the Mumbai Municipal and Maharashtra AIDS Control organizations offers an enabling environment for introducing low-cost program components into public-health clinics and programs in the target communities and elsewhere in Mumbai. In addition, the collaborating university conducts HIV research and evaluation and has a commitment to continue working in the local area. Overall, the components for institutionalization and the intent to institutionalize are in place. Plans for doing so will be developed in the 4th and 5th years of the study.

A final example of a local HIV intervention study that offers the potential for sustainability and institutionalization through multilevel intervention strategies and ongoing partnerships is the NIDA-funded Risk Avoidance Partnership project at the Institute for Community Research. This study, developed by researchers working with active drug users, reduces HIV-related drug risk behavior by diffusing risk-reduction messages and strategies through trained active drug users (peer level) into the sites they use and their peer user networks. It is also supporting the development of an advocacy group of active drug users who can articulate their needs and interests to policy makers (community level). Effects will be measured at the individual level by monitoring changes in behavior of network members, and through cross-sectional surveys to determine the diffusion of risk-reduction messages and reduction in risk behavior of individuals associated with peer health advocates. Potential for institutionalization exists through transference of the model to other HIV prevention organizations that work with active drug users and the formalization of the drug users' advocacy group. One advantage with respect to this program model is its location at the Institute for Community Research, an organization with a long-term commitment to research for HIV prevention in Hartford and the surrounding area that can work with other organizations to seek funds to institutionalize research and intervention efforts.

These studies described above are among the best available models for community-based intervention research with high potential for institutionalization. However, none of the research teams can or could in the future be faulted for failing to sustain results locally or to institutionalize their projects because neither duration of results nor institutionalization were among the research questions and research strategies that framed the studies. These studies demonstrate clearly how intervention research ideology, theory, practice, and funding are all geared toward the implementation and replication of experimental interventions. The matter of sustaining local intervention infrastructure to ensure durability of intervention effect is left to others or to the political will of the collaborating partners. With careful forethought and only modest additional project expenditure and attention to the acquisition of local funding, however, these projects could be locally institutionalized while at the same time contributing to the replicability and generalizability of findings in prevention science.

SUSTAINABILITY AS LOCAL SCIENCE-BASED PROBLEM-SOLVING CAPACITY

In the face of individual, cultural, or structural change affecting risk behavior, implementers must be able to adapt a program to respond to new conditions rather than maintain the same strategies with diminishing effects. Institutionalization alone does not guarantee the presence of this capacity (cf. Jackson et al., 1994; Schensul, 1999; Schensul & LeCompte, 1999). The same challenge faces organizations encouraged to use "evidence-based" programs and practices, only to find that they must adapt them to meet local needs (cf. Miller, Klotz, & Eckholdt, 1998). Both of these circumstances require the assessment of new conditions, modification of intervention strategies, and evaluation of results to sustain positive outcomes (Gilliam et al., 2003).

Wong and colleagues describe the efficacy of a multilevel participatory HIV prevention intervention carried out by a partnership that brought together the National University of Singapore, the Singapore Department of STD Control, brothel managers, and commercial sex workers and clients (Wong, Chan, & Koh, 1998). Based on a local needs assessment, brothel keepers learned about STDs and HIV and the "benefits of an STD-free brothel." They were also encouraged to support sex workers in their efforts to refuse unprotected sex and insist on condoms (p. 894). In addition, health facilitators trained sex workers. This was reinforced by experienced sex workers who motivated their peers to take risks and require condom use and to share their skills.

The intervention was evaluated using a quasi-experimental design at baseline and 5 months post intervention, showing a posttest increase in condom referrals. A time-series design that followed the treatment group for 2 years showed a significant increase in condom use in the treatment group during that period. During this period, researchers and project facilitators provided counseling, assisted peer educators to promote vigilant warnings from the AntiVice Control to brothels refusing to allow women to use condoms, provided individual counseling to sex workers, and assisted them in overcoming their reluctance to ask clients to use condoms. They also facilitated discussions where peer educators shared ways of dealing with problems associated with condom use.

To the question "What led to the sustained consistent condom use over time?" project facilitators responded: "It was probably due to the maintained contacts with the sex workers, continual appraisal of their problems to develop prompt and appropriate solutions, and ongoing support from health staff, peers and brothel keepers" (p. 898). In other words, the critical ingredient was *constant problem solving* through the continuing partnership between the university, local health department, and constituencies involved in commercial sex work after the intervention study ended. This perspective on successful sustainability as constant problem solving challenges the notion of sustainability as the continuation of a specific, prescribed set of programmatic activities over time.

Robin Miller's fine-grained and thoughtful evaluation of the process of adapting the Kelly and St. Lawrence peer opinion leader–intervention model to bar settings in New York shows how theory-driven, science-based HIV prevention strategies can be adopted, adapted, and evaluated by community organizations. Further, her essay describes the ways the adaptation process can be used to question and modify both theory and methods utilized in the original study. Her experience as a trained research psychologist and her capacity to work as an applied researcher and activist at the GMHC provided the disciplinary and conceptual skills to articulate what implementers do, but rarely describe and never evaluate. This experience, like the previous one, suggests that proper technology transfer and intervention adaptation calls for a partnership between prevention researchers and committed community change agents (Miller, 1995; Miller et al., 1998).

But can community residents themselves learn to engage in environmental assessment and the construction of interventions they themselves develop? Can intervention science be democratized? An example from the Institute for Community Research illustrates how research technology transfer empowers community activists to develop an intervention-research conceptual model, transform it into an intervention, and participate in implementing, evaluating, disseminating, and adapting it. In 1997, a consortium that included ICR; the Institute for the Hispanic Family, a mental health service provider; and El Centro, an early childhood center, received funding to replicate one of six "science-based" early childhood family strengthening models for drug and sexual risk prevention with preschoolers. The local consortium took the position that Latino parents should devise their own prevention theory, test it through research with other Hispanic families, and choose intervention components based on the results of their research.

ICR research staff and preschool parents formed a community research team that developed its own indigenous prevention research model using modeling techniques derived from Rossi, Freeman, and Lipsey (1999) and Schensul, Schensul, and LeCompte (1999); they also learned and implemented qualitative and survey research, analyzed the results, and used them to verify their model and to choose intervention components. Together with ICR research staff, the parents tested the instruments, consolidated the intervention components into a manual, and participated in the intervention and a short-term evaluation.

This process transferred critical thinking and research-based problem-solving and assessment skills from researchers to parents. It enabled parents to learn about prevention science and developed their capacity to generate their own science-based intervention drawing from existing interventions that matched their own model. Like Miller's adaptation of the Opinion Leader model of intervention in gay bars, this model also involved university-trained researchers working together with community agencies. Differences lie in the engagement of participants in learning and using research technology to develop and test their own prevention theory against national models, a process they were then able to replicate.

Such stakeholder-based capacity-building approaches, although labor intensive, enable communities to gain and utilize the skills to develop or adapt interventions to changing conditions. Beeker refers to community capacity building in HIV prevention as a community empowerment approach to primary prevention (Beeker et al., 1998). Adding research skills to the primary prevention toolkit enhances community capacity to adapt to new situations and to access the new resources required to do so. Still, these efforts represent but pieces of the longer range process of sustainability defined as the ability to assess changing conditions and adapt interventions to them as circumstances require.

DISCUSSION

The primary mission of community-based intervention research in HIV/ AIDS has been to develop and test programmatic preventive or intervention approaches with demonstrated effects that can be replicated and scaled up elsewhere. In the process of doing so, community researchers must engage with communities because partnership with community leaders, organizations, and networks is required to develop and test these approaches. In addition to pragmatism, the ethics of community-based research support sustaining intervention results over time and in the study location, rather than pursuing short-term results and replication elsewhere. So what must be done to integrate scientific integrity with long-term local sustainability?

First, researchers who engage in community-based intervention studies that call for local partnerships should be supported and encouraged to build these partnerships for local sustainability at the beginning of a project, in anticipation of positive outcomes. Indeed, such partnerships may themselves be seen as increasing the chances of positive outcomes.

Developing the infrastructure for multilevel HIV/AIDS community-intervention research requires considerable investments of time, personnel, and resources to secure the required partnerships and cooperation in the field. Sustaining this infrastructure is critical in order to ensure that results persist and that communities develop the capacity and tools to address new HIV-related challenges (Bartholomew, 2001; Bartholomew, Parcel, & Kok, 1998; Gilliam et al., 2003). Allocating resources to community partnerships through which research-based problem solving can be transferred to the community represents one way to resolve the contradictions between the normative prevention science paradigm and the goal of sustainability (Stevenson & White, 1994).

Social scientists should be guided and supported to engage in technology transfer to enable local communities to assess the continued efficacy of interventions when contextual changes occur. Technology transfer, as well as the continued availability of researchers, can prevent mindless continuation of interventions that no longer work because communities, risk behaviors, and settings have changed. Intervention research trainees should be trained to engage with local communities, using ethnographic techniques for gaining rapport and trust. Training should include the capacity to learn from and take local suggestions seriously, rather than depending solely on externally derived theory and methods.

Not enough is known about the process of building and conducting community-based HIV/AIDS interventions. Process evaluation should be required in all intervention studies to capture not only treatment fidelity but also unexpected aspects of an intervention that develop spontaneously or over time, and the process of implementing and maintaining working partnerships in the field. This would allow scientists to gain deeper understanding of the complexities of intervention implementation, and to catalogue, analyze, and interpret "best practices" in community partnership research.

Longitudinal studies that assess duration of outcome in local sites are both scientifically important and ethically sound because both scientists and local sites are concerned about the long-term effects of the projects in which they participate. More studies that follow intervention results beyond the period of 6 months to 2 years are called for.

With proper attention to issues of sustainability, as described above, HIV/AIDS infection rates can decline, and treatment rates can improve. These challenges are sufficiently pressing that, in the face of entrenched and sensitive behaviors involving drug injection and various forms of unprotected sex, programs that show initial, even marginal, effects, should be sustained over time. Such an effort would allow an examination of the sustainability process as reflected in the promotion and assessment of the changes in social organization, cultural beliefs, and social norms that, together, bring about reductions in HIV infection rates.

To address questions of continuing financial support, AIDS and public-health research activists should court the commitment of private and state funders as long-term partners in intervention research. These funders should be encouraged to support and follow the evolution of successful local interventions over time. Rather than viewing federal funding as competitive or external to their interests, they should be encouraged to develop complementary priorities that focus on the community impact or sustainability of local interventions over time.

Finally, sustainability methods such as permanent links between communities and academically situated research and intervention resources, programmatic grant writing, and activities to stabilize coalitions, could be required in intervention studies in much the same way that "data monitoring" plans have now become integral to NIH funded interventions.

CONCLUSION

Local sustainability calls for "situated commitment" or political will on the part of professional researchers, their organizational bases, and their organizational partners to make a long-term research and development commitment to local research sites (Altman, 1995; Stoecker, 1999). Political will is very different from the administrative infrastructure required to support intervention durability and institutionalization. It calls for researchers' decisions that challenge received wisdom with respect to career development: commitment to long-term community development in a local setting rather than partnerships of convenience with respect to a specific intervention program (Schensul, 1998, 1999). It calls for commitment to active field work and engagement with local organizations, community leaders, residents, and issues rather than singling out specific individuals representing good partnership organizations for single-interest interventions. It calls for commitment to situating intervention research within the broader spectrum of concerns held by local communities. Finally, it requires commitment to providing organizational and interorganizational technical assistance, grant writing, and advocacy with respect to needed policy and service changes, thus expanding the researcher's responsibilities beyond reporting study outcomes and generalizing results.

On the community side, political will to venture into sustainable intervention research relationships calls for another set of commitments (cf. Altman, 1995). These include overcoming inherent biases against research and researchers, especially when there are ethnic, educational, and institutional differences between them and community partners. Critical factors in political will and organizational readiness are also expressed in a willingness to question or test received knowledge of what works to try something new, as well as engaging in intellectual debate and critique with researchers about program process and outcomes. Community organizations and community residents with vested interests must be prepared to allocate resources (time, personnel, and financial resources) to make sure that research design, process, and outcome evaluation are appropriate.

Sustainability requires building new social, political, and cultural infrastructure that can monitor with vigilance and address with conviction both the continuing and the new cultural, social, and economic circumstances that promote infection and transmission and group and individual responses. In other words, the issue of sustainability cannot be separated from capacity building and community- and structural-level interventions in health research and problem solving (cf. Blankenship, Bray, & Merson, 2000; Hawe, Noort, King, & Jordens, 1997; Roberts, Dematteo, King, & Read, 2002; Sweat & Denison, 1995).

A growing body of literature on community-based participatory research (CBPR) for health and development, framed as a movement, positions itself as an ethical alternative to positivist experimental intervention science (cf. Minkler & Wallerstein, 2003). CBPR involves communities or sectors of communities in various aspects of public-health research, intervention, and social change partnerships, emphasizing social validity, community acceptability, local social change, and community empowerment. Partnerships between universities and communities do not, however, guarantee research or problem solving technology transfer, when technical aspects of research are owned and conducted by university partners. Nor do they necessarily address issues of institutionalization of approach or persistence of effect over time. The approach does not address the role of local communities in replication/adaptation and generalizability, scaling up, or the important question of communities' contribution to science. And the critical issue of resource acquisition, which underlies most efforts to sustain good programs, is not necessarily addressed in CBPR case studies either. Thus, despite the best intentions of CBPR activists, the gap between prevention research and community-based action research remains.

It is not, however, a substantial stretch to suggest the following: the process of building research partnerships that enhance acceptability, integrity, social validity, and outcome durability of interventions should be also seen as building research-based health problem–solving capacity; that transfer of the skills that mark research-based health problem–solving capacity—conceptualization (model building), intervention (program design), and evaluation (research design)—can occur in intervention studies; and that the traditional notion of "dissemination" of research results could be expanded and redefined to include principles and practices of local sustainability. Developing local capacity for research-based problem solving through ethical research partnerships can address simultaneously scientific rigor, generalizability, *and* long-term local sustainability through institutionalization and science-based problem solving. In the field of HIV prevention research, we should be doing nothing else.

REFERENCES

Adelman, H. S. & Taylor, L. (2003). On sustainability of project innovations as systemic change. *Journal of Education and Psychological Consultation, 14*(1), 1–25.

Altman, D. G. (1986). A framework for evaluating community-based heart disease prevention programs. *Social Science and Medicine, 22*(4), 479–487.

Altman, D. G. (1995). Sustaining interventions in community systems: On the relationship between researchers and communities. *Health Psychology, 14*(6), 526–536.

Bartholomew, L. K. (2001). *Intervention mapping: Designing theory—and evidence-based health promotion programs.* Mountain View, CA: Mayfield.

Bartholomew, L. K., Parcel, G. S., & Kok, G. (1998). Intervention mapping: A process for developing theory- and evidence-based health education programs. *Health Education and Behavior, 25*(5), 545–563.

Becker, M. H. & Joseph, J. G. (1988). AIDS and behavioral change to reduce risk: A Review. *American Journal of Public Health, 78*(4), 394–410.

Beeker, C., Guenther-Grey, C., & Raj, A. (1998). Community empowerment paradigm drift and the primary prevention of HIV/AIDS. *Social Science and Medicine, 46*(7), 831–842.

Blankenship, K. M., Bray, S. J., & Merson, M. H. (2000). Structural interventions in public health. *AIDS, 14*(Suppl. 1), S11–S21.

Booth, R. E. & Watters, J. K. (1994). How effective are risk-reduction interventions targeting injecting drug users? *AIDS, 8*(11), 1515–1524.

Booysen, F. l. R. & Arntz, T. (2003). The methodology of HIV/AIDS impact studies: A review of current practices. *Social Science and Medicine, 56*(12), 2391–2405.

Bourgois, P. (1995). *In search of respect: Selling crack in el barrio.* New York: Cambridge University Press.

Burrell, G. & Morgan, G. (1979). *Sociological paradigms and organisational analysis.* London: Heinemann.

Choi, K.-H. & Coates, T. J. (1994). Prevention of HIV infection. *AIDS, 8*(10), 1371–1389.

Coates, T. J., Grinstead, O. A., Gregorich, S. E., Sweat, M. D., Kamenga, M. C., Sangiwa, G., et al. (2000). Efficacy of voluntary HIV-1 counselling and testing in individuals and couples in Kenya, Tanzania, and Trinidad: A randomised trial. *Lancet, 356*(9224), 103–112.

Coyle, S. L., Needle, R. H., & Normand, J. (1998). Outreach-based HIV prevention for injecting drug users: A review of published outcome data. *Public Health Reports, 113*(Suppl. 1), 19–30.

Deetz, S. (1996). Describing differences in approaches to organization science: Rethinking Burrell and Morgan and their legacy. *Organization Science, 7*(2), 191–207.

Ekstrand, M. L. & Coates, T. J. (1990). Maintenance of safer sexual behaviors and predictors of risky sex: The San Francisco's men's health study. *American Journal of Public Health, 80*(8), 973–977.

Felix Aaron, K. & Bass, E. B. (2002). A call for papers: Community-based participatory research. *Journal of General Internal Medicine, 17*(1), 84.

Fisher, W. A. & Fisher, J. D. (1993). A general social psychological model for changing AIDS risk behavior. In J. B. Pryor & G. D. Reeder (Eds.), *The Social Psychology of HIV Infection* (pp. 127–153). Hillsdale, NJ: Erlbaum.

Gibson, D. R., Flynn, N. M., & McCarthy, J. J. (1999). Effectiveness of methadone treatment in reducing HIV risk behavior and HIV seroconversion among injecting drug users. *AIDS, 13*(14), 1807–1818.

Gibson, D. R., McCusker, J., & Chesney, M. (1998). Effectiveness of psychosocial interventions in preventing HIV risk behaviour in injecting drug users. *AIDS, 12*(8), 919–929.

Gilliam, A., Barrington, T., Davis, D., Lacson, R., Uhl, G., & Phoenix, U. (2003). Building evaluation capacity for HIV prevention programs. *Evaluation and Program Planning, 26*(2), 133–142.

Groseclose, S. L., Weinstein, B., Jones, T. S., Valleroy, L. A., Fehrs, L. J., & Kassler, W. J. (1995). Impact of increased legal access to needles and syringes on practices of injecting-drug users and police officers, Connecticut, 1992–1993. [comment]. *Journal of Acquired Immune Deficiency Syndromes and Human Retrovirology, 10*(1), 82–89.

Grosskurth, H., Mosha, F., Todd, J., Mwijarubi, E., Klokke, A., Senkoro, K., et al. (1995). Impact of improved treatment of sexually transmitted diseases on HIV infection in rural Tanzania: Randomised controlled trial. *Lancet, 346*(8974), 530–536.

Guba, E. G. & Lincoln, Y. S. (1994). Competing paradigms in qualitative research. In N. K. Denzin & Y. S. Lincoln (Eds.), *Handbook of qualitative research* (pp. 105–117). Thousand Oaks, CA: Sage.

Hawe, P., Noort, M., King, L., & Jordens, C. (1997). Multiplying health gains: The critical role of capacity-building within health promotion programs. *Health Policy, 39*(1), 29–42.

Hays, R. B., Rebchook, G. M., & Kegeles, S. M. (2003). The Mpowerment Project: Community-building with young gay and bisexual men to prevent HIV. *American Journal of Community Psychology, 31*(3-4), 301–312.

Hurley, S. F., Jolley, D. J., & Kaldor, J. M. (1997). Effectiveness of needle-exchange programmes for prevention of HIV infection. *Lancet, 349*(9068), 1797–1800.

Jackson, C., Fortmann, S. P., Flora, J. A., Melton, R. J., Snider, J. P., & Littlefield, D. (1994). The capacity-building approach to intervention maintenance implemented by the Stanford Five-City Project. *Health Education Research, 9*(3), 385–396.

Jemmott, J. B., 3rd, Jemmott, L. S., & Fong, G. T. (1998). Abstinence and safer sex HIV risk-reduction interventions for African American adolescents: A randomized controlled trial. *Journal of the American Medical Association, 279*(19), 1529–1536.

Kahn, J. G., Kegeles, S. M., Hays, R., & Beltzer, N. (2001). Cost-effectiveness of the Mpowerment Project, a community-level intervention for young gay men. *JAIDS: Journal of Acquired Immune Deficiency Syndromes, 27*(5), 482–491.

Kalichman, S. C., Carey, M. P., & Johnson, B. T. (1996). Prevention of sexually transmitted HIV infection: A meta-analytic review of the behavioral outcome literature. *Annals of Behavioral Medicine, 18*(1), 6–15.

Kalichman, S. C., Rompa, D., & Cage, M. (2000). Sexually transmitted infections among HIV seropositive men and women. *Sexually Transmitted Infections, 76*(5), 350–354.

Kamali, A., Quigley, M., Nakiyingi, J., Kinsman, J., Kengeya-Kayondo, J., Gopal, R., et al. (2003). Syndromic management of sexually transmitted infections and behaviour change interventions on transmission of HIV-1 in rural Uganda: A community randomised trial. *Lancet, 361*(9358), 645–652.

Kamb, M. L., Fishbein, M., Douglas, J. M., Jr., Rhodes, F., Rogers, J., Bolan, G., et al. (1998). Efficacy of risk-reduction counseling to prevent human immunodeficiency virus and sexually transmitted diseases: A randomized controlled trial. Project RESPECT Study Group. *Journal of the American Medical Association, 280*(13), 1161–1167.

Kegeles, S. M. & Hart, G. J. (1998). Recent HIV-prevention interventions for gay men: Individual, small-group and community-based studies. *AIDS, 12*(Suppl. A), S209–S215.

Kegeles, S. M., Hays, R. B., & Coates, T. J. (1996). The Mpowerment Project: A community-level HIV prevention intervention for young gay men. *American Journal of Public Health, 86*(8 Pt 1), 1129–1136.

Kelly, J. A., St Lawrence, J. S., Diaz, Y. E., Stevenson, L. Y., Hauth, A. C., Brasfield, T. L., et al. (1991). HIV risk behavior reduction following intervention with key opinion leaders of population: An experimental analysis.[comment]. *American Journal of Public Health., 81*(2), 168–171.

Kelly, J. A., St Lawrence, J. S., Stevenson, L. Y., Hauth, A. C., Kalichman, S. C., Diaz, Y. E., et al. (1992). Community AIDS/HIV risk reduction: The effects of endorsements by popular people in three cities. *American Journal of Public Health, 82*(11), 1483–1489.

Latkin, C. A., Mandell, W., Vlahov, D., Oziemkowska, M., & Celentano, D. D. (1996). The long-term outcome of a personal network-oriented HIV prevention intervention for injection drug users: The SAFE study. *American Journal of Community Psychology, 24*(3), 341–364.

LeCompte, M. D. & Schensul, J. J. (1999). *Designing and conducting ethnographic research* (Vol. 1). Walnut Creek, CA: AltaMira Press.

Leonard, N. R. Lester, P., Rotheram-Borus, M. J., Mattes, K., Gwadz, M., & Ferns, B. (2003). Successful recruitment and retention of participants in longitudinal behavioral research. *AIDS Education and Prevention, 15*(3), 269–281.

Lincoln, Y. S. & Guba, E. G. (2000). Paradigmatic controversies, contradictions, and emerging confluences. In N. K. Denzin (Ed.), *Handbook of Qualitative Research* (2nd ed., pp. 163–188). Thousand Oaks, CA: Sage.

Madison, S. M., McKernan McKay, M., Paikoff, R. L., & Bell, C. C. (2000). Basic research and community collaboration: Necessary ingredients for the development of a family-based HIV prevention program. *AIDS Education and Prevention,* 12(4), 281–298.

McCormick, A., McKernan McKay, M., Wilson, M., McKinney, L., Paikoff, R. L., Bell, C. C., et al. (2000). Involving families in an urban HIV preventive intervention: How community collaboration addresses barriers to participation. *AIDS Education and Prevention,* 12(4), 299–307.

Miller, R. L. (1995). Assisting gay men to maintain safer sex: An evaluation of an AIDS service organization's safer sex maintenance program. *AIDS Education and Prevention,* 7(Suppl. 5), 48–63.

Miller, R. L. & Kelly, J. G. (2002). Community-level approaches to preventing HIV: Guest 'editors' introduction. *Journal of Primary Prevention,* 23(2), 151–156.

Miller, R. L., Klotz, D., & Eckholdt, H. M. (1998). HIV prevention with male prostitutes and patrons of hustler bars: Replication of an HIV preventive intervention. *American Journal of Community Psychology.,* 26(1), 97–131.

Minkler, M. & Wallerstein, N. (2003). *Community based participatory research for health.* San Francisco, CA: Jossey-Bass.

Nastasi, B. K., Moore, R. B., & Varjas, K. M. (2003). *School-based mental health services: Creating comprehensive and culturally specific programs* (1st ed.). Washington, DC: American Psychological Association.

Needle, R. H., Genser, S., & Trotter, R. (1995). Social Networks, Drug Abuse and HIV Transmission. *NIDA Research Monograph Series, No. 151.*

Oakley, A., Fullerton, D., & Holland, J. (1995). Behavioural interventions for HIV/AIDS prevention. *AIDS,* 9(5), 479–486.

Office of Technology Assessment. (1995). *The Effectiveness of AIDS Prevention Efforts.* Office of Technology Assessment: Washington, DC.

O'Neill, K., Baker, A., Cooke, M., Collins, E., Heather, N., & Wodak, A. (1996). Evaluation of a cognitive-behavioural intervention for pregnant injecting drug users at risk of HIV infection. *Addiction,* 91(8), 1115–1126.

Paikoff, R. L. (1996). Adapting developmental research to intervention design. Applying developmental psychology to an AIDS prevention model for urban African American youth. *Journal of Negro Education,* 65(1), 44–59.

Paikoff, R. L., Parfenoff, S. H., Williams, S. A., & McCormick, A. (1997). Parenting, parent-child relationships, and sexual possibility situations among urban African American preadolescents: Preliminary findings and implications for HIV prevention. *Journal of Family Psychology,* 11(1), 11–22.

Rapkin, B. D. (2002). Ecologically-minded reconstruction of experiments in HIV prevention: Reduce, reuse, and recycle. *Journal of Primary Prevention,* 23(2), 235–250.

Rhodes, T. & Quirk, A. (1995). Where is the sex in harm reduction? *International Journal of Drug Policy,* 6(2), 76–81.

Roberts, J., Dematteo, D., King, S. M., & Read, S. (2002). Involving participants in the dissemination of HIV research results. *Canadian Psychology,* 43(2), 112–114.

Rossi, P. H., Freeman, H. E., & Lipsey, M. W. (1999). *Evaluation: A systematic approach* (6th ed.). Thousand Oaks, CA: Sage.

Sagrestano, L. M. & Paikoff, R. L. (1997). Preventing high-risk sexual behavior, sexually transmitted diseases, and pregnancy among adolescents. In R. P. Weissberg & T. P. Gullotta (Eds.), *Healthy children 2010: Enhancing children's wellness Issues in children's and families' lives* (Vol. 8, pp. 76–104). Thousand Oaks, CA.: Sage.

Schensul, J. J. (1998). Community-based risk prevention with urban youth. *School Psychology Review,* 27(2), 233–245.

Schensul, J. J. (1999). Building community research partnerships in the struggle against AIDS. *Health Education and Behavior, 26*(2), 266–283.

Schensul, J. J. & Berg, M. (in press). Youth participatory action research: A transformative approach to service learning. *Michigan Journal of Community Service Learning (Special Issue on Anthropology and Service Learning).*

Schensul, J. J. & LeCompte, M. D. (1999). *The ethnographer's toolkit: A seven volume set on ethnographic methods.* Walnut Creek, CA: AltaMira Press.

Schensul, S. L., Schensul, J. J., & LeCompte, M. D. (1999). *Essential ethnographic methods: Observations, interviews, and questionnaires* (Vol. 2). Walnut Creek, CA: AltaMira Press.

Shadish, W. R., Cook, T. D., & Campbell, D. T. (2002). *Experimental and quasi-experimental designs for generalized causal inference.* Boston, MA: Houghton Mifflin.

Shain, R. N., Piper, J. M., Newton, E. R., Perdue, S. T., Ramos, R., Champion, J. D., et al. (1999). A randomized, controlled trial of a behavioral intervention to prevent sexually transmitted disease among minority women. *New England Journal of Medicine, 340*(2), 93–100.

Sikkema, K. J., Kelly, J. A., Winett, R. A., Solomon, L. J., Cargill, V. A., Roffman, R. A., et al. (2000). Outcomes of a randomized community-level HIV prevention intervention for women living in 18 low-income housing developments. *American Journal of Public Health, 90*(1), 57–63.

Slonim-Nevo, V., Auslander, W. F., Ozawa, M. N., & Jung, K. G. (1996). The long-term impact of AIDS-preventive interventions for delinquent and abused adolescents. *Adolescence, 31*(122), 409–421.

Stanton, B. F., Li, X., Kahihuata, J., Fitzgerald, A. M., Neumbo, S., Kanduuombe, G., et al. (1998). Increased protected sex and abstinence among Namibian youth following a HIV risk-reduction intervention: A randomized, longitudinal study. *AIDS, 12*(18), 2473–2480.

Stevenson, H. C., & White, J. J. (1994). AIDS prevention struggles in ethnocultural neighborhoods: Why research partnerships with community based organizations can't wait. *AIDS Education and Prevention., 6*(2), 126–139.

Stoecker, R. (1999). Are academics irrelevant?: Roles for scholars in participatory research. *American Behavioral Scientist, 42*(5), 840–854.

Strawn, C. (1994). Beyond the buzz word: Empowerment in community outreach and education. *Journal of Applied Behavioral Science, 30*(2), 159–174.

Stryker, J., Coates, T. J., DeCarlo, P., Haynes-Sanstad, K., Shriver, M., & Makadon, H. J. (1995). Prevention of HIV infection: Looking back, looking ahead. *Journal of the American Medical Association, 273*(14), 1143–1148.

Sweat, M. D. & Denison, J. A. (1995). Reducing HIV incidence in developing countries with structural and environmental interventions. *AIDS, 9*(Suppl. A), S251–S257.

Trickett, E. J. (2002). Context, culture, and collaboration in AIDS interventions: Ecological ideas for enhancing community impact. *Journal of Primary Prevention, 23*(2), 157–174.

Trotter, R. (1999). Friends, relatives, and relevant others: Conducting ethnographic network studies. In J. J. Schensul, M. D. LeCompte, R. Trotter, E. K. Cromley, & M. Singer (Eds.), *Mapping Social Networks, Spatial Data, & Hidden Populations* (Vol. 4, pp. 1–49). Walnut Creek, CA: AltaMira Press.

Trotter, R. & Schensul, J. J. (1998). Applied ethnographic research methods. In H. R. Bernard (Ed.), *Handbook of Ethnographic Methods.* Walnut Creek, CA: AltaMira Press.

Valdiserri, R. O., Lyter, D. W., Leviton, L. C., Callahan, C. M., Kingsley, L. A., & Rinaldo, C. R. (1989). AIDS prevention in homosexual and bisexual men: Results of a randomized trial evaluating two risk reduction interventions. *AIDS, 3*(1), 21–26.

Valdiserri, R. O., Ogden, L. L., & McCray, E. (2003). Accomplishments in HIV prevention science: Implications for stemming the epidemic. *Nature Medicine, 9*(7), 881–886.

Valleroy, L. A., Weinstein, B., Jones, T. S., Groseclose, S. L., Rolfs, R. T., & Kassler, W. J. (1995). Impact of increased legal access to needles and syringes on community pharmacies' needle and syringe sales, Connecticut 1992–1993. *Journal of Acquired Immune Deficiency Syndrome and Human Retrovirology, 10*(2), 73–81.

van Empelen, P., Kok, G., van Kesteren, N. M. C., van den Borne, B., Bos, A. E. R., & Schaalma, H. P. (2003). Effective methods to change sex-risk among drug users: A review of psychosocial interventions. *Social Science and Medicine, 57*(9), 1593–1608.

Weeks, M. R., Clair, S., Borgatti, S. P., Radda, K., & Schensul, J. J. (2002). Social networks of drug users in high-risk sites: Finding the connections. *AIDS and Behavior, 6*(2), 193–206.

Weinhardt, L. S., Carey, M. P., Johnson, B. T., & Bickham, N. L. (1999). Effects of HIV counseling and testing on sexual risk behavior: A meta-analytic review of published research, 1985–1997. *American Journal of Public Health, 89*(9), 1397–1405.

Wiebel, W. W., Jimenez, A., Johnson, W., Ouellet, L., Jovanovic, B., Lampinen, T., et al. (1996). Risk behavior and HIV seroincidence among out-of-treatment injection drug users: A four-year prospective study. *Journal of Acquired Immune Deficiency Syndromes and Human Retrovirology, 12*(3), 282–289.

Winkleby, M. A. (1994). The future of community-based cardiovascular disease intervention studies. *American Journal of Public Health, 84*(9), 1369–1372.

Wohlfeiler, D. (2002). Community-level interventions: Are we asking the right questions? *Journal of Primary Prevention, 23*(2), 251–257.

Wong, M. L., Chan, K. W., & Koh, D. (1998). A sustainable behavioral intervention to increase condom use and reduce gonorrhea among sex workers in Singapore: 2-year follow-up. *Preventive Medicine, 27*(6), 891–900.

9

Transferring HIV Prevention Technology to Community-Based Organizations: How Can HIV Prevention Scientists Play an Effective Role in Practice?

Robin Lin Miller & George J. Greene

> The central public health lesson of the epidemic is that it is impossible to offer effective prevention and care services without becoming involved in community development, and thus in forms of political intervention.
>
> (Altman, 1994, p. 51)

The purpose of this chapter is to explore the contextual conditions that affect why AIDS-related community-based organizations might welcome research-based HIV prevention technologies or view them skeptically and as failing to serve community development aims. Our purpose is to try to characterize the environment in which AIDS community-based organizations perform their work and how preventing AIDS is viewed from the standpoint of the community-based organizations to which researchers seek to disseminate their research and HIV prevention programs. Our hope is to promote greater dialogue among researchers and staffs of community-based organizations about how to marry scientific aims to disseminate research-based HIV prevention technologies, hereinafter referred to as "technology transfer," with the social change, service provision, community development, and survival concerns of community-based organizations.[1]

Over the past two decades, scientists and practitioners have each made substantial progress toward the goal of identifying prevention strategies that can assist individuals and communities to reduce their HIV risk. However, advances in the typically distinct realms of HIV prevention science and practice have not always been tightly coupled and mutually informative (Haynes-Sanstad, Stall, Goldstein, Everett, & Brousseau, 1999; Kelly, Sogolow, & Neumann, 2000; Miller, 2001; Mitchell, Florin, & Stevenson, 2002). Integrating research and practice remains an ongoing challenge for the field of HIV prevention and one that is of increasing importance for community-based organizations as the push from funding institutions toward evidence-based practice mounts.

In our view, a major obstacle to the integration of science and practice is that existing models of technology transfer ignore important contextual contingencies in communities that ought to guide the design, implementation, and dissemination of programs. The reigning paradigms do not help researchers understand the interests, ideologies, contexts, and capacities of community-based organizations as they relate to the adoption of evidence-based practice. Moreover, recent technology transfer efforts take inadequate account of the philosophical, conceptual, and practical fit between the research upon which prevention technologies were based and the history, capacity, and operating context of prospective recipient organizations. Further, current approaches to technology transfer fail to consider the organizational risks associated with changing, adding, or replacing programs. Lastly, although the implicit assumption in much of the evidence-based practice literature is that practices that evolve from the community are inferior to those that have been scientifically derived, there is little evidence to verify this assumption. As a result, the existing ways of thinking about technology transfer limit researchers' abilities to have a positive community impact.

In this chapter, we first provide an overview of the historical emergence of AIDS-related community-based organizations in the United States. We then describe the role of research in the community-based organizational environment. Lastly, informed by organizational theories and existing knowledge of HIV-related community-based organizations, we present and critique perspectives on technology transfer as a method for uniting the interests and goals of scientists.

THE AIDS-RELATED COMMUNITY-BASED ORGANIZATION

The Historical Evolution

There are considerable historical, regional, and neighborhood differences in when, where, and why voluntary and nonprofit groups emerge. These organizations differ according to the political, social, and economic environments within which they operate and as a result of the principles on which they were founded. These historical factors also affect whether organizations see themselves as part of or as an alternative to mainstream public health and social service entities. Here, we briefly trace the historical roots of community-based AIDS organizations in United States.

At the beginning of the AIDS epidemic in the United States, AIDS-focused social movements developed out of the gay and lesbian civil rights movements in cities such as New York, San Francisco, and Los Angeles (Altman, 1994; Epstein, 1996; Patton, 1990; Perrow & Guillen, 1990; Shilts, 1988). The first United States AIDS-related community-based organization, Gay Men's Health Crisis (GMHC), was founded in 1982 in New York City by a group of grassroots activists and concerned citizens of the gay community. These men first met in playwright Larry Kramer's living room in 1981 to learn about what was then called gay cancer and to raise funds for biomedical research. In January of 1982, six of these men—Larry Kramer, Paul Popham, Nathan Fain, Lawrence Mass, Paul Rapopport, and Edmund White—named themselves the Gay Men's Health Crisis. By May of that year, they had established a volunteer-staffed hotline. It received 100 calls its first night of operation. In part because they had few places to which to refer callers, the group then began to develop basic patient and education services. Among the earliest of GMHC's services was the buddy program for people diagnosed with AIDS. Buddies helped people with AIDS meet day-to-day needs, such as house cleaning and shopping, and served as patient advocates. Buddies often completed duties that nurses who feared contact with patients with AIDS were unwilling to perform, including changing hospital bed linens and bringing patients' meals into their hospital rooms. GMHC also quickly took on the tasks of fighting stigma associated with AIDS and political advocacy.

The San Francisco AIDS Foundation, which grew out of San Francisco's gay community, emerged almost simultaneously with the founding of GMHC. Shortly thereafter, the AIDS Project Los Angeles was established. These three organizations, on which many later organizations would model themselves, served as early advocates on behalf of the gay community and people affected by AIDS. As many AIDS community-based organizations would come to do, these organizations challenged medical and public health conceptions of AIDS (and homosexuality) and decried government inaction.

Other early participants in the community-based provision of AIDS-related services were gay and lesbian health clinics, such as the Howard Brown Health Center in Chicago and the Whitman Walker Clinic in Washington, DC. These clinics were established prior to the advent of AIDS to provide alternatives to mainstream health care clinics that were ill-informed of gay and lesbian health concerns and insensitive to the needs of these men and women. Because AIDS had such a dramatic impact on gay men, institutions such as these were quick to provide AIDS-related services.

Grassroots activism also spawned the development of many AIDS-related community-based organizations outside the gay community. For example, the first underground needle exchange was founded by activist Dave Purchase in Tacoma, Washington in 1988. Several small community-based organizations were launched in the early and mid '80s by Haitian politicians and physicians who were concerned by stigma applied to Haitians by public health authorities. Organizations founded in other communities of color, such as the Balm in Gilead, Hispanic AIDS Forum, and Asian Pacific Islander Wellness Center, quickly arose. Once sex workers became targeted by public health officials as "vectors of transmission," they founded groups such as the California Prostitutes Education Project to engage in AIDS-related activism and programming.

In reviewing the history of AIDS social service and community-based organizations, Altman (1994) contends that the two major variables driving the establishment of AIDS organizations are *epidemiological* (i.e., the extent to which the disease is concentrated in and identified with particular groups and the extent to which such groups have the ability to develop their own organizations) and *political* (i.e., existing traditions of organizing outside government and the amount of space available for community mobilization). Formed in the absence of available services, the creation of AIDS organizations provided fertile ground for innovative prevention strategies. For example, safer sex parties modeled after Tupperware parties, "carnal carnivals" featuring live safer sex demonstrations in bathhouses, explicit safer sex videos, living room discussion groups, condom police, safer sex workshops, and needle exchanges are among the many innovative strategies that emerged from the community-based sector. These organizations also pioneered innovative services for those living with HIV, from treatment newsletters designed to help individuals understand medical information pertinent to their health status to social and nutritional programs to legal and financial advocacy services. Innovations and ideas developed in these new, HIV-focused, nonprofit organizations later informed the programs and services of larger, more mainstream groups (Chambre, 1995).

The community-based organizations that emerged from these various grassroots efforts differ from other health and human service organizations that have come to include AIDS in their mission (Perrow & Guillen, 1990). Many of the founding AIDS community-based organizations had underlying social change agendas that were intricately linked to human and civil rights movements (Altman, 1994; Wilson, 1995). The relationship between these organizations and the government was often charged with conflict. According to Vaid (1995, p. 227), "Gay and AIDS organizations exist because of the abdication of gay people by mainstream society." For many AIDS-related community-based organizations, preventing AIDS is a political act. Protecting constituent communities from risk of exposure to HIV involves addressing fundamental rights issues such as discrimination and political marginality.

For mainstream human service providers, providing services related to AIDS may be a charitable act, consistent with a service mission. Caring for those who are among the less fortunate members of society is a typical focus of such organizations. Perrow and Guillen (1990) argue that mainstream providers have been far less successful in addressing HIV competently, particularly in the realm of prevention, because organizations resist diverting resources to AIDS or allowing AIDS to affect organizational missions. Mainstream organizations may prefer to insulate themselves from AIDS because AIDS brings with it a complex morass of socially challenging issues such as homosexuality, sexuality, drug use, and poverty that many organizations would prefer to ignore.

The Professionalization of AIDS Community-Based Organizations

Several of the nation's largest AIDS organizations have evolved from small, volunteer-run agencies, dependent mainly on resources raised from their own communities, to large, professional service organizations that are funded by federal, state, and international agencies, or major donors, and controlled by professional staff rather than by members or volunteers (Altman, 1994; Cain, 1997). Patton (1990) aptly refers to the burgeoning AIDS industry as a move from grassroots to business suits. An emerging tension in these organizations is whether the professionals or the indigenous workers who have volunteered their efforts to address their community's needs know best how to address the many challenges created by AIDS (Altman, 1994; Cain, 1997; Wilson, 1995). According to Lipsky and Smith (1989–1990), the tension between professionalization and community groundedness is an almost inevitable consequence of institutionalization via government support.

The professionalization of AIDS community-based organizations has been critiqued from several angles. Caceras (in Altman, 1994) pointed to an increasing demand for services and adoption of a "self-legitimizing narcissistic strategy, losing self-critical capacity and turning their attention to the possibilities of funding for organizational stability" (p. 98). From the perspective of the feminist health movement, Vaid (1995) argued that AIDS service organizations molded themselves into traditional health care bureaucracies vying for the same funds, creating the same structures, and adopting discriminatory attitudes toward patients. Further, Vaid (1995) criticized the AIDS service movement's reproduction of the dominant class, race, and gender biases within the organizations, laws, and delivery systems it created, shying away from a broad antipoverty health care reform movement. More moderate critics acknowledge the delicate dance these organizations must perform, balancing survival as a legitimated actor and guarding against selling out to mainstream authorities (Cain, 1993, 1995; Wilson, 1995). To be sure, the evolution of AIDS community-based organizations has come at a cost. Organizations that grew out of affected communities are struggling to maintain their ties with those they claim to represent while moving almost inexorably into dependent relationships with government and/or major donors (Altman, 1994; Cain, 1993, 1995, 1997; Patton, 1990; Wilson, 1995).

Tensions Faced by AIDS Community-Based Organizations

The critiques leveled at the AIDS community-based organization industry underscore many of the tensions faced by AIDS service providers. These tensions include striking a balance between service delivery and activism (Altman, 1994; Vaid, 1995) and emphasizing treatment, care, and prevention issues for people who are infected with HIV versus the need for education and outreach for those who are not infected (Altman, 1994; Patton,

1990). However, the primary tension for community-based organizations emerges from their reliance on governmental funding and the need to survive in their local communities of identity.

How community-based organizations are funded has enormous political ramifications. The creation and growth of AIDS social service agencies was facilitated by the expansion of public and private funding (Chambre, 1999). Delivery of many government services through contracts with non-profit groups also contributed to the growth of newly founded AIDS organizations and the often reluctant entry of non-AIDS organizations in the AIDS service system (Chambre, 1995; Perrow & Guillen, 1990). As the scope and number of services offered by community-based organizations grows and the costs of providing those services increase, organizations become more dependent on those who are willing to fund their efforts (Altman, 1994). The more reliant a provider becomes on a particular source of funding, the more power that source has over the activities of the provider (Emerson, 1962; Frederickson & London, 2000; Lipsky & Smith, 1989–1990; Saidel, 1989, 1991). Arguably, to the extent that such groups depend on the government for their financial survival, they will not challenge the government and will never be forces for progressive social change (Altman, 1994; Riger, 1984; Wilson, 1995).

For many community-based organizations, the primary source of their dependence has shifted from their volunteer base and the financial support of their constituent community to the government (Cain, 1993, 1995). McCormack and Associates (1997) report that, on average, about 50% of the funds supporting a national sample of 142 AIDS and gay and lesbian organizations are from government. Community-based organizations may no longer be able to retain a participatory model of control appropriate to volunteer-staffed and volunteer-led organizations and also provide millions of government dollars worth of services (Altman, 1994; Lipsky & Smith, 1989–1990). Organizations may have to choose between rejecting government resources and becoming cheap sources of labor for programs directed by the state (Altman, 1994; Frederickson & London, 2000; Lipsky & Smith, 1989–1990). This phenomenon is sometimes referred to as the problem of the hollow state, a reference to government's attempt to fulfill its public service mission by contracting the services of the not-for-profit sector. The hollow state provides the means for government to promulgate its values through legitimizing the replacement of programming originally developed by nongovernmental organizations with versions of programs acceptable to the government.

The kinds of tensions that arise for organizations with government funding and activist roots are evident in both recent and distant events. Principal among these are government attempts to defuse activism within these organizations, control the organizations' work, and censorship.

Recent examples of these tensions illustrate the dilemma these organizations face:

- At the July 2002 International AIDS Conference in Barcelona, activists disrupted United States Secretary of Health and Human Service's Tommy Thompson's address. Some of the activists are believed to be employees of AIDS community-based organizations that receive government support. By congressional mandate, these organizations have been subject to investigation by the Inspector General of Health and Human Services and face loss of government funds. A specific concern in the audit is whether government funds have been used to promote sexual activity or provide sexually explicit education (Meckler, 2002).
- Materials and programs produced with government funds by Stop AIDS San Francisco, an organization founded to meet the HIV prevention needs of adult gay men, have been judged obscene by the inspector general (Meckler, 2002). These materials and the processes by which they were produced were audited by the Centers for Disease Control (CDC) at the urging of members of Congress, echoing the battle begun in 1987 between Senator Jesse Helms and the Gay Men's Health Crisis. Out of disgust with HIV prevention materials produced by the organization, Helms amended federal legislation to prevent federal funds from being used on AIDS education efforts that affirmed homosexual sex. The ACLU and GMHC litigated against the amendment, winning their case in May of 1992.
- In 1993, producers of a Texas public access program that provided viewers with explicit and erotic information for gay men on how to practice safer sex were arrested for violating obscenity laws. The convictions were upheld by the Texas courts (Luckenbill,1998).
- A St. Louis AIDS organization lost government funding after sponsoring an erotic AIDS prevention event that featured a gay porn star. Several staff members were fired for organizing the event. (CDC HIV/STD/TB Prevention News Update, November 6, 2002).

Although these cases highlight the more dramatic tensions that arise for organizations with activist roots, more subtle cooptation has also been described. Censorship may occur when community-based organizations are restricted from mentioning homosexuality or condoms in presentations at schools or businesses (Cain, 1997). In order to access youth, organizations may need to acquiesce to the mores of local school boards. Cain argues that although the short-term benefits of acquiescing include access to an important target population and meeting accountability demands, the long-term losses are far greater: youth may not receive accurate preventative information. Efforts to promote evidence-based practice exist in a climate of government efforts to control and water down the content of HIV prevention programs, including those promoted by arms of government such as the CDC.

In sum, involvement with the state and the receipt of regular funding contribute to the formalization and bureaucratization of community organizations (Singer et al., 1990; Singer et al., 1991; Singer, 1996). Such institutionalization has commonly been described as a threat to creativity, a first step to depoliticalization, and a major threat to the effectiveness of AIDS community-based organizations in promoting an activist agenda (Cain, 1993; Patton, 1990; Singer, 1996). The initial goals of many community groups may become displaced by concerns with organizational maintenance and by the career interests of their workers. Further, funding agencies may attain the power to set the agendas of the organizations and institutions they support with grant dollars rather than allow the activists and leaders of the organization to determine priorities (Singer, 1996). Funding institutions' priorities, including funding institutions' concerns with the latest research or programmatic zeitgeist, tend to drive the general areas in which work is undertaken.

The Changing Environment

The HIV/AIDS epidemic has changed rapidly, affecting the organizations that serve affected populations in a variety of ways. One of the most significant shifts in the epidemic has resulted from medical progress (Chambre, 1995). Over the prior 2 decades, conceptions of the disease have shifted from a fatal to a chronic disease. Assuming access to appropriate medical care, the length of time over which an individual can live with HIV without significant impairment to health has dramatically increased. Prevention has become an infinitely more complex and challenging task in the face of medical progress. Rather than the simple education/care dichotomy of the early and mid '80s, services must now form a continuum. Prevention must meet the needs of those who are HIV-positive and will lead active sexual lives for decades, as well as meet the needs of those who are known or presumed to be HIV-negative (see, for example, Odets, 1995). Many organizations were founded to be "one-stop shops" for HIV-related issues. However, what comprised a one-stop shop in 1984 is inadequate to meet the needs of an increasingly diverse population of people affected by HIV in 2003. Changes in the epidemic and in the political, economic, and cultural context in which organizations seek to provide services suggest that the one-stop shop is not a static entity; it must be routinely reformulated.

A second shift in the epidemic concerns AIDS demographics. In the United States, recognition of those whom AIDS affects most dramatically has expanded from being overwhelmingly focused on gay men to people with hemophilia, to injection drug users and their sexual partners, to an ethnically and economically diverse population of men, women, and children. For some organizations founded in gay communities, programs for gay men have become diluted or marginalized, as other communities compete for limited prevention resources. For other organizations, services and programs have been stretched in new ways to accommodate an increasingly diverse array of clients (Perrow & Guillen, 1990). Despite these changes, allocation of AIDS-related resources still corresponds poorly to the demographics of the disease in many municipalities. For example, in the 1990s a *majority* of California's AIDS cases were concentrated among gay men, but a *minority* of its AIDS-related financial resources was devoted to gay men's prevention programs (Stall, 1994). In many parts of the United States, AIDS is now defined by poverty and race, including among gay men (Altman, 1994).

Given the shift in populations affected by HIV/AIDS, and the lack of available services for these populations, there has been a rise of AIDS community-based organizations in communities of color. Vaid (1995) has argued that the AIDS movement was poorly equipped to deal with an influx of diverse people. She asserts that people of color who turned to mainstream AIDS organizations for culturally specific and sensitive services experienced racial insensitivity, resistance to being served, and racial prejudice. AIDS organizations based in minority communities have emerged amid critiques that ethnic minority communities have been slow to respond to the epidemic. Against this misperception, Singer et al. (1990, 1991) argued that many Latino organizations were mobilizing at the beginning of the epidemic. Their "delayed" response can be seen as the effects of battling against limited financial resources, bureaucratic indifference, discrimination, and multiple health and social problems. Similarly, Stevenson and White (1994) articulated several barriers to the involvement of minority community-based organization in doing AIDS work. These include the following: 1) lack of funds; 2) lack of community-sensitive and language-appropriate teaching and education materials; 3) community denial of AIDS as a major health threat; 4) community mistrust of mainstream service provider institutions; 5) misinformation about AIDS; and 6) community mores that block consideration of some prevention strategies. Perrow and Guillen (1990) echo this view, noting that for minority communities, AIDS was not just one more problem to add on to a list that included poverty and unemployment, but served to magnify all of the problems on this list. Although minority community-based organizations have encountered sociocultural barriers to AIDS work in their communities, they have been more strongly hampered by a lack of resources, trained personnel, and receptivity to their involvement by institutional health and social service providers (Perrow & Guillen, 1990; Singer et al., 1990, 1991).

The experiences of organizations such as those described by Singer et al. (1990, 1991) and Perrow and Guillen (1990) are echoed in the small but growing empirical literature on AIDS community-based organizations. Ethnic minority community-based organizations have reasonably small annual budgets, and an overwhelming scope of work. In a study of 181 AIDS community-based organizations in California, Casteneda and Collins (1997) illustrated how Latino agencies fared less favorably in personnel and monetary resources than did mainstream organizations. Funding cuts, personnel shortages, and lack of basic material resources were among the leading barriers to providing prevention programs for these organizations. Chng et al. (1998) report the median annual prevention budget for 49 AIDS-related community-based organizations serving Asian and Pacific Islanders was under $100,000.

In general, the HIV prevention budgets of AIDS community-based organizations are not especially impressive. For example, Miller (2001) reports a median annual prevention budget of $56,121 among a random sample of providers in Illinois. The median prevention budget for community-based organizations with an exclusive mission to serve ethnic minorities was $83,138; community-based organizations that were not ethnically focused had median prevention budgets of $50,000. In a sample of the largest citywide providers of HIV prevention services in the United States, DiFranciesco et al. (1999) report a median annual budget for HIV prevention of $175,000. In all of the studies cited above, service providers used these limited dollars to provide multiple prevention programs to multiple target populations.

RESEARCH AND AIDS-RELATED COMMUNITY-BASED ORGANIZATIONS

Who Is the AIDS Expert and Why it Matters

In the early 1980s, AIDS medical professionals, government officials, affected communities, and traditional sources of moral authority (e.g., churches) all vied to be seen as experts on the new disease. How AIDS was conceptualized was a major tool in this struggle (Altman, 1994; Epstein, 1996; Gagnon, 1992; Patton, 1986). Conceptualized as a biomedical problem, AIDS would be under control of the medical establishment. Conceptualized as a social and political issue, as community-based groups argued, AIDS would require expertise in social and political activism.

Until community-based groups and those from radically different social environments were able to define social problems for themselves, the dominant discourse around the epidemic would inevitably reflect the experiences of certain groups within the mainstream society (Altman, 1994; Patton, 1986, 1990). Some have argued that scientists and community-based organizations are engaged in waging fundamentally different battles (Gagnon, 1992), with community-based organizations focused principally on issues of civil and human rights and scientists focused principally on how particular scientific tools and perspectives can contribute to solving the medical and behavioral problems presented by the epidemic. Even when community-based organizations and scientists express similar concerns and goals, historical disagreements, such as the medical community's portrayal of homosexuals and drug users as diseased, make for an uneasy and fragile alliance (Epstein; 1996). The ground has long been laid for many community-based organizations and the communities from which they originate to view scientific claims about prevention and treatment with skepticism. At the same time, the seriousness and scope of the epidemic has reinforced the power of science to claim its authority to define AIDS truths (Gagnon, 1992). That each views the epidemic differently should be unsurprising, as people evaluate their world according to their group and individual interests (Aronson, 1984; Hilgartner & Bosk, 1988; Spector & Kitsuse, 1973; Stewart & Rappaport, this volume).

Determining who the expert is and how the disease and epidemic are conceptualized is also important because the way the disease is defined determines the sort of responses that are possible (Altman, 1994; Perrow & Guillen, 1990). For example, if the disease is seen as a foreign import, then screening and quarantine become attractive measures. If the disease is understood as private behavior, there is likely to be an emphasis on education and skill development. Understood as a symptom of social and economic oppression, grassroots organizing in the name of social reform and structural and policy change are viewed as appropriate responses.

A clear example of the tensions involved in defining AIDS lies in the social and behavioral sciences research literatures. The need for a better understanding of how effective changes in behavior can be generated has produced both demands for more research and ongoing criticism of the orthodox methodologies of psychological, sociological, and educational researchers (Altman, 1994). Early survey-style research (based on knowledge-attitude-behavior-practices models) was set aside for qualitative research that yields more information about the ways in which sexual (or drug use) meanings, identities, and practices are constructed within social settings, and how these relate to larger social and cultural constraints (Altman, 1994; Elwood, 1999; Herdt & Lindenbaum, 1992). These lines of research challenged the value of objectivity in social and behavioral research. However, the idea that expertise may grow as much from lived experience and reflection as from objective academic study is still far from universally accepted.

According to Patton (1990), community organizations have tended to fluctuate between an acceptance of science as 'above and outside the polis' and a suspicion of the scientific and academic and establishment. Along with the gay community, criticism of social scientific research has come from other particularly marginalized groups, such as from communities of color (Altman, 1994). Social scientists are viewed by some as defining the larger AIDS agenda and as agents of government and medical surveillance (Altman, 1994; Epstein, 1996; Patton, 1990). Collaboration between social researchers and community organizations all too often means no more than providing researchers with a better opportunity to recruit subjects for study (Altman, 1994), a phenomenon that Riger (1999) refers to as "drive-by data collection." The stress on mainstream academic standards of scholarship—researchers will receive far more kudos for publishing in a refereed journal than for devising imaginative ways of reporting back to the people whose lives are being assessed—means that even well-intentioned research merely enforces existing discrepancies of power (Altman, 1994). Altman (1994) urges that, "A radical critique of AIDS research would stress the diverse forms of expertise and the different ways in which it is created, would acknowledge in other words that there are needs and bases for expertise" (p. 122). In short, research has not always been conducted using a community lens or for the purpose of serving community aims. As Jim Kelly noted to community psychologists in 1971, "We have been protagonists for change and have been invested in interventions without regard for the goals of the community. Our statements regarding community goals have been limited to our own entrepreneurial interests (p. 128)."

Community-Based Organizations' Use of Science

Given the tenuous relationships between academic researchers and community-based organizations, Goldstein and colleagues (1998) examined the extent to which service providers used the results from behavioral science research to inform prevention programs. In a nation-wide survey of 284 program managers of AIDS prevention programs, Goldstein et al. (1998) found that the three most important sources for HIV prevention information were peers and colleagues (53%); departments of public health (44%); and the CDC (40%). Most program managers did not turn to research, nor did they perceive it as an important source of information.

Goldstein et al. (1998) posited that inaccessibility, rather than a basic resistance to research itself, may be the main reason research findings are not widely used by community-based organizations. Most program prevention managers in community-based organizations are not trained in science (Goldstein et al., 1998). On the other hand, Goldstein et al. (1998) added, scientists are not trained in or usually experienced in prevention program design and implementation. They typically disseminate research findings via academic meetings and publications where they rarely address program implications in an applied or practical way. As noted most recently by Mitchell, Florin, and Stevenson (2002), technology pushed through traditional means will be inadequate to promote the use of scientific findings.

Current attempts to disseminate effective HIV prevention programs to practitioners have focused on developing replication packages, disseminating these packages to select community-based organizations, and providing these agencies with varying levels of support and assistance to adopt the interventions (see, for example, Kelly et al., 2000; Neumann, Sogolow, & Kelly, 2000). The principal scientific aim of these efforts is to inform prevention scientists about how they can package interventions to increase the likelihood that their programs are easily adopted and faithfully implemented by community-based organizations. These efforts have not taken full account of organizational theory or theory guiding the use of scientific information, relying instead upon theories of communication and cognitive theories of individual behavior.

The theoretical underpinnings of HIV prevention technology transfer efforts originate from diverse fields and disciplines (Backer, David, & Soucy, 1995). The paradigm that guides most recent work in technology transfer originates from Rogers's (1995) Diffusion of Innovations and similar theories that trace the adoption decision-making process from the perspective of prospective adopters. Kraft, Mezoff, Sogolow, Neumann, and Thomas (2000) conducted a recent review and theoretical synthesis of the literature on technology transfer and diffusion of innovations in public health. Kraft et al., provide an integrative overview of the common tenets of this paradigm, which we will briefly summarize.

Kraft and colleagues (2000) propose that the technology transfer process begins with preimplementation activities. These activities include identifying the need for an intervention, learning about prospective interventions, and assessing the prospective interventions' fit with identified needs. Preimplementation activities may include a range of actors (e.g., prevention planning group members, advisory board members) who are jointly focused on the tasks associated with collecting and gathering information. Preimplementation activities also include assessing the feasibility of implementing the intervention and its overall fit with the organization's mission and philosophy. Assuming an organization decides to adopt an intervention, the organization will then make necessary preparations for its adoption. Creating organizational readiness can include preparing staff to adopt the intervention though training activities. Other preparatory activities may include obtaining the political and fiscal support to import the intervention successfully. Adapting the program to fit organizational requirements and meet target population members' needs may also occur at this stage.

The second phase in the technology transfer process is implementation. Implementation efforts focus primarily on obtaining necessary technical assistance to ensure that the intervention is executed appropriately. This phase also includes monitoring program implementation through process evaluation activities. This phase could be characterized as a pilot stage in which the organization is learning about the program's proper implementation and acquiring basic experience carrying it out.

Should an organization decide to continue the program after its initial implementation, a maintenance and evaluation phase will follow the implementation phase. In this final phase, organizations work toward institutionalizing the program. Activities in this phase might include seeking ongoing financial and political support, conducting further evaluation activities, and developing means to allow the program to evolve in response to changing conditions.

Despite its heuristic appeal for guiding the prevention scientist through a dissemination effort, the dominate technology transfer paradigm has significant limitations and is poorly informed by literature on how organizations actually work. More important, the acontextual nature of the paradigm fails to accommodate the unique ecological space occupied by activist, volunteer-based or professionalized AIDS-related community-based organizations. In this next section, we critique the dominant paradigm and draw implications for technology transfer theory in HIV prevention in light of these critiques and our earlier discussion of the historical and current conditions in which AIDS organizations carry out their work.

The Myth of the Rational Decision-Making Model In her critique of prevailing views of research use, Carol Weiss (1981) argues against assuming a rational decision–making model within organizations. She claims that the following is untrue:

> ... that organizations make decisions according to a rational model: define problems, generate options, search for information about the relative merits of each option, and then, on the basis of the information, make a choice. As our colleagues who study organizations tell us, this is a patently inaccurate view of how organizations work. When we implicitly adopt this as our underlying theory of organizations in studying research use, we inevitably reach distorted conclusions. (1981, p. 26)

The technology transfer paradigm assumes that organizational decision-making processes are influenced largely by considerations of the efficiency and effectiveness of specific programs and that it is always obvious whether a new technology is equal to or better than what it might replace. To the scientist, it would be rational to select the prevention program that enjoys scientific support and is cost-efficient. From an organizational perspective, however, factors such as the extent to which the organization can maintain its current ratio of energy to product, can continue to operate consistent with its values and norms, can offer programs that aid in maintaining good community relations and legitimacy, and can appease regulatory bodies may be more central to the decision-making process and to long-term organizational survival (Abrahamson, 1991; Baldridge & Burnham, 1975; Katz & Kahn, 1966; Meyer & Rowan, 1993; Miller, 2001; Miller, 2003; Oliver, 1991; Zibalese-Crawford, 1993) than selecting a program or activity that has scientific support. And, it may not be evident that an outside program would be more effective than what is currently provided, even if merely because so few programs offered by community-based organizations have undergone rigorous evaluation (Miller, 1995). Although the implicit assumption in much of the evidence-based practice literature is that the practices that evolve from the community are substandard to those that have been scientifically derived and assessed, there is little evidence as yet to verify that this assumption is true.

In addition to its naive portrayal of organizational decision-making processes, the technology transfer paradigm contains a strong proinnovation bias (Abrahamson, 1991). It assumes that innovations are good for prospective adopter organizations and will improve their status quo. Yet, innovations have the potential to harm organizations in numerous ways

(Abrahamson, 1991). Some innovations may be effective and efficient under field laboratory conditions, but inefficient in practice. For example, small-group behavioral skills workshops have enjoyed widespread support in the prevention research literature (Johnson et al., 2002; Kalichman, Carey, & Johnson, 1996). Anecdotal evidence suggests, however, that at best these programs reach very small numbers of highly motivated volunteers and, as a result, may be an inefficient means for many community-based organizations to fulfill the mandate of widespread community-level prevention of HIV. These programs also require highly skilled staff people who are familiar with cognitive-behavioral techniques and can use the principles that underlie this approach to behavior modification. As such, these programs may only benefit organizations that have and can afford to maintain such staff. Employing highly skilled professional staff may also cost the organization its community base by necessitating the displacement of indigenous workers or removing them from hands-on prevention roles. The shift to professional staff changes the maintenance requirements of the prevention system in the organization, because the worker that is now required must fulfill different role requirements, manifest different professional motivations, and respond to different organizational inducements. Absorbing the costs of a professional staff may also necessitate reduced efforts elsewhere in the organization. Finally, these changes may prompt social costs to the organization, such as lowering its legitimacy to some constituent groups.

Researchers have sought to identify how aspects of organizational social networks and characteristics of the actors within them influence dissemination of innovation. Our understanding of the function and composition of organizations' interorganizational networks has been largely limited to exploring the communication channels via which information about innovations may diffuse and the characteristics of those who have influence within the network (see, for example, Goldstein et al., 1998). The impact of other aspects of organizational network structure and function, such as power imbalances, reciprocity, competition, cooperation, and interorganizational interdependency has been poorly captured in theory and research using the dominant technology transfer paradigm. For example, an organization may resist adopting a particular program because it duplicates what a local peer organization already provides or fails to preserve an organization's unique local identity (Barton-Villagrana, Bedney, & Miller, 2002; Miller, 2001).

Technologies may be harmful when organizations are asked to implement them rapidly (Abrahamson, 1991). The next new technology may be imposed on the field before organizations have had adequate time to figure out how to make the older programs work. Rather than become expert at a small number of highly specialized efforts, organizations may find themselves following the latest trend and doing so poorly. In their case study of prevention programs implemented by community-based organizations during the 1980s, Freudenberg and Zimmerman (1995) note that funding institutions are often too impatient to allow programs adequate time to be fine tuned and fully integrated into organizations' programmatic arsenal. Mitchell and colleagues (2002) also note the complex and time-consuming nature of establishing and operating new programs within organizations.

Technologies may also become harmful when they are so widespread and regulated that the field as a whole is homogenized or isomorphic and innovation and bottom-up development of technology is suppressed (DiMaggio & Powell, 1983). Although evidence-based practice and research can be a source of rejuvenation (see, for example, Singer & Weeks, this volume; Singer, 1994), it can limit creativity both by promulgating a particularly narrow world view of prevention and by creating the mistaken impression that equifinality in addressing HIV is impermissible. The concept of equifinality suggests that multiple approaches are viable, can coexist, and be mutually informative toward the end of preventing the spread of HIV. The existing paradigm fails to recognize these possibilities. Its reliance on rational decision–making models, proinnovation bias, ignorance of organizational network structures and functions, and preference for homogeneity limit its usefulness in the real world context of AIDS organizations.

TOWARD A NEW TECHNOLOGY TRANSFER PARADIGM

The Impact of Ecological Context on Organizational Functioning

As we have previously discussed, AIDS-related community-based organizations exist within complex organizational fields (i.e., sets of organizations that produce similar services and have similar suppliers and consumers; DiMaggio & Powell, 1983; Morrill & McKee, 1993). This ecological complexity governs an organization's basic functioning. A host of factors may limit organizations' freedom of choice regarding programming, encourage organizations not to change, cause organizations to reject or abandon effective programs, and enable resistance to pressure to follow trends or become institutionalized (Abrahamson, 1991; DiMaggio & Powell, 1983; Hira & Hira, 2000; Katz & Kahn, 1966; Meyer & Rowan, 1993; Oliver, 1991; Salem, Foster-Fishman, & Goodkind, 2002). Drawing on institutional theory and our earlier discussion of AIDS organizations, we identify several of these salient ecological forces here.

Institutional Controls

Coercive forces in the external environment, typically institutions on which organizations are dependent, impose practices and controls on organizations (DiMaggio & Powell, 1983). For example, state and city government funding entities establish accountability standards to comply with standards set by the federal institutions through which they obtain funds. Community-based organizations that comprise the organizational field that receive these funds are bound by the same governmental mandates and requirements. The operating constraints and requirements associated with federal mandates exert strong pressure on community-based organizations that mold their programs and services in similar ways. Requests for Proposals that reflect the local Planning Groups' funding priorities, accountability requirements, and the threat of loss of funds are among the primary mechanisms by which funding institutions exert coercive control on community-based organizations. This control shapes what and how organizations provide prevention programs and that may ultimately limit programmatic diversity. Lipsky and Smith (1989–1990) argue that among the most common types of organizational changes prompted by government contracting is compromise of the original mission to government priorities. Oliver (1991) contends that compliance with coercion is most probable when the self-serving benefits of acquiescing are obvious.

Host Community Norms

For community-based organizations, coercion may also emerge from the local community in which the organization is embedded. Communities may possess limits of tolerance for particular types of preventive interventions that may or may not coincide with organizations' ideal approaches to prevention. For example, a community newspaper may refuse to run advertisements targeting gay and lesbian teenagers because it does not want to "promote" homosexuality among youth, forcing a program to reach its audience through other means. Schools may require that presentations omit information about condom use or anal sex, fearing parent complaints. Communities may protest the presence of needle exchanges, fearing that they endorse and encourage drug use. Some organizations may need to find ways to offer stealth prevention programs to remain locally viable. At the same time, communities may seek to hold organizations accountable to defend their civil rights.

Professional Norms

Professionalizing processes impose pressure on organizations. Professionalization standardizes the ways in which services are delivered across institutions, conferring particular brands of legitimacy on organizations. Professional networks and associations enable rapid diffusion of information across organizations and lead to the common socialization of staff. Normative pressures create staff who view problems and solutions in similar ways and who accept the types of organizational myths that promote organizational stability and prestige (Meyer & Rowan, 1983). Adherence to professional norms, standards, and principles limit programmatic choice (DiMaggio & Powell, 1983). Professionalization also has the potential to co-opt the organization and corrupt its social change and community-based mission (Lipsky & Smith, 1989–1990; Wilson, 1995; Wohlfeiler, 2002). Professionalization may mean that the progressive and system-challenging way of addressing citizen-defined social problems drifts toward the paternalistic, top-down model against which the self-same movements originally reared up in protest, creating internal strain within the organization. According to Lipsky and Smith (1989–1990), professionalization may also have the negative effect of displacing staff and eroding the organization's ability to be responsive to emergent community concerns and needs. As the field progresses, the organizations that comprise it may find it increasingly challenging to remain radical. Organizations such as Act UP were founded in part out of frustration that existing AIDS community-based organizations had lost their adversarial edge and had given in to becoming service organizations.

Peer Relationships

The behavior of peer organizations is a fourth constraint on organizations, creating pressure to imitate and model what select organizations do. DiMaggio & Powell (1983) assert that the tendency to imitate another organization is often born out of uncertainty in the field. When a particular organization is perceived as more legitimate than or superior to other organizations, is a known and trusted player in the field, and the best way of responding to a situation is unclear; copying the practices of the well-regarded or model organization would confer legitimacy on those organizations that mimic it. In the early years of the epidemic, fledgling AIDS organizations looked to the "big six"—the six large, old, financially well-off, and established AIDS organizations—for ideas about how to provide assistance to those living with AIDS and for programs that served prevention aims. Terms such as "safe sex" on the West coast and "safer sex" on the East coast emerged from these organizations. In the early 1980s, variations on Gay Men's Health Crisis's buddy program and its "Men Meeting Men" and "Eroticizing Safer Sex" workshops, on San Francisco AIDS Foundation's earliest social marketing campaigns, and on AIDS Project Los Angeles's AIDS Walk, among many other early efforts, rapidly spread to organizations throughout the country. Activities and efforts that are legitimated among organizational peers may be powerful influences on what programs and services other organizations might provide.

D'Aunno, Vaughn, & McElroy (1999) explored the extent to which these homogenizing processes have influenced service providers to become similar in their HIV prevention practices and adopt particular programs. D'Aunno and his colleagues surveyed a nationally representative sample of outpatient substance use treatment units in a mixed-panel design, which combined cross-sectional and longitudinal elements. Results of D'Aunno and his colleagues' study suggest that counseling and testing practices and outreach diffused rapidly and widely among substance use providers over a 7-year period. Adoption of these practices was strongly associated with linkages to licensing and accrediting bodies (coercive and professionalizing influences). Strong time effects were also evident in the data, suggesting that units rapidly began to imitate one another in adopting these activities. Interestingly, the stronger a unit's ties were to its local community, the *less* likely it was to have adopted counseling and testing programs. D'Aunno et al. hypothesize that strong local ties may promote organizations' abilities to refer their consumers to other providers, reducing the need to offer services that might duplicate what is already locally available. It is also possible that strong local ties may enable organizations to resist normative pressures.

Acceptance, Acquiescence, or Resistance to Technology Transfer

Oliver (1991) contends that organizations do not merely acquiesce to external forces such as those we have just described. She argues that organizations' responses to pressures may include acquiescing, compromising, avoiding, defying, and manipulating. She hypothesizes that conformity and acquiescing to pressure is likely to occur when at least seven conditions exist. The first condition is that the social legitimacy and economic gains an organization might obtain from giving in to external pressure is high. In other words, when the monetary and social benefits of succumbing to pressure are great, organizations are most likely to give in to such pressure. The second condition described by Oliver is that an organization's constituents have similar expectations of the organization. Homogeneity in expectations provides for consensus about resistance or acquiescence to pressure. Oliver's third condition is that conformity to pressure is voluntary rather than imposed. Self-determination and autonomy in decisions may engender more favorable attitudes toward demands from external sources. Uncertainty about what to do is the fifth condition identified by Oliver. As argued by DiMaggio and Powell (1983), when uncertainty about the best course of action is high, organizations are more likely to respond to external pressures to act in particular ways. Oliver's sixth condition concerns interconnectedness among organizations. She argues that when organizations are not strongly connected to one another, they are more likely to give in to external pressures. Finally, Oliver argues that acquiescence to external pressures is greatest when the specific conformity demands imposed from outside converge with the organization's mission and ideology.

These conditions outlined by Oliver are rarely met in current efforts to create conformity through efforts at technology transfer, though important exceptions exist. By and large, however, it is a relatively rare case in which the costs of evidence-based programs are fully supported so that prospective gains in cost-efficiency can be realized; adoptions of evidence-based programs are voluntary, rather than compulsory; evidence-based programs are convergent with organizational ideology; and organizations' Boards, staffs, local community constituents, funding agents, and other key stakeholders agree on how prevention ought to be carried out. Further, how an organization can best garner legitimacy from its community may be in direct conflict with how it can acquire legitimacy from other social agents. Given the activist roots of many AIDS organizations, conflict of this kind is likely to occur when technology transfer efforts are

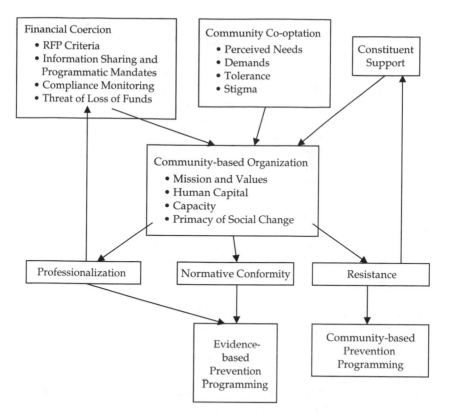

Figure 9.1 Ecological Pressures on AIDS Organizations' Programming

forced. Recent studies provide preliminary evidence for the usefulness of Oliver's hypotheses in explaining technology transfer and resistance to it among HIV prevention providers and other organizations founded to pursue collective action (see Barton-Villgrana et al., 2002; Campbell, Baker, & Mazurek, 1998; Miller, 2001; Milio, 1971; Salem et al., 2002).

To summarize, AIDS-related community-based organizations are situated within complex organizational fields. This ecological complexity governs an organization's basic operations, the probability that an organization may resist evidence-based practice, and the organizational consequences of using research in the form of receiving research technology. In Figure 9.1, we illustrate how these forces may coalesce to lead an organization to accept or resist new programs.

CONCLUSION

AIDS organizations in the United States typically emerged from collective action efforts that were designed to challenge mainstream inaction about AIDS. Being outside the mainstream may be a cardinal organizational value and one that organizations seek to maintain. In this context, HIV prevention is seen as a political act and one that is intimately connected to the human rights of particular communities that are also often socially marginalized and may have multiple other needs. Taking on the issues associated with HIV often also means adopting an organizational stance on issues that are nationally and locally controversial, such as homosexuality, drug use, and teenage sexuality. Further, underlying political and social change concerns may create real and perceived tradeoffs when faced with pressures to professionalize and accommodate funding requirements in order to improve what is usually a very small financial resource base. These contextual factors bear directly on the kinds of HIV prevention programs that organizations will, can, and do provide.

How can the HIV prevention scientist play an effective role in the practice of community-based organizations? How can we have an impact on local communities through technology transfer efforts? An important starting place is the sheer recognition that historical and environmental factors exert a powerful influence on the development and implementation of HIV-related prevention projects in community-based organizations. HIV-related community-based organizations are not a passive audience that eagerly awaits the latest well-tested program or piece of prevention research. Rather, these organizations are currently implementing HIV prevention activities in a demanding, dynamic environment that profoundly shapes the nature of the prevention programming they can and do provide. To survive, community-based organizations model what they perceive are successful, legitimate, and credible strategies and practices, carefully balancing the quest for innovation against demands of funding institutions and their local communities. Organizations balance the differing and sometimes contradictory demands of their funding institutions and their host communities, struggling to enact programs that simultaneously correspond with their funding institutions' prevention frameworks and their own beliefs about what makes for an effective prevention program. They do so in communities that may resist programs derived from principles that are most responsive to the organizations' target populations, as many of these organizations were founded as a challenge to the mainstream perspectives in their local community regarding sexuality and drug use.

Carol Weiss (1983) argues that ideological commitments and political interests are strong indicators of whether or not social science information has a chance of making an organizational impact. Whether the goal is to persuade people to adopt a particular policy position, evolve a new conceptual understanding of an issue, or improve implementation of a particular program, self-interests and guiding ideologies are powerful forces affecting information use. For example, research and prevention programs that challenge the underlying ideological base of an organization and undermine or refute its core values, is research that an organization is unlikely to welcome. Similarly, research that plays no role in furthering the self-interests of the organization may also be perceived as of little relevance and value. Technology transfer efforts that fail to situate themselves within the context of the mission, commitment and role of the organization as part of a social movement may have little impact. If the prevention program to be adopted can play no role in the dynamism of the organization or in sustaining the political movement on which the organization is built, it may have little appeal. Further, research and new programs create risks for organizations. By-products of research endeavors and new programs may be changes in an organization's safely guarded image, its credibility, and its legitimacy. These changes may not always be positive.

To succeed in advancing an HIV prevention practice that is reciprocally beneficial, researchers must know the histories and cultures of the community-based organizations with which they desire to work and how they are placed within their local social and political contexts. Researchers must begin to learn more about what organizations currently do, what benefits, if any, accrue to those who are the intended beneficiaries of the organization's efforts, and what programmatic improvements might enhance the likelihood that these indigenous efforts succeed. To the extent that specific evidence-based programs generated by HIV prevention scientists are likely to be better than or complement what is already being implemented, the design of these programs ought to consider the implementation context and actors fully, including financial and nonfinancial resources, synergy with other efforts, and the political and philosophical organizational stance toward prevention and the constituent communities. It must also be said, however, that evidenced-based practices may not always be positive or more effective than community-based efforts. As noted earlier, extant research does not tip the scales, one way or another. In both cases, the harms associated with implementing HIV prevention programs must be fully considered and researched, including those that concern the relationship between programming and organizational survival.

For AIDS activists, service providers, and researchers, one significant lesson of the epidemic is that community development is necessary to create effective prevention and treatment services (Altman, 1994). The epidemic has given an extraordinary impetus to the organization at the grassroots level of groups who have been largely marginalized, whether because of gender, race, poverty, or behavior (Altman, 1994; Wilson, 1995). Often, the struggle for political rights has become interwoven with AIDS work. Miller (1996) highlights the following:

> Since community-based organizations are by definition engaged in the process of representing constituents while also providing services, the model of disease prevention and care that these organizations have created is fundamentally political and has human rights at its core. These organizations are rooted in traditions of volunteerism and social activism; the cultivation of community and empowerment are key principles of the organizations themselves and of the actual programs they provide. (p. 544)

The future of successful technology transfer lies in its ability to serve these same community development aims.

NOTE

1. We recognize that the term "technology transfer" is not ideal to describe the process of disseminating complex social programs. Lacking a succinct, appropriate label, we default to this terminology.

REFERENCES

Abrahamson, E. (1991). Managerial fads and fashions: The diffusion and rejection of innovations. *Academy of Management Review, 16,* 586–612.

Altman D. (1994). *Power and community: Organizational and cultural responses to AIDS.* Bristol, PA: Taylor & Francis.

Aronson, N. (1984). Science as a claims-making activity: Implications for social problems research. In J. W. Schneider & J. I. Kitsuse (Eds.), *Studies of the sociology of social problems,* (pp. 1–30). Norwood, NJ: Ablex Publishing.

Backer, T. E., David, S. L., & Soucy, G. (1995). *Reviewing the behavioral science knowledge base on technology transfer.* Rockville, MD: National Institute on Drug Abuse.

Baldridge, J. V. & Burnham, R. A. (1975). Organizational innovation: Individual, organizational, & environmental impacts. *Administrative Science Quarterly, 20,* 165–176.

Barton-Villagrana, H., Bedney, B. J., & Miller, R. L. (2002). Peer relationships among community-based organizations providing HIV prevention services. *Journal of Primary Prevention, 23,* 217–236.

Cain, R. (1993). Community-based AIDS services: formalization and depoliticization. *International Journal of Health Services, 23,* 665–684.

Cain, R. (1995). Community-based AIDS organizations and the state: dilemmas of dependence. *AIDS and Public Policy Journal, 10,* 83–93.

Cain, R. (1997). Environmental change and organizational evolution: reconsidering the niche of community-based AIDS organizations. *AIDS Care, 9,* 331–344.

Campbell, R. C., Baker, C. K., & Mazurek, T. L. (1998). Remaining radical? Organizational predictors of rape crisis centers' social change initiatives. *American Journal of Community Psychology, 26,* 457–483.

Casteneda, D. & Collins, B. (1997). Structure and activities of agencies providing HIV and AIDS education and prevention to Latina/Latino communities. *AIDS Education and Prevention, 9,* 533–550.

Chambre, S. M. (1995). Creating new nonprofit organizations as response to social change: HIV/AIDS organizations in New York City. *Policy Studies Review, 14,* 117–126.

Chambre, S. M. (1999). Redundancy, third-party government, and consumer choice: HIV/AIDS organizations in New York City. *Policy Studies Journal, 27,* 840–854.

Chng, C. L., Sy, F. S., Choi, S. T., Bau, I., & Asutdillo, R. (1998). Asian and Pacific Islander American HIV community-based organizations: A nationwide survey. *AIDS Education and Prevention, 10*(Suppl. A), 48–60.

D'Aunno, T., Vaughn, T. E., & McElroy, P. (1999). An institutional analysis of HIV prevention efforts by the nation's outpatient drug abuse treatment units. *Journal of Health and Social Behavior, 40,* 175–192.

DiFranciesco, W., Kelly, J. A., Otto-Salaj, L., McAuliffe, T. L., Somlai, A. M., & Hackl, K. (1999). Factors influencing attitudes within AIDS organizations toward the use of research-based HIV prevention interventions. *AIDS Education and Prevention, 11*, 72–86.

DiMaggio, P. J. & Powell, W. W. (1983). The iron cage revisited: Institutional isomorphism and collective rationality in organizational fields. *American Sociological Review, 48*, 147–160.

Elwood, W. N. (1999). *Power in the blood: A handbook on AIDS, politics, and communication*. Mahwah, NJ: Lawrence Erlbaum Associates.

Emerson, R. E. (1962). Power-dependence relations. *American Sociological Review, 27*, 31–41.

Epstein, S. (1996). *Impure science: AIDS, activism, and the politics of knowledge*. Berkeley, CA: University of California Press.

Fredericksen, P. & London, R. (2000). Disconnect in the hollow state: The pivotal role of organizational capacity in community-based development organizations. *Public Administration Review, 60*, 230–239.

Freudenberg, N. & Zimmerman, M. A. (Eds.). (1995). *AIDS prevention in the community: Lessons from the first decade*. Washington, DC, American Public Health Association.

Gagnon, J. H. (1992). Epidemics and researchers: AIDS and the practice of social studies In G. Herdt & S. Lindenbaum. *The time of AIDS: Social analysis, theory, and method* (pp. 27–40). Newbury Park, CA: Sage.

Goldstein, E., Wrubel, J., Faigeles, B., & DeCarlo, P. (1998). Sources of information for HIV prevention program managers: A national survey. *AIDS Education and Prevention, 10*, 63–74.

Haynes-Sanstad, K., Stall, R., Goldstein, E., Everett, W., & Brousseau, R. (1999). Collaborative community research consortium: A model for HIV prevention. *Health Education and Behavior, 26*, 165–170.

Herdt, G. & Lindenbaum, S. (1992). *The time of AIDS: Social analysis, theory, and method*. Newbury Park, CA. Sage.

Hilgartner, S. & Bostk, C. L. (1988). The rise and fall of social problems: A public arenas model. *American Journal of Sociology, 94*, 53–78.

Hira, A. & Hira, R. (2000). The new institutionalism: Contradictory notions of change. *American Journal of Economics and Sociology, 59*, 267–282.

Johnson, W. D, Hedges, L. V., Ramirez, G., Semaan, S., Norman, L. R., & Sogolow, E., et al. (2002). HIV prevention research for men who have sex with men: A systematic review and meta-analysis. *Journal of Acquired Immune Deficiency Syndromes, 30*, S118–S129.

Kalichman, S. C., Carey, M. P., & Johnson, B. T. (1996). Prevention of sexually transmitted HIV infection: A meta-analytic review of the behavioral outcome literature. *Annals of Behavioral Medicine, 18*, 6–15.

Katz, D. & Kahn, R. L. (1966). *The social psychology of organizations*. New York, NY: Wiley.

Kelly, J. G. (1971). The quest for valid preventive interventions. In G. Rosenblum (Ed.) *Issues in Community Psychology and Preventive Mental Health* (pp. 109–139). New York, NY: Behavioral Publications.

Kelly, J. A., Sogolow, E. D., & Neumann, M. S. (2000). Future directions and emerging issues in technology transfer between HIV prevention researchers and community-based service providers. *AIDS Education and Prevention, 12*(Suppl. 5A), 126–141.

Kelly, J. A., Somlai, A. M., DiFranciesco, W J., Otto-Salaj, L. L., McAuliffe, T. L., Hackl, K. L., Heckman, T. G., Holtgrave, D. R., & Rompa, D. (2000). Bridging the gap between the science and service of HIV prevention: Transferring effective research-based HIV prevention interventions to community AIDS service providers. *American Journal of Public Health, 90*, 1082–1088.

Kraft, J. M., Mezoff, J. S., Sogolow, E. F., Neumann, M. S., & Thomas, P. (2000). A *technology* transfer model of effective HIV/AIDS interventions: Science and practice. *AIDS Education and Prevention, 12*(Supplement 5A), 7–20.

Lipsky, M. & Smith, S. R. (1989–1990). Nonprofit organizations, government, and the welfare state. *Political Science Quarterly, 104*, 625–648.

Luckenbill, W. B. (1998). Eroticized AIDS/HIV information on public access television: A study of obscenity, state censorship, and cultural resistance. *AIDS Education and Prevention, 10*, 229–244.

McCormack & Associates. (1997). *The McCormack Survey: A national survey of executive directors of AIDS service organizations and gay and lesbian social service agencies.* Los Angeles, CA: Author.

Meckler, L. (2002, October 1). HIV prevention groups says Bush administration is targeting their work. *Associated Press.*

Meyer, J. W. & Rowan, B. (1993). Institutional isomorphism and informal social control: Evidence from a community mediation center. *Social Problems, 40*, 445–463.

Milio, N. (1971). Health care organizations and innovations. *Journal of Health & Social Behavior, 12*, 163–173.

Miller, R. L. (1995). Assisting gay men to maintain safer sex: An evaluation of an AIDS service organization's safer sex maintenance program. *AIDS Education and Prevention, 7*(Suppl. 5), 48–63.

Miller, R. L. (1996). Review of *Power and Community: Organizational and Cultural Responses to AIDS. Health Education Quarterly, 23*, 543–547.

Miller, R. L. (2001). Innovation in HIV prevention: Organizational and intervention characteristics affecting *program* adoption. *American Journal of Community Psychology, 29*, 195–205.

Miller, R. L. (2003). Adapting an evidence-based intervention: Tales of The Hustler Project. *AIDS Education and Prevention, 15*(Suppl. 1), 127–138.

Mitchell, R. E., Florin, P., & Stevenson, J. F. (2002). Supporting community-based prevention and health promotion initiatives: Developing effective technical assistance systems. *Health Education and Behavior, 29*, 620–639.

Morrill, C. & McKee, C. (1993). Institutional isomorphism and informal social control: Evidence from a community mediation center. *Social Problems, 40*, 445–463.

Neumann, M. S., Sogolow, E. D., & Kelly, J. A. (Eds.). (2000). Turning HIV prevention research into practice [Special issue]. *AIDS Education and Prevention, 12*(Suppl. 5A).

Odets W. (1995). *In the shadow of the epidemic: Being HIV negative in the age of AIDS.* Durham, NC: Duke University Press.

Oliver, C. (1991). Strategic responses to institutional processes. *Academy of Management Review, 16*, 145–179.

Patton, C. (1986). *Sex and germs: The politics of AIDS.* Montreal, Canada: Black Rose Books.

Patton, C. (1990). *Inventing AIDS.* New York, NY: Routledge.

Perrow, C. & Guillen, M. F. (1990). *The AIDS disaster: The failure of organizations in New York and the nation.* New Haven, CT: Yale University Press.

Riger, S. (1984). Vehicles for empowerment: The case of feminist movement organizations. *Prevention in Human Services, 3*, 99–117.

Riger, S. (1999). Working together: Challenges in collaborative research on violence against women. *Violence Against Women, 5*, 1099–1117.

Rogers, E. M. (1995). *Diffusion of innovations* (4th ed). New York, NY: The Free Press.

Saidel, J. R. (1989). Dimensions of interdependence: The state and voluntary-sector relationship. *Nonprofit and Voluntary Sector Quarterly, 18*, 335–347.

Saidel, J. R. (1991). Resource interdependence: The relationship between state agencies and nonprofit organizations. *Public Administration Review, 51*, 543–553.

Salem, D. A., Foster-Fishman, P. G., & Goodkind, J. R. (2002). The adoption of innovation in collective action organizations. *American Journal of Community Psychology, 30*, 681–710.

Shilts, R. (1988). *And the band played on: Politics, people, and the AIDS epidemic*. New York: Penguin.

Singer, M. (1994). Community-centered praxis: Toward an alternative nondominative applied anthropology. *Human Organization, 53*, 336–344.

Singer, M. (1996). The evolution of AIDS work in a Puerto Rican community organization. *Human Organization, 55*, 67–75.

Singer, M., Castillo, Z., Davison, L., & Flores, C. (1990). Owning AIDS: Latino organizations and the AIDS epidemic. *Hispanic Journal of Behavioral Sciences, 12*, 196–211.

Singer, M., Flores, C., Davison, L., Burke, G., & Castillo, Z. (1991). Puerto Rican community mobilizing in response to the AIDS crisis. *Human Organization, 50*, 73–81.

Spector, M. & Kitsuse, J. I. (1973). Social problems: A reformulation. *Social Problems, 21*, 145–159.

Stall, R. (1994). How to lose the fight against AIDS among gay men declare victory and leave the field. *British Medical Journal, 309*, 685–686.

Stevenson, H. C. & White, J. J. (1994). AIDS prevention struggles in ethnocultural neighborhoods: Why research partnerships with community-based organizations can't wait. *AIDS Education and Prevention, 6*, 126–139.

Vaid, U. (1995). *Virtual equality: The mainstreaming of gay and lesbian liberation*. New York: Doubleday.

Weiss, C. (1981). Measuring the use of evaluation. In J. A. Ciarlo (Ed.), *Utilizing evaluation: Concepts and measuring techniques* (pp. 17–33). Beverly Hills, CA: Sage.

Weiss, C. (1983). Ideology, interest, and information: The basis of policy decisions. In D. Callahan & B. Jennings (Eds.), *Ethics, the social sciences, and policy analysis* (pp. 213–245). New York, NY: Plenum.

Wilson, P. A. (1995). AIDS service organizations: Current issues and future challenges. *Journal of Gay and Lesbian Health Services, 2*, 121–144.

Wohlfeiler, D. (2002). From community to clients: The professionalisation of HIV prevention among gay men and its implication for intervention selection. *Sex Transm Infect, 78*(Suppl. 1), 176–182.

Zibalese-Crawford, M. (1993). Improving service delivery in HIV/AIDS organizations. In V. J. Lynch & G. A. Lloyd, (Eds). *The changing face of AIDS: Implications for social work practice* (pp. 21–38). Westport, CT: Greenwood.

10

Community HIV Prevention Interventions: Theoretical and Methodological Considerations

Ralph J. DiClemente, Richard A. Crosby, & Gina M. Wingood

OVERVIEW

Despite advances in biomedical research, there is still no preventive vaccine or medical cure for HIV/AIDS. Consequently, efforts to change high-risk behaviors remain the best available means to prevent HIV transmission. Because HIV is largely transmitted through sexual behavior and shared injection drug use, it can be prevented through appropriate behavioral changes. However, changing HIV risk behavior is particularly difficult because an individual's propensity to adopt and maintain behaviors occurs in the context of their social relationships and lifestyles. As such, these behaviors represent the endpoint of a complex decision-making process that weighs the following relevant internal and external influences: interpersonal, social, economic, and psychological influences within a cultural context superimposed over traditions, values, and patterns of social organization. While such a complex decision-making process is not easily amenable to modification, HIV-associated risk-taking is not random, uncontrollable, or inevitable and, of particular importance, many of the factors that influence these behaviors are modifiable.

Historically, individual-level interventions (i.e., including small-group, face-to-face interventions) have been designed to maximize direct interactions between those involved in implementing a prevention program and the recipients of that program. The assumption underling this approach is that these programs can be intensive, personalized, and can specifically target recipients' barriers to adopting and maintaining HIV-protective behaviors. An alternative, and potentially more efficacious approach, would broadly target pockets of at-risk individuals within communities rather than specific individuals.

Community HIV prevention programs build upon and extend the more traditional individual approaches. The fundamental premise or rationale for using multidimensional community interventions is that disease etiology stems from multiple sources, and thus requires many different approaches to prevention. Given the magnitude of preventable human immunodeficiency virus (HIV) infections, expanding program delivery to the community may amplify the likelihood that substantial numbers of people will ultimately be "exposed" to the intervention and, as a consequence, will subsequently adopt HIV-protective behaviors (Sweat & Denison, 1995; Waldo & Coates, 2000).

This chapter examines community interventions in the context of HIV prevention. Initially, we describe the contextual framework of these interventions and describe the rationale underlying their implementation. We also describe how community interventions can effectively reduce HIV-associated risk behavior, as well as key characteristics of community interventions in contrast to individual-level approaches. Subsequently, we delineate five essential steps for planning and implementing community interventions. We then devote a substantial portion of the chapter to methodological issues in the design of community intervention trials. Finally, we offer future directions for the design and implementation of community HIV prevention interventions.

RATIONALE FOR THE DEVELOPMENT AND IMPLEMENTATION OF COMMUNITY INTERVENTIONS

Health and illness, historically, have been perceived largely as a function of an individual's behavior. This *individualistic perspective* has dominated the field of health promotion and disease prevention (Crosby, Kegler, & DiClemente, 2002; McLeroy, Bibeau, Steckler, & Glanz, 1988). As psychological theories of behavior change, such as Theory of Reasoned Action (Ajzen & Fishbein, 1980), Social Cognitive Theory (Bandura, 1977; 1997), and Stages of Change (DiClemente & Prochaska, 1998) were adapted to health behaviors, individual-level HIV risk-reduction interventions based on these theories began to address important proximal antecedents of risk behaviors such as knowledge, attitudes, beliefs, motivation, peer norms, risk-reduction, self-efficacy, and skill acquisition. These types of interventions have demonstrated evidence, albeit modest, of effectiveness in reducing HIV-risk behaviors (CDC, 1999).

In recent years, the recognition of the multiplicity of social, environmental, familial, and relational influences that affect an individual's decision-making calculus has contributed to an evolving paradigmatic shift from an individual focus to a focus on the individual-within-community (Sweat & Denison, 1995; Waldo & Coates, 2000). This broader contextual perspective recognizes the importance of targeting the multiple sources of influences that impact individual decision-making processes and, in turn, affect their behavior.

A substantial body of research indicates that characteristics of communities may have an important influence on health outcomes and individual risk behaviors (Robert, 1998; Cohen, Scribner, & Farley, 2000). Ecological studies have documented associations between community-level social and economic conditions and a variety of health outcomes (Acevedo-Garcia, 2001; Cohen et al., 2000; Kaplan et al., 1996; Lynch et al., 1998; Friedman, Perlis, & Des Jarlais, 2001; Kawachi, Kennedy, & Glass, 1999;

Kawachi, Kennedy, Lochner, & Prothrow-Stith, 1997; Kreuter & Lezin, 2002). Moreover, community characteristics are associated both directly and indirectly with individuals' risks for poor health outcomes, even after controlling for the effects of individual characteristics (Diez-Roux et al., 1997; O'Campo, Xue, Wang, & Coughy, 1997).

Emerging HIV prevention research has begun to recognize the importance and relevance of a adopting a broader prevention perspective designed to address an array of modifiable influences that may impact individuals' likelihood of adopting HIV-preventive or risk behaviors. In their assessment of the relative advantages of the system versus the individual approach for changing health behaviors, Green & Raeburn (1990) suggested that the most appropriate and feasible method for stimulating health enhancing behavior is at the community-level through multi-dimensional, community interventions.

There are a number of advantages of community interventions relative to individual-level interventions. One important advantage of delivering programs at the community-level is that reaching a broad proportion of the community may result in changing existing community norms to be more supportive of health protection behaviors. In turn, these new norms may prompt continued diffusion of health protective behaviors, reaching beyond individuals directly exposed to the intervention (Farquhar, 1978). Community strategies may also be more effective than individual- or group-level intervention strategies because they integrate multiple levels of influence (Sweat & Denison, 1995). For example, community strategies may involve institutional, organizational, community, and policy changes designed to amplify the adoption of HIV-preventive behaviors, as well as factors designed to affect intrapersonal and interpersonal influences on behavior (Emmons, 2000; McLeroy et al., 1988). Such changes in community organizations, social structures, and norms may promote the long-term maintenance of HIV-preventive behaviors. Though the promise of community interventions is considerable, relative to the field of chronic disease prevention, which has initiated a number of large-scale community intervention trials (Feinlab, 1996), far fewer have been developed, implemented and evaluated in the field of HIV prevention.

Definition and Rationale for Community Interventions

Despite growing consensus that the community may be the most appropriate level at which to intervene with HIV prevention interventions, there has been little agreement in what constitutes "community." While community has been defined in numerous ways by social science researchers, most definitions shared some common components such as geographic location, shared social institutions or interactions, and personal or health characteristics and/or interests of more or less homogeneous groups of people who share common goals or purposes (Haglund, Weisbrod, & Bracht, 1990; Jewkes & Murcott, 1996; Minkler, 1990). Internal strata may also define community, with the levels based on biological attributes such as age, gender, disease status, or risk behavior, or on sociological characteristics such as education or income. As used here, community HIV prevention interventions are programs designed to promote the adoption and maintenance of HIV-preventive behaviors in either subgroups or localized populations. The interventions do not target the entire community per se, but rather are tailored to at-risk segments within the broader community (e.g., injection drug users).

Regardless of how the community is defined or segmented, it should be remembered that communities are themselves part of the larger context of the system or society in which they exist, and are thus subject to influences from outside forces. Nevertheless, defining a community is a basic requirement to intervention planning in that it permits the definition of a more or less delimited setting in which to implement HIV-prevention activities.

The community intervention approach (i.e., targeting an identified at-risk subgroup) is a marked departure, philosophically, from the medical model of disease and its prevention. That is, the community intervention approach seeks to change not simply individuals but the distribution of risk (and, by inference, the probability of disease and resulting morbidity and mortality) in the at-risk subgroup within the broader population. Within this paradigm, interventions target structures or social networks rather than specific individuals. Stated differently, community-level interventions are designed to promote widespread behavior change by utilizing naturally occurring channels of influence (e.g., social/friendship networks) and social institutions (e.g., media, social venues) while simultaneously providing supportive environmental structures that encourage the adoption and maintenance of health-protective behaviors. These interventions may be "expert driven" or they may be based on collaborative efforts between experts and members of a given community.

Unlike individual-level HIV interventions, the primary purpose (i.e., the desired outcome) of community interventions is to shift—in a downward direction—the mean level of risk factors in a given subgroup within the population (Rose, 1985, 1992). This approach is based on the concept of population-attributable risk: that is, the amount of disease in a given population attributable to a specified level of exposure (Hennekens & Buring, 1987). Population-attributable risk is typically greatest in the central part of a disease distribution (i.e., in the bell part of a normal curve). Thus, the majority of the cases may be observed among individuals with only moderate levels of risk factors.

Consequently, the community-level approach seeks to identify and alter the underlying forces within communities that make the disease prevalent in a given subgroup within the population. That is, rather than attempt to identify characteristics of individuals that place them at risk for a particular disease, the community-level approach identifies socio-environmental factors that are likely to (1) predispose individuals to the adoption of risk

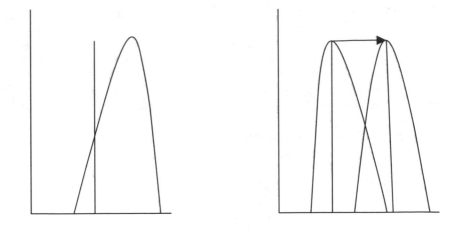

← risky sex behavior/safer sex behavior →

Figure 10.1 The Individual-Level   The Community-Level Approach to
Approach to HIV Prevention   HIV Prevention

behavior; (2) prevent individuals from adopting protective behavior; or
(3) lead directly to increased risk for disease, regardless of individuals' risk
behaviors (Link & Phelan, 1995).

Figure 10.1 (left side) schematically depicts the individual-level approach to HIV prevention. Individual-level HIV interventions commonly
target those persons identified as "at-risk," based on some constellation of
behavioral or other characteristics, and efforts are directed specifically toward changing an individuals' risk behavior. Individual-level approaches to
HIV prevention, unfortunately, are usually not developed on a scale capable of reaching large segments of the at-risk population. Thus, while the
individual-level approach offers a treatment advantage for small numbers
of program recipients, large numbers of people are: (1) at-risk for HIV but
never identified, (2) at-risk for HIV and identified but do not participate in
an individual-level intervention program, or (3) not currently at-risk for
HIV who—in the absence of exposure to a preventive intervention program—might subsequently acquire HIV-associated risk behaviors and
move into the at-risk population.

Figure 10.1 (right side), conversely, schematically depicts the
community-level approach to HIV prevention. Community-level interventions target an at-risk subgroup within the community, however defined,
with HIV prevention messages, often delivered simultaneously through
multiple channels. The primary objective to is change risk behaviors
among a larger segment of the target community. The increase in safer sex
within a community, typified in Figure 10.1 (right side), effectively shifts
the bell portion of the curve; reducing the population-attributable risk. The
end result is an overall shift in risk behaviors from risky sex (left) to safer

sex (right), reducing the risk trajectory of a community thereby reducing the incidence rate of HIV infections.

Understanding the pathways through which community interventions effect behavior change (i.e., reduce HIV-associated behaviors) is critical for intervention planners and evaluators. Below we describe two broad pathways of behavior change. Both pathways are derivatives of the community intervention approach.

COMMUNITY INTERVENTIONS CAN FACILITATE BEHAVIOR CHANGE THROUGH TWO PATHWAYS

Community interventions can facilitate the adoption of HIV-preventive behaviors through two pathways: direct intervention effects (effects produced through methods used in individual-level programs) or indirect intervention effects (effects produced through methods unique to community intervention programs). In the case of direct intervention effects, community participants actually interact with program interveners/change agents or are directly exposed to HIV prevention messages. For instance, direct intervention effects would be palpable in street outreach interventions where trained outreach works or health educators approach and provide brief, tailored counseling and prevention materials, usually stage-matched or other motivational-tailored print media, to individuals.

In the case of indirect intervention effects, participants in a target community do not have to actually interact with behavior change agents for the intervention to have an impact their behavior. Within the framework of community interventions, the indirect pathway is most critical to programmatic efficacy, with respect to both the adoption of HIV-protective behaviors and the maintenance of these behaviors over protracted time intervals. Nonetheless, it is the synergy created as a function of both pathways that magnifies the potential of community interventions to produce the desired outcome: a downward shift in the mean level of risk factors found in a given community (see Figure 10.1).

Community interventions also differ from individual-level forms of interventions in that they commonly utilize a broader array of strategies designed to target and integrate multiple levels of influence. HIV-associated risk and preventive behaviors reflect learned responses shaped largely through social, political, economic, cultural, and environmental factors, Thus, promoting behavior change usually requires a simultaneous, multifaceted intervention, delivered through many different channels before the individual, embedded within the community, can make and sustain healthful behavior changes (Flora, Saphir, Schooler, & Rimal, 1997). Such HIV community strategies may involve institutional, organizational, community, and policy influences designed to amplify the adoption and maintenance of health promoting behaviors, as well as activities designed to affect intrapersonal and interpersonal influences on HIV-risk behavior (Sweat & Denison, 1995; Waldo & Coates, 2000).

COMMUNITY INVOLVEMENT: A CORE CHARACTERISTIC
OF COMMUNITY INTERVENTIONS

The emphasis on community involvement has evolved over the past few decades, from programs imposed on the community (usually by well-meaning public health officials) to interventions developed with the active involvement of community stakeholders. Such community involvement is intended to serve multiple goals. It ensures "buy-in" by community members, increases avenues for dissemination of intervention components, and promotes trust between interventionists and consumers. Furthermore, community ownership increases the likelihood that the program will be sustained after the initial intervention has been completed and outside resources (i.e., funding and trained personnel) have been withdrawn (Butterfoss & Kegler, 2002). In addition, community interventions are more likely to be successful when they are part of a community initiative rather than a program imposed from the outside (Thompson & Kinne, 1990). In the field of HIV prevention, for example, many of the initial community interventions were developed by grassroots service organizations.

The primary core characteristic, then, is to empower the local community (however it is defined) to change lifestyle behaviors detrimental to health by their inclusion in efforts to alter political, social, economic, and environmental structures to promote rather than hinder needed changes (Guldan, 1996). Developing a sense of ownership for community interventions usually begins with an initial organizing effort. Thus, it is often assumed that the success of any community intervention is dependent on how much community involvement the intervention generates. No intervention can be optimally successful without being accepted by the audience for which it was designed. To facilitate the community organization process, Bracht and Kingsbury (1990) have proposed a five-stage process that involves members of the community in the following aspects of the community intervention: community analysis, design and initiation, implementation, maintenance and consolidation, and dissemination and reassessment of the process.

While there is some research focusing on the role of community involvement in community interventions (Butterfoss & Kegler, 2002), empirical evidence establishing the value of such involvement in the successful implementation of community interventions has not been provided. For example, it is unclear what level of community involvement is needed, at a minimum, to achieve and sustain intervention effects. As the field of community intervention research matures, we can begin to develop a coordinated program of research designed to address this key issue.

PLANNING COMMUNITY INTERVENTIONS

The following five fundamental planning factors enhance the success of community interventions:

1. *Conduct a thorough and comprehensive needs assessment.* A thorough and comprehensive qualitative and quantitative needs assessment should be conducted by individuals knowledgeable in these procedures. Determining the social character of the intended intervention community or target population and analyzing educational needs, readiness, and support, facilitate the design and success of the community intervention. When engaging in community assessment, and when implementing and evaluating the intervention, it is important to be aware of and sensitive to the culture, beliefs, and needs of the target population. In this aspect of planning, community involvement ensures a better understanding of the community and garners the local support that is essential to program success. When conducting randomized controlled trials, community involvement is typically designed to facilitate the development and implementation of an effective intervention rather than shape the research design, measurement instruments, or evaluation criteria.

   Assessment procedures should include modes that ensure a multidimensional analysis of the target community, including data on social, educational, epidemiological, and organizational factors that serve to directly or indirectly influence health status. Social issues essential to a community assessment include, but are not limited to, socio-economic characteristics of the proposed target population and access to health and other support facilities. A determination of health or other needs as perceived by community members is perhaps the most important part of a needs assessment. Actual patterns of morbidity and premature mortality are identified in the epidemiological component of the assessment. Having a theoretical framework on which to base the needs assessment can help to ensure that all relevant information is gathered (see below).

2. *Adopt a theoretical framework for guiding development, implementation, and program evaluation of community HIV prevention interventions.* Knowledge and utilization of an appropriate planning framework gives structure to the community intervention by facilitating the assessment process and guiding the development of subsequent intervention components. It focuses on assessing intrapersonal, interpersonal, institutional, community and/or public policy factors that may influence individual and community health morbidity (Haglund et al., 1990). Unlike psychosocial theories that describe individual cognitive factors and predispositions associated with behavior, community planning frameworks guide and tailor the design, implementation, and evaluation of interventions for specific at-risk subgroups within a population or community.

   A number of models can be used to facilitate the planning, implementation, and evaluation of specific community health interventions. Perhaps the most influential planning model is PRECEDE-PROCEED, developed by Green and Kreuter (1991). PRECEDE is an acronym that stands for "predisposing, reinforcing and enabling causes in educational diagnosis and evaluation". The PROCEED component of the model stands for "policy, regulatory, organizational constructs in educational and environmental development". The model can guide the interventionist through a multidimensional diagnosis of the population, its needs, and other factors that may influence health status in both individuals and the community. Application of the PRECEDE-PROCEED model requires the intervention plan to evaluate social, educational, and organizational factors that can influence health status potential. In addition, it helps in negotiating with organizational structures to access available resources.

A similar model often used to facilitate the development of community interventions is PATCH, or "planned approach to community health". Developed by the United States Public Health Service in 1981, PATCH provides a structured approach to developing interventions that are truly community programs, adapted to local characteristics and needs. The model has three major components: (1) community mobilization, (2) community diagnosis, and (3) community intervention. PATCH stresses horizontal and vertical collaborations among local, state, and federal agencies to provide the resources and support needed to implement the community intervention.

Another useful, and more recent, planning framework is MATCH ("multilevel approach to community health"; Simons-Morton, Greene, & Gottlieb, 1995). MATCH is also concerned with involving the local community in planning and implementation of community health interventions. Both PATCH and MATCH provide for a structured assessment of various factors that may influence the health status of individuals and communities alike. Each model shares common elements with PRECEDE-PROCEED. However, PRECEDE- PROCEED focuses predominantly on an extensive needs assessment, while PATCH emphasizes collaboration between the community and local, state, and federal partners (Kreuter, 1992; Simons-Morton et al., 1995), and MATCH stresses implementation of an intervention.

3. *Integrate socio-ecological theories of behavior change into the intervention program.* In addition to the planning models mentioned above, a number of theories of behavior change have been used to plan and structure community interventions, in both the field of chronic diseases and the field of HIV prevention. These theories are used to predict and explain why people do or do not engage in preventive health behaviors. Most can be subsumed under the category of social learning models; including the health belief model

(Becker, 1974; Rosenstock, 1990; Janz & Becker, 1984), Bandura's (1994) social cognitive theory, the theory of reasoned action (Ajzen & Fishbein, 1980) and its extension, the theory of planned behavior, and the transtheoretical model (Prochaska, DiClemente, Norcross, 1992). There is substantial evidence that the use of behavior change theories is instrumental for the design of effective HIV risk-reduction interventions across diverse populations (Peterson and DiClemente, 2000).

However, a major limitation of these theories is their overemphasis on intrapersonal influences (i.e., attitude, beliefs, intentions) and a lack of recognition of the integral role that ecological and cultural influences play in influencing behavior. While the core constructs of some psychosocial theories (i.e., social cognitive theory, transtheoretical model of behavior change) do, in fact, include environmental influences and constraints, they are rarely assessed and, when assessed, they are poorly operationalized. Thus, as noted in preceding sections of this chapter, behavior change theories alone, though useful for guiding individual-level interventions, lack robustness of effects given their limited focus on intrapersonal influences.

Newer models of behavior change that address the socioecological causes of risk and protective behaviors across different levels of causation are sorely needed to explain more fully the complexity of health behavior, including HIV-associated risk and protective behavior (Crosby et al., 2002; McLeroy et al., 1993). An emerging generation of social and ecological models explicitly assess the impact of the social environment as a key determinant of individual's behavior (Hovell, Wahlgren, & Gehrman, 2002; Wingood & DiClemente, 2002; Crosby et al., 2002). In addition, they view individual behavior as resulting from a transaction between individuals and their environment, sometimes referred to as "reciprocal causation".

Taken together, the models shift attention to interventions directed at changing interpersonal, organizational, community, and public policy. They follow the indirect pathway of behavior change outlined earlier and assume that appropriate changes in the social environment will produce changes in individuals. They also include community involvement as integral for implementing environmental changes. Because these newer models address the social causes of risk and protective behaviors across different levels of causation, they may be better suited to guide community interventions, given their broader, contextual focus.

4. *Use implementation models to guide intervention delivery.* Often overlooked in the design of community interventions is the use of implementation models. Implementation models are used to structure and execute the intervention. Methods and techniques

typically used in individual behavior change interventions, such as one-on-one counseling or small-group intervention sessions, would be prohibitively expensive if applied to an entire community. Hence, other strategies are necessary when implementing community intervention programs where the need is to reach a wide audience, either the general population or one or more specific target groups. Messages for a broad, diverse audience are by definition, less personalized and easier for the individual to ignore. Thus, reaching a community audience requires that the message be repeated through as many channels as possible and as often and in as many different forms as possible. Selection of channel delivery and diversity of message channels is therefore vital to reaching different audience segments.

Print media, often referred to as small media in HIV community interventions, has been an integral component of many interventions. Use of print media is supported by Flora et al. (1997), who present research suggesting that print media channels produce higher-involvement cognitive processing of information than television and demonstrate larger increases in knowledge and greater behavior changes. Nevertheless, not all individuals will respond to print material either because of problems with reading and interpretation, primarily attributable to low literacy, lack of exposure to printed material, or other reasons. Therefore, it is essential to know the socio-demographic profile of the target community or group for whom the message is intended in order to design a message or messages that are pertinent and effective for a particular audience.

Two theoretical models used to guide the implementation of community interventions for HIV prevention are social marketing (Kennedy & Crosby, 2002) and diffusion of innovation (Rogers, 1995). Social marketing is a process by which specifically designed programs, messages, or ideas are promoted to a particular audience, using advertising techniques originally designed to sell consumer goods. Targeted messages, formulated to bring about behavioral change, are disseminated throughout a selected site and via a given mode to increase their probability of acceptance by the target population (Lefebvre & Flora, 1988). Use of social marketing strategies enables greater penetration and promotion of a message to various segments of a community. The success of social marketing efforts depends on the consumer's interpretation of the message and his or her belief that the message is beneficial. The message content, clarity, presentation, and delivery channels are vitally important and must be thoroughly researched as to appropriateness and effectiveness for the target population. Knowledge of optimal communication and distribution strategies is also essential.

While social marketing interventions are not widely evaluated in the U.S., there is evidence that social marketing (particular media-based approaches) can help increase awareness of the HIV epidemic and encourage public funding for prevention, treatment and social services. In a number of European countries, as well as in Canada, New Zealand and Australia, social marketing campaigns have been instrumental in creating a social climate that makes a wide spectrum of prevention strategies more acceptable. In addition, messages about HIV disseminated through the social marketing, particularly the use of mass media, may facilitate more open discussion of sexuality in circumstances where this was previously not possible. The widespread promotion of condoms, for example, that is now common in most countries of Western Europe may reflect, to some extent, the attention given to the HIV epidemic by mass media (Rivers & Aggleton, 2000).

Social marketing and media interventions are not a panacea. Whether such media campaigns would enjoy support and success in the United States is arguable. However, media programs, even those that may be less candid or innovative, may still serve to create a social climate conducive to open discussion about sex, STDs and HIV. Media messages may also reinforce prevention messages for individuals exposed to other, more intensive interventions (i.e., individual-level, relational-level, or family-level). In this way, media campaigns may directly impact individuals' behavior and may indirectly influence behavior by affecting social norms to help sustain newly adopted HIV-preventive behaviors or reinforce maintenance of low risk behaviors in the face of countervailing social pressures.

Diffusion of innovation theory attempts to explain how a change or innovation is disseminated throughout cultural or social systems (Oldenburg, Hardcastle, & Kok, 1997; Rogers, 1995). The innovation may be a product, a new way of doing things, or an idea about appropriate health behaviors. This theory centers on the distribution of a message or innovation to one or more groups or subgroups in a community over a selected and predetermined period of time. The theory suggests that change is adopted by a sequential process of awareness of the innovation, persuasion of the benefits of the making the change, making the decision and implementing change, and finally, confirmation that the innovation is beneficial (Rogers, 1995).

The diffusion process is enhanced by identifying specific interventions, channels, methods, and modalities likely to reach the greatest proportion of the target community (Bracht, 1990). Most importantly, diffusion is fostered by initially promoting adoption among key opinion leaders who then influence others to adopt the innovation. As progressively larger numbers of people adopt the innovation, the behavior becomes more normative and thus lends itself to further dissemination. Many community HIV interventions have successfully utilized variants of diffusion of innovation as the guiding dissemination model.

5. *Use diverse intervention modalities.* As the review of theoretical models above indicates, community interventions may optimize their efficacy by using a diverse array of intervention modalities, strategies, and techniques delivered through a broad spectrum of implementation channels. Using a variety of intervention strategies and methodologies increases the probability that the intervention messages will reach, and be understood by, members of the target population. This, of course, requires a detailed community assessment and formative research to identify and characterize those strategies and implementation channels that may be most relevant, appropriate and effective at accessing the target community and encouraging behavior change.

Table 10.1 summarizes five representative studies to outline the intervention strategies and channels commonly utilized in community HIV interventions. Programs universally relied on two primary strategies: dissemination of HIV-prevention education materials and the use of peer educators. The latter method may be one of the most important activities in that it creates the possibility of a diffusion effect. Ideally, key opinion leaders foster "buy in" from members in the target community because they are people who are trusted and respected by members of the target population. In addition, they are also people with whom the target population could identify, thus enhancing the credibility and salience of the prevention messages. In turn, these community members may influence others to adopt and advocate HIV preventive behaviors. While the goal of adopting the protective behavior is the desired study endpoint, the goal of convincing people to also become advocates of others' behavior change accelerates the trajectory of the diffusion process. Of interest, an important study noted that persons who agree to advocate condom use to others are especially likely to become regular condom users (Stone et al., 1994).

Outreach has also been a common method. Unlike peer diffusion techniques, outreach is based on the efforts of project staff members (who may or may not be key opinion leaders of the community). Consistent with the peer diffusion model, evidence suggests that employing outreach workers who are also respected community members may be especially effective (Eng & Parker, 2002). Although outreach workers diffuse HIV-prevention messages, they may also conduct small-group sessions and organize "community events" that are designed to attract members of the target audience. Events may include safer sex parties, community workshops, (Lauby et al., 2000), musical events, and potluck dinners (Sikkema et al., 2000). Selecting venues and themes for these events is a process best addressed by member-driven project advisory boards. For example, in a study reported

Table 10.1 Implementation Methods Reported in Five Selected Trials of Community-Level HIV Intervention Programs

Study	Education Materials	Peers	Business Involvement	Outreach[1]	Events	Condoms	Media	Groups
Kelly et al., 1997	X	X				X		
Sikkema et al., 2000	X	X		X	X	X		X
Lauby et al., 2000	X	X	X	X	X	X		X
Kegeles et al., 1996	X	X		X	X		X	X
CDC, 1999	X	X		X		X	X	

[1] Involves the use of trained staff or community members who specifically agree to diffuse HIV prevention messages.

by Kegeles et al. (1996), a "core group" of community members served as the primary decision-making body for all project-related activities.

Finally, two other methods of community intervention are shown in Table 10.1: condom distribution and media promotion of HIV-prevention messages. While the former is common in the context of individual-level HIV prevention programs, the latter is unique to and, in fact, defines community programs. Each method may contribute to promoting condom use and other forms of HIV-protective behavior as normative. Indeed, a hallmark of community HIV prevention interventions is to foster community-wide norms that support the practice of safer sex. As described in many behavior change theories such as the theory of reasoned action, the theory of planned behavior, and the transtheoretical model; increasing individuals' perceptions of supportive norms may be an important catalyst of behavior change. While each of the methods provides a distinctive contribution to community-level HIV/ASIDS intervention, it is the use of multiple methods in concert that define the distinctive community-level approach.

METHODOLOGICAL CONSIDERATIONS

Rigorous evaluation of community interventions is critical to assessing program efficacy and providing feedback to enhance program performance. Community intervention trials necessarily require acute attention to design and analysis. It is beyond the breadth and scope of this chapter to present an in-depth analysis of the methodological issues in the design and analysis of community intervention trials in general, or HIV community intervention trials in particular. We will, however, describe some of the fundamental methodological issues that impact the design and analysis of community HIV intervention trials.

Community Intervention Trials May Include Nonrandomized or Randomized Designs

Nonrandomized Designs Nonrandomized community intervention trials employ identifiable groups as the unit of assignment but do not employ randomization. As such, they represent a form of quasi-experimental design. Analogous to other nonrandomized individual-level designs, these community intervention trials face substantially greater threats to internal validity than do randomized trials. At the same time, if circumstances prevent randomization, a nonrandomized group trial may be the only design alternative. Although such quasi-experimental designs lack the internal validity provided by experimental designs, they may be a better approximation of the "real world" and therefore have greater external validity. Indeed, HIV interventions have not typically randomized communities to treatment conditions because doing so would present insurmountable practical and political barriers.

Table 10.2 Key Differences Between Randomized, Controlled, Clinical Trials and Community
Intervention Trials

	Clinical Trials	Community Trials
1	Single layer structure (the person is the unit of assignment and observation)	Hierarchical structure (the person is only the unit of observation)
2	Strong internal validity	Strong external validity
3	Bias is random	Bias may be systematic
4	Random assignment	Matched assignments
5	Statistical power can be strong	Statistical power is generally problematic
6	Usually based on a convenience sample	Communities are purposefully selected

Group-randomized Trials   Group-randomized trials represent a subset of a larger class of designs referred to as *nested, hierarchical, multilevel,* or *clustered* designs. Units of observation are typically nested within identifiable groups or clusters, which are in turn nested within study conditions. As used here, the label group-randomized trial refers to a design in which identifiable groups are assigned to study conditions for the express purpose of assessing the impact of one or more interventions on study endpoints. The terms nested, hierarchical, multilevel, and clustered designs refer more broadly to any data set that has a hierarchical structure, as well as comparative studies (Bryk & Raudenbush, 1992).

In public health and medicine, the standard for assessing the efficacy of an intervention has been the randomized clinical trial, a tightly controlled experiment designed to maximize the investigator's ability to draw a causal inference about the effect of the treatment(s) on trial endpoint(s). Although similarities between clinical trials and community interventions exist, numerous differences define the two strategies (see Table 10.2).

The clinical trial in which individuals are randomly assigned to condition is well-known (e.g., two eminently readable texts are by Piantadosi, 1997; Pocock, 1983). These trials are characterized by randomization of individuals to study conditions, often after extensive screening for eligibility. They often have strong internal validity, allowing clearer causal inference, but weak external validity, or the ability to generalize the findings to individuals outside the trial. The participants may or may not represent any identifiable population or subpopulation, but they are always randomized as individuals to the study conditions. The study conditions may not reflect the "real world" well; however, the design hallmark of these trials is optimal experimental control.

By contrast, in community trials the unit of assignment is an identifiable group rather than an individual. Such groups are not formed at random, but rather through some connection among their members. Groups may be defined by their physical structure, as is the case for schools, bars, clinics, etc. In other cases, the groups may be defined by geography, as with whole communities and counties. Alternatively, groups may be characterized by HIV-associated risk behaviors (e.g., injection drug users). Other examples are neighborhoods or, in other cases, the groups may be defined by a social connection, as with a church or other social organization.

Community trials employ random allocation of identifiable groups to study conditions; as a result, they are true experiments. Randomization provides a statistical basis for the assumption of independence of errors at the level of the unit of assignment and serves to distribute potential sources of bias evenly across the study conditions. If a sufficient number of groups are randomized to each condition, inferences based on a valid analysis can be as strong as those obtained from a randomized trial of individuals. For this reason, the community-randomized trial is the standard in public health when identification of specific groups is feasible.

However, while the units of observation (i.e., the source of measurement) are individuals comprising the groups that serve as units of assignment, they typically involve only a limited number of assignment units in each study condition. Because only a limited number of discrete groups are typically available, there is usually an insufficient number of assignment units to ensure that randomization has an opportunity to evenly distribute potential sources of bias across the intervention conditions. This increases the potential for bias in community-randomized trials.

Key Design and Analytic Issues

The design of community-level HIV prevention interventions is intimately linked to a host of analytic issues; thus, design and analysis should be planned concurrently. First, as mentioned above, community-level trials are unique in that they typically involve few units of analysis. This creates multiple problems of analysis and interpretation. For example, Murray (1998) noted that even with random assignment of communities in community-level trials, randomization might not always be effective, particularly in trials involving small numbers of communities. The few units of analysis in community-level interventions also give rise to low statistical power.

Several solutions have been suggested to remedy problems associated with low statistical power. Murray (1998) emphasized measurement of all possible sources of variance, assuring that all statistical assumptions are met, and designing the study to focus on a single, primary endpoint. An additional solution is to analyze the unit of observation (i.e., individuals) and statistically control for similarities within the unit of randomization (i.e., account for the intraclass correlation often observed within clusters such as communities). Fishbein (1996) suggested that precisely defining the behavioral endpoint of the community-level intervention and defining/ clarifying the outcome measure with equal precision could enhance power.

Despite methods of compensating for low statistical power, the majority of community-level interventions have been underpowered, resulting in only modest evidence to support effectiveness (Fishbein, 1996). Indeed, Fishbein has noted that community interventions often lack power to detect even medium effect sizes, let alone small effect sizes. This is unfortunate because small effect sizes in community-level interventions may be very meaningful at the population level (Fishbein, 1996).

Koepsell, Diehr, Cheadle, and Kristal (1995) pointed out that loss of statistical power in community-level interventions commonly results from matching communities on variables that are not strongly correlated to the outcome measures. Accordingly, they advocated matching communities based on careful assessments of associations between community characteristics and trial endpoints. This process requires time and resources to conduct thorough preliminary analyses of the communities. Although it can result in increased statistical power, this practice is not usually included in the design of community interventions.

Second, community HIV interventions typically use nested cross-sectional designs, nested cohort designs, or a combination of the two designs. Nested cohort studies follow members, "nested" within selected communities. In the context of nested cohort designs, a common problem is high attrition rates. Alternatively, nested cross-sectional studies require successive waves of surveys administered to random samples of community members. One problem with this approach is that the time of the year when the survey is administered must be common across each community (Murray, 1995). In addition, measures should be taken to avoid an interactive effect between the community and the person administering the survey (Murray, 1998).

An additional issue with community interventions is community selection. Community selection should be based on several criteria, including ample distance (including nonoverlapping media markets) between selected communities to avoid contamination effects. If communities are to be randomized, then all communities involved must first express willingness to be assigned to any of the intervention conditions, including any "no-treatment" or "wait-list" condition included in the study design.

When communities are matched, it is critical to assess comparability with respect to potential socio-demographic confounders, for example, race, age, income and education. When differences between matched communities are discovered, they should be controlled for statistically. A particularly important confounding variable that should be avoided is the existence of similar programs in either the intervention or comparison communities. Similar programs in the comparison communities create a bias toward the null hypothesis (i.e., no difference between the intervention and comparison communities) and result in Type-2 error; whereas, similar programs in the intervention communities may complement or amplify planned intervention activities and, thus, create a bias toward

Type-1 error (i.e., falsely rejecting the null hypothesis in favor of the research hypothesis).

Effectiveness versus Efficacy

Efficacy, a measure of impact under ideal circumstances, is more characteristic of individual-level randomized interventions. Alternatively, effectiveness, a measure of impact under ordinary circumstances, more aptly describes community interventions. Thus, findings from community interventions are much more likely than those from individual-level interventions to reflect the "true" effect of the intervention on the target population.

INTERPRETING FINDINGS FROM COMMUNITY INTERVENTIONS

Community trial design and the analytic methods may over-represent or under-represent efficacy of the intervention. Several critical factors should be considered subsequent to observing significant or insignificant results. Some of the more important factors follow:

1. In nested cohort designs, findings may be biased by differences between the cohort recruited from a target community and the greater community. This may be particularly problematic when cohort participation rates are low and attrition rates are high. For example, when cohort participation is low, there is the potential for a selection bias (i.e., individuals who have elect to participate in the cohort differ on some measured or unmeasured characteristics from those who chose not to participate). In this instance, the cohort may or may not be representative of the target community. High attrition rates in the cohort may also jeopardize the validity of the findings. In this case, individuals who drop out of the trial may differ on measured or unmeasured characteristics from those who complete the trial (i.e., those remaining in the cohort may not be representative of the entire cohort or the greater community.

2. The use of biological endpoints in HIV prevention intervention trials is becoming increasingly more desirable because they provide an objective and quantifiable measure of intervention effects (DiClemente, 2000). However, with respect to community HIV trials, assessed biological endpoints may under-represent the efficacy of the intervention. For example, assume that in a well-designed and carefully implemented community trial, the investigators used sexually transmitted diseases (STDs) as a proxy measure for HIV risk (given the greater prevalence and incidence of STDs relative to HIV infection). The data analysis, equally well-planned and -conducted, observed no treatment effect; that is, there was no difference in the incidence of STDs

between the intervention and comparison communities. However, an analysis of behavior change identifies significant differences (between intervention conditions) in the HIV-associated risk behaviors that were targeted by the intervention, with the intervention communities having significantly higher rates of condom-protected sexual intercourse. Thus, the null findings observed with respect to the biological outcome may not represent lack of an intervention effect. Monitoring changes in HIV risk behaviors (i.e., reductions in risky sex or use of unclean injection equipment) rather than relying on changes in biological outcomes (e.g., STD incidence) may better reflect intermediate levels of intervention efficacy.

Furthermore, as more trials begin to incorporate biological measures to complement behavioral measures of efficacy (Fishbein & Pequegnat, 1999), data analytic strategies will need to assess intervention impact for both intermediate or proximal outcomes (i.e., risk behaviors) and the primary or distal outcome (i.e., disease incidence). Also, behavior change may not necessarily result in decreased incidence of disease because other factors (e.g., social mixing patterns and sexual "bridges" between sociosexual networks) may have a profound influence on disease outcomes independent of increases in sexual-protective behavior. Only by examining both outcomes can we truly evaluate programmatic efficacy.

3. As noted by Lauby et al. (2000), intervention effects may not be observed immediately post intervention, but may take protracted time periods before they occur and can be accurately measured. This is particularly important given that community effects are dependent on a diffusion process that may lag behind implementation of the intervention. Thus, having a narrow follow-up period to monitor intervention impact may result in determining that a "truly" effective intervention is ineffective.

FUTURE DIRECTIONS FOR COMMUNITY HIV PREVENTION RESEARCH

There are many challenges to the use of community HIV prevention trials. Understanding these challenges, their effect on the validity of the findings, and the strategies that are available to meet them is critically important. There is no question that it is more challenging to change the health behavior and risk profile of a whole community than to make similar changes in smaller identifiable groups such as those at worksites, physician practices, schools, and churches. And while no meta-analysis has been published, it is quite possible that the magnitude of the intervention effects reported for community intervention trials have been greater for trials that involved smaller groups than for trials involving such large aggregates as whole communities.

Communities are not homogeneous entities. Rather, they are a mosaic of subgroups and micro cultures, differing in their propensity to engage in HIV-associated risk behaviors. Thus, the occurrence of HIV risk is not evenly distributed in the population but is segmented in pockets of high prevalence. Viewing communities in terms of the risk of identifiable segments and types of social networks should allow us to much better tailor, focus, and deliver community HIV prevention interventions to those at greatest risk. It may also allow us to better understand what community characteristics serve to increase the vulnerability to HIV among population members and what community characteristics seem to protect against risk (Kelly, 1999).

There are several reasons why community HIV intervention trials would do well to focus on discrete groups rather than on whole cities or similar aggregates. Targeting smaller groups allows the inclusion of more groups in the design, thereby improving the statistical power and the validity of the trial. With smaller groups, it is also easier to tailor and focus intervention activities on the target population. Also, with smaller groups, the cost and difficulty of the implementation of the study generally are reduced.

Community HIV intervention trials, as noted above, confront a host of theoretical and methodological challenges. However, they hold great promise for accessing and modifying HIV-associated risk behaviors, in a cost-effective way, among large segments of the population. Clearly, we should gather the knowledge necessary to refine our approaches (Susser, 1996). For scientific reasons we prefer community HIV randomized trials over quasi-experimental designs. We need to develop increasingly sophisticated ways to construct such trials so that they are (1) sufficiently rigorous to avoid the pitfalls common to all comparative trials, as well as those peculiar to group-randomized trials, (2) powerful enough to provide an answer to the question of interest, and (3) inexpensive enough to be practical. For example, research could investigate 1) the use of continuous surveillance as a method that would allow monitoring of trends in the endpoints, 2) the use of community indicators as endpoints (i.e., collective self-efficacy), 3) the use of frequent but small surveys in lieu of infrequent but large surveys, 4) improved data analytic methods, and 5) analytic methods for the comparison of model-based and randomization-based methods to identify the conditions under which one approach is preferred over the other.

There is every reason to expect that continuing methodological improvements will lead to better trials and that better trials will have more satisfactory results. For example, Rooney and Murray (1996) presented the results of a meta-analysis of community intervention trials in the smoking-prevention field. One of the findings was that stronger intervention effects were associated with greater methodological rigor. Stronger intervention effects were reported for studies that planned from the beginning to employ the unit of assignment as the unit of analysis, that randomized a sufficient number of assignment units to each condition, that adjusted for baseline differences in important confounding variables, that had extended follow-up, and that had limited attrition.

Future HIV community trials will be stronger and more likely to report satisfactory results if they (1) address an important and very specific research question, (2) employ an intervention that has a strong theoretical base and preliminary evidence of feasibility and efficacy, (3) randomize a sufficient number of assignment units to each study condition so as to have good power, (4) are designed in recognition of the major threats to the validity of the design and analysis of group-randomized trials, (5) employ good quality-control measures to monitor fidelity of implementation of intervention and measurement protocols, (6) are well-executed, (7) employ good process-evaluation measures to assess effects on intermediate endpoints, (8) employ reliable and valid endpoint measures, (9) are analyzed using methods appropriate to the design of the study and the nature of the primary endpoints, and (10) are interpreted in light of the strengths and weaknesses of the study.

Concomitantly, improvements in methodological rigor, while necessary, will not be sufficient. No matter how well-designed and -evaluated a community HIV trial may be, strengths in design and analysis cannot overcome a weak intervention. Future trials will need to draw on a deeper understanding, now lacking, of methods for bringing about social change (Susser, 1995), and the nature of the change process in a broader societal context. To some extent, HIV community interventions, though effective, have not fully captured the complexity of community dynamics, the intricacies of formal, as well as informal community structures, and the effects of countervailing societal and economic forces that impact change processes. Thus, HIV community trials will benefit from a deeper understanding of (1) the array of community influences that impact and reinforce individual's HIV-preventive and risk behaviors for diverse populations (DiClemente, Wingood, & Crosby, 2003; DiClemente & Crosby, 2003), (2) the nature of resistance to change and sources of this resistance, and (3) how to measure change in the HIV prevention fabric of a community (Kelly, 1999).

CONCLUSION

Community HIV interventions marshal new kinds of data, ask new and broader questions regarding the range of influences that affect risk of HIV, and most importantly, create new and promising options for HIV prevention. Just as the chronic disease community demonstration programs enriched our knowledge base, the recently concluded community HIV intervention programs may give us impetus to uncover the complex dynamics that govern the adoption and the long term maintenance of HIV-preventive behaviors. As community HIV interventions become an increasingly promising weapon in our prevention armamentarium, further development of these interventions is an essential public health priority (Kelly, 1999). However, for the science of community HIV interventions to progress more rapidly with respect to theory, behavior change strategies, and design and analytic methodology, a comprehensive and coordinated infrastructure to conceptualize, stimulate and support community HIV intervention research remains of critical importance.

REFERENCES

Acevedo-Garcia, D. (2001). Zip code-level risk factors for tuberculosis: Neighborhood environment and residential segregation in New Jersey, 1985–1992. *American Journal of Public Health, 91*(5), 734–741.

Azjen, I. & Fishbein, M. (1980). *Understanding attitudes and predicting social behavior.* Englewood Cliffs, NJ: Prentice Hall.

Bandura, A. (1977). Self-efficacy: Toward a unifying theory of behavioral change. *Psychological Review, 84*(2), 191–215.

Bandura, A. (1994). Social cognitive theory and exercise of control over HIV infection. In R. J. DiClemente & J. L. Peterson (Eds.), *Preventing AIDS: Theories and methods of behavioral interventions. AIDS prevention and mental health.* New York: Plenum Press; 25–59.

Bandura, A. (1997). *Self-efficacy: The exercise of control.* New York: W.H. Freeman.

Becker, M. H. (1974). The health belief model and personal health behavior. *Health Education Monographs, 2,* 324–473.

Bracht, N. (1990). *Health promotion at the community level.* Newbury Park, CA: Sage.

Bracht, N. & Kingsbury, L. (1990). Community organization principles in health promotion: A five-stage model. In N. Bracht (Ed.), *Health promotion at the community level.* Newbury Park, CA: Sage; 66–88.

Bryk, A. S. & Raudenbush, S. W. (1992). *Hierarchical linear models: Applications and data analysis methods.* Newbury Park, CA: Sage.

Butterfoss, F. D. & Kegler, M. C. (2002). Toward a comprehensive understanding of community coalitions: Moving from practice to theory. In R. J. DiClemente, R. A. Crosby, & M. Kegler (Eds.), *Emerging theories in health promotion practice and research: Strategies for improving public health.* San Francisco: Jossey-Bass; 157–193.

Centers for Disease Control and Prevention (CDC). (1999). *Compendium of HIV prevention interventions with evidence of effectiveness.* Atlanta: Centers for Disease Control and Prevention.

Cohen, D. A., Scribner, R. A., & Farley, T. A. (2000). A structural model of health behavior: A pragmatic approach to explain and influence health behaviors at the population level. *Preventive Medicine, 30*(2), 146–154.

Cohen, D., Spear, S., Scribner, R., Kissinger, P., Mason, K., & Wildgen, J. (2000). "Broken windows" and the risk of gonorrhea. *American Journal of Public Health, 90*(2), 230–236.

Crosby, R. A., Kegler, M. C., & DiClemente, R. J. (2002). Understanding and applying theory in health promotion practice and research. In R. J. DiClemente, R. A. Crosby, & M. Kegler (Eds.), *Emerging theories in health promotion practice and research: Strategies for improving public health.* San Francisco: Jossey-Bass; 1–15.

DiClemente, R. J. (2000). Looking forward: Future directions for HIV prevention research. In J. L. Peterson & R. J. DiClemente (Eds.), *Handbook of HIV Prevention*. New York: Kluwer/Plenum; 311–324.

DiClemente, C. C. & Prochaska, J. O. (1998). Toward a comprehensive, transtheoretical model of change: Stages of change and addictive behaviors. In W. R. Miller & N. Heather (Eds.), *Treating addictive behaviors applied clinical psychology* (2nd ed.). New York: Plenum Press; 3–24.

DiClemente, R. J., Wingood, G. M., & Crosby, R. (2003). A contextual perspective for understanding and preventing STD/HIV among adolescents. In D. Romer (Ed.), *Reducing adolescent risk: Toward an integrated approach*. Thousand Oaks, CA: Sage; 366–373.

Diez-Roux, A. V., Nieto, F. J., Muntaner, C., Tyroler, H. A., Comstock, G. W., Shahar, E., et al. (1997). Neighborhood environments and coronary heart disease: A multilevel analysis. *American Journal of Epidemiology, 146*(1), 48–63.

Emmons, K. M. (2000). Health behaviors in a social context. In L. F. Berkman & I. Kawachi (Eds.), *Social epidemiology*. New York: Oxford University Press; 242–266.

Eng, E. & Parker, E. (2002). Natural helper models to enhance a community's health and competence. In R. J. DiClemente, R. A. Crosby, & M. C. Kegler (Eds.), *Emerging theories in health promotion practice and research: Strategies for improving public health*. San Francisco: Jossey-Bass; 126–156.

Farquhar, J. W. (1978). The community-based model of life style intervention trials. *American Journal of Epidemiology, 108*(2), 103–111.

Feinlab, M. (1996). New directions for community. *American Journal of Public Health, 86*, 1606–1698.

Fishbein, M. (1996). Great expectations, or do we ask too much from community-level interventions? *American Journal of Public Health, 86*(8), 1075–1076.

Fishbein, M. & Pequegnat, W. (1999). Evaluating AIDS prevention interventions using behavioral and biological outcome measures. *Sexually Transmitted Diseases, 27*(2), 101–110.

Flora, J. A., Saphir, M. N., Schooler, C., & Rimal, R. N. (1997). Toward a framework for intervention channels: Reach, involvement, and impact. *Annals of Epidemiology, 7*(Suppl. 7), S104–S112.

Friedman, S. R., Perlis, T., & Des Jarlais, D. C. (2001). Laws prohibiting over-the-counter syringe sales to injection drug users: Relations to population density, HIV prevalence, and HIV incidence. *American Journal of Public Health, 91*(5), 791–793.

Green, L. W. & Kreuter, M. W. (1991). *Health promotion planning: An educational and environmental approach* (2nd ed.). Palo Alto, CA: Mayfield.

Green, L. W. & Raeburn, J. (1990). Contemporary development in health promotion: Definitions and challenges. In N. Bracht (Ed.), *Health promotion at the community level*. Newbury Park, CA: Sage.

Guldan, S. C. (1996). Obstacles to community health promotion. *Social Science and Medicine, 43*(5), 689–695.

Haglund, B., Weisbrod, R. R., & Bracht, N. (1990). Assessing the community: Its services, needs, leadership, and readiness. In N. Bracht (Ed.), *Health promotion at the community level*. Newbury Park, CA: Sage; 91–108.

Hennekens, C. H. & Buring, J. E. (1987). *Epidemiology in medicine*. Boston, MA: Little, Brown.

Hovell, M. F., Wahlgren, D. R, & Gehrman, C. A. (2002). The behavioral ecological model: Integrating public health and behavioral science. In R. J. DiClemente,

R. A. Crosby, & M. C. Kegler (Eds.), *Emerging theories in health promotion practice and research: Strategies for improving public health*. San Francisco: Jossey-Bass; 347–385.

Janz, N. K. & Becker, M. H. (1984). The health belief model: A decade later. *Health Education Quarterly, 11*, 1–47.

Jewkes, R. & Murcott, A. (1996). Meanings of community. *Social Science and Medicine, 43(4)*, 555–563.

Kaplan, G. A., Pamuk, E. R., Lynch, J. W., Cohen, R. D., & Balfour, J. L. (1996). Inequality in income and mortality in the United States: Analysis of mortality and potential pathways. *British Medical Journal, 312*, 999–1003.

Kawachi, I., Kennedy, B., & Glass, R. (1999). Social capital and self-rated health: A contextual analysis. *American Journal of Public Health, 89(8)*, 1187–1193.

Kawachi, I., Kennedy, B., Lochner, K., & Prothrow-Stith, D. (1997). Social capital, income inequality, and mortality. *American Journal of Public Health, 87(9)*, 1491–1498.

Kegeles, S. M., Hays, R. B., & Coates, T. J. (1996). The Mpowerment project: A community-level HIV prevention intervention for young gay men. *American Journal of PublicHealth, 86*, 1129–1136.

Kelly, J. A. (1999). Community-level interventions are needed to prevent new HIV infections. *American Journal of Public Health, 89(3)*, 299–301.

Kennedy, M. G. & Crosby, R. A. (2002). Prevention marketing: An emerging integrated framework. In R. J. DiClemente, R. A. Crosby, & M. C. Kegler (Eds.), *Emerging theories in health promotion practice and research: Strategies for improving public health*. San Francisco: Jossey-Bass; 255–284.

Koepsell, T. D., Diehr, P. H., Cheadle, A., & Kristal, A. (1995). Invited commentary: Symposium on community intervention trials. *American Journal of Epidemiology, 142(6)*, 594–598.

Kreuter, M. W. (1992). PATCH: Its origin, basic concepts, and links to contemporary public health policy. *Journal of Health Education, 23(3)*, 135–139.

Kreuter, M. W. & Lezin, N. A. (2002). Social capital theory: Implications for community-based health promotion. In R. J. DiClemente, R. A. Crosby, & M. C. Kegler (Eds.). *Emerging theories in health promotion practice and research: Strategies for improving public health*. San Francisco: Jossey-Bass; 228–254.

Lauby, J. L., Smith, P. J., Stark, M., Person, B., & Adams, J. (2000). A community-level HIV prevention intervention for inner-city women: Results of the women and infants demonstration projects. *American Journal of Public Health, 90(2)*, 216–222.

Lefebvre, R. C. & Flora, J. A. (1988). Social marketing and public health intervention. *Health Education Quarterly, 15*, 299–315.

Link, B. G. & Phelan, J. (1995). Social conditions as fundamental causes of disease. *Journal of Health and Social Behavior, (Extra Issue)*, 80–94.

Lynch, J. W., Kaplan, G. A., Pamuk, E. R., Cohen, R. D., Heck, K. E., Balfour, J. L. et al. (1998). Income inequality and mortality in metropolitan areas of the United States. *American Journal of Public Health, 88(7)*, 1074–1080.

McLeroy, K. R., Bibeau, D., Steckler, A., & Glanz, K. (1988). An ecological perspective on health promotion programs. *Health Education Quarterly, 15(4)*, 351–377.

Minkler, M. (1990). Improving health through community organization. In K. Glanz, F. M. Lewis, & B. K. Rimer. (Eds.), *Health behavior and health education*. San Franciso: Jossey-Bass; 257–287.

Murray, D. M. (1995). Design and analysis of community trials: Lessons from the Minnesota Heart Health Program. *American Journal of Epidemiology, 142*(6), 569–575.

Murray, D. M. (1998). *Design and analysis of group-randomized trials.* New York: Oxford University Press.

O'Campo, P., Xue, X., Wang, M., & Coughy, M. O. (1997). Neighborhood risk factors for low birth weight in Baltimore: A multilevel analysis. *American Journal of Public Health, 87*(7), 1113–1118.

Oldenburg, B., Hardcastle, D. M., & Kok, G. (1997). Diffusion of innovations. In K. Glanz, F. M. Lewis, & B. K. Rimer (Eds.), *Health behavior and health education* (2nd ed.). San Franciso: Jossey-Bass; 270–276.

Peterson, J. L. & DiClemente, R. J. (2000). *Handbook of HIV prevention.* New York: Kluwer/Plenum.

Piantadosi, S. (1997). *Clinical trials: A methodological perspective.* New York: John Wiley& Sons.

Pocock, S. J. (1983). *Clinical trials.* New York: John Wiley & Sons.

Prochaska, J. O., DiClemente, C. C., & Norcross, K. C. (1992). In search of how people change: Applications addictive behaviors. *American Psychologist, 47*(9), 1102–1114.

Rivers, K. & Aggleton, P. (2000). HIV prevention in industrialized countries. In J. L. Peterson & R. J. DiClemente (Eds.), *Handbook of HIV prevention.* New York: Kluwer/Plenum; 245–263.

Robert, S. A. (1998). Community-level socioeconomic status effects on adult health. *Journal of Health & Social Behavior, 39*(1), 18–37.

Rogers, E. M. (1995). *Diffusion of innovations* (4th ed.). New York: Free Press.

Rooney, B. L. & Murray, D. M. (1996). A meta-analysis of smoking prevention programs after adjustment for errors in the unit of analysis. *Health Education Quarterly, 23*(1), 48–64.

Rose, G. (1985). Sick individuals and sick populations. *International Journal of Epidemiology, 14*(1), 32–38.

Rose, G. (1992). *The strategy of preventive medicine.* New York: Oxford University Press.

Rosenstock, I. M. (1990). The health belief model: Explaining health behavior through expectancies. In K. Glanz, F. M. Lewis, & B. K. Rimer (Eds.), *Health behavior and health education.* San Franciso: Jossey-Bass; 39–62.

Sikkema, K. J., Kelly, J. A., Winett, R. A., Solomon, L., Cargill, V., Roffman, R., et al. (2000). Women living in 18 low-income housing developments. *American Journal of Public Health, 90,* 57–63.

Simons-Morton, B. G., Greene, W. H., & Gottlieb, N. H. (1995). *Introduction to health education and health promotion.* Prospect Heights, IL: Waveland Press.

Stone, J., Aronson E., Crain, A. L., Winslow, M. P., & Fried, C. B. (1994). Inducing hypocrisy as a means of encouraging young adults to use condoms. *Personality and Social Psychology Bulletin, 20,* 116–128.

Susser, M. (1996). Some principles in study design or preventing HIV transmission: Rigor or reality. *American Journal of Public Health, 86,* 1713–1716.

Sweat, M. D. & Denison, J. A. (1995). Reducing HIV incidence in developing countries with structural and environmental interventions. *AIDS, 9*(Suppl. A), S251–S257.

Thompson, B. & Kinne, S. (1990). Social change theory: Applications to community health. In N. Bracht (Ed.), *Health promotion at the community level.* Newbury Park, CA: Sage; 45–65.

Waldo, C. R. & Coates, T. J. (2000). Multiple levels of analysis and intervention in HIV prevention science: Exemplars and directions for new research. *AIDS* *14*(Suppl. 2), S18–S26.

Wingood, G. M. & DiClemente, R. J. (2002). The theory of gender and power: A social structural theory for guiding the design and implementation of public health interventions to reduce women's risk of HIV. In R. J. DiClemente, R. A. Crosby, & M. C. Kegler (Eds.), *Emerging theories in health promotion practice and research: Strategies for improving public health*. San Francisco: Jossey-Bass; 313–347.

11

Comprehensive Dynamic Trial Designs for Behavioral Prevention Research With Communities: Overcoming Inadequacies of the Randomized Controlled Trial Paradigm

Bruce D. Rapkin & Edison J. Trickett

In considering how behavioral prevention research could best lead to sustained risk reduction at community or population levels, we focus on the following question: How does the prevention research paradigm help or hinder our ability to develop sustainable community-level change? "The prevention research paradigm" refers to the routine way in which our scientific community identifies, tests, and draws conclusions about strategies to reduce HIV risk behavior (Wandersman, 2003).

The heart of this paradigm is the randomized controlled experiment to compare one or more prevention approaches (DesJarlais et al., 2004). The randomized controlled trial (RCT) paradigm is so central to the work that we do that it often treated as synonymous with science and rigor (Black, 2001; Stephenson & Imrie, 1998; Victoria, Habicht, & Bryce, 2004). Prevention approaches in such trials are most often cast in a standard or "manualized" form. Evaluation includes at least one baseline assessment prior to the intervention, followed by one or several post-intervention reassessments. This behavioral prevention paradigm has become increasingly sophisticated, often including direct measures of psychological mediators and checks of fidelity to protocols (Neumann et al., 2002; Semaan et al., 2002).

When asked to address how the RCT might relate to the community impact of HIV prevention research, one of us (Rapkin) found himself derailed by two incidents. First, a colleague and I were seeking biostatistical consultation on an intervention trial to help newly diagnosed women make decisions about disclosing their HIV status. We wanted to see whether our intervention helped women optimize outcomes in all relevant life domains, a choice necessitating multiple potential outcome variables. However, our consultant insisted that since we were conducting an RCT, we needed to specify a primary outcome. We pointed out that the most important outcomes for women who choose to conceal their status might be irrelevant to others who chose to disclose. Nonetheless, rules of the RCT dictated that there had to be a "primary outcome" so we would know how to power the study. Rather than have outcomes that address the context of women's lives as we had hoped, we had to settle on psychological distress as the primary variable of interest, equally applicable to all women, but also several steps removed from the decisions we were interested in.

Second, another colleague presented a proposed intervention study using a two-arm RCT to compare spirituality-based patient support groups to standard mutual support groups. Pilot work had suggested that many patients would prefer spirituality-based coping strategies. For rigor's sake, he proposed to randomly assign patients to these two intervention arms. The following question arose: If this new method is intended to accommodate patient preferences, does it make sense to ignore them in testing the program? If people are not "neutral" about their spiritual beliefs and practices, randomly assigning them to a condition that they would not choose could grossly affect the results. Patients who feel strongest about their placement may drop out, refuse randomization, or choose not to respond to study advertisements and would thus be underrepresented in the research. The investigator acknowledged this problem but was concerned about how grant reviewers would respond if he deviated from the RCT paradigm.

Why do researchers have to simplify or distort their questions for the sake of the RCT design? If we know that patients' preferences matter, why is it more scientific to ignore them when we compare interventions? Should investigators design studies that conform to the RCT template simply to satisfy review committees? Is the RCT always the strongest design for studying interventions? What are the unintended consequences of subscribing to the RCT paradigm? What other paradigms might we consider?

This chapter explores the RCT paradigm using the following structure: First, we consider the scientific rationale for using the RCT design when studying phenomena as complex as community-based HIV prevention interventions. Second, we examine the "investigator-subject" relationship presupposed by the RCT paradigm, to highlight potential unintended consequences engendered by this relationship in HIV prevention research. Third, we outline a series of alternative research designs to demonstrate how we might begin to advance and broaden our research agenda. Finally, we discuss the place of the RCT in a more inclusive scientific paradigm that may better serve public health by promoting more responsive and sustainable approaches to HIV prevention.

DOES THE RCT DESIGN ENSURE SCIENTIFIC RIGOR IN TESTS OF HIV PREVENTION INTERVENTIONS?

To evaluate the scientific merits of RCT for testing HIV prevention interventions, it is useful to examine four concepts central to this paradigm: random assignment, experimental treatment effects, independence, and generalization. Each poses particular problems when considering current understanding of HIV risk, behavioral change, and community-level processes (Oakley, 1990; Victoria et al., 2004).

Random Assignment

The purpose of random assignment is to ensure that all other plausible known and unknown causes for an outcome are equally distributed among experimental conditions, effectively isolating the effects of a given independent variable (Campbell & Stanley, 1963). But how tenable is this assumption? In commenting on discrepancies concerning the benefits of mammography, Strauss (2000; Strauss & Dominioni, 2000) argues that the failure to replicate findings across trials may in part be due to the complex nature of error. Complex outcomes, like occurrence and early detection of a tumor or health behavior, are determined by many different variables, some known and measurable, and some not. These factors can interact with one another in a myriad of ways, creating multiple possible paths to a single outcome.

Strauss contends that so many different combinations of health status, genetic, and environmental risk factors underlie breast cancer that randomization may fail, even in trials including tens of thousands of people. How much more of this problem exists in trials examining sexual risk behavior, which are influenced by the preferences and histories of partners rather than individuals, depend on outcome measures aggregated across multiple situations, and usually include several hundred participants?

We conducted a simulation to look at how well randomization handles underlying factors. Using SPSS for Windows (2002), we generated a "population" of 100,000 cases. Each case was assigned a score of 1 or 0 on three binary variables, A, B, and C, representing three confounds or correlates of risk. Variable A occurs at 50% prevalence, variable B at 33.3% prevalence, and variable C at 66.7% prevalence. Values to these variables were assigned to cases at random. We next drew at random 100 samples of 250 cases each (without replacement), half randomly assigned to an "experimental" arm and the other half designated as "controls".

Random assignment did a good job in forming equivalent groups on confounds A, B, and C, taken independently. However, to examine how well randomization produces samples that were relatively comparable in terms of combinations of A, B, and C, we calculated the proportion of each combination of AxBxC (8 possible combinations) in both the experimental and the control group. The important question was whether random assignment to condition split each sample evenly. To test this, we computed the ratio of cases assigned to the experimental arm versus the control arm for each of the 8 AxBxC combinations. If the arms were comparable, this ratio would be close to 1 (for example, 6% divided by 6%). We decided to see how often assignment of the cases displaying any given combination differed by 50% or more. Random assignment achieved reasonably high comparability in only 5% of the 100 random samples of 250 cases (125 per arm). Random assignment yielded experimental arms that were noncomparable on one of the eight combinations in 24% of the samples, noncomparable on two combinations in 37% of the samples, and noncomparable on three to five combinations in 34% of the samples.

What this simulation demonstrated is that when we randomly assign people to intervention arms, we cannot guarantee that groups are truly comparable in terms of combinations of variables that influence treatment responses and outcomes (Black, 1996; 2001; DesJarlais et al., 2004; Victoria et al., 2004). The implication is that human diversity, evident in the interplay of determinants of complex behavior, may preclude reliance on evaluation techniques that depend solely upon comparisons of group responses to isolate the effects of treatment.

Treatment Effect

Hypotheses in RCTs are generally framed in terms of single monolithic models and outcomes. The notion that people will respond in a lock step fashion to treatment may be a major impediment to discovery. For example, some people may do just fine in an intervention group while others do not. Some people may benefit from sexually explicit materials and models that embarrass or offend others. Our methodological infatuation with "THE" treatment effect precludes considering these likely scenarios.

Fortunately, the RCT design *per se* does not limit our ability to explore treatment effects in some detail. In an earlier paper, Rapkin (2002) discusses empirical techniques that can be used to identify patients who respond to interventions in different ways. For example, participants may demonstrate different trajectories on key outcome variables, including different rates of response or responses in different areas on a multivariate profile of outcomes (Hedeker & Mermelstein, 2000; Zeger & Liang, 1992).

Although we need to reexamine interventions to understand different outcome patterns and trajectories, our goal should be to anticipate and model these effects. One challenge may be to formulate families of hypotheses associated with different possible expected trajectories, and then to specify variables that predict which trajectory people will follow. For example, participants who are in a brand new relationship, or who live with a partner, or who have a friend recently diagnosed with HIV, *all* may have beneficial outcomes from a given intervention. The *same* intervention may lead participants in new relationships to start using condoms, participants in established relationships to get tested, and participants with HIV+ friends to initiate conversations about their needs and risks.

Another factor in understanding differential responses to interventions involves "response shift". Response shift refers to a property of all evaluative scales that are subject not only to change in the behavior or attribute of interest, but also to changes in the understanding or meaning of that behavior or attribute. In quality of life research, Sprangers and Schwartz (1999) posit three different types of response shift: recalibration, or changes in the use or understanding of a rating scale; reprioritization, or changes in the relative importance of different factors involved in making

Table 11.1 Response Shift Phenomena That Can Attenuate the Apparent Treatment Effects of HIV Prevention RCTs

Response Shift Construct	Applicability to the Evaluation of HIV Prevention RCTs
Recalibration	Intervention makes participants more critical of their own risk behavior; respondents use rating scales in a more nuanced or precise manner.
Reprioritization	Intervention leads participants to become more aware of risk; respondents pay attention to events and activities that they might have previously ignored;
Reconceptualization	Intervention causes participants to see behavior in a new way; things that they might not have "counted" as sex or drug use is now considered.

a rating; and reconceptualization, or changes in the very meaning of the construct of interest. Rapkin and Schwartz (2004) discuss changes in frame of reference, standards of comparison, and implicit rules for recalling and prioritizing experience that account for response shifts.

Although developed most recently in the context of quality of life research, the response shift model has direct relevance for understanding risk behavioral outcomes in RCTs. Almost all of the behavior that we consider in HIV prevention RCTs cannot be directly observed. Thus, we are dependent upon self-reported outcomes of sexual activity and substance use. Clearly, interventions may do more than affect these behaviors; they can also influence the criteria people use to appraise these behaviors, changing the sensitivity and even the meaning of our outcome measures. (see Table 11.1).

A traditional RCT analysis that directly compares arms without considering and correcting for differential response shifts in risk appraisal may obscure treatment effects. A remedy would be to include direct measures of response shifts in risk appraisal as moderators of the RCT evaluation or any other design. Schwartz and Sprangers (2000) recommend such approaches as the "retrospective pretest" that asks participants to rerate past behavior using current standards; think aloud techniques to get people to explicate the criteria they use to rate key items; and measures of degree of comfort in discussing highly personal and stigmatized behavior to examine self-censuring. Rapkin and Schwartz (2004) discuss assessment and design options for dealing with response shift in quality of life outcomes research that can be adapted to studies of perceived risk.

Independence, Contamination, and the Individual Level of Analysis

There is a troubling paradox inherent in the use of RCT to foster HIV prevention. Even though our goal is inevitably to change the behavior and the norms of large groups of people, we often design and evaluate programs in a way that precludes "contamination" between experimental and control groups. In the ideal case, we would want to develop programs that are so good that they even help the people who receive the program indirectly. However, requirements of independence and concerns about contamination essentially require us to operate with one hand tied behind our proverbial back.

If we were testing the effects of a drug, the fact that participants inhabit common settings and have social relationships would not be expected to influence its biological effects (although these factors might affect self-reports of symptoms, side effects etc.). However, when it comes to HIV risk behavior, nonindependence may come into play in ways rarely considered in RCT studies.

1. Social facilitation of sampling: If participants are attracted to studies by like participants, then the composition of a sample does not approximate a population. People may sign up because they see other people in the setting doing so (cf. Suarez et al., 1994).
2. Change in ambient norms within networks and settings: Even if intervention participants follow the rules and don't talk about the program, they may express beliefs or model behavior that demonstrates the influence of the intervention. If Suzie breaks up with Jimmy because she doesn't like that he is pressuring her to have unsafe sex, you can bet her friends will know.
3. Partnering within bounded networks: If an intervention targets a relatively self-contained setting or delimited subgroup (e.g., a church, linguistic minority group, the gay community in a specific locale), over time, a study will be more likely to sample new participants who have had partners that have already experienced the intervention. Prior exposure to a program participant may restrict range on outcome measures of interest because prior participants may have influenced the risk behavior of new participants through contact.

The most important examples of nonindependence arise in studies where interventions are administered to people in groups (Murray, Varnell & Blitstein, 2004). It is a testament to the power of the RCT model and its emphasis on the individual level of analysis that virtually all studies of group HIV interventions focus exclusively on cognitive mediators of change and examine effects solely at the individual level of analysis (Neumann et al., 2002; Semaan et al., 2002). Even though programs are administered by common leaders in a group context, and participants are encouraged to share their stories, we virtually ignore group process in our understanding of outcomes.

Table 11.2 outlines a variety of social processes that occur in group-administered HIV prevention interventions (Shinn & Rapkin, 2000; Rapkin & Dumont, 2000) along with hypotheses that might influence the outcome of the intervention and suggested methods to examine how these

Table 11.2 Social Processes That May Account for Individual Differences in Response to
          Group-Administered HIV Prevention Interventions

Social Interactions and Group Relationships	Hypothesized Impact on HIV Prevention Effect	Methods to Examine within Experimental Arms
Friends may enroll in a study and attend a group together.	Attending together will foster retention in the program and sustained change.	Assess ties at enrollment; Correlate ties with retention and magnitude of change; Test intraclass correlation in outcomes;
People in a program may get to know one another, and stay in touch afterward.	Relationships that form in group programs will help to sustain intervention effects; more connected experience most benefit.	Post-assessment of group members as a network; Correlate support, density, and contact after program with outcomes.
Individuals will feel more or less similar to others in their group, according to salient characteristics.	Group "outliers" in terms of age, ethnicity, religion, neighborhood etc. will benefit less from program.	Define outliers on variables of interest and/or measure identification. Correlate with change in behavior.
Individuals will achieve status within their group, based on education, communication skills, sexual experience, etc.	Members with attributes that impart special status within a group will tend to benefit more.	Ethnographic or sociometric peer nomination techniques to identify members' status. Correlate status variables with change in behavior.
Members may actively try to help one another deal with problems and to succeed with the intervention.	Groups that are aware of and respond to members' problems adhering to intervention will have fewer treatment "failures."	Observation to determine group responses to members' difficulties and specific support directed members with problems.
Performance of the group may enhance or inhibit performance of individual members.	Group members' skill acquisition will be correlated; Individuals will benefit from overall group improvement in skill, above and beyond their own gain.	HLM analysis to determine level of effect. Regression to see if group changes in mediators explains individual outcomes.

processes influence outcomes. The different examples address individuals'
connectedness prior to joining a group, relationships that form within the
group, relative diversity and status of group members, the groups targeted
or discretionary response to members' difficulties, and group enhancement (or attenuation) of individual outcomes.

Just because the prevailing HIV prevention RCT paradigm treats people as being isolated and independent from one another doesn't mean that they are. The potent role that social processes may play in HIV prevention supports the rationale for programs that explicitly encourage and capitalize upon diffusion of intervention effects from the outset, such as network interventions, opinion leader models, and peer-based interventions.

Generalizability

The entire RCT edifice exists to produce a treatment condition by time effect: that the intervention is likely to be associated with a change in risk behavior that is different from zero in the population. But how meaningful or definitive is a treatment effect estimated in a RCT (Sackett et al., 1996; Strauss, 2000)? Given the potential for unknown moderators or combinations of moderators, it may be more meaningful to think of an observed effect as an amalgam of influences, highly sensitive to sample characteristics and constraints, rather than as an estimate of some universal population parameter. For example, an intervention to reduce unsafe sex may reliably have one kind of effect (E1) on participants who start new relationships during the program and reliably have another effect (E2) on participants with stable partners throughout the program. No matter how strong the treatment effect, the results of any prevention trial are contingent upon particular conditions that hold sway in a given sample.

This argues for repeating key experiments in multiple settings and samples. Such repeated experiments should be viewed as "corroborative" studies, designed to determine contextual and historical factors that modify intervention effects (Popper, 1959). If a particular treatment effect associated with a given intervention holds up in sample after sample under different circumstances and surrounding conditions, then we should feel more confident about its generalizability to a broader population. Alternatively, if results are difficult to corroborate in different samples, they suggest a need to look across studies to better understand the circumstances necessary for a given intervention to succeed.

This need for corroboration raises an additional set of issues related to generalizability: exactly what constitutes an "intervention" (Backer, 2001; Bauman, Stein and Ireys, 1991)? Which critical components and transactions are essential to the intervention, which are secondary, and which are unimportant? Table 11.3 lists a number of the factors that may vary in a replication study.

Clearly, it would be impractical if not impossible for every single HIV prevention intervention RCT to be repeated varying every one of these features. Even if resources were available for such an exercise, we simply could not keep up with the epidemic.

It may be helpful to reframe this problem by recalling our original question, what constitutes an intervention? The universe of existing HIV prevention programs draw on a finite set of theoretical models and processes

Table 11.3 Variables in the Implementation of an Intervention

- Curricular Components
- Leader Characteristics
- Intervention Format (group, individual, dyad)
- Number of Sessions
- Length of Sessions
- Timing of Sessions
- Population Characteristics
- Recruitment and Sampling Procedures
- Incentives
- Intervention Setting
- Participants' Relationship to Setting
- Background Seroprevalence and Incidence
- Community "Standard of Care" for HIV Prevention

of change. Programs may try to impart similar information for similar reasons, but one uses a video to convey the message, another uses a peer, and another uses a family planning nurse. Are these different curricula or merely different media? Some programs ask people to practice refusal skills in five sessions while others do this in two. Are these different interventions, or just different doses? At some level, each manualized program can be thought of as an application of a fundamental set of principles of behavior change. Samples of programs would have to be thoughtfully defined, taking into account theoretical orientations or features that invoke unique principles of change. Meta-analysis can then be employed to identify variables associated with sample composition and program implementation that modify treatment effects (Wilson, 2000).

Summary

This section began with the question, "Does the RCT design ensure scientific rigor in tests of HIV prevention interventions?" The answer to this question is "no" (albeit with qualifications, discussed below). The RCT cannot guarantee intervention arms that are balanced in terms of factors that can potentially bias or confound results. Intervention effects measured using quantitative outcomes may be subject to response shifts in the meaning of the outcome indicator itself. Further, the same intervention may manifest different outcomes for different individuals and subgroups, depending upon interplay of personal circumstances and intervention features. In addition, HIV preventive interventions cannot and probably should not attempt to meet the assumption of independence and individual level of effect that is fundamental to the classical RCT. The notion that an RCT can provide a definitive test of the efficacy of an intervention breaks down when we consider limits to the generalizability of any one experiment, and the large number of factors that must be considered in corroborating a particular result.

While this may appear to be an overly pessimistic take on the HIV prevention RCT, we find it to be liberating. By calling into question the "tyranny" of the RCT, we level the "playing field" for other research designs and methods, such as natural history studies, case studies, intervention process analysis, health services research, qualitative research and participatory action research. All these research methods need to be used in tandem to open up the "black box" of the randomized experiment.

DOES THE RCT ENCOURAGE EFFECTIVE PARTNERSHIPS FOR THE PROMOTION OF PUBLIC HEALTH?

This question assumes that academic-community partnership is ultimately needed to translate findings of HIV prevention research so that communities can adapt and apply the findings of studies to the greatest possible effect (Israel et al., 1998). But how does the RCT paradigm affect this partnership?

Generally, HIV intervention researchers approach communities at two different junctures. The first is when researchers want to test a new intervention and want a place to implement the program and/or recruit participants (Susser, 1995). The second is when researchers want to disseminate an already developed intervention (Green, 2001). Scientific issues relating to the RCT paradigm constrain what researchers can and must do in each of these situations.

It is important to put a discussion of these two points in context. First, the "community" side of the partnership refers to those individuals and organizations involved in making decisions or providing resources necessary to carry out an RCT in a given locality. This may pertain to potential study subjects, to their intermediaries (such as parents or employers), local service agencies, and formal and informal leaders and gatekeepers in a setting. Second, it would be easy but wrong to depict a "straw man" caricature of the ivory tower academic interested only in the next paper or grant. As a rule, that is not who is in this field. Over the past 20 years, many very committed people have taken on the problem of HIV in diverse communities using the best tools that science has had to offer. They enter communities with an honest intention to learn better ways to promote health, seek to empower people by providing them with accurate information, necessary skills, and needed resources, and strive to be respectful, culturally sensitive, and as responsive as possible to local context and concerns. However, there is an often unexplored tension between the values of committed and responsible researchers and the prevailing scientific paradigm of the RCT (Green, 2001; Wandersman, 2003).

Undertaking a New HIV Prevention Trial

The RCT paradigm can and often does interfere with two imperatives of effective prevention programs: the need to address diversity and to empower people to act on their own behalf.

Problem 1: Randomization Creates Inequities In medical treatment research, the ethical justification for randomization is "therapeutic equipoise." This means that there is a balance between what is known about the likely benefits and the likely risks involved in the decision to apply a new treatment. The research is designed to tip that balance one way or the other. This balance is determined by making comparisons to the best available standard of care. Ideally, this standard of care is well-established and widely accepted. At minimum, the comparison treatment would be well-defined according to a protocol. Placebos or substandard comparisons are not ethically acceptable when known effective treatments are available (Victoria et al., 2004).

Equipoise is an applicable criterion in HIV prevention studies because prevention research trials must hold up under public scrutiny. In any RCT, we ask people to trust that random assignment is imperative and in their overall best interest. Participants' understanding of the justification for randomization figures into decisions about getting involved in a given study. Thus, it is worthwhile to examine the ethical justification for random assignment in prevention trials in light of the need for equipoise. Consider the following options:

- No Treatment: Although we may not know whether a new intervention will work, it strains credulity to suggest that a new program that has received hundreds of thousands of dollars of grant money to test may be no better than nothing at all.
- Standard of Care: The standard of care comparison is often ill-defined. In some instances, "standard of care" may mean that no special skill-building or support for prevention is offered. Other times, the effective "standard of care" may vary widely from participant to participant.
- Waitlist Control: It takes many months to observe program outcomes in HIV prevention studies. Withholding assistance for months from interested participants is difficult to justify as the no treatment comparison.
- Attention Placebo: Many HIV prevention programs approximate an attention placebo by comparing HIV programs to such non-HIV alternatives as social support, general wellness, or smoking prevention. While this appears to resolve the problem of therapeutic equipoise, it is like saying two wrongs make a right: 100% of participants get something they need, but 100% of participants also remain underserved in some regard.

In each of these cases, the RCT paradigm pits an HIV prevention program against a comparison that must be viewed as substandard care. There are several approaches that have been used to work around this problem (DesJarlais et al., 2004). In some instances, it is possible to make the case that random assignment is necessary due to scarce resources, although scarcity of resources is a different justification than a scientific decision based on equipoise. The most defensible position is to offer two (or more) active arms, so that everyone gets the best available program or a viable experimental alternative. Unfortunately, the RCT paradigm takes substantial statistical power to distinguish differences among nonzero aggregate treatment effects, and "the best available program" may not be well-defined.

Problem 2: Personal Preferences Are Ignored   Randomization means that people do not get to choose conditions (Brewin & Bradley, 1996; Stephenson & Imrie, 1998). The logic of this approach is elusive at best. Almost all of our interventions seek to give people a greater sense of control, self-efficacy, and empowerment, yet we start by denying them that control. For some participants, that lack of control may not be salient; for others, it may matter a great deal. Of course, people can drop out if they do not like their condition assignment or avoid research altogether because they do not like having no choice. However, this raises the issue of ecological validity: When an intervention program is implemented outside of the research context, presumably most if not all the people who receive the program will do so by choice. Thus, to the extent that research samples are disproportionately made up of individuals who don't care what treatment they receive, studies cannot represent the clients that will attend a program in practice.

In addition, the need to get participants to accept a study without regard to preference may encourage researchers to present relatively little information about study conditions during recruitment. How often, for example, are participants given an opportunity to examine a study protocol or measures prior to making a decision to consent to join a study (Agre et al., 2003)? This stance can communicate that what the community wants does not matter, that researchers know what is good for them. At worst, it contributes to lack of trust between the researcher and community and decreases the potential for positive community impact. (Israel et al., 1998).

Problem 3: RCT Is Antagonistic to the Value of Diversity   There is another, more subtle implication of randomization. Random assignment is intended to negate the need to attend to potential confounds by creating groups that are equivalent on all factors accept the experimental manipulation. Individual and situational differences are not supposed to matter. Each participant is simply a case, supposedly equivalent to any other. Human diversity is noise. Contextual variation in resources is noise. By directing our attention away from particulars in favor of universals, the RCT paradigm assumes that everyone should respond in the same way and be treated in the same way (Simmons et al., 2002).

For example, a one-size-fits-all protocol means that interventions are finished after a set number of sessions. Rarely are provisions made to vary the length of an intervention contingent upon individual needs. Although it might be possible to refer individuals for additional assistance after completion of a program, this would be construed as a deviation from the protocol or contaminating the follow-up data. To the extent that the RCT paradigm leads us to say "no" when a participant still wants or needs help, we are subverting our relationship with the community for methodological reasons (Minkler & Wallerstein, 2003).

Problem 4: RCTs Cannot Readily Change in Response to Feedback   Once begun, HIV prevention trials have a momentum of their own. Protocols are essentially frozen and fixed at the beginning of a study. Participants on day one are supposed to receive the same intervention as participants on the last day. Unfortunately, RCT protocols do not fully incorporate concepts of continuous quality improvement to take advantage of lessons learned (Berwick, 1989; 1996; Wandersman, 2003). Fundamental modifications of the protocol are not permitted.

The inability to modify a program once it is in the field can greatly constrain the ways that prevention researchers relate to program participants and communities. The collective wisdom of clients, community partners, and line staff must be saved up for the next study and are not usually presented by investigators in their formal evaluations. Thus, the RCT paradigms makes it unlikely that mechanisms for continued program innovation responsive to local input are accessible to the community on an ongoing basis.

Disseminating a Tested HIV Prevention Trial   The RCT rules and conditions that hold sway when we try to replicate or scale up an intervention create further constraints on partnerships between HIV prevention researchers and communities. These constraints further limit our ability to increase the impact of community-based prevention interventions.

Problem 5: Emphasis on Fidelity Impedes Local Innovation   Consistent with the rules of the medical model, the preferred approach to intervention dissemination is to adhere to the original program model as closely as possible. High fidelity is seen as requisite to program dissemination, and deviations from fidelity as diluting intervention potency (Backer, 2001; Bauman Stein & Ireys, 1991). Unfortunately, high fidelity comes at a cost. To the extent that we enter settings with a prepackaged, highly scripted intervention protocol, we preempt, discourage, or greatly constrain, local creativity. Moreover, we are in the position of having to deflect or attenuate community suggestions to modify an intervention in order to conform to the original protocol.

The rationale for fidelity boils down to two primary assumptions: (1) sticking to the protocol guarantees a particular outcome, and, (2) sticking to the protocol allows us to compare what happens from setting to setting. Is this rationale warranted in the case of community prevention protocols?

The rationale emanates from the medical model, where the active intervention is generally a specific drug, procedure, or finite combination of such treatments. Medical protocols presume a standard, highly regulated, clinical infrastructure that includes patients seeking care from providers able to administer and monitor treatment. Such protocols can be closely followed in such settings. Further, such circumscribed and tightly scripted medical interventions are likely to work in consistent way across a similar group of patients, allowing a direct comparison across findings from multiple settings.

However, in community prevention interventions that have appropriated this paradigm it is difficult to single out active ingredients (Black, 1996; Blumenthal & DiClimente, 2004; Victoria, Habicht, & Bryce, 2004). Any prevention curriculum is probably best viewed as an omnibus intervention, including many, many transactions expected to increase a variety of skills and enhance motivation to use these skills. Further, there are multiple pathways to change in response to a preventive intervention and multiple mechanisms at work. It is hard to argue that fidelity to an intervention will necessarily yield the same outcome in new settings because what happens simply depends on too many variables (Green, 2001).

The assumption that fidelity permits comparability from setting to setting is also problematic. As listed in Table 11.3, relatively arbitrary aspects of intervention administration can differ from setting to setting. At the point of dissemination, aspects of intervention setting history, existing programs and services, relationships with the community, staffing, and accessibility can all interact with and change the results of a prevention trial. Behavioral outcomes are affected by these surrounding conditions.

We may or may not be able to get communities to buy into the idea of fidelity for the sake of science, but even if we can, our rationale so may be specious. When we insist on conformity to protocols developed elsewhere, we ignore local norms and expectations about how programs and services happen. In addition, our insistence on conformity may preclude dissemination to communities with the greatest need and least resources to implement a protocol in a way that conforms to the original RCT.

If the rationale for rigid conformity to protocols breaks down in the context of community-based prevention trials, what are we left with? Laurie Bauman et al. (1991) make the case for maintaining fidelity to the essential theoretical ingredients of interventions, but allowing local conditions to dictate how programs are carried out. Her arguments suggest that we begin to discuss implementation standards for the dissemination of community-based prevention trials. An emphasis on implementation standards would invite a dialogue between researchers and communities. The idea would be to raise questions about implementation, and to suggest a process by which settings and researchers would reach satisfactory answers.

In a study of the dissemination of family-focused programs to frontline AIDS care providers, Rapkin, Lounsbury, and Murphy (2003) have developed a "Memorandum of Understanding" procedure that lays out the key choice points with community collaborators before the study begins. Although each location has instituted somewhat different procedures and approaches, all of them have maintained *fidelity to a process* of implementation. This approach has been welcomed by different settings, is highly replicable, and explicitly draws upon local expertise.

Problem 6: The Process of Discovery is Artificially Separated from the Diffusion of Innovation   Thus far we have not challenged a prevailing assumption of the RCT paradigm: that the process of scientific discovery is essentially a top-down enterprise, with researchers developing ideas, testing them with experiments, and sending them out into communities. The top-down approach to prevention does not invite community input into the design of studies, articulation of local theories and beliefs about HIV risk behavior, or even homegrown techniques and strategies to promote change. Alternatively, emerging participatory action research and empowerment models centrally involve the community in the process of discovery.

The lessons of participatory research and empowerment have certainly been heeded by many who do work in HIV prevention (cf. Bauman, Stein, & Iyers, 1991; Hays, Rebchook, & Kegles, 2003; Yoshikawa et al., 2003). Development of interventions often involves members of the community in various substantive roles. Input is solicited and efforts are made to incorporate cultural norms and other features to welcome and engage participants. However, after we have framed, developed and tested such a community-oriented intervention, is it appropriate to disseminated it in a top-down manner, such as the Center for Disease Control and Prevention's national initiative on "Replicating Effective Programs" (Centers for Disease Control [CDC], 2004)? Once a prevention program has been manualized, can it be directly translated to other settings, and, if so, what is the community's role in the subsequent recipient communities? How is the process of discovery embedded in the process of diffusion? These issues are dealt with below where we propose alternative designs to the RCT for community-based HIV preventive interventions and community impact.

Summary

This section dealt with the question of whether the RCT design fosters effective partnerships between communities and researchers. Even with the best intentions, researchers burdened with design-driven obligations to limit and control community choice, access to information, programmatic decisions, and responsiveness to special circumstances run the risk of alienating communities. Added to this is the intrinsic top-down nature of the RCT, including the need to discount local experience and expertise for the sake of standardization. It is truly a testament to the ingenuity and commitment of HIV prevention researchers that they have been successful in making inroads and accomplishing all they have, given these constraints.

Analysis of the scientific basis underlying these constraints on our community partnerships is telling. Use of randomization is ethically problematic due to the difficulty in achieving true equipoise. Random assignment also ignores choice at the expense of ecological validity, a factor that can significantly bias trial samples and attenuate outcomes. The RCT design assumption that one size must fit all, and that people will respond to interventions in uniform and consistent ways does not correspond to what we know about human diversity, multiple pathways and mechanisms of change, and differential trajectories in response to outcomes. The emphasis on fidelity to fixed protocols ignores the inherent changes and opportunities for continuous quality improvement that naturally arise over time in the conduct of any trial. Emphasis on rigid fidelity also ignores the local contexts and meanings that arise in efforts to disseminate RCTs. Finally, the top-down nature of the RCT precludes other modes of discovery related to intervention development and determining mechanisms of change.

ARE THERE VIABLE ALTERNATIVES TO THE RCT DESIGN?

Analysis of the limits of the RCT in HIV prevention research points to several valuable lessons. First, designs must take into account diversity inherent in the determinants of health and risk behavior. Second, designs must recognize that different people can respond to the same intervention in different ways, or in the same way for different reasons. Third, designs must accommodate personal choice and preference. Fourth, designs must anticipate nonindependence and significant potential benefits associated with contamination across arms. Fifth, designs must avoid ethical dilemmas associated with substandard treatment of some participants. Sixth, designs must be responsive to evolving understanding of how to best administer an intervention, and to local innovations and ideas. Seventh, designs must contribute to community capacity building and empowerment at every step of the research process.

With these lessons and ideals in mind, we propose a class of designs that we call comprehensive dynamic trials or CDT. They are "comprehensive" in that they make use of complete information from multiple sources to understand what is happening in a trial. They are "dynamic" in that they build in recurring mechanisms for feedback in order to respond to different needs and changing circumstances (cf. Schulz, Krieger, & Galea, 2002; Williams & Lykes, 2003). The three examples of CDTs summarized in Table 11.4 bear similarities to observational studies of utilization and outcome from health services research and action research. By formalizing these designs, explicitly linking them to intervention processes and surrounding them with sufficient assessment, CDT approaches may offer a strong alternative for community prevention research anchored by the RCT.

Table 11.4 Characteristics of Three Comprehensive Dynamic Trials Designs

Design Characteristics	I. Continuous Quality Improvement	II. Titration-Mastery Algorithms	III. Collaborative Consultation and Empowerment
Dynamic Intervention Processes	Reinvent the intervention by modifying the manual until desired quality of service achieved	Continually assess stage of adoption of participants; treat individuals as indicated until results achieved	Provide "cafeteria" of options plus tools to make choices and to evaluate implications of those choices
Theoretical Foundation	Diffusion of Innovation	Stages of Change	Empowerment via mediating structures
Business Model	Total quality management	Medical care; Psychotherapy	Cooperative extension; library
Values Maximized	Input, shared decision making	Beneficence	Autonomy, diversity, preference
Comprehensive Assessment of Response Variables	Maximize retention, attendance, client satisfaction, staff productivity and satisfaction, as well as risk reduction	Not risk reduction *per se* because goal is 100% response rate, but time and steps needed to achieve reduction	Level of risk is both outcome and input to subsequent steps. Interest in how people make use of resources
Major Analytic Paradigm	Multilevel Modeling of persons nested within intervention "epochs," which have parameters that vary over time	Survival Analysis and Event History Analysis to predict time to attainment of criterion	Growth curve analysis—determine how differential use of resources shapes trajectories for different individuals
Potential to Increase and Sustain Community Impact	Evolutionary mechanisms built into intervention—optimized and tailored to specific contexts	Resources allocated most efficiently, so those with greatest need get most help	Flexible resources, with on-going encouragement of self-monitoring to motivate and sustain behavioral change
Potential for Dissemination	Intervention may be planted as a "seed" in many communities, can evolve according to context	Appropriate algorithm needed to suit community. Mix of individuals may require more or less intensive levels	Intrinsically amenable, because of focus on responding to preferences
Novel Resources and Capacities Needed	Intervention process analysis; Decision making body; Rapid procedures for revision	Monitoring; Feedback; Multiple interventions; Client navigation	Education; Knowledge base; Monitoring; Feedback

Continuous Quality Improvement Design (CDT-QI)

The first design incorporates the concept of continuous quality improvement, familiar in clinical care (Berwick, 1989; 1996), to refine and tailor manualized interventions (Wandersman, 2003). Interventions throw off an enormous amount of information concerning their performance: acceptability of the program, attendance, use of curricular material, interactions among clients and between clients and staff, draw on existing resources and new resources, and reactions to the program from participants, providers and the surrounding community. In the RCT, there is no systematic way to capture these "lessons learned" and incorporate them back into the trial. CDT-QI takes advantage of lessons learned as an intervention progresses (Leshan et al., 1997).

The first step is the formation an oversight body capable of making ongoing decisions about trial modifications. Intervention researchers, agency staff, community members, consumer advocates, and other interested parties should meet while a program is being developed to determine the major performance variables to be monitored and develop procedures for monitoring them (Harrison, 2001). For example, in an intervention to promote safer sex among young adult heterosexual couples, indicators of program outcomes (e.g., negotiated safer sex), unintended consequences (e.g., using repeated HIV testing without condom use as a "prevention" method) and adverse events (e.g., increased conflict between partners related to the intervention) would be monitored. For each of these indicators, assessment criteria would be built directly into the protocol, using a combination of qualitative, quantitative, and archival methods.

Program implementation of the CDT-QI would be based on theory, pilot work, prior intervention experience, practice standards, available resources, and local custom, exactly analogous to the RCT. Initial implementation would be considered the "reference epoch," a term chosen to indicate a finite period of time during which an intervention is conducted under a given set of operating conditions. Data on all quality and performance indicators would be gathered and tracked from the onset of the "reference epoch" using a routine schedule for program review developed by the project advisory committee (Shortell, Bennett, & Byck, 1998; Spencer et al., 1999).

If program modifications are warranted, the program advisory committee would initiate a quality improvement planning process, including development of an acceptable problem definition about what is happening with the reference epoch, brainstorming solutions, weighing consequences, and developing a plan to modify the intervention accordingly (Berwick, 1989; Green & Kreuter, 1999). Modifications might involve scheduling and timing, intervention group composition, eligibility criteria, curricular components, and the like. The program advisory committee would subsequently prompt intervention developers to amend the protocol, initiating a new epoch in the intervention. Successive epochs would occur, incorporating lessons learned and retooling as needed. Over successive epochs, it is likely that the need for modifications would diminish.

Ultimately, such continuous quality improvement could be a component built into all HIV prevention intervention manuals. Because the emphasis is optimizing an intervention, use of a no-treatment control group would add relatively little. It would be more beneficial to try out the program over a larger number of cases, to have more examples under different epochs. Therapeutic equipoise is achieved because earlier participants benefit from getting the program sooner, while later participants benefit from earlier lessons learned.

The CDT-QI lends itself directly to replication and dissemination. In general, one would start with the final epoch of a prior incarnation of an intervention and take it from there. Although the machinery for adaptation is already built into a CDT-QI protocol, it would be necessary to compose a new advisory body for each new local community. In addition to the study results and manual, dissemination of the intervention should include tracking data on the various quality indicators, as well a record of the earlier advisory committee's problem solving deliberations. Dissemination of a single CDT-QI intervention would likely yield somewhat different programs in different places, in response to local context and resources. Fidelity to the original program is much less important than optimizing program performance indicators in each site.

Titration-Mastery Algorithm Designs (CDT-TM)

If the metaphor for CDT-QI is quality improvement in service industries, the second example of a CDT design draws its inspiration from clinical practice such as primary care or psychotherapy. The goal of the "titration-mastery algorithm" intervention design is to develop optimal algorithms for coordinating a multi-component intervention, including procedures for adding services and making "dose" adjustments (cf. McMahon & Puett, 1999). The purpose is to ensure that each participant receives the services needed to reach the desired outcome in mastery of skills and ability to reduce HIV risk behavior (Block & Burns, 1976; Dolan, 1986; Guskey, 1985). In the RCT, the intent is to test a single intervention to determine whether and how well it works for different individuals. In the CDT-TM, the intent is to develop a hierarchy of interventions to help every participant attain their best possible outcome.

One of the most challenging aspects of the CDT-TM design is to develop an appropriate hierarchy of interventions (Jumper-Thurman et al., 2004). It is first necessary to identify a range of candidate interventions and approaches, and organize them in terms of level of intensity and effort. To carry out titration of the dose or intensity of the intervention, it is also necessary to implement ongoing assessment of client response to determine whether they benefited from a given level of intervention or whether more intensive work is necessary. Pilot work would require intervention researchers to enter the community, prepared to experiment with different combinations and sequences of programs. Through clinical experience, hypotheses concerning the different types of interventions could be developed about the types of interventions that should be routinely offered and criteria to trigger movement along the algorithm.

A second challenge facing CDT-TM studies involves the development of mechanisms to engage study participants. In order to accomplish successive steps of intervention and assessment to achieve appropriate titration of services, the intervention team must maintain a close alliance over time with participants. One way to achieve this is to implement the CDT-TM in the context of stable settings where many potential intervention participants have sufficiently long-term roles, such as schools, workplaces, religious institutions, and primary care settings (cf. Winett et al., 1999). Since CDT-TM trials are designed to support participants' efforts to achieve a particular prevention goal, different individuals will receive only those program components necessary. Outcome variables would involve the time and resources necessary to help clients attain this goal.

The real appeal of the CDT-TM design is the opportunity to offer comprehensive services to all participants involved (Pruett & Jackson, 1999). Efforts to replicate and disseminate titration-model programs would involve finding communities interested in offering a similar mix of services. It would be necessary to verify that criteria used to screen participants and direct them to services can translate directly from setting to setting. In addition to dissemination across settings, it could be useful to periodically repeat CDT-TM campaigns within the same, already treated, community, as individuals may change their risk status or encounter new surrounding concerns.

CDT-TM designs challenge our traditional notion of what constitutes an intervention. Rather than focus on testing a single component manual, the idea is to mount a comprehensive and multifaceted effort, intended to efficiently address individuals according to the difficulties they encounter in changing their HIV risk behaviors (Lafferty & Mahoney, 2003). The particular mix of HIV and supportive services would be dictated by local needs. Whatever the mix of services, there is a considerable advantage gained by organizing a common point of entry, administering methods to level of need, coordinating transitions between levels of care, and engaging participants in an ongoing relationship to maximize benefits of preventive services.

Collaborative Consultation and Empowerment Designs (CDT-CE)

This final example of a comprehensive dynamic trial design employs a third metaphor for community intervention: the library or the cooperative extension. Unlike the titration or quality improvement models, which preserve much of the intervention researchers' control over program content and organization (Wallerstein, 1999), the CDT-CE design is explicitly a vehicle to promote transfer of intervention technology (Arcury, 2000;

Brakefield-Caldwell & Parker, 2000; Green, 2001). However, rather than transfer one manual at a time, the intervention researcher is charged with making the state of the art in prevention science available for communities to learn, query, and challenge. In this design, the researcher brings information about best practice intervention approaches, manuals, videos, and research findings to the community. The task is to facilitate a process in which community members are guided and supported in using information to craft and then evaluate their own strategies to address HIV transmission (Lantz et al., 2001; Shadish et al., 1999).

This approach is intended to empower the community to find the intervention(s) that work best for them (Syme, 2004). The intervention researcher's role is to facilitate a process of program planning, implementation, and evaluation intended to lead to interventions that are highly responsive to local needs and conditions and highly sustainable because they are developed "in place."

With respect to community impact, it is best to gear this model toward community-based organizations. Community organizations can serve as intermediaries for their members or clients through deploying resources to meet public health needs in a way that is most responsive to local context, culture, values and needs. Thus, a critical task involves identification of a sample of potential "mediating structures" (Berger & Neuhaus, 1996). Criteria for serving as a mediating structure involve community organizations' readiness and capacity to fulfill a variety of roles, depending upon the goals of a particular CDT-CE trial (Edwards et al., 2000; Oetting et al., 2001). Such roles might include providing oversight, supplying connections to populations of interest, and assisting in program evaluation. It is preferable to partner with existing organizations within the community, to draw on their experience, expertise and infrastructure. If community partners able to serve as mediating structures cannot be identified, it would be necessary to bring people and groups together to establish this community base (Jones, 2000).

There are several considerations involved in mounting CDT-CE studies (Foster-Fishman et al., 2001; Rapkin et al., n.d.; Schulz et al., 1998). It is most effective to identify several key representatives of community agencies to serve as primary contacts and to work with partner organizations to develop and extend their capacity to engage in this work. Partner organizations and intervention researchers must also work out memoranda of understanding regarding what a CDT-CE involves: expectations, timelines, problem solving mechanisms, issues of privacy for organization, staff, and members/clients, use of data, mechanisms for feedback, and even authorship.

In addition to primary contacts, the CDT-CE design requires that each community organization form an advisory committee to work in tandem with intervention researchers. Unlike the single overall advisory body required recommended for the CDT-QI, the CDT-CE requires each participating community organization to form an advisory panel so that each organization can make independent program decisions best suited to the local community.

A fundamental task to conducting CDT-CE is the assembly of a knowledge base that organizes what we know about reducing HIV risk and provides the raw material for carrying out the intervention trial. Communities may benefit from both academic and popular articles pertaining to HIV transmission and relevant interventions for the population of interest, including meta-analyses, relevant intervention programs, manuals, videos, public service ads, and brochures. In addition, the knowledge base ought to provide access to local expertise. The goal of CDT-CE is to make this knowledge base useful and accessible to the community, including creation of searchable retrieval records, and providing physical access to desirable information.

With partnerships, advisory bodies, and knowledge base in place, the CDT-CE trial involves a cycle of activities, including the following:

1. Obtaining elicitation data concerning clients' HIV prevention needs and preferences, as well as review of any existing data on HIV and STI prevalence.
2. Reviewing this data with a partner's advisory committee to determine local problems, trends and conditions that shape HIV transmission and risk behavior.
3. Searching the knowledge base for pertinent research findings and intervention examples best suited to the community-based organizations' target population.
4. Drawing on the curricular materials, local resources, and academic expertise in the database to develop a preliminary intervention program suited to the agency.
5. Obtaining or creating necessary materials and resources plus conducting staff orientation and training as needed to mount the intervention.
6. Gathering predata from a sample of agency members, clients, or other constituents on HIV risk behavioral, beliefs, and other relevant variables.
7. Implementing the program for an agreed upon period.
8. Gathering post-data to determine intervention reach and impact.
9. Reviewing quantitative, qualitative, and anecdotal data on program results with the local advisory panel to formulate plans for next steps.
10. Planning bodies may decide to repeat some of the planning steps (1–4) above to prepare for subsequent steps.

This cycle of planning, implementation, development can be continued until desired intervention objectives are achieved. Empowerment is reflected in increased community capacity to direct and undertake more and better programs and do so with greater control of resources necessary to do so (Minkler et al., 2003; Silka, 2000).

The CDT-CE design completely and intentionally blurs distinctions between initial planning of a trial and program dissemination. Every new trial represents "dissemination" in the sense that it build upon (or is a reaction to) what is available in the library. Replications of CDT-CE studies would not require new communities and settings to use the same materials as their predecessors, but to replicate the process. As with the titration design, community impact may be sustained by perpetuating or reintroduce the CDT-CE design in the same community over a number of repeated planning cycles. Ideally, over time we should be able to assess and encourage organizations' creativity and effectiveness in their roles as mediating structures.

Threats to Validity in Comprehensive Dynamic Trials

Given the novelty of the CDT designs, it is reasonable to ask, "Is this science?" Our reply is, "We don't see why not." These designs are complex, but no more so than the randomized trial. As we gain experiences with these approaches, norms and standards for how to accomplish certain regular steps will be established, just as RCT research has customs around fidelity, pilot testing or data safety. The rules of evidence in CDT studies are not based on statistical inference, but on comprehensive in-depth understanding based on direct experience. However, findings based on the designs proposed above will be subject to a variety of threats to validity, including the following:

1. Choices based on incomplete information: Community advisory groups and planning may make decisions based on incomplete elicitation procedures or a partial search of the knowledge base Titration decisions may be made using data that does not fully capture risk. Steps must be taken to minimize these problems.
2. The appropriate role of community or client preference in driving interventions: In the CDT designs, community decision makers are given considerable latitude in choosing what they think is best. There is no guarantee that this is optimal. Ideally, built in procedures for feedback and review of data should serve a corrective function.
3. Close (unblinded) relationship between the conduct of the intervention and the ongoing analysis of data: Communities, clients, and researchers all have a vested interest in things going well. Given the complete absence of blinding in all of the CDT models, there is the potential that evaluations will be biased.
4. Potential for "contamination" within bounded networks: Like the RCT, effective CDTs are subject to contamination within bounded networks. As noted above, analytic models that can look at potential temporal and social network effects in data may be especially important in CDTs.
5. Accounting for the huge number of combinations of choice points and branches CDT implies: There are clearly many possible

decisions and choice points involved throughout the CDT-QI and CE studies, and in establishing the initial service mix in TM studies. CDT studies will have to develop a methodology for describing principles of intervention planning and decision-making processes to determine whether the planning processes are sound.

The Role of the Intervention Researcher in Comprehensive Dynamic Trials Research

Just as the RCT presupposes and shapes the relationship between investigators and communities, the CDT also requires certain standards and activities. Perhaps the most important feature of this type of design is the need for investigators (or centers) to anticipate and maintain close, long-term working relationships with communities. Established relationships with advisory groups, the awareness that they can rely on the researcher to provide promised support, opportunities to solve problems together and effectively address community needs, all contribute to trust. From the perspective of the CDT, building and strengthening community relationships for prevention are more important than the results of any one iteration of an intervention trial.

Supporting this sort of relationship will entail the development of new types of funding mechanisms, new funding cycles, and new models of accountability. CDT interventions require support that balances a high-level of accountability with a high-level of flexibility to make on-line decisions and change direction as they go. Year-to-year funding decisions ought to be based on criteria that include the functioning and potential of the community-academic relationship along with the scientific yield.

Comprehensive Dynamic Trials and the Scientific Enterprise

This paper makes the case that the scientific enterprise has largely been shaped by the RCT model. The CDT paradigm invites an opportunity to reconsider how our discipline functions and how we work with one another. It will be useful to close this discussion by reflecting on several ways that our field might change if we broaden our views about what counts as science (Aguinis, 1993).

1. Primary evaluation criteria for studies will include soundness of researchers' relationships with communities.
2. Multiple sources of data will gain increasing importance
3. New norms will be invented around authorship to include community members
4. Case studies regarding the use of different processes for planning, decision making and community involvement will be highly important
5. Significant results of any single trial will be important, but will not be given undue weight because of the awareness of how dependent such results are on local conditions

6. Investigators may work together in tandem to create more effective titration-mastery service suites and more useful knowledge bases for community empowerment studies.
7. Meta-analysis will grow increasingly important as a way of integrating information from multiple sources and multiple types of studies.

What is the role of the RCT in this new paradigm? Rather than be the centerpiece for HIV prevention research, the RCT may be applied as an "embedded experiment" in the context of an ongoing CDT program. If an advisory body chooses to test whether one focal approach works better than another in a given context, the RCT is a sound way to get that information. However, the research edifice that we need to do effective community intervention research should not be driven by large-scale RCTs but by large scale and high-quality relationships with necessary community partners. The opportunities for discovery before, during, and after any one focal experiment are manifold (Sarason, 2003). The only way that we will increase the community impact of HIV prevention research in underserved and at-risk communities is by finding systematic ways to fully capitalize on the lessons and the expertise to be found there.

REFERENCES

Agre, P., Campbell, F. A., Goldman, B. D., Boccia, M. L., Kass, N., McCullough, L., et al. (2003). Improving informed consent: The medium is not the message. *IRB: Ethics & Human Research, Supplement* 25(5), S11–S19.

Aguinis H. (1993). Action research and scientific method: Presumed discrepancies and actual similarities. *Journal of Applied Behavioral Science, 29*, 416–431.

Arcury T. (2000). Successful process in community-based participatory research. In L. R. O'Fallon, F. Tyson, & A. Dearry (Eds.), *Successful models of community-based participatory research*. Washington, DC: National Institute of Environmental Health Sciences; 42–48.

Backer, T. (2001). *Finding the balance: Program fidelity and adaptation in substance abuse prevention*. Rockville, MD: Center for Substance Abuse Prevention.

Bauman, L. J., Stein, R. E., & Ireys, H. T. (1991). Reinventing fidelity: The transfer of social technology among settings. *American Journal of Community Psychology 19*(4), 619–639.

Berger, P. & Neuhaus, J. (1996). *To empower people: From state to civil society* (2nd ed.). Washington, DC: American Enterprise Institute Press.

Berwick, D. M. (1989). Continuous improvement as an ideal in health care. *New England Journal of Medicine, 320*, 53–56.

Berwick, D. M. (1996). Quality comes home. *Annals of Internal Medicine, 125*, 839–842.

Black, N. (1996). Why we need observational studies to evaluate the effectiveness of health care. *British Medical Journal, 312*, 1215–1218.

Black, N. (2001). Evidence based policy: Proceed with care. *British Medical Journal, 323*, 275–279.

Block, J. & Burns, R. (1976). Mastery learning. In L. Shulman (Ed.), *Review of research in education* (Vol. 4). Itasca, IL: F.E. Peacock.

Blumenthal, D. S. & DiClemente, R. J. (2004) *Community-based health research: Issues and methods*. New York: Springer Publishing Company.

Brakefield-Caldwell, W. & Parker, E. (2000). Successful models combining intervention and basic research in the context of community-based participatory research. In L. R. O'Fallon, F. Tyson, & A. Dearry (Eds.), *Successful models of community-based participatory research*. Washington, DC: National Institute of Environmental Health Sciences; 55–61.

Brewin, C. R. & Bradley, C. (1996). Patient preferences and randomised clinical trials. *British Medical Journal, 299*, 313–315.

Campbell, D. T. & Stanley, J. C. (1963). *Experimental and quasi-experimental designs for research*. Chicago: Rand McNally College Publishing; 1963.

Centers for Disease Control. (2004). Replicating effective programs. www.cdc.gov/hiv/projects/rep/default.htm.

Des Jarlais, D. C., Lyles, C., & Crepaz, N., the TREND Group. (2004). Improving the reporting quality of nonrandomized evaluations of behavioral and public health interventions: The TREND statement. *American Journal of Public Health, 94*, 361–366.

Dolan, L. (1986). Mastery learning as a preventive strategy. *Outcomes, 5*(2), 20–27.

Edwards, R. W., Thurman, P. J., Plested, B., Oetting, E. R., & Swanson, L. (2000) Community readiness: Research to practice. *Journal of Community Psychology 28*, 291–307.

Foster-Fishman, P. G., Berkowitz, S. L., Lounsbury, D. W., Jacobson, S., & Allen, N. A. (2001). Building collaborative capacity in community coalitions: A review of integrative framework. *American Journal of Community Psychology, 29*(2), 241–261.

Green, L. W. (2001). From research to "best practices" in other settings and populations. *American Journal of Health Behavior, 25*(3), 165–178.

Green, L. W. & Kreuter, M. (1999). *Health promotion planning: An educational and ecological approach* (3rd ed.). Mountain View, CA: Mayfield.

Guskey, T. (1985). *Implementing mastery learning*. Belmont, CA: Wadsworth.

Harrison, B. (2001). *Collaborative programs in Indigenous communities: From fieldwork to practice*. Walnut Creek, CA: AltaMira Press.

Hays, R. B., Rebchook, G. M., & Kegles, S. M. (2003). The MPowerment project: Community-building with young gay and bisexual men to prevent HIV. *American Journal of Community Psychology, 31*(3/4), 313–328.

Hedeker, D. & Mermelstein, R. J. (2000). Analysis of longitudinal substance use outcomes using ordinal random-effects regression models. *Addiction 3*(Suppl.), S381–S394.

Israel, B., Schulz, A., Parker, E., & Becker, A. (1998). Review of community-based research: Assessing partnership approaches to improve public health. *Annual Review of Public Health, 19*, 173–202.

Jones, L. Partnership building. (2000). In L. R. O'Fallon, F. Tyson, A. Dearry (Eds.), *Successful models of community-based participatory research*. Washington, DC: National Institute of Environmental Health Sciences; 35–41.

Jumper-Thurman, P., Edwards, R. W., Plested, B. A., & Oetting, E. R. (2004). Honoring the differences: Using community readiness to create culturally valid community interventions. In G. Bernal, J. Trimble, K. Burlew, & F. Leong (Eds.), *Handbook of ethnic and racial minority psychology*. Thousand Oaks, CA: Sage; 591–607.

Lafferty, C. K. & Mahoney, C. A. (2003). A framework for evaluating comprehensive community initiatives. *Health Promotion Practice, 4*(1), 31–44.

Lantz, P. M., Viruell-Fuentes, E., Israel, B., Softley, D., & Guzman, R. (2001). Can communities and academia work together on public health research? Evaluation results from a community-based participatory research partnership in Detroit. *Journal of Urban Health, 78*(3), 495–507.

Leshan, L. A., Fitzsimmons, M., Marbella, A., & Gottlieb, M. (1997). Increasing clinical prevention efforts in a family practice residency program through CQI methods. *Joint Commission Journal on Quality Improvement, 23,* 391–400.

McMahon, P. & Puett, R. (1999). Child sexual abuse as a public health issue: Recommendations of an expert panel. *Sexual Abuse: A Journal of Research and Treatment, 11,* 257–266.

Minkler, M., Blackwell, A. G., Thompson, M., & Tamir, H. (2003). Community-based participatory research: Implications for public health funding. *American Journal of Public Health, 93*(8), 210–1213.

Minkler, M. & Wallerstein, N. (Eds.). (2003). *Community-based participatory research for health.* San Francisco: Jossey-Bass.

Murray, D. M., Varnell, S. P., & Blitstein, J. L. (2004). Design and analysis of group randomized trials: A review of recent methodological developments. *American Journal of Public Health, 94,* 423–432.

Neumann, M. S., Johnson, W. D., Semaan, S., Flores, S., Peersman, G., Hedges, L., et al. (2002). Review and meta-analysis of HIV prevention intervention research for heterosexual adult populations in the United States. *Journal of the Acquired Immune Deficiency Syndrome, 30*(Suppl.1), S106–S117.

Oakley, A. (1990). Who's afraid of the randomized trial? Some dilemmas of the scientific method and "good" research practice. In H. Roberts (Ed.), *Women's health counts.* London: Routledge.

Oetting, E. R., Jumper-Thurman, P., Plested, B., & Edwards, R. W. (2001). Community readiness and health services. *Substance use and misuse, 36*(6-7), 825–843.

Popper, K. S. (1959). *The logic of scientific discovery.* London: Hutchinson.

Pruett. M. K. & Jackson, T. D. (1999). The lawyer's role during the divorce process: Perceptions of parents, their young children, and their attorneys. *Family Law Quarterly, 33,* 283.

Rapkin, B. D. (2002). Ecologically minded reconstruction of experiments in HIV prevention: Reduce, reuse and recycle. *Journal of Primary Prevention, 23*(2), 235–250.

Rapkin, B. D. & Dumont, K. A. (2000). Methods for identifying and assessing groups in health behavioral research. *Addiction, 95*(Suppl. 3), S395–S417.

Rapkin, B. D., Lounsbury, D., & Murphy, P. (2003). Protocol for the family access to care study. *Memorial Sloan-Kettering Cancer, 3*(008).

Rapkin, B. D., Massie, M. J., Jansky, E. J., Lounsbury, D. W., Murphy, P. D., & Powell, S. (in press). Developing a partnership model for cancer screening with community-based organizations: The ACCESS breast cancer education and outreach project. *American Journal of Community Psychology.*

Rapkin, B. D. & Schwartz, C. E. (2004). Toward a theoretical model of quality-of-life appraisal: Implications of findings from studies of response shift. *Health and Quality of Life Outcomes, 2*(14), 1–12.

Sackett, D. L., Rosenberg, W. M. C., Gray, J. A. M., Haynes, R. B., & Richardson, W. S. (1996). Evidence based medicine: What it is and what it isn't. *British Medical Journal, 312,* 71–72.

Sarason, S. (2003). The obligations of the moral-scientific stance. *American Journal of Community Psychology, 31*(3/4), 209–212.

Schulz, A., Krieger, J., & Galea, S. (2002). Addressing social determinants of health: Community-based participatory approaches to research and practice. *Health Education and Behavior, 29*(3), 287–295.

Schulz, A. J., Parker, E., Israel, B., Becker, A., Maciak, B., & Hollis, R. (1998). Conducting a participatory community-based survey: Collecting and interpreting data for a community health intervention on Detroit's East Side. *Journal of Public Health Management and Practice, 4*(2), 10–24.

Schwartz, C. E. & Sprangers, M. A. G. (Eds.). (2000). *Adaptation to changing health: Response shift in quality of life research.* Washington, DC: American Psychological Association.

Semaan, S., Kay, L., Strouse, D., Sogolow, E., Mullen, P., Neumann, M., et al. (2002). A profile of U.S.-based trials of behavioral and social interventions for HIV risk-reduction. *Journal of the Acquired Immune Deficiency Syndrome, 30*(Suppl. 1), S30–S50.

Shadish, W. R., Newman, D. L., Scheirer, M. A., & Wye, C. (Eds.). (1999). *New directions for program evaluation: Guiding principles for evaluators.* New Directions for Program Evaluation Series, No. 66. San Francisco: Jossey-Bass.

Shinn, M. & Rapkin, B. D. (2000). Cross-level research without cross-ups in community psychology. In J. Rappaport, E. Seidman (Eds.), *Handbook of community psychology.* New York: Kluwer Academic; 669–695.

Shortell, S. M., Bennett, C. L., & Byck, G. R. (1998). Assessing the impact of continuous quality improvement on clinical practice: What it will take to accelerate progress. *Milbank Quarterly, 76,* 593–624.

Silka, L. (2000). Evaluation as a strategy for documenting the strengths of community-based participatory research. In L. R. O'Fallon, F. Tyson, & A. Dearry (Eds.), *Successful models of community-based participatory research.* Washington, DC: National Institute of Environmental Health Sciences; 49–54.

Simmons, R., Bennett, E., Schwartz, M. L., Sharify, D. T., & Short, E. (2002). Health education and cultural diversity in the health care setting: Tips for the practitioner. *Health Promotion Practice, 3*(1), 8–11.

Spencer, E., Swanson, T., Hueston, W. J., & Edberg, D. L. (1999). Tools to improve documentation of smoking status: Continuous quality improvement and electronic medical records. *Archives of Family Medicine, 8,* 18–22.

Sprangers, M. A. G. & Schwartz, C. E. (1999). Integrating response shift into health-related quality-of-life research: A theoretical model. *Social Science and Medicine, 48,* 1507–1515.

SPSS for Windows (Release 11.5). (2002). Chicago: SPSS, Inc.

Stephenson, J. & Imrie, J. (1998). Why do we need randomised controlled trials to assess behavioural interventions? *British Medical Journal, 316,* 611–613.

Strauss, G. M. (2000). Randomized population trials and screening for lung cancer: Breaking the cure barrier. *Cancer, 89*(Suppl. 11), 2399–2421.

Strauss, G. M. & Dominioni, L. (2000). Perception, paradox, paradigm: Alice in the wonderland of lung cancer prevention and early detection. *Cancer, 89*(Suppl. 11), 2422–2431.

Suarez, L., Lloyd, L., Weiss, N., Rainbolt, T., & Pully, L. (1994). Effect of social networks on cancer-screening behavior of older Mexican-American women. *Journal of the National Cancer Institute, 86*(10), 775–779.

Susser, M. (1995). The tribulations of trials intervention in communities. *American Journal of Public Health, 85,* 156–159.

Syme, S. L. (2004). Social determinants of health: The community as an empowered partner. *Preventing Chronic Disease Public Health Research, Practice, and Policy, 1*(1), 1–5.

Victora, C. G., Habicht, J-P., & Bryce, J. (2004). Evidence-based public health: Moving beyond randomized trials. *American Journal of Public Health, 94,* 400–405.

Wallerstein, N. (1999). Power between evaluator and community: Research relationships within New Mexico's healthier communities. *Social Science & Medicine, 49,* 39–53.

Wandersman, A. (2003). Community science: Bridging the gap between science and practice with community-centered models. *American Journal of Community Psychology, 31*(3/4), 227–242.

Williams, J. & Lykes, M. B. (2003). Bridging theory and practice: Using reflexive cycles in feminist participatory action research. *Feminism & Psychology. 13*(3), 287–294.

Wilson, D. B. (2000). Meta-analyses in alcohol and other drug treatment research. *Addiction, 3*(Suppl.), S419–S438.

Winett, R. A., Anderson, E. S., Whiteley, J. A., Wojcik, J., Rovniak, L., Graves, K., et al. (1999). Church-based health behavior programs: using social cognitive theory to formulate interventions for at-risk populations. *Applied Preventive Psychology, 8,* 129–142.

Yoshikawa, H., Wilson, P. A., Hsueh, J., Rosman, E. A,. Chin, J., & Kim, J. H. (2003). What front-line CBO staff can tell us about culturally-anchored theories of behavior change in HIV prevention for Asian/Pacific Islanders. *American Journal of Community Psychology, 32*(1/2), 143–158.

Zeger, S. L. & Liang, K. Y. (1992) An overview of methods for the analysis of longitudinal data. *Statistics in Medicine, 11,* 1825–1839.

12

Toward the Next Generation of AIDS Interventions With Community Impact

Willo Pequegnat

Risk for HIV transmission and other public-health problems with a be-havioral component have multiple causes that are embedded in the social organization of society. The effort to prevent further HIV infections is of-ten compared to the smoking campaign that has resulted in a change in the social norms and rules about smoking. Entrenched norms about smok-ing that are supported by the culture, reinforced by personal addiction, and strongly sustained by commercial interests finally gave way to public-health interests. It has taken time for the evidence from research and community-level interventions to lead to these changes in social policy and personal habits. In the 1950s, it would have been unthinkable to envi-sion a smoke-free environment.

If AIDS prevention efforts are going to use lessons from the smoking cessation movement, they should be the following:

- Changes in social norms and personal behaviors take a long time;
- intervention must occur at multiple levels (individual, family, insti-tutional, community, media, and social policy).
- While community interventions may be more difficult to mount, measure, and achieve, they are essential to ensuring widespread impact of AIDS prevention programs.

Almost 20 years of AIDS prevention research have demonstrated that we can change individual behavior (Coutinho & Cates, 2000). Changing individual behavior is necessary, but not sufficient, to make an impact on a public-health epidemic like AIDS. It is time to develop prevention models at the community level so that each new generation adopts safe behaviors from the beginning rather than needing to change high-risk behaviors.

In the same way that the level of readiness to mobilize for change may vary between individuals, the preparedness of various communities to launch an effective AIDS prevention campaign directed at these multiple levels may differ. First, the community must be aware that it has a major health problem. Then, this awareness of the problem must be translated into concern. Next, a community-wide initiative must be developed, and the infrastructure for connecting the different components for an effective

The views expressed in this chapter and this book do not necessarily represent the views of the National Institutes of Health or of the United States Government.

AIDS prevention campaign must be put in place. Finally, the campaign must become an ingrained part of the social community, and evaluation of its effectiveness must be made so that it can constantly be fine tuned in response to changing conditions.

AIDS prevention researchers and community leaders can work effectively together during different phases of this process. Effective ways for alerting communities about major health problems and making them a personal, local concern can be addressed; community leaders know what will be acceptable to the community and who the key people at the different levels are. AIDS prevention researchers have experience developing AIDS interventions that are appropriate for different populations; community leaders know who will be heard and who has the most relevant experience. AIDS prevention researchers have experience in program evaluation and can help community leaders identify the components.

While federal and state governments can establish AIDS prevention policy and develop models, it is at the community level that action must be taken to develop appropriate plans that address the confluence of complex issues at the local level. The traditional approach to community health has often been embedded in a social and psychological approach that evaluates success as changes in risk behaviors of individuals. A newly emerging approach is that of social ecology where changing individual risk behavior is considered within the social and cultural context in which it occurs. Prevention programs developed using this paradigm are directed more at the social forces that are operative in the environment than at individual motives, attitudes, and knowledge.

CONCEPT OF COMMUNITY

In AIDS research, the concept of community has often been invoked but has not been well-defined. In order to develop the next generation of AIDS prevention with community impact, it is important to reach consensus on the definition of terms such as community-based research, community collaboration, community-level research, community-implemented programs, and community impact. To begin this dialog, the following sections propose some definitions of these terms.

Community-Based Programs

While research has often been developed in laboratories where constructs can be well-controlled and a strict experimental design can be implemented, AIDS research has a tradition of being community based. That is, the recruitment and conduct of the prevention programs have been tested in STD clinics, nongovernment organizations (NGOs), and public-health agencies. An example of a community-based research study is the National Institute of Mental Health (NIMH) Multisite HIV Prevention Trial that was conducted in 37 clinics and women's health clinics nationally (NIMH Multisite HIV Prevention Trial Group, 1998).

Community Collaboration

Community collaboration involves the participation of community members in the development of the research protocol and the conduct of the study. The Chicago HIV Prevention and Adolescent Mental Health Project (CHAMP), which is overseen by a collaborative partnership of community parents, school staff, and university-based researchers, is an example of community collaboration (McKay et al., 2000). The community collaborative boards actively participate in all aspects of the research (recruiting subjects, reviewing all aspects of the protocol, coding behavior in videotapes, interpreting data), and some have even become employees of the university.

Community-Level Research

Community-level research involves prevention programs that are delivered to the community rather than to individuals. One such program is the Popular Opinion Leader (POL) intervention developed by Kelly et al. (1997), which is based on the Theory of Innovations (Rogers, 1983). Leaders in a community are identified and trained to deliver prevention messages to their friends and neighbors. These messages diffuse throughout the social networks in the community, and gradually the community norms about safer HIV-related behavior change. Changing community norms, attitudes, collective self-efficacy, and risk-behavior practices in populations vulnerable to AIDS are essential to mounting a social movement (Kelly, 1999).

Community-Implemented Programs

Community-implemented programs are conducted under real-world circumstances. After prevention programs have been demonstrated to be efficacious in Phase 3 studies (RCT), Phase 4 (effectiveness) studies are critical in demonstrating that a prevention program works in a community when the rigorous design components of a clinical trial are relaxed. It is extremely important to demonstrate that these programs can work in the real world in order to have them widely adopted.

Community Impact

Community impact indicates the extent to which an AIDS prevention program has a broad effect on the largest number of people in the community. Even interventions focused on individuals, couples, or a school can diffuse into the community and have a tremendous affect on the risk behaviors of people who did not directly receive the intervention.

The preceding chapters have suggested future research efforts that focus on enhancing community impact in HIV/STD prevention. This strategy involves the development of basic knowledge about understanding the varied ways that community-level factors may affect the sexual risk behavior of individuals (Yoshikawa, Wilson, Peterson, & Shinn, this volume) as well as planned efforts to chang the aspects of the community context that shape the norms, opportunities, and constraints related to risk behavior. The preceding chapters provide examples of work needed to develop HIV/STD interventions that can achieve community impact. In this chapter, the important themes in those chapters are discussed and a research agenda that can serve as an action plan for HIV/STD prevention investigators to enhance community impact is presented.

THE MULTILEVEL IMPACT OF HIV/STD PREVENTION PROGRAMS

One major theme underscores the importance of multilevel influences on individual behavior: While individuals must change their behaviors in order to stop the HIV/STD epidemic, interventions intended to impact the individual can be delivered at the couple, family, community, or societal levels. The shift from an individual perspective to a community one raises many methodological and measurement challenges. A case could be made that multilevel interventions may be the only effective way to develop the kind of social movement that has been so successful in the antismoking campaign.

This approach raises multiple research questions:

- How can the community-level impacts of multilevel interventions be measured?
- How can the independent effect of multilevel intervention designs be assessed?
- How can multiple methods be coordinated in the design, implementation, and assessment of community-impact interventions?
- How can existing data from efficacious interventions be explored to assess group and community-level effects?
- How is individual sexual behavior affected by factors such as community cohesion, peer group norms, or the presence or absence of an organized community support network at higher levels of analysis?
- What are the community contexts within which risk is greatest for different sociocultural groups and people of different ages?
- What institutional norms support risky behavior and therefore undermine efforts to sustain change conducted at the individual level?

CULTURAL INFLUENCES ON THE COMMUNITY IMPACT OF INTERVENTIONS

Another theme is the perspective that, regardless of level of analysis, it is important to understand the role of cultural and social context when attempting to either replicate programs or transfer programs developed in one context to another. The role of cultural influences over all aspects of community interventions is increasingly appreciated in AIDS research.

The following questions warrant further investigation:

- How do culturally defined gender roles affect interventions designed to change social norms related to risk behavior?
- In what ways does the concept of culture affect the feasibility and impact of community interventions in diverse communities?
- How are cultural differences related to efforts to replicate interventions across cultural and social contexts?

THE LONG-TERM IMPACT OF COMMUNITY-LEVEL INTERVENTIONS

Another theme is the need to document not only the immediate but also the long-term community impact of HIV/STD prevention efforts, which involves two concepts. One concept assesses the sustainability of the original impact of the intervention. The second concept involves identifying the continuing benefits to the community that may evolve from the original intervention over a longer period of time. Ethnographic research methods can assess the congruence of the intervention with the local setting and population and identify local resources that may sustain the intervention. This is critical because the effects of interventions on communities can be expected to occur over a protracted time period, not solely in the immediate aftermath of the intervention itself. Such outcomes may be positive (e.g., the development of subsequent community-based programs stimulated by the success of the original intervention) or negative (e.g., increased antagonism to outsiders because of promising more than was delivered).

The following are questions about sustaining community impact and assessing permutations of the intervention over time:

- How can the fit between the intervention and the community context be assessed, and what effect does the fit between the prevention program and the context have on the intervention's community impact and sustainability?
- What resources are left in the community when the intervention ends and how does this affect the sustainability?
- How do cultural and contextual community differences contribute to the diffusion of intervention over time in one population but not in others?
- What mechanisms need to be developed to follow the impact of community-level interventions over a significant time period?
- How can the continuing and evolving effects of interventions on individuals, their social networks, and community norms be identified?
- How can intended and unintended outcomes of community interventions be assessed?

REPLICATING COMMUNITY-LEVEL INTERVENTIONS

Research should be initiated that transfers interventions developed under one set of circumstances to another so that the interventions can be successful and sustained. The factors that determine whether an intervention is generalizable to other communities should be identified. Journals and other publications should be encouraged to publish process issues related to program implementation in differing contexts.

Additional research questions related to linking programs and context remain:

- What components must be adapted to replicate an intervention in another setting, and how does this impact the fidelity?
- How do the resource assumptions of the intervention mesh with the community resources available to carry it out over time?
- How can interventions be designed to assess the effects of components across diverse populations and levels of analysis so they can be replicated?
- What community and organizational factors affect the adoption of HIV/STD prevention programs?
- What strategies might be developed to balance existing, locally developing programs with a plan to replicate HIV/STD prevention programs?
- How can efficacious, individually based programs be constructed to increase their community impact when they are replicated?
- What methods can be developed to describe the interaction and mutual influence of investigators and local service providers in program design and implementation?

NATURALLY OCCURRING EXPERIMENTS

Another theme is that naturally occurring experiments are continually happening in communities as new programs are implemented, new laws are passed, and natural disasters occur that disrupt community services. Documenting baseline data prior to the event is critical in assessing the impact on the community HIV/STD prevention program of naturally occurring experiments. RADAR (Rapid Action Deployment of AIDS Research) is a program announcement that accepts grant proposal submissions at any time in order to capture a naturally occurring experiment.

Some of the research questions that might be addressed are the following:

- What impact will the passage of laws on HIV testing, sterile needle sales, or aspects of care have on the community HIV/STD prevention effort?
- What impact will the infusion of new populations into a community (e.g., the presence of a student with AIDS in a high school or the influx of a refugee group into a neighborhood with preexisting high

rates of HIV/STD prevalence) have on community norms about HIV/STD risk behaviors?

- What impact will a natural disaster, such as a fire, tornado, hurricane, or earthquake have on risky behaviors in the community?
- What is the synergy between the initiation of HIV/STD research programs and the local community programs designed to have broad community impact as a basis for further program development?

RELATIONSHIP BETWEEN INVESTIGATORS AND COMMUNITY MEMBERS

The importance of the relationship between investigators and communities is a pervasive theme. The research agenda associated with this issue includes the following questions:

- What is the impact of the researcher/community relationship on (a) program development relevant to local issues and responsiveness to local definitions of problem solutions; (b) the provision of evaluation and consultative activities that affect service delivery in local agencies; and (c) the opportunity for developing guidelines about tailoring programs to local contexts?
- What effect does the nature of this relationship have on the success and sustainability of HIV/STD prevention programs?
- How can collaborations between investigators and community agencies be sustained over time and across projects?

CONCLUSION

This book has presented a description of AIDS prevention programs developed over the past 20 years and has laid out a research agenda for the future. The zeitgeist for behavioral HIV/STD prevention research is clearly multilevel interventions that have community impact.

Even if a vaccine were to be developed in the next few years, it is doubtful that it would approach 90% to 100% efficacy. There will be a continuing role for behavioral interventions, especially those that have community impact and serve to support individual resolve to engage in safer HIV/AIDS behaviors.

REFERENCES

Coutinho, R. & Cates, W. (2000). Interventions to prevent HIV risk behaviors. *AIDS, Supplement 2.*

Kelly, J. A. (1999). Community-level interventions are needed to prevent new HIV infections (Editorial). *American Journal of Public Health, 89,* 299–301.

Kelly, J. A., Murphy, D. A., Sikkema, K. J., McAuliffe, T. L., Roffman, R. A., Solomon, L. J., et al. (1997). Randomized, controlled, community-level HIV prevention intervention for sexual risk behaviour among homosexual men in U.S. cities. *The Lancet, 350,* 1500–1505.

McKay, M. M., Baptiste, D., Coleman, D., Madison, S., Paikoff, R., & Scott, R. (2000). Preventing HIV risk exposure in urban communities: The CHAMP family program. In W. Pequegnat & J. Szapocznik (Eds.), *Working with families in the era of AIDS* (pp. 67–88). Thousand Oaks, CA: Sage.

National Institute of Mental Health (NIMH) Multisite HIV Prevention Trial Group (1998). The NIMH multisite HIV prevention trial: Reducing HIV sexual risk behavior. *Science, 280,* 1889–1894.

Rogers, E. M. (1983). *Diffusion of innovations* (2nd ed.). New York: Free Press.

Index